Environmental Politics and Policy

Eleventh Edition

For Ashley, Leanna, and Carly.

Sara Miller McCune founded SAGE Publishing in 1965 to support the dissemination of usable knowledge and educate a global community. SAGE publishes more than 1000 journals and over 800 new books each year, spanning a wide range of subject areas. Our growing selection of library products includes archives, data, case studies and video. SAGE remains majority owned by our founder and after her lifetime will become owned by a charitable trust that secures the company's continued independence.

Los Angeles | London | New Delhi | Singapore | Washington DC | Melbourne

Environmental Politics and Policy

Eleventh Edition

Walter A. Rosenbaum

University of Florida

FOR INFORMATION:

CQ Press

An Imprint of SAGE Publications, Inc.

2455 Teller Road

Thousand Oaks, California 91320

E-mail: order@sagepub.com

SAGE Publications Ltd.

1 Oliver's Yard

55 City Road

London EC1Y 1SP

United Kingdom

SAGE Publications India Pvt. Ltd.

B 1/I 1 Mohan Cooperative Industrial Area

Mathura Road, New Delhi 110 044

India

SAGE Publications Asia-Pacific Pte. Ltd.

18 Cross Street #10-10/11/12

China Square Central

Singapore 048423

Library of Congress Cataloging-in-Publication Data

Names: Rosenbaum, Walter A., author.

Title: Environmental politics and policy / Walter A. Rosenbaum, University of Florida.

Description: Eleventh Edition. | Washington, D.C. : CQ Press, a DIVISION OF SAGE, [2019] | Previous edition: 2017. | Includes bibliographical references and index.

Identifiers: LCCN 2019003075 | ISBN 9781544325040 (paperback : acid-free paper)

Subjects: LCSH: Environmental policy—United States.

Classification: LCC GE180 .R66 2019 | DDC 363.7/05610973—dc23 LC record available at https://lccn.loc.gov/2019003075

Acquisitions Editor: Scott Greenan

Editorial Assistant: Lauren Younker

Production Editor: Andrew Olson

Copy Editor: Diane Wainwright

Typesetter: C&M Digitals (P) Ltd.

Proofreader: Alison Syring

Indexer: Will Ragsdale

Cover Designer: Dally Verghese

Marketing Manager: Jennifer Jones

19 20 21 22 23 10 9 8 7 6 5 4 3 2 1

CONTENTS

FIGURES, TABLES, BOXES, AND MAPS

Figures

Tables

Boxes

Maps

PREFACE

We are now living in an extraordinary period, perhaps *the* most extraordinary period, in American environmental governance since the first Earth Day. What happened in the twenty-four hours of the 2016 presidential election initiated the most abrupt, radical revision of U.S. environmental policymaking in fifty years. Donald Trump's administration has quickly redefined, and certainly intensified, policy discourse in every domain of environmental policymaking discussed in this book. This transformation in environmental governance is recognized by timely revisions in substance and detail throughout each of the following chapters. Still, readers familiar with *Environmental Politics and Policy* will recognize a continuity with previous editions in conceptual framework and substantive policy concerns.

The foundational chapters that explain and illustrate the essential components of the policymaking process (Chapters 2 and 3) still cover these key areas, but they have been carefully reorganized for greater clarity and continuity. Chapter 2 now focuses entirely on the policymaking process, whereas Chapter 3 covers the institutions and politics of policymaking. Throughout the book, case studies and other examples have been updated comprehensively, where appropriate, to ensure timeliness and relevance. Each chapter has been edited rigorously to eliminate material from previous editions that is no longer essential. The result is a more concise narrative that does not sacrifice fundamentals, such as the conceptual design, the careful explanation of substantive policy, and the abundant illustrations, that have appealed to the readers of previous editions. As always, a major subtext is the continuing challenge, inherent to environmental policymaking, of reconciling sound science with practical politics.

The revisions emphasizing the strategic transformations that have taken place in domestic environmental governance from the Obama to Trump administrations appear in every chapter. These revisions include:

- A new discussion in Chapter 1 of the radical transition from the Obama to the Trump environmental policy agendas, with particular attention on the Trump environmental deregulatory initiatives and energy policies in contrast to the evolution of national environmental policy since Earth Day 1970.

- A recurring discussion of the nationally publicized controversies over the Trump administration's alleged misuse of scientific information for environmental policymaking, particularly by the Environmental

Protection Agency (EPA, Chapter 3) and, most notably, in issues related to climate-warming regulations (Chapter 10).

- An updated narrative about the policymaking process. This includes in Chapter 2 a new case study illustrating environmental decision-making in the federal government's decision to list a bumblebee species as endangered. This chapter also notes the shifting texture and discontinuities of public opinion concerning the environment and its impact on environmental policymaking and voting behavior. The chapter also includes new public opinion polls about public environmental concerns in the 2016 presidential election and new data about increasing polarization of opinion between Republican and Democratic partisans over important domestic energy issues, such as climate change, as well as a discussion of the important Republican "war on coal" campaign theme in the 2016 election and data on political spending and activism by environmental groups.

- A recognition of continuing change in environmental trends and indicators. The shelf life of environmental data is short. Data need continual updating and pruning to remain relevant. Tables and figures from earlier editions that are no longer useful have been removed. The remaining tables and figures presenting the most essential data—current trends in national air pollution emissions, water quality, and toxic waste discharges, for example—have been updated as much as possible.

- A description of major Trump changes in the organization of executive environmental agencies, illustrated in Chapter 3 by a rewrite of the introductory case study to include the suspension of EPA's new, stricter Clean Water Act regulations for surface water. Other updates include a description of the Trump administration's controversial reorganization of EPA's scientific advisory committees and reductions in EPA budget, staff, and regulatory resources.

- An updated discussion of environmental justice issues, including a new case study in Chapter 4 concerning the discovery of drinking water contamination in Flint, Michigan, and the resulting political controversy.

- A comprehensive discussion of the Trump administration's highly controversial suspension of the Obama Clean Power Plan to control domestic climate-warming emissions and the crucial scientific and political implications. The analysis includes a Chapter 6 summary of the plan, the critical Trump revisions, and implications of these revisions scientifically and politically.

- A description of the changes in national energy policy created by the Trump administration's increased promotion of fossil fuel exploration and production on federal lands (Chapter 9) and by related efforts to rapidly increase domestic coal production and combustion (Chapter 8). A related discussion of the challenges involved in creating "clean coal" technologies has also been added (Chapter 8).

- The Trump administration's rejection of U.S. participation in the international Paris Accord to limit global climate warming emissions and the implications for national climate diplomacy are discussed (Chapter 10) in an extensively updated chapter on U.S. climate change policy.

I have tried to keep faith with colleagues, students, reviewers, and others who have found the narrative design informative, accessible, and durable. That includes an implicit commitment to material that is interesting as well as balanced and teachable—in the end, a book that is both a good read and a fair read.

ACKNOWLEDGMENTS

As usual, the talents of many other people were enlisted in the writing of this new edition, and I am deeply indebted to them for the continuing acceptance of this book. Like most teachers, I recognized long ago that my students are often my best instructors and critics. To them, I express my continuing gratitude. A number of reviewers made constructive suggestions during the revision and writing of this edition. I thank Marjorie Hershey, Indiana University; Dr. Ninian R. Stein, Environmental Studies and Anthropology, Tufts University; and Robert Holahan, Associate Professor, Environmental Studies and Political Science, Binghamton University, for their thorough reviews. To my current CQ Press editor Scott Greenan and to copyeditor Diane Wainwright, I offer a well-deserved thanks for the many hours of planning, reviewing, and patience invested in the work. Faults of omission and commission—alas!—are my own.

—Walter A. Rosenbaum

ABOUT THE AUTHOR

 **Walter A. Rosenbaum** is professor emeritus of political science at the University of Florida and director emeritus of the University of Florida's Bob Graham Center for Public Service. His recent activities include an analysis of the EPA's capacity for climate change regulation, prepared for the Brookings Institution; an examination of the data requirements for a new Federal Environmental Legacy Act; preparation of an energy policy text for CQ Press; and an analysis of U.S. energy governance for MIT Press. He has also served as a staff member of the U.S. Environmental Protection Agency and an adjunct professor in the School of Public Health, Tulane University Medical College. In addition to his teaching and research, he has been a consultant to the EPA, the U.S. Department of Energy, the Federal Emergency Management Agency, and the South Florida Ecosystem (Everglades) Restoration Project. He is currently the Editor-in-Chief of the *Journal for Environmental Studies and Sciences.*

AFTER EARTH DAY

A few miles north from Denver, along Colorado's Front Range, the busy urban corridor straddling Interstate 25 along the eastern range of the Rocky Mountains, lies the small, picturesque town of Erie. In 2005, Erie was little more than an historic, old coal town consisting of two paved roads, a miniature urban center with a few restaurants, a handful of retail stores, a post office, and a bar boasting continuous service since 1926. Then along came fracking, and everything changed.

Within a few years, Erie and surrounding Weld County were suddenly, uneasily, riding the crest of an economic boom. Since 2005, more than 23,000 active oil and gas production wells, mostly fracking sites, have appeared in Weld County, so numerous they seemed to one journalist "more common than trees."[1] In Erie, the population tripled from 6,291 to 19,723 in little more than a decade. The explosive growth of oil and gas production rapidly transformed the town's retail economy, workforce, and households. By 2015, the median family income was $103,796, almost double the national average. The surge of new residents produced a thriving and expensive market for housing construction—many homes costing in excess of $300,000. New homes? "They'll sell in a night," one local businesswoman told a reporter. "I'll have people come in here and say, 'Yup, it was up there for two hours and it sold.'"[2] Rising tax revenues, retail sales, and many other economic windfalls from robust oil and gas production have brought new wealth and a multitude of desirable community amenities to Erie and Weld County. But less than a decade after fracking arrived, middle school children and their parents were parading through a drilling site chanting "Hey, hey! Ho, Ho! These fracking wells have got to go."[3]

By 2015, the *Washington Examiner* reported that controversy over Erie's fracking sites "has grown so bitter that Erie residents don't tell neighbors if their spouse works for the oil industry. Many won't discuss the issue with reporters . . . " Remarked one woman to a reporter: "You don't tell them your husband works for an oil company. When they say, 'Hey, what does your husband do?' you just smile and change the subject." Fracking technology has brought Erie, like numerous other communities across the United States, not only prosperity but divisive controversy, environmental disruption, and a problematic future. In 2014, Erie was selected among "The Best Places to Live" in America.[4] The same year, the fracking battle catapulted Erie into national attention and earned it the unwelcome distinction as "ground zero for the disputes over property rights and environmental protection that fracking has unleashed."[5] Most important, the fracking conflict is U.S. environmental politics in the present tense. The rapidly enlarging contention is a showcase for many issues inseparable from environmental policymaking and certain to appear in variation throughout later chapters.

"FRACK, BABY, FRACK"

By 2009, when the drilling sites first appeared in Erie, fracking technology had already spread rapidly across the United States. More than thirty-five major oil shale formations exist beneath the United States and the Gulf of Mexico. Virtually every U.S. state is or could become a fracking site for natural gas and petroleum. The fracking rigs arriving in Erie were the leading edge of the fracking boom rapidly expanding to exploit Colorado's Niobrara shale deposit, the fourth largest oil and gas shale formation in the United States.

A Spreading Technology

A relatively recent innovation called high-volume hydraulic fracturing and horizontal drilling has greatly increased fracking's efficiency and economic profitability, thus dramatically accelerating its growth across the natural gas industry into what many industry experts now call a revolution in oil and natural gas production. Like almost all environmental issues, fracking is a complex mix of politics, economics, technology, science, and health risks—in Erie's case, with a generous seasoning of neighborhood conflict and intergovernmental dissention.

Oil shale is a densely packed sedimentary material formed millions of years ago containing oil and natural gas combined like an egg in cake batter within the densely packed rock. Fracking technology is designed especially to reach and capture these petroleum resources locked in deep sedimentary layers.

Fracking involves igniting underground explosives to fracture oil shale. Engineers then combine a vertical pipe, often miles deep, with a horizontally drilled pipe to pump into the shale millions of gallons of heated, salty water mixed with numerous chemicals to produce a brine, under pressure high enough to penetrate the fractures. The heated brine releases petroleum and natural gas embedded in the shale. The whole mix is captured, pumped to the surface, and separated into petroleum materials and wastewater.[6] Fracking involves massive water consumption, the potential contamination of surface and subsurface water resources by the drilling brine, and disposal of the millions of gallons of wastewater. Most drilling companies assert that the drilling brine is environmentally safe and that the brine's diffusion through the oil shale and its eventual disposal above ground pose few ecological hazards. (One mining company executive even publicly—and harmlessly—drank a small glass of the drilling brine to demonstrate its safety.)[7] Most drillers believe that any additional environmental regulation, when needed, can be provided by the relevant state or local governments.

Contested Environmental Impacts

There is little doubt, however, that the newest fracking technology can pose significant health risks and create potentially severe ecological damage, unless properly managed by mining companies and carefully regulated by government. An extensive review of the available research, reported by the highly respected National Academies of Science, concluded that oil shale mining "is much more costly, energy intensive, and environmentally damaging than drilling for conventional oil. The processes . . . involve significant disturbance of the land, extensive use of water (a particular concern in dry regions where oil shale is often found), and potential emissions of pollutants to the air and groundwater. . . ."[8]

Fracking's potential impact upon the nation's rivers, lakes, streams, and underground water has become especially contentious. Even a relatively small drilling site pours millions of gallons of chemically treated water into a fracking well. Fracking sites currently operating or planned near large urban drinking water sources or infrastructure, for instance, might create significant contamination and extremely costly remediation. Small, repeated earthquakes have occasionally been linked to fracking operations. Farmers near fracking operations have complained about methane-contaminated wells, poisoned cattle, and drilling access roads destroying timber and isolating croplands. Clear and convincing evidence of these and other environmental impacts attributed to fracking technology, however, is fragmentary and controversial. A 2015 EPA investigation of fracking's geologic impact found no evidence that fracking had created "widespread, systemic impacts on drinking water resources in the United States" but admitted the conclusion was very tentative.[9] Some limited university studies have found no evidence of groundwater contamination at a few southwestern fracking sites; other research reveals no earthquakes associated in other regions. Illness directly linked to fracking-contaminated soil and water among farmers and ranchers remains unproven. Thus, the fracking boom advances, even as government regulators, property owners, the drilling companies, health scientists, and environmentalists debate when, where, and how to regulate it.

Neighbor Against Neighbor

Whatever else fracking's impacted, it has divided communities and governments while setting neighbors against each other. It also has produced substantial income for property owners living atop a shale formation and for local governments. In Erie, for example, property owners with mineral rights received an average of $25,000 to lease their land for drilling. Local retail sales and new store openings rapidly increased. Controversy began, however, with construction of the earliest among more than 200 drilling sites erected within the city by 2016 and has continued unabated.

The Erie controversy was incited by many events. In 2012, an early drilling site near Red Hawk Elementary School, within the range permitted by state law, soon provoked teachers, parents, and neighbors to complain that the noise disrupted school work and the sleep of nearby residents. Truck traffic crowded local roadways. Concern about possibly hazardous emissions from drilling sites and geologic disturbances, based upon news from other communities, circulated among residents. In 2014, the National Oceanic and Atmospheric Administration released a study revealing that propane levels in Erie were ten times higher than the recommended limits for high-extraction communities.[10] That same year, a new drilling site produced noise twenty-four hours daily, violating state regulations and forcing some residents to cover their bedroom windows with four-inch upholstery foam to smother the noise.[11]

Governments in Conflict

Erie's government, the fracking corporations, local residents, community business, and state regulators have struggled to find a satisfactory political strategy to reconcile their often dissonant interests. The controversy is intensified by federalism. Environmental regulation involves federalism, which usually proceeds with considerable cooperation among federal, state, and local governments. But federalism has raw edges, exposed when federal and state governments disagree about regulation. In Erie, local, state, and federal governments all have asserted competing claims to regulatory authority over fracking. The state, not Erie's city government, regulates all oil and gas drilling sites and resists regulation by local authorities; state officials, in turn, resist Washington preempting state regulation. Colorado's property law separates property rights above ground from mineral rights below. Thus, a landowner with property overlying shale deposits may refuse to allow fracking at the surface, but it can—and does—happen that "a person or company who wants to develop the minerals can go to a more willing neighbor and bore laterally underneath the property of the recalcitrant anti-fracker."[12] Some residents want fracking entirely prohibited; some just want the drilling off their property, and others, citing Erie's sudden prosperity, oppose any prohibition of local drilling.

Local community activists, a coalition of longtime residents and new middle-class arrivals, organized public forums and informal gatherings and hosted wine-and-cheese house parties where strategies were developed to pressure local and state governments to resolve the fracking issues. Since then, local efforts have failed to persuade Erie's state and congressional representatives to invest Erie and Weld County with authority to regulate local drilling. Both a local and a state referendum to freeze further drilling have failed. The drillers have worked diligently to earn Erie's acceptance and to mitigate, if not eliminate, many of the problems arousing community criticism. One drilling corporation, for example, has spent about $3.3 million in Weld County since 2007 on philanthropic endeavors, such as buying solar panels to power the Erie Community Center.[13] At some drilling pads, the company has voluntarily moved beyond required boundaries, and others removed or rescheduled drilling hours to diminish the neighborhood noise.

A Continuing Controversy

The collision of community and corporate interests remains, and some conflicts defy compromise. By early 2018, Colorado's energy regulators had received more than 900 complaints about fracking from Weld County, and Erie's local government had passed an ordinance—which drillers claim is illegal—intended to control objectionable odors originating at drilling sites.[14]

The issue has outgrown Erie. The simmering political conflict has provoked attention and engagement from national advocacy groups representing a multitude of environmental, petroleum industry, and state and local government interests that regard Erie and Colorado as a showcase for the larger national debate over which governments should regulate fracking and how it should be done. As the Colorado fracking conflict evolves, however, it could be overtaken by the sudden, rapid decline in global petroleum prices starting in 2014—an economic shock already driving many small fracking operations out of production. In Colorado, as elsewhere in the United States, communities like Erie seem perched precariously between an economic boom and a potential bust.

Whatever the outcome, the fracking battles, wherever fought across the United States, have become environmental politics in the present tense, testimony that environmental issues are bundled inextricably in economic, political, scientific, and social issues certain to appear in variation throughout later chapters. These are a permanent legacy of an American Environmental Era hardly a generation old.

AMERICA'S ENVIRONMENTAL LEGACY

By the time Donald Trump entered the White House, America's environmental movement had transformed the nation's environment and its politics in many enduring ways. Perhaps most impressive has been the improvement of the nation's air quality. Ambient concentrations of sulfur oxides, carbon monoxide, nitrogen oxides, particulates, and ozone—all associated with serious human health disorders—had decreased by 73 percent between 1970 and 2016, and many more acutely dangerous ambient air toxics, especially formaldehyde and lead, have been reduced or virtually eliminated.[15] Dangerous chemical and biological pollutants of major U.S. waterways, such as the Mississippi, Potomac, and Ohio rivers, have been reduced sharply.

Aggressive regulatory programs have reduced significantly the number of abandoned hazardous waste sites across the United States and, for the first time, compelled the manufacturers and distributors of hazardous or toxic chemicals to comply with national standards for their transport and disposal. National testing programs now require more rigorous screening and testing of newly manufactured chemicals to protect human health and the environment. Numerous plant and animal species that were threatened with extinction, including the American bald eagle and the American panther, have been protected and, in a few instances, restored to vitality. Equally important, the United States was committed to numerous regional and international treaties, such as the Montreal Protocol, to reduce the global ozone hole, testifying to a growing recognition that the quality of the nation's domestic environment and global environmental quality have become interdependent. Most important politically, these transformations seemed securely grounded in a durable national consensus that environmental protection must now be a first-order public concern—a remarkable emergence of a national ecological consciousness that was nonexistent a few decades ago.

Despite these transformations, the U.S. environment remains significantly degraded in critical respects. In 2017, more than 123 million Americans lived in a county where one or more of eight regulated air pollutants exceed National Air Quality Standards.[16] More than half the total area of the nation's biologically essential estuaries and almost half the nation's river miles are considered unacceptably polluted. The primary cause of this water degradation is still largely unregulated. Surprisingly little information is available about the extent to which Americans are exposed to thousands of existing chemicals or about the possible health risks involved. Federal government estimates suggest that information on public exposure is available for less than 6 percent of more than 1,400 naturally occurring and manufactured chemicals considered to pose a human health threat.[17] The EPA has been able to assess the public health risks for an even smaller proportion of the about 1,500 new chemicals introduced annually into commerce and industry. "EPA's review of new chemicals provides only limited assurance that health and environmental risks are identified," according to a report by the U.S. Government Accountability Office (GAO; formerly the Government Accounting Office), "because the agency has limited information with which to review them."[18] In fact, one of the most compelling national environmental problems is the pervasive lack of reliable scientific information about current environmental quality and human exposure to environmental contaminants—data that are absolutely essential for sound environmental policymaking.[19]

It is increasingly apparent that the scope and scale of this ecological degradation were often gravely underestimated and that the social and economic costs of pollution regulation were frequently miscalculated badly when the nation's major environmental policies were enacted. For instance, when Congress wrote legislation in 1976 requiring the EPA to ban or regulate any chemicals posing an unreasonable risk to human health, it did not anticipate that more than 62,000 chemical substances might have to be evaluated to determine their toxicity. Nor did Congress predict when it wrote the Comprehensive Environmental Response, Compensation, and Liability Act of 1980 (CERCLA, popularly known as Superfund) to clean up the nation's worst abandoned chemical waste sites that more than 40,000 sites would be discovered, that 500 new sites would be identified annually, and that the initial funding would be virtually exhausted by the mid-1990s, thus requiring annual additional appropriations of $1.2 billion through at least 2015.[20] We know now that the seemingly inexorable expansion in the scale and costs of environmental restoration is often the consequence of better environmental monitoring and research revealing, often to considerable surprise, the true reach and complexity of environmental problems. Thus, environmental protection is a work in progress.

THE EVOLUTION OF U.S. ENVIRONMENTALISM

The first Earth Day in April 1970 was the big bang of U.S. environmental politics, launching the country on a sweeping social learning curve about ecological management never before experienced or attempted in any other nation. No challenge has been more fundamental to U.S. environmentalism since Earth Day 1970 than the constructive adaptation of the original vision of environmental conservation and a renewal, once written into law and embedded into the political and economic structure of U.S. life, to domestic and global changes.

The Environmental Decade: From Richard Nixon to Ronald Reagan

The 1970s, the decade spanning the presidencies of Richard Nixon, Gerald Ford, and Jimmy Carter, remain the most remarkably creative legislative period in the history of U.S. environmentalism.[21] During this decade, almost all of the major environmental laws, federal environmental regulatory institutions, and environmental interest groups that now define the contours of the nation's environmental politics and policy appeared.

A Republican, Richard Nixon himself was no environmentalist, nor were most congressional Republicans. But both congressional parties recognized the enormous political capital to be gained by riding the crest of the upwelling public concern for environmental protection. In Congress, a vigorous, broad coalition of Democrats and Republicans in both chambers collaborated in creating the legislative majorities essential to firmly establish the legal and political foundations of the U.S. environmental era.[22]

By the time Richard Nixon's presidency abruptly ended in 1974, Congress had written the National Environmental Policy Act of 1969, which required all federal agencies to prepare environmental impact statements for any significant actions affecting the environment, declared a national policy "to encourage productive and enjoyable harmony between man and his environment," and created the Council on Environmental Quality within the White House to advise the president on environmental matters. During this period, the Clean Air

Amendments of 1970 for the first time mandated national air pollution standards and regulatory laws to enforce them. Two years later, the Federal Water Pollution Control Act Amendments of 1972 (Clean Water Act) set national water quality goals, established a national pollution discharge permit system, and created federal grants to the states to improve municipal waste treatment plants. To administer these new laws, Nixon created by executive order the EPA, the largest federal regulatory agency and the first of its kind in any national government.

A cascade of environmental legislation continued throughout the 1970s. The Endangered Species Act (1973) broadened federal authority to protect all endangered and threatened species, and the Safe Drinking Water Act (SDWA, 1974) authorized the federal government for the first time to set standards protecting the quality of the nation's drinking water. The Toxic Substances Control Act of 1976 (TSCA) required premarket testing of chemical substances and authorized the EPA to regulate or ban the manufacture, sale, and use of chemicals posing "an unreasonable risk of injury to health or to the environment," and the Resource Conservation and Recovery Act of 1976 (RCRA), requiring the EPA to set national standards for hazardous waste treatment, storage, and disposal.

By the time Jimmy Carter entered the White House in 1977, public support for environmental protection had become so broadly and deeply founded that it was, in effect, a part of the national consensus—that array of issues publicly accepted as an essential and priority concern of government. Carter's term began with his successful promotion of the Surface Mining Control and Reclamation Act (1977), establishing for the first time federal standards for strip mining and requiring mine operators to environmentally restore mined lands. Carter was also instrumental in the congressional passage of amendments to the Clean Air Act (CAA) and Clean Water Act in 1977. Powerfully aided by national revelation of the extensive, buried toxic waste dump discovered under the suburban settlement at New York's Love Canal, Carter was able to collaborate with Congress in the creation of CERCLA.

But Carter's administration was also beset from the outset by an energy crisis, created when the Organization of Petroleum Exporting Countries (OPEC) in 1973 imposed an embargo on U.S. imports of Middle Eastern petroleum.[23] The economic shock of the embargo and the political turbulence in its aftermath compelled the federal government for the first time since World War II to regulate domestic petroleum prices and supply, to set energy-efficiency standards for transportation and consumer products, and to create a national energy plan. Carter proposed and Congress enacted legislation establishing the new Department of Energy (DOE).

Policy Deadlock: From Ronald Reagan to George W. Bush

The environmental movement had prospered through the 1970s. That changed with the advent of the Reagan administration (1981–1989). Reagan and his advisers, abetted by a new cadre of sympathetic congressional Republicans and the collapse of bipartisan congressional environmentalism, believed they had been elected to bring regulatory relief to the U.S. economy, and environmental regulations were an early priority on their hit list of laws needing regulatory reform. The environmental movement regarded the Reagan administration as the most environmentally hostile in a half century and Reagan's regulatory reform as the cutting edge of an implacable assault on the institutional foundations of federal environmental laws enacted during the 1970s.[24]

The Reagan years severely tested the foundations of the environmental movement. Although the foundations held, little was done to advance the implementation of existing policies or to address new and urgent environmental issues. Accompanied by polarizing partisan infighting and protracted legislative delays, Congress was able to pass important amendments to the Clean Water Act, the SDWA, CERCLA, and the RCRA. The future of commercial nuclear power seemed to plunge from bleak to barren when the deadly 1984 reactor meltdowns at the Soviet Union's Chernobyl nuclear power facility released a catastrophic cloud of high levels of atmospheric radioactivity over the Soviet Union and its adjacent European neighbors.

President George Bush (1989–1993) ended the pernicious policy impasse of the Reagan years. The EPA's morale and resources, severely depleted during the Reagan years, improved. The Bush administration sponsored and adeptly promoted the CAA Amendments of 1990, a long-overdue reform of the CAA of 1970. The Energy Policy Act of 1992 for the first time created a comprehensive federal energy plan to reduce U.S. dependence on imported oil, encouraged energy efficiency and conservation, and promoted renewable energy.

The environmental movement expected much of Bill Clinton, especially because Vice President Al Gore was an outspoken environmentalist and Clinton had cultivated the environmentalist vote. In the end, the Clinton administration was distinguished more by its ambitions than by its accomplishments.[25] Clinton generally reinvigorated environmental regulation and installed aggressive environmentalist administrators in strategic executive agencies such as the Department of the Interior and the EPA. He revived U.S. engagement in international environmental policymaking, eventually committing the United States to the Kyoto Protocol to control global climate change (which the U.S. Senate, for its part, refused to ratify).

But Clinton confronted throughout most of his administration a hostile Republican congressional majority that thwarted most of his legislative initiatives.[26]

Environmental Leadership Revived: From George W. Bush to Barack Obama

Then came Republican George W. Bush (2001–2009). To the wary environmental movement, Bush's succession to the White House seemed to announce a profoundly unsettling new regime emerging from the shadows of the bitterly remembered Reagan administration, and it enthusiastically embraced its environmental attitudes. The environmental movement and most passionate environmentalists vigorously opposed Bush's election, even though Bush strongly represented himself as a moderate environmentalist, a prudent reformer rather than an anti-environmental zealot.

Bush's relationship with the environmental movement was confrontational from the outset. His appointment of individuals closely associated with energy production and natural resource consumption to strategic leadership positions in the executive branch, especially in the Department of the Interior and the DOE, and the close association of Vice President Dick Cheney with the oil and gas industry provoked deep misgivings among environmentalists.[27] The Energy Policy Act of 2005 and the subsequent Energy Independence and Security Act of 2009 exemplified the Bush administration's ambitious effort to create a long-term energy strategy for the United States. Although the environmental community generally welcomed these initiatives aimed at increasing energy efficiency and developing renewable energy resources, environmentalists continued to criticize the heavy emphasis on accelerated fossil fuel exploration, new commercial nuclear power, and coal-fired utilities in the Energy Independence and Security Act.

During the Bush administration, the EPA did strengthen national air pollution controls on particulates and mercury emissions, but to environmentalists, these and other administration initiatives were too laggard and limited. Christie Todd Whitman, Bush's first EPA administrator, had complained at the end of her term that the Bush administration seemed condemned to "an eternal fistfight" with environmental groups.[28] Her remark became prophetic.

A Collision of Expectations: The Obama Presidency

The election of Barack Obama and the return of Democratic majorities to both congressional chambers in 2009 seemed to signify a renewed White House commitment to innovative and new environmental initiatives and a relief from the adversarial, polarizing environmental legislative politics of the Bush administration. Obama's first term began with a bold program of ambitious environmental legislation, regulations, and other initiatives that never quite materialized. The White House environmental agenda was soon depleted by a severe economic recession and embattled by a tenacious partisan deadlock afflicting Congress for the duration of his presidency.

During its first term, the Obama administration created a significant record of environmental achievements. Among the most important legislation was the administration's American Recovery and Reinvestment Act of 2009, the massive economic recovery program that included more than $100 billion in spending, tax incentives, and loan guarantees to promote energy efficiency, renewable energy development, fuel-efficient cars, and control of climate-warming emissions, among other programs appealing to environmentalists. The administration promoted new congressional initiatives to create a regulatory program to control domestic climate-warming emissions. The EPA enacted numerous new and revised environmental regulatory programs, including revised regulations to limit mercury emissions from industrial fossil fuel combustion, further regulations to improve control of other toxic air pollutants, and new, stricter mileage standards for automobiles and light trucks. White House guidelines were written to strengthen protection of federal scientific research and regulation from White House political interference.

The president, however, inherited the most severe economic recession since the Great Depression and was compelled to weaken or eliminate many regulatory and legislative environmental initiatives in order to reduce federal expenditures and regulatory costs. Moreover, the 2010 congressional elections returned to the House of Representatives a Republican majority hostile to most White House environmental initiatives and preoccupied with reducing federal spending and regulation. A divided congress virtually assured legislative deadlock and the failure of almost all Obama's environmental legislative proposals.

The White House effort to enact new legislation to control climate-warming emissions failed despite an enormous investment of time and political resources. The EPA postponed its widely anticipated reform of regulations controlling atmospheric ozone and weakened its initial plan to strengthen regulation of atmospheric soot (particulates). Facing continuing budget deficits, the administration reduced the EPA's budget for three successive years.[29] Thus, the Obama administration, caught between conflicting demands to revive a severely weakened economy, to achieve legislative leadership in a bitterly divided Congress, and to satisfy the environmentalist expectations, was almost predestined to create disappointment and division within the environmentalist community. The second term, however, was a very different matter.

By the end of his second term, Obama had created an unprecedented environmental presidency he expected would endure. This legacy was crafted almost entirely through the exercise of the president's inherent executive powers, which did not require congressional collaboration to implement—a strategy that increased Republican determination to revoke most of Obama's regulatory enactments if they won the White House in 2016. Obama became the first president to actively and consistently promote climate change as a major priority in his regulatory agenda, legislative initiatives, and public speeches.

The foundation of Obama's second-term climate agenda was the president's regulatory power created by the Clean Air Act and exercised through the EPA. Using this authority, in 2015 the EPA drafted the Clean Power Plan, a rule establishing state-by-state goals for carbon emission reductions from electric utilities—a major source of climate-warming gases—and permitting states great discretion in determining how to meet goals. The EPA estimated that the rule would reduce these national emissions by an estimated 32 percent below 2005 levels by 2030.[30] This rule, coupled with a 2015 EPA rule mandating tougher emission rules for trucks and heavy-duty vehicles and an agreement with China to jointly reduce national carbon emissions significantly, constituted the fundamentals of the climate agenda. Late in his second term, to the satisfaction of environmentalists, the president rejected the Keystone XL pipeline proposal, the long-disputed plan to build a 1,179-mile pipeline to transport 800,000 barrels a day of carbon-heavy petroleum from the Canadian oil sands to the Gulf Coast.

Virtually all these and other environmental regulations enacted during Obama's second term, however, have been challenged by a great diversity of opponents in most of the federal court venues, a strategy that seemed certain to delay their implementation and mire them in prolonged legal wrangling. Whether all or part of the Obama administration's environmental legacy would endure under this siege of litigation remained an open question when Obama exited the White House.

A Radical Redirection: The Trump Environmental Agenda

A year after his startling election, Donald Trump appeared in the White House before the national media and beside six piles of office paper six-feet tall to dramatize his "war on Washington's regulatory industry."[31] One relentless target of the Republican presidential campaign had been federal environmental regulations that, Trump asserted, created unemployment, inhibited economic growth, and inflicted excessive, unnecessary costs upon American industry. And no federal agency epitomized all that Trump and congressional Republicans considered wrong with environmental management more than the EPA. Trump promised a sweeping "regulatory rollback" at the EPA and across a vast expanse of other environmental agencies and laws, creating what Republicans believed was a long overdue, radical retrenchment of excessive federal authority.

The Trump initiatives struck especially hard at the Obama administration's major environmental enactments to control domestic climate-warming emissions, to accelerate renewable power development, and to enlarge the scope of national air and water pollution standards. Trump also promised to liberate domestic fossil fuel industries from production restrictions, to open previously restricted public lands for energy exploration, and to revoke the Obama administration's Clean Power Plan and the Paris Climate Agreement, the foundations of the federal government's program to reduce domestic climate-warming emissions. And the president promised concurrently to reduce drastically the personnel and regulatory power of the EPA.[32] Trump's agenda seemed blessed by political circumstances. Republican majorities, enlarged by the 2016 presidential elections, controlled both congressional chambers and responded enthusiastically to Trump's attacks on environmental regulation. Powerful business and industrial interests vigorously supported the Trump deregulation agenda. Additionally, voters showed scant interest or concern about environmental issues, thus apparently giving Republicans considerable latitude to propose comprehensive policy reforms.[33]

The White House environmental agenda also created the most politically toxic relationship between environmentalists and the White House since the first Earth Day. The scope and vehemence of Trump's assault on environmental regulation alarmed and deeply angered environmentalists who overwhelmingly opposed Trump's election, which they considered the prelude to a massive subversion of the nation's environmental quality. The Trump agenda "takes a wrecking ball to agencies that protect our health, safety and environment," asserted the president of the Union of Concerned Scientists.[34] The Sierra Club's executive director, Michael Brune, exemplified the mood of most national environmental organizations. "Trump can't reverse our clean energy and climate progress with the stroke of a pen," he warned, "and we'll fight Trump in the courts, in the streets, and at the state and local level across America to protect the health of every community."[35]

By the end of the administration's second year, practically every federal environmental agency's staff and authority, especially the EPA's regulatory programs, had been critically altered by the Trump administration's regulatory rollback. The first year box score: twenty-nine regulatory rules cancelled, twenty-four additional rollbacks underway, and seven more regulations rewritten.[36] Among Trump's most important executive orders were a cancellation of the EPA's Clean Power Plan restricting national climate-warming emissions, an end to the moratorium on federal coal leases on public land, and a cancellation of the mandate that federal officials consider climate-change impacts during decision making. The president had also ordered a severe reduction of references to climate change, renewable energy, and related issues across federal agency websites, and the virtual elimination of the EPA's climate-warming website with climate data links. The president also repeated his promise to withdraw the U.S. commitment to the Paris Climate Agreement limiting international climate-warming emissions.

The Trump administration, however, faced a long, contentious political struggle with environmentalists and their allies if the promised regulatory rollbacks were to succeed. Revising existing EPA regulations, for example, involves extensive procedural requirements sure to mobilize strong opposition. Opponents of major regulatory revisions have also turned to the courts, launching a flood tide of litigation that may delay, and perhaps defeat, many proposed regulatory reforms. Many important White House legislative initiatives will require uncertain congressional collaboration to succeed.

ONGOING CHALLENGES: PRESENT AND FUTURE

On that first Earth Day in 1970, more than half the Americans living today had not been born. A whole new generation has matured. Americans now have more than fifty years of collective experience with unprecedented experimentation in environmental management. The ultimate test of the ambitious U.S. regime of environmental regulation will be not how well it was conceived but how well it endures. That endurance depends largely on how well U.S. science, political culture, and environmental leadership can learn from past experience and creatively apply the lessons learned to several profound problems now recognized as inherent in all environmental policymaking.

Keeping Environmentalism Contemporary

The environmental movement is now almost a half century old. Environmentalism is no longer the fresh, growing, politically ascending force that propelled environmental issues to unprecedented importance in national politics and policy. The Trump environmental program is the latest among many challenges environmental organizations face that have come with a now-familiar presence of environmentalists among the nation's major advocacy groups. Environmental organizations continually struggle to keep environmental issues a priority on the national policy agenda, to sustain a large, politically robust membership base, and to keep their messages politically relevant to a new generation of Americans. These challenges are especially significant because the membership of many major environmental organizations has been aging. (One of the largest and most influential conservation organizations, for example, reported that the average age of their membership is sixty-five, and only 5 percent of its million members are younger than fifty.)[37] In politics, moreover, public perceptions can become more important than environmental realities in creating priority for environmentalism on the national policy agenda. Many environmental problems, such as visibly polluted air and water, public pesticide exposures, and threatening toxic waste sites, that effectively dramatized the immediate need for environmental regulation now may seem—whatever the reality—less publicly important. Many newer, profoundly important environmental issues, such as global climate change or the relentless decline in the quality and quantity of fresh water, are difficult to characterize with a powerful, persuasive imagery that makes them immediately important and relevant to the public.

Thus, among the nation's environmental leadership, a growing, often heated discussion has evolved concerning whether environmentalist language is stale, the issues no longer compelling, and the major advocacy groups too unimaginative and complacent about delivering their political messages. A vigorous constituency within the environmental community is advocating new strategies and a fresh language to inspire a more contemporary image and wider public appeal for environmentalism, especially among the young, ethnic minorities, the economically underprivileged, and middle-income Americans recovering from a severe economic recession.

Modernizing Environmental Laws

The nation's environmental management is grounded on an essential but aging legal foundation of federal legislation and regulations. Many of these laws need updating and adaptation to remain relevant to contemporary environmental conditions and responsive to a rapidly enlarging and diversifying body of new knowledge created by environmental science. "Our environmental laws," environmental journalist and advocate Greg Esterbrook has noted, "are a generation or more out of date," and he cites what he believes are compelling examples: "The Clean Air Act, signed by President Richard M. Nixon in 1970, has not been amended since 1990, a quarter-century ago. The Clean Water Act, passed in 1972, has not been updated since 1987. The Endangered Species Act, passed in 1973, was last amended in 1982. The National Environmental Policy Act, the law that mandates environmental impact statements, was passed in 1970 and last amended in 1982."[38]

When the Toxic Substances Control Act was written in 1972, for example, it was unrecognized that more than 50,000 chemicals would be subject to its review and possible regulation, and consequently, complete and faithful implementation of the legislation has been impossible—an impasse long recognized and requiring a revised, updated regulatory strategy to relieve.[39]

Modernizing these laws has been difficult for several reasons. Party polarization over environmental regulation has become deeply entrenched within Congress and between Republican and Democratic presidents since 2000, imposing a policy deadlock that forestalls any sustained and comprehensive partisan collaboration to revise comprehensively existing environmental laws. Additionally, the nation's slow recovery from the severe 2008 economic recession, health care issues, and a growing national preoccupation with terrorism and national security have driven environmental issues down the list of governmental and public priorities. Without a compelling national emergency or a timely emergence of party collaboration on national environmental issues, modernizing the nation's environmental governance will continue to be slow and extremely incremental.

Implementing Policy

The character and pace of policy implementation changes continually in response to shifting public moods; to ebbs and flows in crucial resources, such as money and personnel invested in carrying out environmental policies; to changes in political party control of Congress, the White House, and state governments; and to other changes discussed in later chapters. In short, policy implementation is unfolding and variable, powerfully driven by economic, political, and cultural forces. Practically every important environmental ill has been targeted by a major federal law, but the majority of important environmental laws have been implemented at a plodding pace, and portions of all the laws exhibit regulatory rigor mortis.

One reason for this plodding pace is the growing complexity of the regulatory process. The average size of major environmental statutes has inflated from about fifty pages in the 1970s to more than 500 pages currently. The original CAA (1970) was sixty-eight pages, the CAA Amendments of 1990 weighed in at 788 pages, and the regulations required for their implementation will exceed 10,000 pages. Like an augury of the future, the American Clean Energy and Security Act (2009), the first climate change regulatory legislation to be proposed by the House of Representatives, bloated to more than 1,400 pages. To create the elephantine regulations necessary to implement these complex laws and to apply the procedures in the appropriate instances can consume an enormous amount of time.[40]

Another important source of regulatory delay is the increasing mismatch between the responsibilities assigned to environmental agencies and the budgetary resources required to accomplish them. Although the EPA's workload has increased enormously since its creation in 1970, its budget has failed to keep pace.[41] Decades of underfunding has left the EPA overwhelmed by the scientific and administrative complexity of its regulatory tasks. For example, by 2018 the EPA was decades behind in the required risk assessment—each of which might require eight years—for hundreds of chemicals on a growing list for which it was responsible.[42]

Enforcement of most environmental legislation also depends on voluntary compliance by regulated interests, public and private, but the responsible federal and state agencies often lack the resources to monitor compliance with the law. Few states, for example, routinely inspect public and private drinking water systems, even though such inspections are required by the SDWA (1974).[43] Many states lack the technical resources to develop numerical standards for many groundwater contaminants and, instead, depend on evidence of environmental damage or public health risks before acting to control these substances.

Controlling Costs

By most estimates, the national cost of environmental regulation does not seem excessive, particularly when compared with estimated economic benefits, nor likely to inhibit healthy economic growth.[44] Currently, the United States spends about $120 billion annually for environmental control or about 2 percent of the gross national product.[45] Overall, the annual proportion of national expenditures invested in pollution control appears to have decreased since 1990.[46] But these expenditures sometimes conceal troublesome details. The cost of individual regulatory programs is soaring, often inflicting heavy, unanticipated costs on specific economic sectors, depleting regulatory resources, and compelling a search for scarce, new funding sources, as the following examples illustrates:

- *Superfund* was created to clean up the nation's numerous abandoned hazardous waste sites. After originally authorizing $1.6 billion for the project, Congress was compelled in the mid-1980s to increase spending to $15.2 billion, and estimates suggest the program will require annual congressional supplements of at least $1.5 billion after 2010.[47]

- *Federal storm water runoff regulations* will require the District of Columbia to spend $1.9 billion to completely renovate its antiquated sewer system.[48]

The roster of inflationary programs has become a virtual catalog of the nation's major environmental laws. Unanticipated environmental problems, unexpected scientific complexities, and inexperience with new regulations are the common causes of cost overruns. The litany of other inflationary provocations includes administrative delay, litigation, bureaucratic bungling, waste, missing information, and political obstruction. Whatever the reasons, excessive costs divert public and private capital from more productive investment, promote economic inefficiency, impair competitiveness in some industries, and increase consumer costs. Bloated budgets become a cudgel in the hands of opponents eager to beat back demands for essential improvements in environmental management.

Environmentalists traditionally suspect, often correctly, that the estimates of regulatory costs produced by businesses or other regulated interests are inflated deliberately. (However, they are seldom dubious about the considerably lower estimates they usually produce.) They also believe that benefit–cost comparisons applied to environmental policies are usually biased, because it is much easier to monetize the costs of regulation than the benefits. Leaving aside predictable and usually unresolvable arguments over the "real" costs of environmental regulations, the fact of sharply rising costs has compelled many major environmental leaders to seek creative strategies for reducing the expense and to collaborate in this effort with the businesses and industries being regulated.

Responding to Evolving Science

When the political leadership of U.S. environmentalism set out its initial policy agenda following Earth Day 1970, the ozone hole, global climate change, genetically altered foods, endocrine disrupters, leaking underground toxic storage tanks, ionizing radiation, indoor air pollution, and a multitude of other environmental issues—as well as many thousands of chemicals now common in U.S. commerce and industry—were unknown. All these matters and many more currently on the environmental movement's priority list are largely the product of scientific research in the past several decades. In later chapters, we observe how science contributes constructively to environmental management through, for example, the discovery of environmentally benign substitutes for more harmful chemicals such as chlorofluorocarbons. But the relentless evolution of scientific research can also frustrate, confuse, and discredit existing environmental policy by producing all sorts of new and unexpected discoveries. For example, to meet the public health standards of the CAA, the EPA in 2006 slightly lowered the short-term threshold for public exposure to particulates (soot) as a result of scientific research conducted since the original standard had been set several decades previously. Although the new standard, described by the EPA as "the most health-protective in U.S. history," is assumed to create from $9 billion to $70 billion in long-term health and visibility benefits, it is also estimated to cost electric utilities alone about $400 million yearly to implement.[49]

A rising tide of ecological science poses several continuing challenges to environmental scientists and policymakers. First, it can produce new data indicating that prior policy decisions may have been based on inadequate information and must be revised—perhaps with great political or legal difficulty and at considerable expense.[50]

Scientific research can also produce ambiguous, fragmentary, or contradictory data concerning the existence or extent of an environmental problem—especially at an early stage in the research—at a time when policymakers feel compelled to do something about the issue. Sometimes a solution—or the appearance of one—seems so urgent that policymakers believe that they cannot wait for additional research or perhaps that additional research may never satisfactorily resolve the issue, because the impact of an environmental regulation will remain inconclusive. The continuing scientific ambiguity about the ecological impact of human-made chemicals mimicking human hormones (often called endocrine disrupters) and the persisting controversy about the ecological impact of species loss illustrate this sort of science problem.

Finally, scientific research can complicate environmental policymaking and, in the process, drive up the cost and time involved in remedying environmental ills by disclosing, instead of timely or quick answers to an ecological problem, the unanticipated need for new information. Pentagon planners call these discoveries the *unk-unks*—the unknown unknowns, the kinds of information they don't know are needed until a problem is investigated. Consider, for instance, the experience of scientists trying to explain the sudden dramatic increase in fish kills between 1991 and 1993 in North Carolina's vast estuaries. Unprecedented millions of fish were floating to the water surface with large, bleeding sores, often accompanied by a strange smell that burned the eyes and throat—not the smell of decaying fish. At first, investigators assumed the familiar explanation—lack of dissolved oxygen in the water, a seasonal deficiency in the estuarine environment that is sometimes fatal to fish. Instead, extensive fish biopsies gradually revealed something wholly unexpected—the presence of enormous quantities of a tiny, one-celled creature, a dinoflagellate of the species *Pfiesteria piscicida,* an apparently harmless organism seldom studied and never associated with extensive fish kills. So biologists began to observe *Pfiesteria* habits intensively. They discovered that, when estuarine nutrient levels of nitrogen and phosphorous increased significantly, *Pfiesteria* can transform into a murderous organism with a personality akin to the star of the science fiction movie *Alien,* multiplying in staggering numbers and aggressively attacking and consuming huge fish populations. Thus, an unk-unk—in this case, the complete life cycle of *Pfiesteria*—was unexpectedly uncovered in the course of investigating a fish kill and became a critical component in understanding and eliminating the problem itself.[51]

The Challenge of Sustainability

In September 2018, the Swedish manufacturer of Legos, the tough, brightly colored little plastic blocks found worldwide, announced it would soon create its toys "sustainably" by replacing with less polluting materials the plastic in the

100 million bricks it produced daily. Across the Atlantic, that same month, the Mayor's Office of Sustainability in New York announced that it was giving to 320,000 students in public and charter high schools a reusable, stainless-steel water bottle to replace single-use plastic bottles in an effort to reduce landfill waste.[52,53] By the time New York's students received their new water bottles, more than 400 American colleges were offering sustainability-related bachelor's degrees and the United Nations had declared Seventeen Sustainable Development Goals as an essential metric to measure national progress globally. Sustainability planning, in one form or another, has become a global enterprise.

The concept of "sustainability" or "sustainable development," as a transcendent vision for public policymaking, has permeated deeply into the philosophy of American environmentalism and its image of a sound civic culture. Yet sustainability is often an imprecise and contested vision, at once compelling and formidable to translate into viable public policy. And Washington's once enlarging commitment to promoting sustainable national development through public policy, culminating with the Obama administration's ambitious national plans, has rapidly receded as the Trump environmental agenda gives priority to other matters.

Sustainability and Federal Policy

In 1987, sustainable development crossed the threshold from an emerging concern to a transcendent goal for many within the national environmental movement. In that year, *Our Common Future* (often called the Brundtland Report) was published by the World Commission on Environment and Development. This report responded to increasing worldwide apprehension about the long-term environmental impact of national growth by concisely proposing that nations balance present and future development by "meeting the needs of the present without compromising the ability of future generations to meet their own needs." While the report's definition has become virtually synonymous with the concept itself, sustainable development in the United States has been translated nationally into a multitude of variations. The EPA, for example, defines sustainability to mean "to create and maintain the conditions under which humans and nature can exist in productive harmony to support present and future generations."[54] Different definitions often imply different policy agendas focused on different resources and development metrics.

Beginning with the Clinton administration (1992–2000), the federal government became increasingly active in promoting national sustainability planning and research. Clinton attained national visibility to sustainability issues by creating the President's Council on Sustainable Development, headed by Vice President Al Gore, to advise the White House on sustainability matters. While sustainability never assumed White House importance during George W. Bush's administration (2000–2008), state and local governments began increasingly to introduce sustainability as an operational concept in land and resource planning. By 2010, a U.S. national directory cited more than 2,700 private or public entities involved with environmental sustainability.[55]

The Obama administration promoted sustainability as a major environmental priority, investing considerable political capital and federal resources in advancing sustainability planning in both the public and private sectors. Among Obama's five executive orders promoting sustainability, the last and most comprehensive, EO 13514, required all federal agencies to publish an annual Strategic Sustainability Plan, mandated that all federal buildings progressively achieve standards for federal sustainable buildings, ordered the federal government to achieve greater energy efficiency and reliance on renewable energy, and committed the federal government to reduce climate-warming emissions.

The election of Donald Trump brought an end to the Obama sustainability initiatives. While Obama's executive orders were not revoked—with the exception of the mandate for federal reduction of climate-warming emissions—sustainability planning appeared to be a White House cast off, unattended, underfunded, and largely unmentioned.

State and Local Government Initiatives

Local governments, and to a lesser extent the states, are gradually introducing sustainability into their planning procedures. A third of American cities have adopted sustainability plans within the last decade, almost a fifth of local governments have specific budget allocations for sustainability-related activities, and about a fifth have dedicated staff for sustainability planning.[56] Efforts continue in numerous state legislatures to create legal mandates requiring some form of statewide sustainability planning or state sustainability staff position. Nonetheless, the states have been slower than local governments to introduce sustainability planning into their governing process.

Sustainability's Many Meanings

Over time, as Jonathan M. Harris, an international environmental scholar, has observed, the definition of a sustainable society has been interpreted to include at least three qualities:

- *Economic:* "An economically sustainable system must be able to produce goods and services on a continuing basis, to maintain manageable levels of government and external debt, and to avoid extreme sectoral imbalances which damage agricultural and industrial production."

- *Social:* "A socially sustainable system must achieve distributional equity, adequate provision for social services including health and education, gender equality, and political accountability and participation."

- *Environmental:* "An environmentally sustainable system must maintain a stable resource base, avoiding over-exploitation of renewable resource systems . . . and depleting non-renewable resources. . . . This includes maintenance of biodiversity, atmospheric stability, and other ecosystem functions."[57]

Sustainability, however, is still loaded with ambiguities that can reduce it to a cliché weighted with goals that can seem competitive, even contradictory. This ambiguity easily leads to dissimilar, sometimes conflicting or contested definitions that become apparent especially when translating sustainability into specific public policy goals or creating a metric to measure progress toward sustainable development.

Protection of nonrenewable resources, for instance, may appear inconsistent with sustained economic production. Adequate provision of health and education services may appear to require reduction of public spending to protect biodiversity. Should sustainable energy consumption be measured by growth of renewable energy production or by reduction in per capita energy consumption? Decisions inevitably involve political, economic, and social trade-offs between competing policy goals and competing stakeholders. Some of the most divisive political controversies within the environmental movement arise from these decisions. Nonetheless, decisions, inspired by some vision of sustainability, are continually being made by American governments, corporations, and educational institutions that do translate sustainability into public policies, corporate growth strategies, and educational curricula.

PLAN FOR THE BOOK

This chapter has introduced, broadly and briefly, the major themes that later chapters explore in more depth and detail. It has also provided a review of many significant events since Earth Day 1970 that define the political setting for environmental policymaking today, thus creating a present sense of place in the rapidly evolving politics of U.S. environmentalism. The chapters that follow progress from a broad overview of the major governmental institutions, private interests, and political forces shaping all environmental policy today to an increasingly sharp focus on the distinctive issues, actors, and interests involved with specific environmental problems.

Chapter 2 (Making Policy: The Process) describes the phases of the policy cycle that shape all major environmental policies. Included is an exploration of the influence of the U.S. Constitution and U.S. political culture on this process. Also discussed is the nature of environmental pressure groups and other stakeholders in the policy process and the important role of public opinion and the scientific community in policymaking.

Chapter 3 (Making Policy: Governmental Institutions and Politics) describes the specific U.S. governmental institutions, private interests, and political forces engaged in environmental policymaking. The narrative includes a discussion of the presidency, the important bureaucracies, Congress, and the courts. Also discussed is the importance of political events such as changing congressional majorities, economic growth or recession, and shifting public moods.

Almost all environmental policymaking entails some common issues. Chapter 4 (Common Policy Challenges: Risk Assessment and Environmental Justice) explores two of the most scientifically contentious and politically controversial of these issues: risk analysis and environmental justice. Risk analysis is concerned with determining whether specific chemicals, industrial processes, consumer products, and environmental contaminants, among many other things, pose a significant threat to public health or the environment and, if they do, how they should be regulated. Environmental justice investigates whether various social groups, particularly minorities of color and economically disadvantaged individuals, are disproportionately exposed to environmental risks or denied reasonable opportunity to protect themselves from such risks.

Among the longest-running and least-resolvable conflicts in environmental policymaking is over the economic cost and fairness of environmental regulations. Chapter 5 (More Choice: The Battle Over Regulatory Economics) looks at two major aspects of this issue: the use of benefit–cost analysis to evaluate environmental regulations and proposals to replace current methods of environmental regulation with policies that rely on market forces to achieve results. Discussed are the major arguments and interests aligned on different sides of these issues together with evidence about the impact of proposed economic reforms when they have been instituted.

Chapter 6 (Command and Control in Action: Air and Water Pollution Regulation) describes the nation's major air and water pollution control laws, evaluates their impacts, and discusses the impact of new Trump administration regulatory reforms. The chapter explains how these laws illustrate the command-and-control style of regulation now common in the United States. Also described are the substantive elements of the CAA (1970) and the Federal Water Pollution Control Act Amendments (1972). The accomplishments and deficiencies resulting from these major air and water pollution laws are reviewed together with characteristic policymaking challenges created by the scientific and economic requirements of air and water pollution control.

Chapter 7 (A Regulatory Thicket: Toxic and Hazardous Substances) focuses on the major regulatory legislation to control environmental dangers posed by chemical, biological, and radioactive agents. The major laws examined include the TSCA (1976), the RCRA (1974), and Superfund legislation. The chapter briefly describes the major elements of these important laws and examines their impacts in the context of determining whether they have accomplished their purpose to control the manufacture and distribution of ecologically harmful chemicals and to safely regulate toxic waste from the cradle to the grave.

Chapter 8 (Energy: America's Energy Politics in Transformation) describes the nation's primary energy resources and increasing reliance on fossil fuels together with the ecological, economic, and political risks entailed. The Trump administration's new fossil fuel regulatory changes and promotion of coal production are explained and evaluated. The chapter focuses special attention on increasing petroleum supplies, the attractions and environmental dangers associated with increased coal production, and the environmental problems linked to nuclear power. Also explored are future energy policy options and the ecological implications, especially in the contentious trade-off between coal and nuclear power as future energy sources and the challenges created by greater reliance on energy conservation and energy efficiency as alternatives to major reliance on traditional energy sources.

Chapter 9 (635 Million Acres of Politics: The Contested Resources of Public Lands) focuses on the historic political battle over the use of more than 600 million acres of public land, mostly controlled by the federal government. The narrative examines the major economic and environmental interests engaged in a century-long battle over access to timber, natural gas, petroleum, grazing land, hydroelectric power, and other important resources on federal land. Described are the major federal agencies caught in the middle of these conflicts, such as the Department of the Interior and the U.S. Forest Service. The chapter also discusses new Trump administration federal land use policies, the major legislation land use agencies are expected to implement in managing these resources, and the resulting problems, including the obstacles to achieving ecosystem management on federal lands.

Chapter 10 (The Politics and Policy of Global Climate Change) focuses on the scientific and political status of domestic climate policy and the Trump administration's impact on national climate regulations. The scientific evidence of global climate change, the political and scientific conflict associated with control of climate-warming emissions, and the impact of climate issues on public opinion and voting is examined. The Trump administration's major revisions of national climate emissions regulations are described and evaluated. The growing importance of states in national climate policy is discussed. The Trump administration's withdrawal from the Paris Accord to control global climate-warming emissions is explained and evaluated.

CONCLUSION

In calendar time, the presidential election of Donald Trump preceded the fifth decade of the U.S. Environmental Era proclaimed in the 1970s. In political time, it commenced an uncertain season for environmentalists now deep into that era, a season of conflicting implications and richly contradictory experiences. From the perspective of policymaking, a sense of frustration and impasse nurtured by often bitterly divisive conflict between organized environmentalism and the White House has permeated the era. Yet evidence is abundant that environmental leaders have enormously enlarged the temporal and geographical scope of their policy vision to embrace sustainable development, ecosystem management, and global ecological restoration. Improvements in environmental quality have become increasingly apparent and sometimes impressive, yet regulatory achievements fall gravely below expectations. Environmentalism has matured to the point where its organizational advocates can reflect critically on past experience and accept the need for rethinking and reforming their policy agendas, especially the need to moderate the escalating cost of environmental protection and to find more effective ways to implement pollution regulation. At the same time, the rapid progress of environmental science reveals with increasing acuteness the need to improve significantly the quality of the science base on which environmental policy is grounded. Environmentalism is now firmly rooted in U.S. political culture, yet its electoral force often seems surprisingly feeble.

The election of Donald Trump, however, has abruptly and radically altered the political trajectory of American environmental policymaking. The Trump administration's ambitious agenda of environmental deregulation, accelerated fossil fuel energy development, and federal divestment of protected public lands constitutes the most pervasive constriction of national environmental governance since Earth Day 1970. While the ultimate impact of these unprecedented White House initiatives may be determined by the federal courts, Congressional elections, and public opinion, the short-term impact has been uncertainty, diminished capacity, and a retreat of federal authority in environmental governance.

Suggested Readings

Andrews, Richard N. L. *Managing the Environment, Managing Ourselves: A History of American Environmental Policy.* 2nd ed. New Haven, CT: Yale University Press, 2006.

Daynes, Byron W., and Holly O. Hughes. *White House Politics and the Environment: Franklin D. Roosevelt to George W. Bush.* College Station: Texas A&M University, 2010.

Gardner, Gary. *Creating a Sustainable Future: The Need for Innovation and Leadership.* Washington, DC: Worldwatch Institute, 2011.

Lomborg, Bjorn. *The Skeptical Environmentalist: Measuring the Real State of the World.* New York: Cambridge University Press, 2001.

Mazmanian, Daniel A., and Michael E. Kraft. *Toward Sustainable Communities: Transition and Transformations in Environmental Policy.* 2nd ed. Cambridge, MA: MIT Press, 2009.

Meadowcroft, James, and Daniel J. Fiorino. *Conceptual Innovation in Environmental Policy.* Cambridge, MA: MIT Press, 2017.

Merchant, Carolyn. *American Environmental History: An Introduction.* New York: Columbia University Press, 2007.

Sachs, Jeffrey D. *The Age of Sustainable Development.* New York: Columbia University Press, 2015.

Shabecoff, Philip. *A Fierce Green Fire: The American Environmental Movement.* Washington, DC: Island Press, 2003.

Notes

1. Zack Coleman, "Freaking Out Over Fracking," *Washington Examiner*, April 27, 2015, available at http://www.washingtonexaminer.com/freaking-out-over -fracking/article/2563518.
2. Ibid.
3. Troy Hooper, "Colorado Fracking Protests Target Drilling Near School," *The Colorado Independent*, June 6, 2012, available at http://www.huffington post.com/2012/06/06/colorado-fracking-protest-school_n_1575816.html (accessed March 13, 2015).
4. "Best Places to Live 2015, Erie Colo.," *Money*, available at http://time.com/ money/3984422/erie-colorado-best-places-to-live-2015/.
5. Mark Jaffe, "Drilling Rigs and Housing Development Face Off in Colorado Suburbs," *Denver Post*, February 13, 2015, available at http://www.denverpost .com/managingtheboom/ci_27522307/drilling-rigs-and-housing-development -face-off-colorado.
6. U.S Department of the Interior, 2012 Oil Shale and Tar Sands Programmatic EIS Information Center, "About Oil Shale," available at http://ostseis.anl .gov/guide/oilshale/.
7. Catherine Tsai, "Halliburton Executive Drinks Fracking Fluid," *Huff Post Green*, August 22, 2011, available at www.huffingtonpost.com/2011/08/22/ halliburton-executive-drinks-fracking-fluid_n_933621.html.
8. Curt Suplee, *What You Need to Know About Energy* (Washington, DC: The National Academies, 2008), 29.
9. U.S Environmental Protection Agency, Office of Research and Development, *Assessment of the Potential Impacts of Hydraulic Fracturing for Oil and Gas on Drinking Water Resources: Executive Summary* (Washington, DC: U.S. Environmental Protection Agency, 2015), E-6.
10. Troy Hooper, "Colorado Fracking Protests."
11. Mark Jaffe, "Drilling Rigs and Housing Development Face Off in Colorado Suburbs," *Denver Post*, February 16, 2015, available at https://getpocket.com/a/ read/845837745; see also Alex Burness, "Erie Neighbors Say They've Been Kept in Dark About 13 Planning Sites," *Daily Camera*, available at http://www.dailycamera .com/erie-news/ci_25968637/erie-neighbors-say-theyve-been-kept-dark-about.
12. Mark Jaffe, "Drilling Rigs and Housing Development Face Off in Colorado Suburbs."
13. Zack Coleman, "Freaking Out Over Fracking."
14. Anthony Hahn, "Vista Ridge Residents, Erie Officials Wary of Fracking Sites, Push Back on Health Reports," *Daily Camera*, May 31, 2017, available at http://www.dailycamera.com/erie-news/ci_31028251/vista-ridge-resident.
15. U.S. EPA, "Air Quality Trends," available at https://gispub.epa.gov/air/ trendsreport/2017/#growth_w_cleaner_air.
16. U.S. EPA, "National Air Quality: Status and Trends of Key Pollutants: Status and Trends Through 2016," https://www.epa.gov/air-trends.

17. U.S. General Accounting Office (GAO), *Chemical Risk Assessment: Selected Federal Agencies, Procedures, Assumptions and Policies,* Document no. GAO 01–810 (Washington, DC, August 2001), 16.

18. GAO, *Chemical Regulation: Options Exist to Improve EPA's Ability to Assess Health Risks and Manage Its Chemical Review Program,* Report no. GAO-05-2005 (Washington, DC, June 13, 2005), 1; see also, GAO, *Chemical Regulation: Observations on the Toxic Substances Control Act and EPA Implementation,* Report no. GAO-13-696T (Washington, DC, February, 2012).

19. Robert O'Malley, Kent Davender-Bares, and William C. Clark, "'Better' Data: Not as Simple as It Might Seem," *Environment Magazine,* March 2003, 9–18.

20. Katherine Probst and David Konisky, *Superfund's Future: What Will It Cost? Executive Summary* (Washington, DC: Resources for the Future, 2001).

21. A comprehensive summary of federal environmental legislation since 1970 is found in Norman J. Vig and Michael E. Kraft, "Major Federal Laws on the Environment, 1969–2008," in *Environmental Policy: New Directions for the Twenty-First Century,* ed. Norman J. Vig and Michael E. Kraft (Washington, DC: CQ Press, 2010), App. 1.

22. Useful analyses of the presidency's role in environmental policymaking can be found in Dennis L. Soden, ed., *The Environmental Presidency* (Albany, NY: SUNY Press, 1999); Norman J. Vig, "Presidential Powers and Environmental Policy," in *Environmental Policy: New Directions for the Twenty-First Century,* ed. Norman J. Vig and Michael E. Kraft (Washington, DC: CQ Press, 2010), 75–98.

23. The Carter administration's difficulties with energy policy are examined from different perspectives in Richard H. K. Vietor, *Energy Policy in America since 1945* (Cambridge: Cambridge University Press, 1984); Pietro S. Nivola, *The Politics of Energy Conservation* (Washington, DC: Brookings Institution, 1986).

24. More detailed analyses of Reagan's environmental policies are found in Michael E. Kraft and Norman J. Vig, "Environmental Policy in the Reagan Presidency," *Political Science Quarterly* 99 (Fall 1984): 414–439; Barry D. Freedman, *Regulation in the Reagan-Bush Era: The Eruption of Presidential Influence* (Pittsburgh, PA: University of Pittsburgh Press, 1995); V. Kerry Smith, *Environmental Policy Under Reagan's Executive Order: The Role of Cost–Benefit Analysis* (Chapel Hill: University of North Carolina Press, 1984); Robert V. Bartlett, "The Budgetary Process and Environmental Policy," in *Environmental Policies in the 1980s,* ed. Norman J. Vig and Michael E. Kraft (Washington, DC: CQ Press, 1984); J. Clarence Davies, "Environmental Institutions and the Reagan Administration," in *Environmental Policies in the 1980s,* ed. Norman J. Vig and Michael E. Kraft (Washington, DC: CQ Press, 1984).

25. On the Clinton presidency, see Campbell Colin and Bert A. Rockman, eds., *The Clinton Presidency: First Impressions* (Chatham, NJ: Chatham House, 1995); "GOP Sets 104th Congress on New Regulatory Course," *Congressional Quarterly Weekly Report,* December 10, 1994, 1693–1719.

26. During Clinton's first term, however, Congress passed the important Food Quality Protection Act of 1996. The act created a new approach to regulating pesticides used in food, fiber, and other crops by requiring the EPA to determine the health risk in foods by considering all the ways in which people were exposed to harmful chemicals and created a reasonable risk health standard for raw and processed food that replaced the earlier standard barring processed food containing even a trace of chemicals thought to cause cancer.

27. The environmentalist indictment of George W. Bush's administration is summarized in Natural Resources Defense Council, *Rewriting the Rules, Year-End Report 2002: The Bush Administration's Assault on the Environment* (Washington, DC: Natural Resources Defense Council, January 2003); U.S. Congress, House of Representatives, Committee on Government Reform—Minority Staff, Special Investigations Division, *Politics and Science in the Bush Administration: Prepared for Rep. Henry W. Waxman* (Washington, DC, August 2003).

28. Quoted in Katherine Q. Seelye, "Whitman Quits as E.P.A. Chief," *New York Times*, May 22, 2003, 1A.

29. Jeremy P. Jacobs and Jean Chemnick, "Obama Proposes Agency's 3rd Consecutive Budget Cut," *E&E Reporter*, February 13, 2012, available at http://www.eenews.net/Greenwire/rss/2012/02/13/2 (accessed May 20, 2012).

30. On details of the Plan, see *U.S. EPA, Clean Power Plan for Existing Power Plants*, available at http://www.epa.gov/cleanpowerplan/clean-power-plan-existing-power-plants; and Union of Concerned Scientists, *The Clean Power Plan: A Climate Changer* (Cambridge, MA: Union of Concerned Scientists, 2015), available at http://www.ucsusa.org/our-work/global-warming/reduce-emissions/what-is-the-clean-power-plan#.VmOm-r_i4oE.

31. Juliet Eilperin, "Trump Pledges To Cut Regulations Down To 1960 Levels—But That May Be Impossible," *Washington Post*, December 14, 2017, available at https://www.washingtonpost.com/politics/trump-pledges-to-whittle-federal-regulations-down-to-1960-levels/2017/12/14/17de13a4-e119-11e7-bbd0-9dfb2e37492a_story.html?utm_term=.005ee64db371.

32. Mark Hand, "Repeal of Obama-Era Environmental Rules Dominates Trump's Regulatory Agenda," *Think Progress*, July 29, 2017, available at https://thinkprogress.org/trump-releases-deregulatory-agenda-6ad07b7dd28a.

33. Andrew Follett, "Poll: Environment Is Least Important Issue to Americans," *The Daily Caller News Foundation*, December 21, 2016, available at http://dailycallernewssfoundation.org; Pew Research Center, People and the Press: "Presidential Election Reactions and Expectations," November 21, 2016, available at http://www.people-press.org/2016/11/21/presidential-election-reactions-and-expectations/.

34. Kate Sheppard and Alexander C. Kaufman, "Donald Trump's Latest Budget Still Takes an Ax to Environmental Protection Agency," May 23, 2017, available at https://www.huffingtonpost.com/entry/trump-budget-environmental-protection-agency_us_592449d8e4b034684b100247.

35. Adam Beitman, "Trump's Attack on Clean Air and Climate Action Targets Policy That Saves Thousands of Lives and Billions of Dollars," Sierra Club, March 27, 2017, available at https://content.sierraclub.org/press -releases/2017/03/trump-s-attack-clean-air-and-climate-action-targets -policy-saves-thousands.

36. Nadja Popovich and Livia Albeck-Ripka, "Environmental Rules on the Way Out Under Trump," *New York Times*, October 6, 2017, available at www .nytimes.com/interactive/2017/10/05/climate/trump-environment-rules -reversed.html?_r=0.

37. Paul Voosen, "Myth-Busting Scientist Pushes Greens Past Reliance on 'Horror Stories,'" *E&E Reporter*, April 23, 2012, available at www.eenews .net/public/Greenwire/2012/04/03/1.

38. Greg Esterbrook, "Let's Modernize Our Environmental Laws," *New York Times*, October 8, 2015, A31.

39. U.S. Governmental Accountability Office (GAO), *Toxic Substances EPA Has Increased Efforts to Assess and Control Chemicals But Could Strengthen Its Approach*, "Report in Brief," Report no. GAO-13-249 (Washington DC: GAO, 2013).

40. GAO, *Status of EPA's Reviews of Chemicals Under the Chemical Testing Program*, Report no. GAO/RCED 92–31FS (Washington, DC, October 1991), 27.

41. J. Clarence Davies, *Nanotechnology Oversight: An Agenda for the New Administration* (Washington, DC: Woodrow Wilson Center, 2008), 10.

42. Sheldon Krimsky, "The Unsteady State and Inertia of Chemical Regulation Under the US Toxic Substances Control Act," *PLOS*, December 18, 2017, available at http://journals.plos.org/plosbiology/article?id=10.1371/journal .pbio.2002404.

43. Michael Decourcy Hines, "Survey Finds Flaws in States' Water Inspections," *New York Times*, April 15, 1993, A14; GAO, *Widening Gap Between Needs and Available Resources Threatens Vital EPA Program*, Report no. GAO/RCED 92–184, Washington, DC, July 1992.

44. See, for example, The White House, Office of Management and Budget, *Draft 2012 Report to Congress on the Benefits and Costs of Federal Regulations and Unfunded Mandates on State, Local, and Tribal Entities*, available at http:// www.whitehouse.gov/omb/inforeg_regpol_reports_congress, for estimated costs and benefit of EPA regulations between 2002 and 2012.

45. U.S. Department of Commerce, Bureau of the Census, *Statistical Abstract of the United States, 1996* (Washington, DC: Government Printing Office, 1997).

46. For estimates on national pollution expenditures and their impact, see William A. Pizer and Raymond Kopp, "Calculating the Costs of Environmental Regulation," Discussion Paper 03–06, Resources for the Future, Washington, DC, March 2003; U.S. Environmental Protection Agency, Office of Policy Planning and Evaluation, *The Costs of a Clean Environment* (Washington, DC: EPA, 1990), v–viii.

47. Jonathan L. Ramseur, Mark Reisch, and James E. McCarthy, "Superfund Taxes or General Revenues: Funding Policy Issues for the Superfund Program I," Document RL 31410, Congressional Research Service, Washington, DC, February 4, 2008, 9.
48. Lisa Rein, "As Pressure Increases, So Do Ways to Control Pollution," *Washington Post,* May 23, 2006, A01.
49. Andrea Fischer, "EPA Tightens Particulate Matter Rule; Manufacturers Concerned With Costs," *Transport Topics,* October 2, 2006, 4, 35.
50. Ibid.
51. Chris Reuther, "Microscopic Murderer: Pollution May Be Motivating *Pfiesteria* to Kill Fish by the Thousands," Academy of Natural Sciences, Philadelphia, May–June 1999, available at www.acnatsci.org/research/kye/pfiester.html.
52. Stanley Reed, "Lego Wants to Completely Remake Its Toy Bricks (Without Anyone Noticing)," *New York Times,* September 1, 2018, B1.
53. James Barron, "320,000 High Schoolers to Get Free Water Bottles. The Goal? 54 Million Fewer Single-Use Containers," *New York Times,* September 24, 2018, A23.
54. EPA, "What is Sustainability?" available at https://www.epa.gov/sustainability/learn-about-sustainability#what.
55. Thaddeus C. Trzyna, Elizabeth Margold, and Julia K. Osborn, *World Directory of Environmental Groups,* 7th ed. (Sacramento, CA: International Center for the Environment and Public Policy, 2005); Harbinger Communications, *National Environmental Directory* (Santa Cruz, CA: Harbinger Communications, 2005), available at www.environmentaldirectory.net/search.htm.
56. International City Managers Association, "Nearly a Third of Local Governments Have Adopted Sustainability Plans," available at https://icma.org/articles/article/nearly-third-local-governments-have-adopted-sustainability-plans.
57. Jonathan M. Harris, "Basic Principles of Sustainable Development," Working Paper 00–04, Global Development and Environment Institute, Medford, MA, 2000, 5–6.

MAKING POLICY

The Process

In 2014, a once common bumblebee had become so uncommon that it earned the attention of the White House. The rusty patched bumblebee, one of the insect pollinators essential to production of American's fruit, nut, and vegetable crops, was rapidly disappearing. All 4,000 U.S. bee species appeared in decline but none so severely as the rusty patched bee.[1] In the previous twenty years, the bumblebee's population had fallen by almost 90 percent, and many scientists predicted that the bee was facing extinction unless the federal government initiated a plan to save it. By 2014, a movement to protect the bee had gathered sufficient political momentum to enlist support of President Barack Obama. Thus, the fate of the rusty patched bumblebee arrived on the federal government's policy agenda.

PROTECTING THE BEE: THE PATHWAYS OF POLICY

The prolonged and contentious effort that followed Obama's decision to protect the bee and the multibillion-dollar economy it supports displayed many of the enduring qualities, and provoked many of the conflicts, deeply embedded in the government's environmental policymaking. This chapter concerns the basic design of this policymaking and the fundamentals that shape most public policies. The bumblebee's Washington odyssey is part of that larger story.

Multiple Agencies Deliberate

The decline of the rusty patched bumblebee resulted in a widely reported presidential policy initiative in mid-2014 to protect America's endangered pollinating insects. "Pollinators contribute more than $24 billion to the United States economy," emphasized the president, "of which honeybees account for more than $15 billion through their vital role in keeping fruits, nuts, and vegetables in our diets."[2] Obama then created a task force to investigate the rapid decline of honeybees and other pollinators. The task force originated in the White House, but like many other White House policy initiatives, this required multiagency collaboration. Obama directed two other executive agencies, the Department of Agriculture and the Environmental Protection Agency, to lead in discovering why the pollinators were declining and to develop a conservation plan.

More executive departments were soon involved. If the rusty patched bee faced extinction, it might be protected by the Endangered Species Act of 1973, intended to preserve any species of wild animal or plant in danger of extinction throughout all or a significant portion of its range. This crucial decision rested with the Fish and Wildlife Service (FWS) in the Department of the Interior. If the FWS determined a species was endangered, the FWS could "list" the species, which would then be protected by the federal government. Only the president or Congress could overrule the decision.

After almost two years' research and consultation with other agencies, the FWS proposed in 2016 to list the bee. By this time, however, the bee's fate had incited an intense controversy between politically important stakeholders deeply divided concerning whether the rusty patched bumblebee should be listed. The embattled stakeholders had organized national campaigns to promote or oppose the "endangered" listing, pressured Congress to intervene, and enlisted the support of federal agencies with which they were closely allied—all common strategies in American public policymaking.

Pressure Groups Mobilize

Support for the endangered listing was widespread among organizations representing environmentalists, biological scientists, conservationists, and public health officials, joined by many congressional Democrats and numerous scientists working in the private sector. They were also joined by political leaders in many northern and midwestern states, where the agricultural economies depended heavily on pollinators, and by the commercial bee industry, whose bees were essential to pollinate major crop production and which had experienced a 44 percent loss of bee population in a single year. These interests looked to government scientists in the EPA, the FWS, the Department of the Interior, and other federal health and conservation agencies for additional support.

Opposition to the bee listing also mobilized a diversity of economically and politically potent interest groups. If the bee were listed, many farmers feared losing income and perhaps their farms because farmers might be forbidden to use powerful pesticides and insecticides that successfully protected crops but unintentionally and predictably killed millions of pollinators like bumblebees.[3] The farm protest, led by national organizations such as the American Farm Bureau

Federation and the National Association of State Departments of Agriculture, was joined by international chemical corporations such as Syngenta and Dow Chemical, which produced pesticides widely used in the United States to protect wheat, barley, corn, rice, sorghum, and potato crops. Other major interests opposed to the listing included the American Petroleum Institute, National Association of Home Builders, and the National Cotton Council of America. Many congressmen from midwestern and western farm districts also joined the antilisting coalition.

Scientific Controversy Prevails

As often happens in environmental policymaking, conflict prevailed over the quality of the science involved in the Obama initiative. Disagreement intensified among government scientists concerning whether the pesticides suspected of endangering the bees threatened the pollinators with extinction. Scientists in the Department of Agriculture, the EPA, the FWS, and the Department of the Interior, for example, advanced conflicting estimates of the pesticides' potency.

The Courts Intervene

Another predictable result of the bee controversy appeared when the federal courts were drawn into the conflict. Several national environmental organizations successfully petitioned federal judges to compel the FWS to hasten its deliberations about the bee listing. Opponents of the listing were also preparing legal strategies to contest the FWS listing if it occurred. Finally, nearing the end of the Obama administration in late 2016, the FWS finally announced its intention to list the rusty patched bumblebee in January 2017.[4] Proponents of the listing, however, had scant time to celebrate. The 2016 elections brought Donald Trump to the White House, much to the satisfaction of the listing opponents who anticipated that Trump would overturn the FWS endangerment finding.

Contested Policy Is Created

On January 20, 2017, Donald Trump, a fierce advocate for reduced governmental regulation, became president and immediately signed an executive order freezing all pending federal regulations—the bee listing included—for sixty days while the new administration reviewed them. "The Trump administration has put the rusty-patched bumblebee on the path to extinction," warned a senior attorney for a major environmentalist organization that promptly filed suit against the FWS, claiming the agency had illegally delayed its bee listing.[5] In mid-February, however, the FWS ruled that the bee was "balancing precariously on the brink of extinction" and announced its intention, despite White House displeasure, to officially list the bee as endangered by mid-March. And so, the rusty patched bumblebee became the first American bee to reach the endangered list.[6]

The bee might be protected environmentally but not yet politically. In February 2018, Congress joined the bee controversy when Senate Republicans organized a committee to consider "modernizing" the Endangered Species Act, which might make it possible to remove species, like the bee, already listed as endangered by the FWS. Also, the pesticides threatening bee populations are still widespread across American agriculture. Congressional Democrats, joined by many conservation, farmworker, and consumer groups, have repeatedly introduced legislation to limit the use of pesticides threatening bee populations. Policymaking, and policy controversy, over bee protection will continue indefinitely.[7]

Policymaking Is a Process

The bee controversy exemplifies the multitude of actors and institutions, the complex fabric of decisions, and the sometimes glacial, disjointed, and frequently contentious sequence of events involved in the making of national environmental policy.

Although environmental policies often develop less tumultuously, the bee listing incident features some characteristics common to environmental policymaking. First, policymaking is a process that involves a number of related decisions originating from different institutions and actors ranging across the whole domain of the federal government and private institutions. Moreover, policymaking is continuous; once made, decisions rarely are immutable. Environmental policy is therefore in some respects fluid and impermanent, always in metamorphosis. Second, policymakers—whether of the legislative, White House, or bureaucratic type—can seldom act without restraint. Their discretion is bounded and shaped by many constraints: the constitutional separation of powers, institutional rules and biases, statutory laws, shared understandings about the rules of the game for conflict resolution, political realities, and more. These constraints collectively are a given in the policy setting, which means government resolves most issues in a predictable style. Third, environmental policymaking is a volatile mixture of politics and science that readily erupts into controversy among politicians, bureaucrats, and scientists over their appropriate roles in the process as well as over the proper interpretation and use of scientific data in policy questions.

One useful way to understand public policy, and environmental policy specifically, is to view the process as a cycle of interrelated phases through which policy ordinarily evolves. Each phase involves a different mix of actors, institutions, and constraints. Although somewhat simplified, this approach illuminates particularly well the interrelated flow of decisions and the continual process of creation and modification that characterizes governmental policy development. This chapter continues by describing the significant phases of environmental policymaking and then examines important constitutional and political influences, deeply embedded in U.S. political culture, that continually animate and shape the environmental policies emerging from this policy cycle.

THE POLICY CYCLE

Governmental response to public issues—the business of converting an issue into a policy—customarily begins when an issue can be placed on the governmental agenda. The successful promotion of issues to the agenda does not ensure that public policies will result, but this step initiates the policy cycle. An environmental issue becomes an environmental policy as it passes through several policy phases.

Agenda Setting

Political scientist Charles O. Jones aptly calls agenda setting "the politics of getting problems to government."[8] It is the politics of imparting sufficient importance and urgency to an issue so that the government will feel compelled to place the matter on the official agenda of government—that is, the "set of items explicitly up for the serious and active consideration of authoritative decision-makers."[9] This means getting environmental issues on legislative calendars, before legislative committees, on a priority list for bill introduction by a senator or representative, on the schedule of a regulatory agency, or among the president's legislative proposals. In brief, getting an issue on the agenda means placing it where institutions and individuals with public authority can respond and feel a need to do so. Especially if an environmental issue is technical and somewhat esoteric, its prospects for making the agenda are bleak unless political sponsors are attracted to it. Former EPA assistant administrator and environmental activist Clarence Davies observes, "New technical information by itself does not significantly influence the political agenda. It must be assisted by some type of political propellant," such as an interest group, congressional committee, or the president.[10] Thus, the discovery of the stratospheric ozone hole and the ability of scientists to portray it in the most literal way—scientific photography enabled the public to see a hole—immensely hastened the Montreal Protocol to completion.

Formulation and Legitimation

The governmental agenda also can be a graveyard for public problems. Few issues reaching the governmental agenda reach the phase of policy formulation or legitimation. Policy formulation involves setting goals for policy, creating specific plans and proposals for these goals, and selecting the means to implement such plans. Policy formulation in the federal government is especially associated with the presidency and Congress. The State of the Union address and the avalanche of bills introduced annually in Congress represent the most obvious examples of formulated policies. Policies, once created, must also be legitimated and invested with the authority to evoke public acceptance. Such legitimation usually is done through constitutional, statutory, or administrative procedures, such as voting, public hearings, presidential orders, or judicial decisions upholding the constitutionality of laws—rituals whose purposes are to signify that policies have now acquired the weight of public authority.

Implementation

Public policies remain statements of intention until they are translated into operational programs. Indeed, the impact of policies depends largely on how they are implemented. What government is doing about environmental problems relates primarily to how the programs have been implemented. Policy analyst Eugene Bardach compares the implementation of public policies to "an assembly process"; according to him, it is

> as if the original mandate . . . that set the policy or program in motion were a blueprint for a large machine that has to turn out rehabilitated psychotics or healthier old people or better educated children. . . . Putting the machine together and making it run is, at one level, what we mean by the "implementation" process.[11]

Policy implementation involves especially the bureaucracy, whose presence and style shape the impact of all public policies.

Impact and Reformulation

All the procedures involved in evaluating the social impact of governmental policies, in judging the desirability of these impacts, and in communicating these judgments to the government and the public can be called impact assessment. Often, the federal courts assume an active role in the process, as do the mass media. The White House, Congress, and the bureaucracy continually monitor and assess the impacts of public policy. As a consequence, once a policy has been formulated, it may pass through many phases of reformulation. All major institutions of government may play major roles in this process of reformulation.

Termination

The "deliberate conclusion or succession of specific governmental functions, programs, policies or organizations" amounts to policy termination, according to political scientist Peter deLeon.[12] Terminating policies, environmental or otherwise, is such a formidable process that most public programs, in spite of intentions to the contrary, become virtually immortal. Policies usually change through repeated reformulation and reassessment.

Policymaking Is a Combination of Phases

Because policymaking is a process, the various phases almost always affect each other, an important reason why understanding a policy often requires considering the whole development pattern. For instance, many problems encountered by the EPA when enforcing the Federal Water Pollution Control Act (1956) arose from the congressional failure to define clearly in the law what was meant by a *navigable waterway,* to which the legislation explicitly applied. Congress deliberately built in this ambiguity to facilitate the passage of the extraordinarily complicated legislation. In turn, the EPA sought early opportunities to bring the issue before the federal courts—to compel judicial assessment of the law's intent—so that the agency might have reliable guidance for its implementation of the provision. Also, many aspects of environmental policy may occur simultaneously. While the EPA was struggling to implement portions of the Superfund legislation allocating grants to the states for cleaning up abandoned toxic waste sites, Congress was considering a reformulation of the law to increase funding authorization to support more state grants.

CONSTITUTIONAL CONSTRAINTS

The design of governmental power intended more than two centuries ago for a nation of farmers still rests heavily on the flow of policymaking in a technological age. Like other public policies, environmental programs have been shaped and complicated by the enduring constitutional formula.

Checks and Balances

The Madisonian notion of setting "ambition against ambition," which inspired the constitutional structure, creates a government of countervailing and competitive institutions. The system of checks and balances disperses power and authority within the federal government among legislative, executive, and judicial institutions and thereby sows tenacious institutional rivalries that are repeatedly encountered in discussions of specific environmental laws. Yet as former presidential adviser Richard E. Neustadt has observed, these are separated institutions sharing power; effective public policy requires that public officials collaborate by discovering strategies to transcend these institutional conflicts.[13]

The U.S. federal system also disperses governmental power by fragmenting authority between the national and state governments. Despite the growth of vast federal powers, federalism remains a sturdy constitutional buttress supporting an edifice of authority—shared, independent, and countervailing—erected from the states within the federal system. "It is difficult to find any governmental activity which does not involve all three of the so-called 'levels' of the federal system."[14] No government institution monopolizes power. "There has never been a time when it was possible to put neat labels on discrete 'federal,' 'state' and 'local' functions."[15]

Regulatory Federalism

Federalism introduces complexity, jurisdictional rivalries, confusion, and delay into the management of environmental problems. Authority over environmental issues inherently is fragmented among a multitude of governmental entities. Moreover, almost all new federal regulatory programs since 1970 permit or require implementation by the states. For instance, thirty-five states currently administer water pollution permits under the Clean Water Act. State implementation of federal laws may vary greatly in scope and detail. The federal government often attempts to reduce administrative complications in programs administered through the states by the use of common regulations, guidelines, and other devices to impose consistency on implementation. However, the practical problems of reconciling so many geographical interests within the arena of a single regulatory program often trigger major problems in implementing the programs.

Federal and state collaboration in environmental regulation is often cooperative but can be contentious. Many state authorities believe that numerous environmental problems now federally regulated would be best managed by state and local governments. Often, as in the emerging national controversy over the environmental impact of fracking to obtain petroleum from oil shale, many states want exclusive authority to regulate and often protest federal plans to assume that responsibility. Many state governments also resent the expense and administrative difficulty they must endure to implement the numerous environmental laws and regulations they believe the federal government has negligently piled on them. In the decade ending in 2010, for example, the EPA's major new environmental regulations imposed a minimum cost upon state governments of at least $23 billion.[16]

Organized Interests

The Constitution encourages a robust pluralism of organized interests. Constitutional guarantees of freedom of petition, expression, and assembly promote constant organization and political activism at all governmental levels among thousands of economic, occupational, ethnic, ideological, and geographical interests. To make public policy in the United States requires public officials and institutions to reconcile the conflicting interests of organized groups who claim not only influence but sometimes even authority in making public policy. The constitutional architecture of the U.S. government also provides numerous points of access to public power for such groups operating in a fragmented governmental milieu. The political influence broadly distributed across this vast constellation of organized private groups clouds the formal distinction between public and private power.[17] Instead, the course of policymaking moves routinely and easily between public institutions and private organizations mobilized for political action.

These constitutional constraints have important implications for environmental policy. It is easier to defeat legislation than to enact it and to frustrate incisive governmental action than to create it. Furthermore, most policy decisions result from bargaining and compromise among institutions and actors all sharing some portion of diffused power. Formulating policy usually means coalition building in an effort to engineer consensus by reconciling diverse interests and aggregating sufficient strength among different interests to support effective policies. As economist James V. DeLong observes, agencies "like to achieve consensus on issues and policies. If they cannot bring everyone into the tent, they will try to get enough disparate groups together so as to make the remainder appear unreasonable. If the interested parties are too far apart for even partial consensus, then the agency will try to give everybody something."[18]

Bargaining and compromise often purchase consensus at the cost of disarray and contradiction in the resulting policies. "What happens is not chosen as a solution to a problem but rather results from compromise, conflict and confusion among officials with diverse interests and unequal influence," notes presidential adviser Graham Allison.[19]

INCREMENTALISM

Public officials strongly favor making and changing policy incrementally. "Policy making typically is part of a political process in which the only feasible political change is that which changes social states by relatively small steps," writes social analyst Charles A. Lindblom.[20] Gus Speth, a former chair of the Council on Environmental Quality and a veteran environmental policymaker, describes incrementalism as "working within the system." He explains:

> When today's environmentalism recognizes a problem, it believes it
> can solve that problem by calling public attention to it, framing policy
> and program responses for government and industry, lobbying for
> those actions, and litigating for their enforcement. It believes in the
> efficacy of environmental advocacy and government action. It believes
> that good-faith compliance with the law will be the norm. . . . Today's
> environmentalism tends to be pragmatic and incrementalist—its actions
> are aimed at solving problems and often doing so one at a time. . . . In
> the end, environmentalism accepts compromises as part of the process. It
> takes what it can get.[21]

Incrementalism is politically seductive. It permits policymakers to draw on their own experiences in the face of unfamiliar problems and encourages the making of small policy adjustments at the margins to reduce anticipated, perhaps irreversible, and politically risky consequences. But incrementalism also can become a prison of the imagination by inhibiting policy innovation and stifling new solutions to issues. Especially when officials treat new policy issues as if they were familiar ones and deal with them in the customary ways, a futile and possibly dangerous repetition of the past can result in the face of issues requiring fresh approaches.

NEPA (1969), the CAA (1970), and the other innovative legislation of the early 1970s came only after Congress repeatedly failed when dealing with environmental issues incrementally.[22] For more than thirty years previously and despite growing evidence of serious environmental degradation, Congress had continued to treat pollution as a "uniquely local problem" requiring a traditional "partnership" between federal and state governments in which Washington gently prodded the states to deal more effectively with pollution. Finally, Congress put an end to this incrementalism with the avalanche of new, forceful federal environmental laws in the 1970s mandating national pollution standards and regulations that compelled state compliance and enforcement. To many observers, this was a sudden outburst of environmental reform. In fact, its rise to the national policy agenda had been achieved by years of increasingly skilled, patient, and persistent promotion by a multitude of groups.

INTEREST GROUP POLITICS

It is an implicit principle in U.S. politics, assumed by most public officials as well as those groups seeking access to them, that organized interests affected by public policy should have an important role in shaping those policies. Few special interests enjoy such pervasive and unchallenged access to government as business, but almost all major organized groups enjoy some measure of influence in public institutions. Many officials, in critic Theodore Lowi's terms, conduct their offices "as if it were supposed to be the practice of dealing only with organized claims in formulating policy, and of dealing exclusively through organized claims in implementing programs."[23]

Structuring Groups Into Government

Arrangements exist throughout governmental structures for giving groups access to strategic policy arenas. Lobbying is accepted as a normal, if not essential, arrangement for ensuring organized interests major roles in lawmaking. More than one thousand advisory committees exist within the federal bureaucracy to give interests affected by policies some access and voice in agency deliberations. Hundreds of large, quasi-public associations bring together legislators, administrators, White House staff, and private-group representatives to share policy concerns, thereby blurring the distinction between public and private interests. The Highway Users Federation for Safety and Mobility, for instance, diligently promotes the interstate highway system; and the Atomic Industrial Forum pursues the interests of commercial nuclear power corporations. Successful organized groups so effectively control the exercise of governmental power that, in historian Grant McConnell's words, significant portions of the U.S. government have witnessed "the conquest of segments of formal state power by private groups and associations."[24] In effect, group activity at all governmental levels has been practiced so widely that it has become part of the constitutional order.

Business: Secure and Effective Access

No interest has exploited the right to take part in the governmental process more pervasively or successfully than has business. In environmental affairs, the sure access of business to government assumes enormous importance because business is a major regulated interest whose ability to represent itself and secure careful hearing before public agencies and officials often delays or complicates such regulation. During the 2013–2014 congressional session, for instance, business and energy organizations were exclusively represented among the top twenty interest groups in lobbying expenditures concerning climate change legislation. In contrast, the combined expenditures of all environmental groups concerning all legislation during the same period was only slightly greater than the total for Koch Industries, the largest business contributor.[25]

Business weighs especially heavily in the deliberations of public officials, because its leaders collectively manage much of the economy and perform such essential economic functions that the failure of these businesses would produce severe economic disorder and widespread suffering. According to Lindblom,

> government officials know this. They also know that widespread failure
> of business . . . will bring down the government. A democratically
> elected government cannot expect to survive in the face of widespread or
> prolonged distress. . . . Consequently, government policy makers show
> constant concern about business performance.[26]

So great is this concern that public officials usually give business not all it desires but enough to ensure its profitability. Out of this grows the privileged position of business in government and its widely accepted right to require that government officials often "give business needs precedence over demands from citizens through electoral, party, and interest-group channels."[27]

Business also enjoys practical political advantages in competition with other interests for access to and influence on government: far greater financial resources, greater ease in raising money for political purposes, and an already existing organization available for use in political action. These advantages in strategic resources and salience to public officials do not ensure the uncompromised acceptance of business's demands on government, nor do they spare business from defeat or frustration by opponents. But business often, if not usually, is able to exploit its privileged status in U.S. politics to ensure that its views are represented early and forcefully in any policy conflicts, its interests are pursued and protected carefully at all policy phases, and its forces are mobilized effectively for long periods of time. These are formidable advantages, often enough to give a decisive edge in competitive struggles with environmental or other interests that do not have the political endurance, skill, or resources to be as resolute in putting pressure on government when it counts.

Environmentalism's Access

Prior to the 1970s, the environmental lobby could claim, with considerable justification, to be political outsiders compared to business. However, environmental groups—along with public-interest groups, consumer organizations, and others advocating broad public programs—were quick to promote a number of new structural and legal arrangements that enlarged their governmental influence. Congress and administrative agencies often created these structural and legal arrangements deliberately for the advantage of environmental interests. These new arrangements, defended ferociously by environmental organizations against continuing assaults by their political opposition, have diminished greatly the disparities in political access and influence that once so conspicuously distinguished environmentalists from their political opponents. Environmental groups, in fact, have acquired the finesse to be formidable adversaries in traditional political confrontations with well-endowed opponents. In 2015, the ten leading environmental organizations, with a collective membership exceeding fifteen million, were estimated to have more than 2,000 staff and a budget of more than $525 million.[28] During the 2016 presidential election year, the League of Conservation Voters, the most important environmentalist political action committee, spent more than $40 million to elect favored candidates.[29]

However, environmentalists gain no advantage when the skilled legislative advocacy of lobbyists is involved. In 2017, for example, environmental organizations reported spending $17.3 million for lobbing while energy and natural resource interests, a frequent political adversary, spent $316.1 million.[30] Still, environmentalism no longer wears the rags of the politically disadvantaged and the establishment outsider. In the vernacular of Washington, D.C., environmentalists are now major players—so major that a closer look at organized environmentalism and its impact on public opinion is essential to understand the fundamental driving forces of environmental policymaking.

THE ENVIRONMENTAL MOVEMENT: CONFRONTING THE CHALLENGE OF CHANGE

In mid-2012, the EPA sent photographers across the United States to once again photograph some of the most dramatic examples of pollution that inspired the environmental movement and dramatized the environmental crisis during the era of the first Earth Day. However, "the clouds of smoke billowing from industrial smokestacks, raw sewage flowing into rivers that had galvanized public concern were gone."[31] And that creates a problem, observed William Ruckelshaus, the EPA's first administrator, who commissioned those early, powerful photographs. "To a certain extent, we are a victim of our own success," he observed. "Right now, EPA is under sharp criticism partly because it is not as obvious to people that pollution problems exist and that we need to deal with them."[32] However, this is one among several other compelling issues facing environmental organizations as the environmental movement ages into a changing political era.

As a political profile of the environmental movement illustrates, environmentalism's political vitality has been sustained by the continuity and political skill of its organizational base. While this has enabled environmentalists to be major players in U.S. politics, these organizations now confront the considerable challenges in staying politically relevant and effective for a new American generation in an era of political change. Among these important challenges are effectively dramatizing emerging environmental problems to the public, recruiting and retaining organizational membership, confronting growing partisan division within Congress over environmental regulation, resolving sometimes intense conflicts within the movement itself, and competing successfully for financial resources in economically difficult times.

Strategies and Tactics

Organization is the bedrock on which the politics of successful environmental policymaking is built. Estimates of environmentalism's organizational membership vary. About 5 percent of Americans report membership in an environmental organization, and between 15 and 21 percent customarily report they have been active in an environmental group. Careful estimates suggest that perhaps 5,600 organized environmental groups are nationally active, together with thousands more transient state, local, and regional organizations defying enumeration.[33] The thousands of organized national, state, and local groups, collectively enrolling millions of members, arm the movement with absolutely essential political resources that only organized groups provide—dependable, active, informed, and experienced advocacy.[34] Organized groups create the kind of constant pressure on policymakers and the continual aggressive surveillance of policy administration required for effective policy influence in government.

Over the years since Earth Day 1970, the number of U.S. environmental and conservation advocacy groups[35] has grown steadily. Accurate estimates of their number are elusive, but these groups, regardless of size and resources, probably exceed twenty-six thousand.[36] Most environmental organizations are quite small in membership and financial resources.[37] No more than a few thousand have incomes sufficient to enable significant, national-scale activities, and the political core of environmentalist organizations—those with the political clout and income to be major presences in national or international environmental policymaking—probably does not exceed one hundred organizations. Most of these highly influential groups, often characterized as the "environmentalist establishment" or BINGOs (big, influential nongovernment organizations) have been important presences since the first Earth Day.

A politically significant change since that Earth Day has been the continuing growth in number of and activism among environmentalist groups at the state and local governmental levels—in fact, these constitute most of the environmental and conservation groups currently active. This growth in membership has enlarged the political clout of environmental interests at the state and local levels at a time when state and local governments have become increasingly important actors in U.S. environmental policymaking.[38] Between 2000 and 2008, for instance, environmental organizations successfully promoted three unprecedented regional agreements to regulate climate change emissions: the Regional Greenhouse Gas Initiative (RGGI), among northeastern states; the Midwest Climate Initiative; and the Western Climate Initiative.[39]

Ideological Consensus and Cleavage

Environmentalism has never been a church of one creed. To the frustration of some leaders, this pluralism is often politically divisive in legislative infighting, especially with formidable opponents, such as business interests. "Business interests are like the Republican Party—they're able to find a message, stay on message and get everyone to talk on the same page," lamented veteran environmental leader Leon Billings. "Environmental groups are like the Democratic Party—50 different states with 50 different messages, and no member who wants to say the same thing more than once."[40] Although pluralism and the conflicts born of it are inherent in environmentalism, this pluralism is still bounded by general values, attitudes, and beliefs—a way of looking at nature, humanity, and U.S. society—widely shared with many nuances by environmental leaders and activists. Although this pluralism lacks the coherence of an ideology, it sets environmentalists apart from mainstream U.S. culture.

Essential Principles

Reduced to essentials, environmentalism springs from an attitude toward nature that assumes humanity is part of the created order, ethically responsible for the preservation of the world's ecological integrity, and ultimately vulnerable, as are all Earth's other creatures, to the good or ill that humans inflict on nature. In the environmentalist perspective, humans live in a world of limited resources and potential scarcities; like the good stewards of an inheritance, they must use their scientific genius to manage global resources. An enlightened approach to managing nature, the environmentalists argue, should stress the interdependency of all natural systems (the ecosystem concept), the importance of ecological stability and resource sustainability," and the enormously long time span in which the impact of ecological change occurs. In its approach to nature, environmentalism emphasizes the sanctity of the created order as a warning against the human assumption that we stand above and apart from the created order by virtue of our intelligence and scientific achievements. All this is summed up for many ecologists in the metaphor of spaceship Earth, the image of a unique and vulnerable ecosystem traveling through space and time, dependent on its crew for survival.

In its cultural stance, environmentalism sharply criticizes marketplace economics generally and capitalism particularly, and it denigrates the growth ethic, unrestrained technological optimism, and the political structures supporting these cultural phenomena. Such an attitude often places environmentalists on a collision course with dominant U.S. values. Environmentalism challenges U.S. confidence in market mechanisms to allocate scarce resources for several reasons. Environmentalists assert that market economics esteem economic growth and material consumption above concern for ecological balance and integrity. Therefore, the market cannot be relied on to signal resource scarcity efficiently enough to prevent possibly catastrophic resource exhaustion.

Environmentalism is less hostile to technology itself than to blind faith in the power of technology to cure whatever ecological ills it begets and to bland confidence in technological expertise to meet humanity's material and spiritual needs. Environmentalists regard the public's confidence in American know-how as responsible for many of the nation's most difficult environmental problems, such as the management of commercial nuclear technologies. The environmental movement's initial political agenda arose from these attitudes toward the natural world and contemporary culture. From its inception, the movement has expressed an ambivalence toward the nation's dominant social structures that frequently translates into calls for major institutional as well as policy reforms. Many environmentalists believe that the nation's dominant political institutions and processes must be reformed, because they are committed to the preservation of ecological, economic, and technological values that are hostile to prudent ecological management. For some, this is summed up as suspicion of the establishment and the traditional institutions and processes associated with it. Political scientist Susan Leeson argues that "If American political ideology and institutions have been successful in encouraging the pursuit of happiness through material acquisition, they appear incapable of imposing the limits which are required to forestall ecological disaster."[41] Many fear the power of an interlocking economic and political structure committed to controlling technology in environmentally reckless ways.

The Ideological Mainstream

Organized environmentalism today is divided into several ideological enclaves. The movement's dominant ideological and political style has been crafted by pragmatic reformers, the largest, most politically active, and publicly visible organizations, represented by national groups such as the Sierra Club and the National Wildlife Federation. These large organizations emphasize political action through government; traditional styles of politics such as bargaining and coalition building; and national environmental agendas focusing on pollution, resource conservation, and land use. Their priorities are "influencing public policy in incremental steps, forging pragmatic alliances issue by issue with those with whom they could agree," explains Michael McCloskey, former executive director of the Sierra Club. McCloskey emphasizes that the pragmatists do not believe "that the entire political or economic system needed to be changed and were confident that environmental protection could be achieved within the framework of existing institutions of governance."[42]

The ideological diversity among the pragmatists, however, makes them appear more an ecumenical movement than a denomination. One important factional conflict pits preservationist groups, such as the Sierra Club and the Wilderness Society, which emphasize the preservation of resources rather than their economic or recreational exploitation, against groups such as the Izaak Walton League and the National Wildlife Federation, which favor prudent resource development for public use and economic growth. Another significant cleavage divides the pragmatists from antiestablishment groups such as Friends of the Earth and Environmental Action, which are impatient with the moderation and slowness of political action among the leading national groups but still committed to traditional forms of political activity. The national leadership in almost all mainstream environmental organizations, in fact, contends with their own grassroots factions, which, in the words of critic Brian Tokar, believe "the voices of 'official environmentalism' [are] hopelessly out of step with the thousands of volunteers who largely define the leading edge of locally based environmental activism."[43] To these critics, the leaders of official environmentalism have become just another political elite, absorbed in promoting their careers and accommodating the corporate interests that they should be opposing. When the World Wildlife Fund, for instance, selected a former executive of Weyerhaeuser Company, an international timber industry giant, for a major management position, the organization was bitterly flayed by one grassroots environmentalist publication:

> The World Wildlife Fund functions more like a corporate enterprise than public interest group. It . . . has made millions upon millions hawking its panda logo, a brand as zealously marketed as Nike's "swoosh." But, of course, it's done almost nothing to save the panda . . . except peddle pictures to trophy wives and innocent third graders. Call it Panda porn. . . . The World Wildlife Fund also rakes in millions from corporations. . . . As a result, WWF's budget has swelled to over $100 million a year. . . . Most of it goes to pay for plush offices, robust salaries, and a tireless direct mail operation to raise even more money.[44]

These critics, who agree on little else, complain about the amount of foundation money flowing into the coffers of pragmatic environmental groups. In 2017, for example, more than eighty foundations, most representing corporate money, contributed to conservation organizations and sixty foundations funded projects or organizations related to climate change.[45] In the opinion of the critics, corporate largesse encourages mainstream environmentalism to "green wash" the environmental record of the donors and to compromise programs and tactics to suit foundation patrons. Undoubtedly, foundations do prod their environmentalist clientele toward political moderation, but such influence is highly variable. The hard-liners, moreover, have had their own foundation angels, and many odd-couple alliances exist between relatively moderate foundation sponsors and aggressive environmental activists, such as the one between the Ford Foundation and Environmental Defense.

Deep Ecologists

Another highly vocal faction within environmentalism comprises individuals and groups ideologically committed to deep ecology or lifestyle transformation. Deep ecologists believe humans are, at best, only a part of nature—and not necessarily the most significant part. They believe that all forms of life have equal claims on existence; that social, political, and economic institutions should promote the ecological vitality of all created orders; and that fundamental changes in national institutions and lifestyles are essential to preserve global ecological integrity. The fundamental political problem, from the deep ecologists' perspective, is that social institutions have become instruments for the human exploitation of the created order for the primary benefit of humans, often through technologies that threaten to destroy essential aspects of the natural order. Deep ecology inherently challenges the fundamental institutional structures and social values on which governments, economies, and societies are presently constituted. Thus, between deep ecologists and what they call the shallow ecology of mainstream environmentalism, there abides a profound philosophical tension, nourished by antagonistic principles and a sharply disparate political imagination.[46]

Deep ecologists, lacking the political leverage of organizational or numerical strength, are presently a vocal, aggressive, and dissenting minority within the environmental movement. Many within the movement, preferring social to political action, have adopted individual and collective lifestyles outside conventional U.S. culture. Nonetheless, deep ecologists continue to be politically active, often to greatest effect at the state and local levels.

Radical Environmentalism

Militant and alienated from the movement's organizational mainstream, radical environmentalism emerged in the 1980s among environmentalists disillusioned with establishment styles and accomplishments. According to environmental historian Bill Devall, the radical environmentalists

> were discouraged by the compromising attitude of mainstream groups, by the bureaucratization of the groups, by the professionalization of leaders and their detachment from the emerging concerns of grassroots supporters, and by the lack of success of mainstream organizations in countering the Reagan anti-environmental agenda.[47]

Radical environmentalists favor direct-action tactics, including the street politics of civil disobedience, nonviolent demonstrations, and political obstruction. To environmental radicals, the harassment of commercial whaling vessels on the high seas by Greenpeace protest vessels, carefully orchestrated to attract media attention worldwide, was better politics than the inhibited, reformist style of the mainstream organizations.

Radical environmentalists share a common sensibility that all life is mortally threatened by an ecological degeneration created by advanced, modern cultures. Thus, radicals espouse a fundamental cultural transformation that rejects the dominant political and economic institutions of most advanced societies as incompatible with global ecological vitality. This preoccupation with transformational politics usually involves a belief in "bearing witness" through lifestyle changes emphasizing harmony with nature, conservation of resources, and cooperative living in reconstructed, ecologically sensitive societies.[48]

Despite a commitment to nonviolence, radicals betray ambivalence about violence—*ecotage* and *monkey-wrenching* are euphemisms—condemned from within and outside the environmental movement. Shadowy groups such as the Animal Liberation Front (ALF) and the Earth Liberation Front (ELF) are suspected of violent property destruction. (The ALF website has contained information on making arson devices, and the ELF claimed responsibility for burning down a Boise Cascade Corporation office in Oregon, causing $1 million in damages.)[49] The small but aggressive movement Earth First! is environmentalism with a fist: "Earth First! has survived attacks by moderates, would-be leaders and the agents of the system, remaining the most diverse, passionate, committed, and uncompromising group of environmental activists," it advertises. "Our direct actions in defense of the last wild places only seem radical compared to an entire paradigm of denial and control, where the individual is convinced they are powerless, and the organizations set up to protect the wilderness continue to bargain it away."[50] Earth First! spokespeople sometimes assert that when defending nature and saving old-growth trees from lumberyards, it may be permissible to spike those trees with metal rods likely to fragment into shrapnel when shattered by commercial logging chain saws.

Other groups, such as Greenpeace and the Sea Shepherd Society, have been accused of nonviolent direct action that provokes violence, such as disabling the nets of commercial fishing vessels whose crews refuse to protect dolphins during deep-sea tuna harvesting. In light of the profound cultural alienation inherent in many radical ideologies, an ambivalence about political violence is inevitable, although radical environmentalism's political strategies still remain—sometimes barely—within the tradition of nonviolent direct action.

Organizational Structures and Strategies

The number and size of environmental organizations fluctuates over time. Nonetheless, the major national organizations retain the numbers and resources needed to ensure their influential presence in national policymaking. By one estimate, the ten leading environmental organizations in 2015 had more than fifteen million members and a collective budget exceeding $525 million.[51] Moreover, to the national membership rolls should be added the thousands of grassroots state and local groups. For instance, one national organization concerned with solid waste identifies seven thousand collaborating state and local groups. Altogether, the number of national, state, and local environmental organizations is estimated to exceed ten thousand.

Membership. In mid-2017, 17 percent of a sample of the American public reported to Gallup that they were "active participants" in the environmental movement.[52] Although social approval for environmentalism is broadly based in the United States, the organizational membership is mostly middle to upper class, white, well educated, and well-off.[53] Such a socially select membership exposes environmentalists to the frequent criticism that the so-called greens are too white and too well-off and that they are racists or elitists indifferent to minorities and the economically disadvantaged. To support these accusations, critics argue that environmentalism fights for clean air but not for equal employment opportunities, promotes wilderness preservation for upscale recreationists but not better schools for the disadvantaged, and condemns pollution in national parks but not inner-city decay. In short, the agenda of environmentalism is largely a wish list from the book of middle-class white lifestyles. Mainstream environmental organizations, increasingly sensitive to such criticism, have struggled to broaden their social constituencies and policy agendas. A number of national organizations have initiated joint action with labor and minority groups intended to make environmentalism relevant to the workplace and neighborhood. Most national environmental organizations, responding to initiatives from minority groups, also have supported the emerging environmental equity movement intended to end discrimination against the economically disadvantaged in environmental policymaking. The emergence of environmental racism as a mainstream environmentalist concern is discussed in Chapter 4.

The Organizational Mainstream. The environmental movement's national leadership is concentrated in a small number of highly visible, politically skilled, and influential organizations. These groups, anointed The Big Green in one survey, typically includes Defenders of Wildlife, Environmental Defense Fund, Greenpeace, National Audubon Society, National Wildlife Federation, Natural Resources Defense Council, the Nature Conservancy, Sierra Club, the Wilderness Society, and the World Wildlife Fund.[54]

These large, mainstream groups, mostly political pragmatists, are thoroughly professionalized and sophisticated in staff and organization. They are armed with the same high-technology tools and modern techniques of policy advocacy as any other powerful national lobby. The large membership rolls of the national organizations demonstrate an aptitude for direct-mail solicitation that is as good as can be found in Washington, D.C.

The economic recession beginning in 2009 created serious funding problems for many environmental organizations. Most of the large "establishment" organizations felt the recession's impact in declining membership numbers, diminished contributions, and reduced income from foundation and government grants from which they were slowly recovering.[55] The election of Donald Trump in 2016, however, produced the "Trump Bump"—a massive surge of new membership and money for mainstream environmental organizations fiercely opposed to Trump's environmental agenda.[56] The Sierra Club, for instance, reported 11,000 new monthly donors in the weeks following the presidential election, nine times the previous record.[57]

Growing professionalization of the leadership of the mainstream groups also continues to provoke accusations from many environmentalists that the national organizations have lost their fire and vision. The critics charge that the national leadership is more bureaucratic than charismatic and that it has lost touch with the movement's grassroots and become too preoccupied with bargaining and compromise.

The Essential Politics of Procedure. Rep. John Dingell, D-MI, a legislator of legendary political skill, once shared a lesson gleaned from thirty years in Congress: "I'll let you write the substance on a statute and you let me write the procedures, and I'll screw you every time."[58] Dingell's axiom illuminates a law as fundamental to policymaking as gravity is to physics—the decision-making rules, as much as the policy outcomes, enlarge or diminish group power. The environmental movement, always respectful of Dingell's axiom, has been as aggressive in promoting advantageous policy procedures as in creating substantive environmental laws.

The politics of procedure is always a fundamental consideration in environmentalist political agendas. Indeed, the movement's power flows, in good part, from success in procedural politics, from aggressively exploiting advantages through the intricate manipulation of policy process. Because so many environmental laws are implemented largely through bureaucracy and the courts, environmental organizations have been especially sensitive to the importance of protecting or enhancing decision-making procedures that work to their benefit in these institutions. The success of this strategy depends on securing these procedural advantages through law: statutory, administrative, or judicial. The public politics of environmentalism could not have succeeded so well and perhaps not at all had environmentalism's political power not been anchored in procedural law during the movement's rise to influence in the 1970s. "To a great extent, environmental group power . . . was legal power," observes political scientist George Hoberg, and environmentalism survived because the new legal arrangements "granted environmental groups institutional and legal foundations that to a large extent solidified their power status within the regime."[59]

Environmental groups have benefited especially from changes in law and administrative procedure that enhance their access to information and their opportunities to participate in the implementation of environmental laws. A major environmental reform was the enactment of NEPA in 1969, requiring federal agencies to prepare environmental impact statements that have become a major source of substantive information and procedural influence in federal environmental policies. Other important reforms include provisions in almost every major environmental law to greatly expand citizen participation in administrative decision-making and to make it easier for citizens to sue administrative agencies for failure to implement environmental laws.

Environmentalism and Political Engagement. Environmental organizations are an active, highly visible, and politically important presence among the major organized interests in U.S. politics at all governmental levels. Environmental groups seldom match in political resources the magnitude of money, organization, and legislative representation available to powerful economic sectors such as business, labor, and agriculture, but the political skill and resources of environmental advocacy is nonetheless considerable. Environmental organizations rarely claim to be partisan, but the reality is that most of their money invested in partisan elections flows to Democrats. During the 2016 congressional elections, for instance, environmental groups reported spending $9.2 million for Democratic candidates but only $365,000 for Republicans.[60]

ENVIRONMENTALISM AND ITS CRITICS

Although environmentalist organizations are committed to defending the public interest and public values, they also represent a constituency with its own ideological and material interests. As environmentalism becomes increasingly organized and politicized nationally, critics assert that it has also assumed the narrow, self-interested viewpoint of every other interest group while promoting policies that often serve no public ends.

Public Interest or Self-Interest?

Critics frequently allege that environmentalism is largely the voice of a social elite hostile to U.S. capitalism, distrustful of science inconsistent to its own viewpoint, and obsessed with imagined or exaggerated ecological problems. To fortify such arguments, critics assert that the environmentalists' passion for controlled economic growth will deprive the economically disadvantaged domestically and internationally, that wilderness preservation usually benefits a handful of naturalists but deprives the average American of access to and enjoyment of wilderness resources, and that locking up resources costs jobs and inhibits economic progress. Moreover, continues the indictment, environmentalists often selfishly obstruct valuable public or private projects like power-generating plants, waste landfills, and even apparently environmentally friendly projects when these might threaten their lifestyles or property values. Critics have delightedly seized on events that seem proof of perverse environmentalism, such as the opposition by some environmental spokespeople to a proposed 130-tower wind farm in Horseshoe Shoal, a shallow portion of Nantucket Sound south of Cape Cod, and the vehement environmentalist battle against a vast solar-energy plant in the Mojave Desert, a very remote and reliably sunny location.[61] In these and many similar instances, however, plausible reasons exist for concern about the biological and ecological impacts of such projects and—as often happens—the environmentalist community itself is often divided over the issues.

Many environmental organizations are striving diligently for greater social diversity in membership and programs. National environmental organizations, for example, are actively seeking, with some success, to build durable alliances with labor unions anchored by a shared concern about workplace safety and worker health, but the stigma of social exclusivity still clings to the movement.[62] In addition, increased professionalization and competition among environmental groups breeds a preoccupation with organizational needs.[63]

Environmental leaders also resort to the rhetoric of crisis so habitually that environmentalism's mother tongue may seem to be the Apocalypse. This hyperbolic style begets the kind of misstatements on which critics often seize to demonstrate environmentalism's distorted vision. There have certainly been errors, as the discussion of the controversies over the chemicals disononyl phthalate (DINP) and dioxin demonstrate (see Chapter 4). Nonetheless, environmentalists have aroused an appropriate sense of urgency about numerous ecological issues such as climate change, air and water pollution, groundwater contamination, radioactive wastes, and surface mining, to cite but a few. The mainstream environmental organizations are sometimes also condemned as shrewd opportunists, promoting policies that enlarge their own political power at public expense. The Superfund program is often cited as a flagrant case in point. The major environmental groups generally insist on the strictest possible standards for all Superfund site cleanups, as required in the original law. Others have suggested that some relaxation of standards would enormously shrink the huge program costs and greatly facilitate site cleanups without significantly increasing risks to public health. But the critics assert that environmentalists insist on the stringent standards because it draws to their side the waste treatment industry and the legal profession, for whom the strictest standards ensure the greatest income.

Pressure Politics: Constructive Opposition and Destructive Obstruction?

It is a political axiom of organized environmentalism that only unremitting pressure on the government will ensure that environmental laws are implemented effectively. This informal ideology of countervailing power is animated by the conviction that government officials cannot be trusted to implement environmental regulations without the coercive force of pressure politics. Distrust of bureaucrats runs so deeply through environmentalism that, next to saving nature for humanity, environmentalists often seem most dedicated to protecting the public from its public servants. This sour assault on environmental regulators, for instance, comes not from regulation's embittered foes but from Michael McCloskey, the former executive director of the Sierra Club:

> [Regulatory programs] need endless follow-through and can go wrong in a thousand places. The relevant bureaucracies have minds of their own and very little loyalty to the ideas of those who lobbied the programs through. Although the bureaucracies are somewhat responsive to Presidential direction, they are not very responsive to outside lobbying and are subject to no self-correcting process if they fail to be productive.[64]

The reliance by those within organized environmentalism on countervailing power is manifest in their customary resistance to the relaxation of strict pollution standards, which critics consider to be stonewalling. Countervailing power also means the continual resort to litigation, administrative process, citizen involvement, and any other procedures that equate with group pressure on government. More than half of all litigation initiated against federal agencies involving compliance with NEPA and the majority of all legal challenges to EPA regulations originate with environmental organizations, often in collaboration with labor unions, consumer groups, and private interests. Environmental organizations are extremely aggressive in challenging federal, state, and local agencies over compliance with Superfund cleanup standards and over the licensing of hazardous waste disposal sites and nuclear utilities, among many other issues.

The skilled exploitation of these and other political processes has invested environmentalists with political power they probably would not otherwise have. Countervailing power can force administrative agencies and their regulated interests to comply with laws they might prefer to ignore and frequently improves the quality of regulatory decision-making. But countervailing power also has produced enormous delays in the implementation of regulations and increased significantly the cost of environmental regulation through litigation and administrative processes. Whether the use of countervailing power is dangerously disruptive to environmental governance is a concern to many within the environmental movement as well as to its critics.

The continuing controversy over environmentalism reveals some political realities—environmentalist organizations have institutional dogmas and self-serving agendas that may not always be compatible with the larger interests of the movement or even with their own professed goals. Although environmental organizations frequently speak in the name of an encompassing public interest, they also speak for a distinctive social and ideological constituency that often does not include the whole public or even a majority of the public. Environmentalism itself is increasingly divided over the goals and social constituencies to which it should be responsive.

THE PUBLIC AND ENVIRONMENTALISM

Whatever its internal dissonances, the environmental movement has been largely responsible for a remarkable growth in public environmental consciousness and acceptance of environmental protection as an essential public policy. These are public assets, essential to the movement's continuing political vitality, and environmental organizations are extremely adept at arousing public concern on environmental matters and turning it into political advantage. How durable and deep this public support may be, especially in times of severe political or economic hardship, is a different matter.

A Core Value

"The transformation of the environment from an issue of limited concern to one of universal concern is now complete," observed opinion analyst Everett Carll Ladd in mid-1996.[65] The strength of public support for environmental protection early in the twenty-first century, as measured by most public opinion polls, appears widespread. On the eve of the 2016 presidential election, for instance, the Pew Research Center reported substantial public majorities expressing strong concern for the environment (Figure 2.1). However, the intensity of this support is variable over time.

Critics sometimes assert that environmental interest groups speak for only a small portion of the public, but most polls seem to suggest otherwise. In general, opinion polls consistently report that substantial majorities in almost all major socioeconomic groups support the environmental movement and governmental programs to protect the environment and have supported them since Earth Day 1970.[66] Environmental activists have been especially gratified that the polls offer little support to the once widespread notion that concern for environmental quality is a "white thing."[67] As long as environmental questions are lofty abstractions, the public's answers can easily imply that environmentalism's roots run deeply

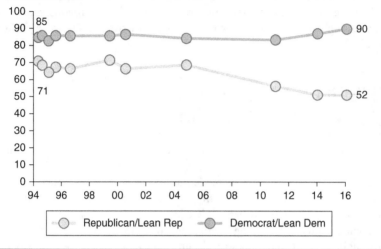

FIGURE 2.1 ■ Public Concern About the Environment, 2016

Should the country do whatever it takes to protect the environment? Most say yes, but party divisions grow wider

% of U.S. adults who say the country should do whatever it takes to protect the environment

Republican/Lean Rep   Democrat/Lean Dem

Source: Monica Anderson, "For Earth Day, Here's How Americans View Environmental Issues," *Facttank,* April 20, 2017, available at http://www.pewresearch.org/fact-tank/2017/04/20/for-earth -day-heres-how-americans-view-environmental-issues/.

Note: Republicans and Democrats include independents and others who "lean" toward one of the parties. Respondents who do not lean toward a political party, gave other responses, or did not give answer are not shown.

as well as broadly across the nation. Certainly, when the political bedrock of environmental regulation seems threatened—when fundamental laws such as the CAA or Clean Water Act seem imperiled—public support for environmentalism has usually been dependable.

Environmentalists have also accomplished what amounts to a massive raising of the public's ecological consciousness through public education about environmental issues facing the United States and the world. On the first Earth Day, ecology and the environment were issues foreign to most Americans. Today, most Americans have a rudimentary understanding of many basic ecological precepts, including the importance of resource conservation and the global scale of environmental problems. And the movement has educated the public and itself into embracing a progressively larger conception of the environment.

How Deep and Broad Is Public Environmentalism?

Despite the public's ecological concern, environmentalism's public impact is still restricted in politically important ways. Environmentalism may now be a consensual value in U.S. politics, but it is what public opinion analyst Riley E. Dunlap calls a "passive consensus"—a situation of "widespread but not terribly intense public support for a goal [in which] government has considerable flexibility in pursuing the goal and is not carefully monitored by the public."[68]

By 2018, several durable patterns had emerged suggesting that the other things to which Americans are turning seldom include sustained interest or reflection about environmental issues at home, at work, or at the voting booth. First, environmental issues have rarely risen to compelling importance or remained among the issues that most concern the public. Thus, while the public often names the environment among issues about which they are concerned in advance of an election, when it comes to voting, the environment seldom ranks among the public's consuming concerns. When a Gallup Poll, for example, asked a sample of the American public in mid-2016 which issues concerned them in the presidential election, less than 4 percent mentioned the environment as a personal concern or one that should be important to the next president.[69]

Second, this low electoral priority for environmental issues prevails even though the public consistently rates Democrats, and especially Democratic presidential candidates, much higher than Republicans on environmental stewardship. In none of the past seven presidential elections, for instance, did more than 11 percent of voters ever state that the environment was the most important issue in casting their ballots.[70] Third, the disconnect between the voters' environmental values and their candidate preferences, especially in presidential elections, seems to result from several enduring assumptions about environmental issues. Duke University's Nichols Institute concluded from a careful survey of voter behavior that most voters

- believe significant progress has been made in environmental protection,

- perceive the environment as "long-term issues that did not warrant the same priority as more 'immediate' concerns such as jobs and health care", and

- assume that environmental policies would have negative economic impacts such as lost jobs and higher taxes.[71]

Sudden surges of public interest or apprehension about the environment predictably rise in the aftermath of widely publicized environmental disasters or emergencies, but public concern is usually evanescent unless the issue is repeatedly dramatized and personalized. At best, deep public engagement with environmental issues is a sometime thing.

Fourth, a deep, apparently growing partisan cleavage now runs like a fault line across public alignments on most domestic environmental matters. On most major issues related to environmental policy—how to regulate, what to regulate, and whether to regulate—Republican and Democratic partisans persistently disagree.[72] The breadth and depth of this gap is evident in the Pew poll found in Figure 2.2 reflecting voter attitudes early in the 2016 presidential election year concerning environmental regulation.[73] This gap is not surprising, considering

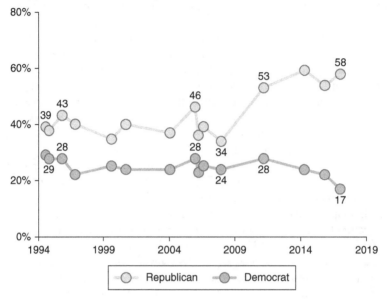

FIGURE 2.2 ■ Partisan Differences About Environmental Regulation

Political parties grow farther apart on impact of environmental regulations

% of U.S. adults who say stricter environmental laws and regulations cost too many jobs and hurt the economy

Source: Monica Anderson, "For Earth Day, Here's How Americans View Environmental Issues," *Facttank*, April 20, 2017, available at http://www.pewresearch.org/fact-tank/2017/04/20/for-earth -day-heres-how-americans-view-environmental-issues/

Note: Republicans and Democrats include independents and others who "lean" toward one of the parties. Respondents who do not lean toward a political party, gave other responses, or did not give answer are not shown.

that Democratic Party identifiers attribute much greater importance to environmental issues and to environmental regulation than Republicans.[74]

Finally, an important trend since 2000 has been increasing public concern about the possible adverse economic impact of environmental regulation. One symptom has been a gradual increase in the proportion of the public that, when asked to make a choice, agreed that economic growth should take precedence over environmental protection—evidence of the nation's growing economic malaise during these years. By 2012, Gallup reported after twenty-seven years of repeated polling that, since 2009, a public majority almost consistently responded that it believed economic growth should be favored over environmental protection if a choice must be made—a sharp departure from prior polls.

The severe recession, which began in late 2007, undoubtedly has fueled the public's growing preoccupation with the economy and demonstrated, once again, the potency of economic issues in commanding public attention and setting national policy priorities. Does this imply that environmental protection has become a hostage to the economy? Not necessarily. It is not yet apparent how opinions similar to those expressed to Gallup translate into decisions by the public and public officials concerning specific policies. In broader perspective, these polls exemplify what most public officials know from experience—the enormous difficulty in persuading the public to accept the substantial costs of environmental management in terms of dollars or lifestyle. (Jimmy Carter, battered by a nasty public backlash after his efforts to manage the 1970s energy crisis with new controls on public energy consumption, compared that struggle to "gnawing on a rock.")[75] It may sometimes appear to environmental leaders that an environmental equivalent of the 9/11 terrorist attack on New York is required to arouse sustained public attention and acceptance for even modest personal costs that might be involved.

THE SPECIAL PLACE OF SCIENCE IN POLICYMAKING

What often distinguishes environmental policymaking from other policy domains is the extraordinary importance of science, and scientific controversy, in the policy process. The growth of environmental legislation since the 1970s is evidence of the federal government's increasing concern with science and technology after World War II. Legislation concerning atomic power, air and water pollution, workplace and consumer safety, and hazardous wastes has put before public officials and agencies the need to make determinations of public policy by depending heavily on scientific evidence and scientific judgments. Environmental issues routinely require administrative agencies, Congress, judges, the White House staff, and even the president to make these determinations.

Science as Law

The range of scientific judgments required of administrative agencies in implementing environmental programs seems to embrace the whole domain of ecological research. For instance,

- the U.S. Coast Guard is authorized "in order to secure effective provisions . . . for protection of the marine environment . . . to establish regulations for ships with respect to the design and construction of such vessels . . . and with respect to equipment and appliances for . . . the prevention and mitigation of damage to the marine environment."[76]

- the EPA is to set effluent standards for new sources of water pollution so that each standard reflects "the greatest degree of effluent reduction . . . achievable through application of the best available demonstrated control technology, process, operating methods, or other alternatives, including, where practicable, a standard permitting no discharge of pollutants."[77]

Congress—and particularly the congressional committees writing legislation—also may have to resolve a multitude of technical issues. When regulating hazardous substances, for instance, what is a reasonable period to specify for chemical manufacturers to produce reliable data on the human effects of potentially dangerous substances? Is it necessary to regulate air emissions from diesel trucks to reduce harmful air pollutants? Is it appropriate to include heavy metals in the list of water pollutants for which standards must be created by the EPA? Eventually, judges will be compelled to weigh scientific evidence and render judgment on environmental issues.

Science as Politics

In policy conflicts, data become weapons, and science becomes a bastion against critics. Torturing technical data to fit some partisan position has become an art form in policy debates. Environmental issues frequently place scientists in a highly charged political atmosphere in which impartiality and objectivity, among the most highly esteemed scientific virtues, sometimes fail.

Scientists are consulted by public officials in good part because the scientists' presumed objectivity as well as their technical expertise makes them trustworthy advisers. But impartiality can be an early casualty in highly partisan and polarizing policy conflicts. Even if scientists maintain impartiality, they cannot prevent the partisans of one or another policy from distorting the technical information to gain an advantage. Scientists suspect (with justification) that their work will often be misrepresented in political debate and their credibility consequently diminished.

In any case, it is characteristic of environmental policy that scientific evidence and opinion often are divided for political reasons and, thus, that expert disagreements will reinforce political conflicts. Especially when political conflict tends to polarize views and force division over issues, an expert can intentionally or unwittingly shade opinions to fit a favored position or manipulate materials until they fit a simplistic policy position. When scientific disputes erupt in the course of environmental decision-making, one need not assume willful deceit on any side to suggest that political and economic bias might play some part in convincing experts of the truth of a position. Unfortunately, few executives or legislative agencies are innocent of data manipulation, deliberate or not, at some time.

Policy Pressures and the Scientific Method

The politician and the scientist live in fundamentally different decision-making worlds. Significant differences exist in the time frames for problem solving. "In his search for truth," biologist Roger Revelle observes, "the scientist is oriented toward the future; the politician's orientation is usually here and now. He desires quick visible pay-offs for which he often seems willing to mortgage the future. For the politician in a democratic society, infinity is the election after the next one."[78] Often, public officials are compelled to act swiftly. The Superfund Amendments and Reauthorization Act, for example, passed in 1986, included among its 150 deadlines a requirement that the EPA issue a plan to implement the act's radon research program, produce an annual report on radon mitigation demonstration programs, and provide a report on its national assessment of the radon problem in less than two years after the legislation was passed.[79]

If a crisis erupts—a newly discovered, leaking hazardous waste dump or a potentially catastrophic oil spill, for instance—information is needed immediately. But scientific information rarely appears on demand, even in urgent situations and especially when it must be sufficiently accurate to point to a clear direction for policy.

Public officials, moreover, often must craft environmental policies amid continuing disagreement between experts and the public over the degree of risk associated with various environmental problems. For instance, whereas the public rated chemical waste disposal as the highest environmental risk, the experts ranked it considerably lower. In contrast, the experts assigned much greater risk to stratospheric ozone depletion and indoor radon than did the public. Critics of current environmental regulation, pointing to these disparate views of ecological risk, often argue that public opinion has intimidated policymakers into following the wrong environmental priorities.

Still, decisions must be made, thus often confronting policymakers with an unwelcome choice between a scientifically risky decision and a politically risky one.[80] Consider, for example, the decision facing EPA Administrator Lisa Jackson and her staff in mid-2012 when confronting a legal requirement that the EPA review the national air-quality standard for fine particulates, often called *soot,* and recommend change from an older standard if more recent scientific research justified it. Particulates are extremely small, solid particles found in air and produced by dust, smoke, fuel combustion, agriculture, and forest cultivation, among other sources. Soot is a recognized public health hazard associated with significant deaths, chronic respiratory illness, infant mortality, and other illness. Confronted with an approaching legal deadline and based upon available EPA research, Jackson had informed the White House that she would recommend that existing permissible particulate levels be reduced—in effect, made more rigorous, a decision the EPA estimated would prevent thousands of premature deaths and other illness. The White House responded to the EPA's recommendation with a suggestion that the particulate requirement be less rigorous but still tougher than the existing standard. Jackson subsequently responded with a new proposal for a less rigorous standard than she had originally advocated.

The EPA's revised decision incited an intense political and scientific controversy. Critics, including many public health organizations, charged that the

White House was interfering with EPA science. Environmentalist organizations were almost unanimously opposed to the White House response. In that spirit, the clean air director of the Natural Resources Council, a major national environmental organization, considered it "obnoxious and untoward that a bunch of economists and politicos in the [White House] evidently told EPA that it had to propose a [weaker standard] as a formally endorsed preference, contrary to EPA's wishes and scientific views."[81] Congressional Republicans, major spokespeople for the petroleum industry such as the American Petroleum Institute, and organizations representing major industries subject to the regulation asserted that the EPA's initial recommendation had been scientifically questionable and economically damaging; many opposing the EPA's new standard asserted that there was no compelling need to change the standard at all, especially at a time when the regulated industries were enduring an economic recession. Moreover, the EPA was aware of concern from political spokespeople from a number of populous urban U.S. counties who expressed displeasure because their counties would be out of compliance with any newly revised standard, resulting in potentially serious political and economic impacts.

As the debate evolved, it became clear that setting the new standard also involved substantial scientific uncertainties. EPA scientists had long acknowledged that setting the particulate standard was difficult because any standard except total elimination of airborne particulates would still create significant public health risks.[82] In short, no scientifically "safe" standard could be created, and any decision would have to be made on the basis of how much estimated risk to public health was considered acceptable.

While the EPA had until December 2012 to make a decision and was not necessarily compelled to heed the White House recommendations, as a practical matter, the agency would almost certainly have to abide by White House preferences. In the end, whatever decision Jackson and her staff eventually made concerning the final standard, there was no safe harbor from a decision loaded with both scientific and political risk and uncertainty—and the same problem will likely arise when the standard has to be reviewed in the future.

CONCLUSION

In an important sense, environmental degradation is a twenty-first century problem resolved according to eighteenth-century rules. Fundamental government arrangements, such as institutional checks and balances, interest-group liberalism, federalism, and much else reviewed in this chapter, are explicitly created by the Constitution or are implicit in its philosophy. The explosive growth of federal environmental legislation and the distinctive role of science in environmental policymaking add distinctly new elements to the federal policy cycle and indicate that environmental management has become a permanent new policy domain within federal and state governments with its own set of institutional and political biases.

Suggested Readings

Ascher, William, Toddi Steelman, and Robert Healy. *Knowledge and Environmental Policy. Re-Imagining the Boundaries of Science and Politics.* Cambridge, MA: MIT Press, 2010.

Kraft, Michael E., and Scott R. Furlong. *Public Policy: Politics, Analysis, and Alternatives.* 6th ed. Washington, DC: CQ Press, 2017.

Layzer, Judith. *The Environmental Case: Translating Values Into Policy.* 4th ed. Washington, DC: CQ Press, 2015.

Lindblom, Charles A., and Edward J. Woodhouse. *The Policy-Making Process.* 3rd ed. Englewood Cliffs, NJ: Prentice Hall, 1993.

Marzotto, Toni, Vicky Moshier Burnor, and Gordon Scott Bonham. *The Evolution of Public Policy: Cars and the Environment.* Boulder, CO: Lynne Rienner, 2000.

Mazur, Alan. *Technical Controversies Over Policy: From Fluoridation to Fracking and Climate Change.* New York: Routledge, 2017.

Notes

1. Kelsey Kopec and Lori Ann Burd, Pollinators in Peril, "Executive Summary," available at https://www.biologicaldiversity.org/news/press_releases/2017/bees-03-01-2017.php.
2. Faith Karimi, "Obama Announces Plan to Save Honey Bees," *CNN Politics*, June 23, 2014, available at https://www.cnn.com/2014/06/22/politics/honey bees-protection/index.html.
3. Sharon Lerner, "Poison Fruit," *The Intercept*, 1/14/17, available at https://theintercept.com/2017/01/14/dow-chemical-wants-farmers-to-keep-using-a-pesticide-linked-to-autism-and-adhd/.
4. Tatiana Schlossberg and John Schwartz, "A Bumblebee Gets New Protection on Obama's Way Out," *New York Times*, January 11, 2017, A14.
5. Rhett Jones, "White House Blocks Listing of Bumble Bee As Endangered Species," *Gizmodo*, 2/12/17 https://gizmodo.com/white-house-blocks-listing-of-bumble-bee-as-endangered-1792271532.
6. Michael Greshko, "First U.S. Bumblebee Officially Listed as Endangered," *National Geographic*, March, 2017, available at https://news.nationalgeo graphic.com/2017/03/bumblebees-endangered-extinction-united-states .html.
7. Center for Biological Diversity, "Conservation Groups, Congressman Blumenauer Call for Action on Pollution-killing Pesticides," http://www .biologicaldiversity.org/news/press_releases/2018/pesticides-.

8. Charles O. Jones, *An Introduction to Public Policy* (North Scituate, MA: Duxbury Press, 1978), 38.

9. Roger W. Cobb and Charles D. Elder, *Participation in American Politics* (Baltimore: Johns Hopkins University Press, 1972), 86.

10. J. Clarence Davies III, "Environmental Regulation and Technical Change," in *Keeping Pace With Science and Engineering: Studies in Environmental Regulation,* ed. Myron F. Uman (Washington, DC: National Academies Press, 1993), 255.

11. Eugene Bardach, *The Implementation Game* (Cambridge, MA: MIT Press, 1971), 36.

12. Peter deLeon, "A Theory of Termination in the Policy Process: Rules, Rhymes and Reasons," paper delivered at the annual meeting of the American Political Science Association, Washington, DC, September 1–4, 1977, 2.

13. Richard E. Neustadt, *Presidential Power* (New York: John Wiley, 1960).

14. Morton Grodzins, "The Federal System," in *American Federalism in Perspective,* ed. Aaron Wildavsky (Boston: Little, Brown, 1967), 257.

15. Ibid. See also Charles E. Davis and James P. Lester, "Federalism and Environmental Policy," in *Environmental Politics and Policy: Theories and Evidence,* ed. James P. Lester (Durham, NC: Duke University Press, 1989), 57–86; James P. Lester, "A New Federalism? Environmental Policy in the States," in *Environmental Policy in the 1990s,* ed. Norman J. Vig and Michael Kraft (Washington, DC: CQ Press, 1990), 59–80.

16. Executive Office of the President, Office of Management and Budget, Office of Information and Regulatory Affairs, *2011 Report to Congress on the Benefits and Costs of Federal Regulations and Unfunded Mandates on State, Local and Tribal Entities,* 13, available at www.whitehouse.gov/sites/default/files/omb/ . . . /2011_cba_report.pdf. Some of these costs were offset by other federal grants. The estimated benefits of these regulations were also estimated to exceed $81 billion.

17. This mingling of private and public power is well explored in Grant McConnell, *Private Power and American Democracy* (New York: Vintage, 1967). See also Helen M. Ingram and Dean E. Mann, "Interest Groups and Environmental Policy," in *Environmental Politics and Policy: Theories and Evidence,* ed. James P. Lester (Durham, NC: Duke University Press, 1989), 135–157.

18. James V. DeLong, "How to Convince an Agency," *Regulation* (September–October 1982): 31.

19. Graham Allison, *The Essence of Decision* (Boston: Little, Brown, 1971), 163.

20. Charles A. Lindblom, "The Science of Muddling Through," *Public Administration Review* (Spring 1959): 86.

21. James Gustave Speth, "Environmental Failure: A Case for the New Green Politics," *Environment 360: Opinion,* October 20, 2008, available at http:// e360.yale.edu/content/feature.msp?id=2075.

22. The reasons for this departure are examined carefully in J. Clarence Davies III and Charles F. Lettow, "The Impact of Federal Institutional Arrangements,"

in *Federal Environmental Law*, ed. Erica L. Dolgin and Thomas G. P. Guilbert (St. Paul, MN: West, 1974), 126–191.

23. Theodore Lowi, "The Public Philosophy: Interest Group Liberalism," *American Political Science Review* 61 (March 1967): 18.

24. McConnell, *Private Power and American Democracy*, 162.

25. Center for Responsive Politics, OpenSecrets.org, "Energy and Natural Resources: Industry Influence in the Climate Debate," and "Environment Industry Profile, Summary 2015," available at https://www.opensecrets.org/news/issues/energy/.

26. Charles A. Lindblom, *The Policy Making Process*, 2nd ed. (Englewood Cliffs, NJ: Prentice Hall, 1980), 73.

27. Ibid.

28. Katherine Bagley, *Infographic: A Field Guide to the U.S. Environmental Movement*, available at http://insideclimatenews.org/news/20140407/infographic-field-guide-us-environmental-movement.

29. Juliet Eilperin "Top Green Group to Spend at Least $40 million This Election, Shattering Past Records," *Washington Post*, October 12, 2016, available at https://www.washingtonpost.com/news/energy-environment/wp/2016/10/10/top-green-group-to-spend-at-least-40-million-this-elec tion-shattering-past-records/?utm_term=.a0a2316f4a17.

30. Center for Responsive Politics, OpenSecrets.org, "Ranked Sectors" and "Environment," available at https://www.opensecrets.org/lobby/indusclient .php?id=Q11&year=2016.

31. Dina Cappiello, "Politics Replaces Pollution as Agency's Top Foe," *Atlanta Journal-Constitution*, April 22, 2012. Quoted in *Greenwire*, April 23, 2012, available at http://www.eenews.net/Greenwire/2012/04/23/6/.

32. Ibid.

33. Robert Brulle, Liesel Hall Turner, Jason Carmichael, and J. Craig Jenkins, "Measuring Social Movement Organization Populations: A Comprehensive Census of U.S. Environmental Movement Organizations," *Mobilization: An International Quarterly Review* 12 (July 2007): 195–210.

34. Dunlap, "State of Environmentalism in the U.S.—Diagnosis: Neither Dead nor Rejuvenated," April 26, 2007, available at www.ecoamerica.typepad .com/blog/2007/04/the_state_of_en.html.

35. Identified as nonprofits by the U.S. Internal Revenue Service.

36. Based on estimates for 2005 in Baird Straughan and Tom Pollak, *The Broader Movement: Nonprofit Environmental and Conservation Organizations, 1989–2005* (Washington, DC: The Urban Institute, 2008).

37. Ibid., 37.

38. Katrina Darlene Taylor, "The Broadening Strategy of Environmental Organizations on the Issue of Global Warming," paper presented at the annual conference of the Western Political Science Association, San Diego, CA, 2008.

39. Committee on Energy and Commerce, "Climate Change Legislation Design White Paper: Appropriate Roles for Different Levels of Government," February 2008, available at http://energycommerce.house.gov/ Climate_Change/white%20paper%20st-lcl%20roles%20final%202-22 .pdf.

40. Jason Plautz and Elana Schor, "Mapping Environmentalism's Road Ahead," *E&E Daily*, December 9, 2013, available at http://www.eenews.net/special_ reports/shades_green/stories/1059991471. February 16, 2015).

41. Susan Leeson, "Philosophic Implications of the Ecological Crisis: The Authoritarian Challenge to Liberalism," *Polity* 11 (Spring 1979): 305.

42. Michael McCloskey, "Twenty Years of Change in the Environmental Movement: An Insider's View," in *American Environmentalism: The U.S. Environmental Movement, 1970–1990*, ed. Riley E. Dunlap and Angela G. Mertig (Philadelphia: Taylor and Francis, 1991), 78–89, quotation on 78.

43. Brian Tokar, "Questioning Official Environmentalism," *Z Magazine* (April 1997): 38.

44. Jeffrey St. Clair, "Panda Porn: The Marriage of WWF and Weyerhaeuser," *Counterpunch Magazine*, December 5, 2002, available at http://www.counter punch.org/stclair1205.html.

45. Inside Philanthropy, "Conservation Funders" and "Climate Change," available at https://www.insidephilanthropy.com/grants-for-conservation/.

46. Bill Devall, "Deep Ecology and Radical Environmentalism," in *American Environmentalism: The U.S. Environmental Movement, 1970–1990*, ed. Riley E. Dunlap and Angela G. Mertig (Philadelphia: Taylor and Francis, 1991), 51–61; G. Sessions, "The Deep Ecology Movement," *Environment Review* 11 (June 1987): 105–125; Rick Scarce, *Eco-Warriors: Understanding the Radical Environmental Movement* (Chicago, IL: Noble Press, 1992).

47. Devall, "Deep Ecology and Radical Environmentalism," 55.

48. David Foreman, *Ecodefense* (Tucson, AZ: Abbzug Press, 1988); G. Grossman, *And on the Eighth Day We Bulldozed It* (San Francisco: Rainbow Action Network, 1988); S. Obst Love and D. Obst Love, eds., *Ecotage* (New York: Bantam, 1972); D. Day, *The Environmental Wars: Reports From the Front Lines* (New York: St. Martin's, 1989).

49. John H. Cushman Jr. and Evelyn Nieves, "In Colorado Resort Fires, Culprits Defy Easy Labels," *New York Times*, October 24, 1998.

50. Web Ecoist, "25 Environmental Agencies and Organizations," available at http://webecoist.momtastic.com/2008/09/24/25-environmental -agencies-and-organizations.

51. The ten organizations: National Wildlife Federation, Credo, Sierra Club, Natural Resources Defense Council, League of Conservation Voters, 350.org, Environmental Defense Fund, Friends of the Earth, Greenpeace, and Rainforest Action. Katherine Bagley, "Infographic: A Field Guide to the U.S. Environmental Movement," *Inside Climate News*,

available at http://insideclimatenews.org/news/20140407/infographic-field
-guide-us-environmental-movement.

52. Jim Norman, "Environmental Activists Put Their Beliefs Into Action,"
www.gallup.com, March 24, 2017, available at http://news.gallup.com/
poll/207104/environmental-activists-put-beliefs-action.aspx.

53. Robert Cameron Mitchell, "From Conservation to Environmental Movement:
The Development of the Modern Environmental Lobbies," in *Government and
Environmental Politics,* ed. Michael J. Lacey (Washington, DC: Wilson Center
Press, 1989), 81–114; Michael deCourcy Hinds, "The Politics of Pollution,"
American Demographics 22 (2000): 26.

54. Center for Media and Democracy, Sourcewatch, "The Big Green," available
at www.sourcewatch.org/index.php/Big_Green.

55. John M. Bridgeland, Mary McNaught, Bruce Reed, and Mark Dunkelman,
The Quiet Crisis: The Impact of the Economic Downturn on the Nonprofit Sector
(Washington, DC: W. K. Kellogg Foundation, 2009); Training Resources for
the Environmental Community (TREC), *Moving to Higher Ground: Funding
Strategies in Challenging Times,* available at http://www.trec.org/resource/
page-report.asp?nMode=1&nLibraryID=32#.

56. John O'Connell, "Election Provides Fund-Raising Windfall for Environmental
Organizations," *Capital Press,* January 19, 2017, available at http://www
capitalpress.com/Nation_World/Nation/20170119/election-provides-fund
-raising-windfall-for-environmental-organizations.

57. BBC News, "Trump Presidency: Opponents Boosted by 'Rage Donation,'"
February 9, 2017, available at http://www.bbc.com/news/world-us-canada
-38909322.

58. George Hoberg, *Pluralism by Design: Environmental Policy and the American
Regulatory State* (New York: Praeger, 1992), ix.

59. Ibid., 198–199.

60. Center for Responsive Politics, OpenSecrets.org, "Environment," available
at www.opensecrets.org/industries/summary.php?ind=Q11&recipdetail=A&
sortorder=U&mem=Y&cycle=2016.

61. Amanda Little, "RFK Jr. and Other Prominent Enviros Face Off Over Cape
Cod Wind Farm," *Grist,* January 12, 2006, available at www.grist.org/arti
cle/capecod; Jeffry Ball, "Power Shift: Renewable Energy, Meet the New
Nimbys—Solar and Wind-Power Proposals Draw Opposition From Residents
Fearing Visual Blight; a Dilemma for Some Environmentalists," *Wall Street
Journal* (Eastern ed.), September 4, 2009, A13.

62. Bryan Mayor, *Blue-Green Coalitions: Fighting for Safe Workplaces and Healthy
Communities* (Ithaca, NY: Cornell University Press, 2009).

63. Marc K. Landy and Mary Hague, "The Coalition for Waste: Private Interests
and Superfund," in *Environmental Politics: Public Costs, Private Rewards,* ed.
Michael S. Greve and Fred L. Smith (New York: Praeger, 1992), 75.

64. McCloskey, "Twenty Years of Change," 86.

65. Everett Carll Ladd and Karlyn Bowman, "Public Opinion on the Environment," *Resources* 124 (Summer 1996): 5.

66. Steven R. Brechin and Daniel A. Freeman, "Public Support for Both the Environment and Anti-Environmental President: Possible Explanations for the George W. Bush Anomaly," *Forum* 2, no. 1 (2004), Berkeley Electronic Press, available at http://www.bepress.com/forum.

67. Paul Mohai, "Dispelling Old Myths: African American Concern for the Environment," *Environment* 45 (June 2003): 11–26.

68. Riley E. Dunlap, "Public Opinion and Environmental Policy," in *Environmental Politics and Policy: Theories and Evidence,* ed. James P. Lester (Durham, NC: Duke University Press, 1989), 131.

69. Gallup Poll, Presidential Election 2016: Key Indicators," http://news.gallup .com/poll/189299/presidential-election-2016-key-indicators.aspx.

70. Ibid.

71. Jim DiPeso, "The 2006 Midterm Elections: An Environmental Perspective," *Environmental Quality Management* (spring 2006), available at www.inter science.wiley.com.

72. See, for example, Riley E. Dunlap, "Climate Change Views: Republican-Democratic Gaps Expand," May 29, 2008, available at http://www.gallup.com/poll/107569/ClimateChange-Views-RepublicanDemocratic-Gaps-Expand .aspx.

73. Pew Research Center for People and the Press, *Social Issues Rank as Lowest Priorities* (Washington, DC: Pew Research Center), 12, available at http://www.people-press.org/2012/04/17/with-voters-focused-on-economy -obama-lead-narrows/.

74. For example, two-thirds of Democratic voters said that the environment would be very important to their vote in the fall 2015. Forty-eight percent of independents and 35 percent of Republicans rated the environment as very important.

75. Quoted in Neil King Jr., "A Past President's Advice to Obama: Act With Haste—Jimmy Carter Says New Administration Needs to Harness the Benefits of a Crisis Mentality to Tame Energy Policy," *Wall Street Journal* (Eastern ed.), December 11, 2008, A16.

76. Ports and Waterways Act of 1972, Pub. L. No. 92–340.

77. Federal Water Pollution Control Act Amendments of 1972, Pub. L. No. 92–500.

78. Roger Revelle, "The Scientist and the Politician," in *Science, Technology, and National Policy,* ed. Thomas J. Kuehn and Alan L. Porter (Ithaca, NY: Cornell University Press, 1981), 134.

79. U.S. General Accounting Office, "Superfund: Missed Statutory Deadlines Slow Progress in Environmental Programs," Report no. GAO/RCED 89–27, Washington, DC, November 1988, chap. 2.

80. The epitome of this decision-making problem is explored in Riley Dunlap, *DDT: Scientists, Citizens, and Public Policy* (Princeton, NJ: Princeton University Press, 1981), esp. chap. 8.

81. Gabriel Nelson, "White House Change to EPA Soot Standards Stirs Debate," *E&E Reporter*, July 18, 2012, available at www.eenews.net/Greenwire/2012/07/18/2.

82. Quoted from U.S. EPA, *Draft Proposal for the Particulate Matter (PM) National Ambient Air Quality Standards (NAAQS): Briefing for Interagency Review, June 4, 2012* (Washington, DC: EPA), available at Gabriel Nelson, "White House Change."

MAKING POLICY

Governmental Institutions and Politics

This is a brief narrative about one of the most important and formidable environmental challenges President Barack Obama encountered during his presidency and his successor inherited. The story concerns six words in the Clean Water Act and the president's attempt to resolve an environmental policy conflict these six words incited, a struggle known as "the water war" and nicknamed WOTUS.

The conflict began shortly after the dawn of the nation's Environmental Era. It involves a confusing but extremely important federal water pollution law, an intense environmental controversy persisting for more than forty years, and a cast of politically and economically powerful stakeholders who have pursued their conflicting policy agendas through all the important institutions inherent to U.S. public policymaking all the way to the Trump administration. In the twilight of his second term, President Barack Obama hoped to enhance his environmental legacy by resolving finally the WOTUS conflict. The task was daunting, progress slow. Adding insult to frustration, one of the president's own executive agencies expertly assisted his opposition. The WOTUS story briefly illuminates much about U.S. public policymaking, about its institutional foundations, their opportunities and hazards, and the complexity, all of which constitute the substance of this chapter.

THE WATER WAR CALLED WOTUS

The conflict that became WOTUS originated only months after the first Earth Day, during the early 1970s when Congress and the White House collaborated to create in rapid succession most of the legislation that has become the foundation of the nation's Environmental Era. Among the most important of these laws is the Clean Water Act of 1972 (CWA), which invested the federal government with authority to regulate water pollution across the nation, identified which pollutants were to be regulated, set datelines and standards for control, and—here the WOTUS controversy began—identified which bodies of water were to be regulated. Identifying which water bodies to regulate meant declaring who would be regulated—in practical terms, who would bear the cost of controlling the pollution and who could be prosecuted, fined, or possibly imprisoned for failure to obey the law. This was a matter involving potentially hundreds or thousands of different public and private entities and incalculable billions of dollars in regulatory costs for the regulated interests over the life of the law. Practically any industry, business, farm, community, governmental entity, corporation—any entity that discharged pollutants into a water body—might be liable for regulation if that water body was encompassed by the law. Thus, enormous importance rested upon how the CWA defined a regulated water body. Here Congress sowed confusion.

Creating WOTUS

WOTUS is shorthand for "waters of the United States" and refers to section 404 of the Clean Water Act, in which Congress defined which water bodies are to be regulated by the Army Corps of Engineers (COE) and the EPA, the two federal agencies responsible for enforcing its provisions. The law states that regulation shall apply to "navigable waters," which are defined to mean "the waters of the United States, including the territorial seas." It is clear that Congress intended these terms to include rivers, lakes, streams, and most wetlands. Unfortunately, Congress would not or could not write into the law a more precise, comprehensible definition of what it meant by "waters of the United States." Section 404, noted an experienced environmental attorney, "doesn't tell you very much. It refers to navigable waters and defines them as waters of the United States. But there are so many possible variations of facts, and the Clean Water Act says so little that there is just so much room for disputes."[1] That room was quickly packed with regulated interests, environmental organizations, state governments involved in enforcement, and other stakeholders contending over the meaning of the law, all attempting to influence EPA and COE to interpret the legislation to their advantage as the agencies wrote the required regulations.

"The Water War"

The agencies followed a common administrative practice by looking at the congressional history of the law to find what guidance they could when interpreting "waters of the United States" and found some help: it appeared that Congress meant to regulate not only large water bodies but also their tributaries. However, the COE and EPA would have to use their environmental expertise and experience to resolve numerous other contentious issues sure to arise, because the law was mined with ambiguities. For instance, was an industry liable for regulation if it discharged pollutants on property that was a wetland only part of a year? Must a dairy farm control its water discharges if it was releasing pollutants into a very small tributary of a much larger river? Did runoff from city streets that flowed from gutters into groundwater and eventually into a lake estuary constitute pollution to "waters of the United States"? What determined that a body of water was "navigable"? These and a multitude of related issues provoked the prolonged and expensive political competition among conflicting stakeholders determined to achieve regulatory interpretations to their own advantage.

So began the water war, the legal battle over the meaning of "waters of the United States." A battlefront rapidly hardened between interests pressing EPA and COE to interpret the law very broadly so that it applied to as many water bodies as possible and those wanting the agencies to limit its scope as much as possible. The proponents of an expansive definition favored active, aggressive enforcement of federal water pollution regulation—environmentalists, public health officials, Democrats in the White House and Congress, some state governments, and their allies. Advocates of more limited water regulation included industrial, commercial, and farming interests opposing what they considered the excessive cost and complexity of federal water pollution regulations; most Republicans in Congress and the White House; state and local governments concerned about a loss of their authority in environmental management; and numerous organizations advocating more restraint on the growth of the federal government powers and bureaucracy.

Once EPA and COE began interpreting the law, the scope of battle widened to include not only Congress and regulatory agencies but also the federal courts. It is an iron law of U.S. politics that stakeholders in major regulatory conflicts sooner or later resort to the courts in an attempt to turn regulatory decisions to their advantage when other means fail. The judges are drawn into such conflicts because the courts are responsible for oversight of administrative agencies to assure that the agencies properly interpret and implement the laws for which they are responsible. Quite often, the courts are compelled to interpret the law, especially when the law is vague or confusing—such was the case with WOTUS. The judges' decisions then become guidelines that administrators must follow as they translate the language of the law into environmental regulations.

By the beginning of the Obama administration in 2008, virtually every major water pollution regulation issued by the EPA and the Corps of Engineers involving an interpretation of "waters of the United States" had provoked litigation usually initiated by interests disadvantaged by an EPA or COE ruling and asserting that the agencies had misinterpreted the law or exceeded their authority when enforcing it. The court battles assured not only income and occupation for a generation of lawyers but also enormous delay and uncertainty concerning when water pollution regulations would be issued and how they would be enforced. By the beginning of Obama's presidency, the Supreme Court had twice struck down major EPA regulations during the previous G. W. Bush administration because, the Court declared, the agency had attempted to regulate waters beyond its authority. The Court's several rulings, however, were confusing and inconsistent, leaving EPA and COE without clear guidelines needed to issue further regulations about WOTUS.

The White House Acts

President Barack Obama, an outspoken advocate of strong federal pollution regulation, intended to resolve the forty-year water war. The president and his EPA leadership were convinced that the federal courts had severely and inappropriately limited the regulatory authority of EPA and COE by the judges' inconsistent and usually conservative interpretation of the agencies' powers to enforce the Clean Water Act. The White House solution was to use the executive authority of the president to instruct EPA and COE to propose a new regulation or "rule" that would interpret "waters of the United States" in a way that greatly enlarged the number of water bodies regulated by Washington. In essence, the new rule represented what the White House, EPA, and the COE believed to be the correct interpretation necessary to assure that the Clean Water Act would be enforced as Congress intended. The new rule was expected to greatly reduce the number of lawsuits involving WOTUS and to hasten enforcement of long-delayed water pollution regulations over an enormous variety of new water bodies.

After several years of deliberation, the EPA and COE jointly proposed the new rule in March 2014, known as the Waters of the United States Rule. The new rule clarified the definition of "waters of the United States" in a way that enlarged regulation to include more than 60 percent of the nation's streams and millions of wetland acres not clearly protected as a result of previous federal court interpretations of the law.[2] Early warning of impending political strife was almost immediate.[3] "With the stakes high, lawyers are already talking about legal assaults on the proposed regulations," noted a Washington political reporter shortly after the rule was publicized.[4] Politically powerful organizations, such as the U.S. Chamber of Commerce, the National Association of Manufacturers, and the American Farm Bureau Federation, announced their opposition. Legislative opponents of expanded EPA authority, primarily congressional Republicans, quickly announced plans to introduce legislation preventing the EPA and COE from enforcing the proposed rule—a tactic thwarted by Obama's threat to veto any attempt to kill the water rule. Nonetheless, opposition to the new rule was organizing for a long opposition campaign.

During the following year, EPA and COE held more than 400 public meetings with concerned interests and considered more than a million public comments about the proposed rule. Finally, in May 2015, the White House announced its final version of the rule, substantially as originally proposed, to the great satisfaction of environmentalists and their allies.[5] "This rule will provide the clarity and certainty businesses and industry need about which waters are protected by the Clean Water Act," Obama stated. "My administration has made historic commitments to clean water, from restoring iconic watersheds . . . to preserving more than a thousand miles of rivers and other waters for future generations. With today's rule, we take another step towards protecting the waters that belong to all of us."[6] The president spoke too soon.

The Water War Revives

The proposed new rule was a trip wire for a renewed assault upon EPA's regulatory power by the tireless, always formidable opponents to any expansion of EPA and COE's regulatory authority. The battle ranged across Congress, the executive branch, the federal courts, interest groups, the states, and the media, including a Twitter skirmish between the critics (#DitchTheRule) and EPA (#DitchTheMyth). The opposition involved interests as diverse as farmers, property developers, fertilizer and pesticide manufacturers, oil and gas producers, the National Cattleman's Association, U.S. Chamber of Commerce, and numerous other business and trade associations. Within a month of the rule announcement, legislative critics from both parties succeeded in passing a joint congressional resolution disapproving (but not suspending) the rule that Republican leaders condemned as a "raw and tyrannical power grab that will crush jobs."[7]

The most unexpected event in the revived water war was the public release of several long, detailed memos written by a top official in the Corps of Engineers to EPA's leadership contending that EPA's version of the new rule was "legally vulnerable, difficult to defend in court, difficult for the Corps to explain or justify, and challenging for the Corps to implement." The memo concluded: "The rule's contradictions with legal principles generate multiple legal and technical consequences that, in the view of the Corps, would be fatal to the rule in its current form."[8] That another administrative agency within the executive branch, especially one supposed to collaborate with the EPA in writing a new regulation the president considered vital, should publicly release such a comprehensive shredding of the president's proposal was remarkable as well as exceedingly useful to the opposition.

The Water War Continues

The campaign against the WOTUS rule gained additional force when the opposition turned predictably to the federal courts for assistance. In June 2015, thirteen states, led by North Dakota, requested the court to halt enforcement of the new regulation because they asserted the rule was an unconstitutional assumption by the federal government of powers belonging to the states. Fourteen additional states had joined the original judicial action by October 2015 when a federal district court issued an injunction temporarily halting enforcement of WOTUS just one day before the rule would take effect. Advocates of the new rule had reason for apprehension when the district court explained the reason for its action. "We conclude that petitioners have demonstrated a substantial possibility of success on the merits of their claims," the judges wrote in their decision, explaining that the EPA's new guidelines for determining whether water is subject to federal regulation . . . "is 'at odds' with a key Supreme Court ruling."[9]

Thus, by early 2016, the water war had returned again to the federal courts, but not for long. In early 2018, Donald Trump took the controversy out of the courts and delivered a victory for opponents of the Obama rule when he used his authority to suspend the Obama rule and instructed his new EPA administrator, Scott Pruitt, to prepare a revised ruling greatly restricting the EPA's authority over domestic water pollution.[10]

As the WOTUS saga demonstrates, policymaking in the federal government is inherently time consuming, frequently highly contentious, and often mined with surprises and uncertainties. It could hardly be otherwise in a government of checks and balances, where institutions exercise competing and shared powers concurrently. In addition, history resonates through the policymaking process. Today's policy discussions are infused with institutional memories of past events and nuanced with expectations for the future. This chapter examines the most important of the institutions involved in this process to exemplify how competing constitutional authority, shared powers, and historical experience shape the character of policymaking in Washington.

THE PRESIDENCY

"Mothers all want their sons to grow up to be president," President John Kennedy once remarked, "but they don't want them to become politicians in the process."[11] The president wields vast constitutional authority and powerful leverage over public opinion, enlarged by a century of growing public tolerance for presidential assertions of additional inherent powers. But to be a successful policymaker, the president must still be a proficient politician. The essential politics of presidential leadership in environmental affairs, as with other policy issues, requires, among other things, the will as well as the ability to bargain and compromise with Congress, to know how to shape public opinion and when to be governed by it, and to know when to respect judicial independence and when to challenge it—in short, a capacity to move a government of divided powers and competitive institutions in the direction that presidential policies require.

Occupants of the White House since Earth Day 1970 have varied greatly in their concern about environmental protection and their ability to translate environmental commitments into practical policy. So-called "green presidents" have often been the least successful environmental policymakers. It is a lesson repeated endlessly in Washington that even presidents committed to the politics of policymaking discover they cannot always command the ends even when they summon the means for policy leadership (see Chapter 1).

Presidential Resources

Environmentalists, long irate at what they perceived to be the George W. Bush administration's dismal environmental record, had awaited prompt signals that the new Obama administration would bring the anticipated friendlier environmentalist agenda to Washington, and they weren't disappointed. Within days of taking office, Obama had exercised his constitutional authority as chief executive to revoke Bush administration policies promoting resource exploration near Utah public lands, to suspend other Bush measures facilitating increased timber production from the national forests, and to order regulators to write stringent new rules for auto emissions and fuel economy. This followed a high-profile "green inauguration" featuring a carbon-neutral ball (another was celebrated on a green carpet made from a recycled rug), hybrid Lexuses for transportation, organic menus, recycled paper invitations, and valet bicycle parking. All of this demonstrated early the president's intention to summon both the inherent constitutional powers of his office and his unrivalled ability to command media attention to advance his environmental agenda. Here were potent presidential resources, a few among many, that could effectively shape the course of White House environmental policymaking—if presidential skill, historical opportunity, congressional and judicial collaboration, the economy, the public, and luck also permitted.

Constitutional Powers

As the nation's chief executive, the president can bring to environmental policymaking a vast array of constitutional powers. A short list of these resources includes the following:

- The authority to propose and to veto legislation

- The ability to propose policy priorities and initiatives to Congress and the nation simultaneously in the constitutional State of the Union message

- The power to draft and to present to Congress the annual federal budget

- The authority to appoint a cabinet of executive department heads and to designate other executive leadership of most major federal environmental bureaucracies, such as the DOI and the EPA

- The power to appoint federal judges when judicial vacancies occur

- The prerogative to issue executive orders, which require no congressional approval, to all federal executive agencies

- An ability to appoint policy advisers to the president's personal staff and to White House advisory committees required by Congress

- The authority to negotiate and to propose international agreements and treaties for congressional approval[12]

This inventory excludes a great deal, such as the talent of creative presidents to transmute traditional authority into new modes of influence. Moreover, presidential power also resides in the president's decision not to use his or her resources of policy leadership—inaction is also policymaking.

In practice, presidential ability to capitalize on the presidency's political resources for environmental purposes has varied greatly. One explanation for this variability is the many ways in which circumstances can alter the political climate surrounding the White House—events such as economic recessions, changing congressional majorities, and other changes in the political "seasons."

Surprise, Crisis, and the Presidency

Sometimes, presidential policymaking is blessed or plagued by the unexpected and the unpredictable. Often, presidents discover that their policy agendas and priorities become captive not only to unexpected events but to crises that force the pace and substance of White House politics. Crises of various kinds have compelled many crucial White House environmental initiatives, such as the Superfund legislation in 1980 regulating abandoned hazardous waste sites and the creation of the Toxics Release Inventory (TRI) in 1984 to track toxic industrial air and water emissions.

The disastrous 2010 oil spill in the Gulf of Mexico is a textbook illustration of how events can shape White House policy. The *Deepwater Horizon* oil rig exploded and incinerated into the Gulf of Mexico on April 20, 2010. It unleashed a catastrophic oil spill, quickly accelerating into an environmental crisis and spilling 210,000 gallons of crude oil daily into the gulf. Within a month, the spill had created a vast underwater oil plume ten miles long and one mile wide, and a surface slick visible to astronauts in the International Space Station, hundreds of miles above Earth. For British Petroleum, the rig's owner, it rapidly became a financial and political crisis exacerbated by the global media's relentless dramatization of the event and its potentially catastrophic environmental consequences.

The *Deepwater Horizon* disaster was an acute embarrassment and a potential political disaster for the Obama administration. Exactly a month before the rig explosion, Obama had announced that he would propose that Congress increase significantly the scale of oil and natural gas exploration in a large portion of the eastern Gulf of Mexico. A month later, the *Deepwater Horizon* disaster compelled Obama to announce that his administration would stop further offshore energy exploration indefinitely—an abrupt policy reversal enthusiastically advertised by his critics as evidence of bad judgment and poor political leadership. Obama's decision to propose new offshore exploration had been a reluctant concession made to Senate Republicans, many of whom had for decades campaigned for increased exploration; it was the price he had to pay for Republican support of the administration's important climate change legislation. But the *Deepwater Horizon* disaster now compelled Obama and Congress as well to focus not on getting more oil from the gulf but on preventing further offshore drilling crises.

The Executive Office of the President

The president is an individual, but the presidency is an institution surrounding the Oval Office with an array of administrative resources, collectively called the Executive Office of the President (EOP), which includes the president's personal staff and has become essential for the president to fulfill his constitutional responsibilities. Most of the EOP's employees are permanent civil service appointees, such as the critically important personnel in the Office of Management and Budget (OMB), who provide expert administrative advice, oversee the implementation of presidential policies, and provide continuity from one presidency to the next.[13] In addition, within the EOP is an entity called the White House, containing other, personally appointed presidential staff and advisers, such as speechwriters and congressional liaison specialists, whom the president selects and who serve at his or her pleasure. Much of the daily work involved with the president's environmental policymaking is done by the individuals and offices within the EOP and by his or her personal staff. Equally important, presidents routinely turn to their personal staff and the professionals in the EOP for advice and assistance. What appears to be a presidential decision often turns out, on close inspection, to be a collaborative White House staff creation. Indeed, it is often an OMB official, not the president, who interprets and represents White House policies to Congress and the federal bureaucracy.

Because the OMB is so frequently the agent for implementing presidential policy within the executive branch, it readily becomes a focus for conflict over White House environmental policymaking. The OMB is sometimes criticized by environmentalists and scientists for excessive, inappropriate political interference in scientific research supporting EPA regulatory decisions.

Other potentially important entities within the EOP are the CEQ (Council on Environmental Quality) and the Office of Science and Technology Policy (OSTP). The mission of the OSTP, created in 1976, includes the following:

- Advise the president and others within the EOP on the impacts of science and technology on domestic and international affairs

- Lead an interagency effort to develop and implement sound science and technology policies and budgets

- Work with the private sector to ensure federal investments in science and technology contribute to economic prosperity, environmental quality, and national security

- Build strong partnerships among federal, state, and local governments; other countries; and the scientific community

- Evaluate the scale, quality, and effectiveness of the federal effort in science and technology

Much of the OSTP's continuing responsibilities are uncontroversial and often commendable in the view of environmentalists—for example, promoting federal support for green energy technologies. The OSTP is, however, an advisory body and the president is free to accept as much, or as little, of its advice as he or she chooses.

Council on Environmental Quality

The National Environmental Policy Act of 1969 created a commission to advise the president on environmental matters. Headed by three members appointed by the president, the CEQ was to be part of the president's staff. Among the major responsibilities prescribed for the council were (1) to gather for the president's consideration "timely and authoritative information concerning the conditions and trends in the quality of the environment both current and prospective," (2) "to develop and recommend to the President national policies to foster and promote the improvement of environmental quality," and (3) "to review and appraise the various programs and activities of the Federal Government" to determine the extent to which they comply with, among other things, the requirement for writing environmental impact statements.[14] The CEQ was created, like other major presidential advisory commissions, primarily to provide policy advice and evaluation from within the White House directly to the president.

The CEQ is a small agency with no regulatory responsibilities or major environmental programs beyond modest research activities, but during its early years, it assumed symbolic importance and political value to environmental interests. Its presence within the White House implied a high national priority given to environmental programs, and the council's opportunities to influence the president directly meant that it might act, in the words of environmental leader Russell Peterson, as "the environmental conscience of the executive branch."[15] The council has a statutory mandate to administer the writing and reviewing of environmental impact statements within the federal government and to advise other executive agencies on environmental issues.

Still, the CEQ exercises no more influence in White House decisions than the president cares to give it. By 2000, the CEQ's early political clout had vanished. Its influence plummeted beginning with the Reagan administration, and CEQ experienced no significant reversal of fortune under the Clinton, George W. Bush, and Obama administrations. Under the Trump administration, the CEQ seemed destined to the political twilight, seen but seldom heard in White House policymaking.

CONGRESS: TOO MUCH CHECK, TOO LITTLE BALANCE

The president may propose, but it is often Congress that ultimately disposes. In a Madisonian government of separated institutions sharing powers, presidents and environmental administrators have good reasons to look warily toward Congress. The Constitution invests Congress with enormous authority over the daily conduct of the president and the executive branch. Under ordinary circumstances, few aspects of presidential and bureaucratic behavior are untouched directly or indirectly by congressional authority and politics.

Despite a panoply of party organizations, legislative leaders, and coordinating committees, Congress is still largely an institution of fragmented powers and divided geographical loyalties. Legislative power is dispersed in both chambers among a multitude of committees and subcommittees; local or regional concerns often tenaciously claim legislative loyalties. The electoral cycle intrudes imperiously on policy deliberations. The public interest and legislative objectivity compete with equally insistent legislative concerns to deliver something from Washington to the folks back home.

The Statutory Setting

The most fundamental congressional responsibility is to craft environmental law. Current federal environmental legislation is a patchwork of several hundred congressional enactments written since the 1950s. Legal scholar Christopher Schroeder's verdict about federal toxic substance laws—that they have "resulted not in a well-designed cabin, but in a pile of logs"[16]—applies as well to the whole of federal environmental legislation. Many controversies prominent since the 1970s result from the inconsistencies, contradictions, confusions, and inadequacies of this statutory welter. At the same time, each law memorializes the success of a major environmental coalition in waging a battle for environmental protection that may have lasted decades. Each law acquires a politically vocal and potent constituency from congressional factions, private interests, bureaucratic agencies, and program beneficiaries. A huge volume of judicial opinions girding each law with court-derived interpretations and justifications further institutionalizes the legislation. These laws are the legal edifice on which environmental policy has been erected.

The major legislative enactments currently on the federal statute books relating to just one category of environmental pollutant—toxic substances—exceed fifteen major laws. Cataloging just this one among the many categories of environmental law is sufficient to emphasize two realities about environmental policy controversies: (1) The existing law becomes a conservative force in policy debate because it is difficult to change, and (2) existing environmental laws also need continual updating and revision as a result of ongoing scientific research and administrative experience with the laws' administration.

Committee Decentralization

Congress has been described as a "kind of confederation of little legislatures."[17] In both chambers, the committees and subcommittees—those little legislatures wielding the most consistently effective power in the legislative system—are dispersed and competitive in environmental matters. William Ruckelshaus, the first EPA administrator, complained in the early 1970s that he had to deal with sixteen different congressional subcommittees.[18] The situation has gotten more complicated. In the 113th Congress (2013–2015), the box score for committees with EPA jurisdiction came to seven full committees including thirteen subcommittees in the Senate and eight full committees with eighteen subcommittees in the House of Representatives. Any major environmental legislation, depending on its content, is predestined to arrive on several, perhaps many, different committee and subcommittee tables during a customarily labored progress through congressional deliberation. Congressional jurisdiction over ocean issues, for instance, is very generously dispersed; the 113th Congress included fifty committees and subcommittees in both chambers with jurisdiction over related research and policy.

With authority over environmental policy fragmented among a multitude of committees in each chamber, competition and jurisdictional rivalry commonly occur as each committee attempts to assert some influence over environmental programs. The result is that, as a rule, environmental legislation evolves only through protracted bargaining and compromising among the many committees. This time-consuming process often results in vague and inconsistent legislation. Divided jurisdictions, however, provide different interest groups with some point of committee access during environmental policy formulation; as a consequence, these groups resist efforts to reduce the number of committees with overlapping jurisdictions and concentrate authority in a few major committees.

Localism

When the national taxpayer organization Citizens Against Government Waste (CAGW) noted in its annual *Pig Book* that Mississippi ranked sixth among the fifty states in the amount of political pork (a common term for wasteful federal spending) its congressional delegation had delivered to the state, Sen. Trent Lott, R-MS, seemed almost pleased with his state's ranking. "The definition of wasteful 'pork' is in the eye of the beholder," he responded. "In my eye, if its south of Memphis, it sure isn't pork. . . . If we must use our political acumen to get part of our money back, then so be it. In this regard, the *Pig Book* indicates Mississippi is doing very well."[19] Many of his Senate colleagues would have added, "Amen." Senators are unapologetically loyal to the practice of voting for each other's local public works projects, the most common political pork.

Localism is driven by a powerful tradition in congressional voting. In U.S. political culture, legislators are treated by constituents—and regard themselves—as ambassadors to Washington, D.C., from their own geographical areas. They are expected to acquire skills in the practice of pork-barrel politics, capturing federal goods and services for their constituencies. They are also expected to be vigilant in promoting and protecting local interests in the national policy arena. Congressional tenure is more likely to depend on a legislator's ability to serve these local interests than on other legislative achievements. Political localism is perhaps the most deeply rooted and most compelling force in shaping voting decisions.

This localism affects environmental policy in different ways. By encouraging legislators to view environmental proposals first through the lens of local interests, localism often weakens sensitivity to national needs and interests. At worst, it drives legislators to judge the merits of environmental policies almost solely by their impact on frequently small and atypical constituencies.

Localism also whets the congressional appetite for federal distributive programs freighted with local benefits. An aroma of political pork can add appeal to an environmental program, especially if other important local issues are involved. This lesson is not lost on the environmental bureaucracies. For instance, when opposition by the powerful House Ways and Means Committee appeared to threaten defeat for the initial Superfund legislation, a program strongly supported by the EPA, the agency worked with sympathetic congressional staff members to create a list of prospective Superfund sites in each committee member's district. The committee members were then reminded of the "ticking time bombs" in their districts and of the potentially great financial benefits from cleanup activities—an almost irresistible double dose of localism.[20] It is not surprising that federal grants to build pollution control facilities, such as sewage treatment plants, also have instant appeal. The robust political pork packaged with the federal government's original program to improve national wastewater quality, for instance, enormously enhanced its congressional appeal because it contained massive funding for local public works. "The huge $18 billion waste treatment facilities program, first authorized in 1972, [was] the second largest public works program in U.S. history . . . EPA estimated that for every $1 billion spent, about 50,900 worker-years of employment would be generated in plant and sewer construction."[21]

Public works are not the only legislative bargaining chips, however. Legislation often enlists congressional votes, because sponsors are alert to write in diverse benefits or projects of all sorts that are attractive to important colleagues and pressure groups. Conversely, pressure groups—including environmentalists—are perpetually vigilant for opportunities to advance their agendas through legislative benefits. For example, the massive Waxman–Markey climate change legislation approved in 2009 by the House of Representatives provoked a virtual feeding frenzy among organized groups intent on gaining a share of the benefits from provisions proposing an auction of greenhouse gas emission rights. "Every line of the text [had] billions and billions of dollars riding on it," observed economist Peter Dorman. "People will do and say anything," he asserted, to get a share of the money, including environmentalists who hope that federal revenues from the eventual auction of emissions permits will help their cause.[22]

Elections

The electoral cycle also dominates the legislative mind. The constitutionally mandated electoral cycles of the federal government—two years, four years, and six years—partition the time available for legislative deliberation into periods bounded by different elections. Within these time frames, policy decisions are continually analyzed for their electoral implications and often valued largely for electoral impacts. This affects congressional policy styles in several ways. First, the short term becomes more important than the long term when evaluating programs; legislators often attribute more importance to a program's impact on the next election than to its longer-term effects on unborn generations. Second, policies are tested continually against public opinion. Although a weak or badly divided public opinion often can be ignored, a coherent majority opinion related to an environmental issue usually wields significant influence on congressional voting, especially when the majorities are in a legislator's own district. Hazardous waste cleanup programs, for example, are hard to oppose whatever their actual merits because the "ticking time bomb" has become a durable, powerful public metaphor in practically every constituency.

Preoccupation with elections, localism, and the other aspects of congressional culture are the givens of policymaking. And congressional policymaking, as much as presidential leadership, has been responsible for creating and maintaining the entire foundation of federal environmental governance—one of Congress's greatest historical achievements. However, Congress has also become a rich source of delay, confusion, and waste in making and implementing environmental policy. These problems arise from excesses and exaggeration in the authority the constitutional framers prudently invested in Congress—a case of checks and balances gone awry. Many of these difficulties could be eliminated or mitigated by a self-imposed discipline, of which Congress may be incapable.

"Ready, Fire, Aim": Crisis Decision-Making

The congressional response to environmental problems is highly volatile, waxing and waning according to changing public moods, emerging environmental crises, economic circumstances, or today's front-page ecological disasters. Congress can easily fall into a pollutant-of-the-year mentality, mandating new programs or sudden changes in existing ones according to what environmental problems currently seem most urgent or according to the public's current mood.

The Ocean Dumping Act of 1988, for example, is the very model of crisis-inspired legislation. During summer 1988, popular bathing beaches along New York's eastern coast frequently were fouled with medical wastes, raw sewage, and other dangerous debris apparently washed ashore from New York City sewage dumped more than one hundred miles offshore. Closed beaches and public revulsion at the widely publicized pollution quickly persuaded Congress to pass, without one dissenting vote, the Ocean Dumping Act, which prohibited additional ocean disposal of urban waste within a few years. Congress was unmoved by expert testimony that held the real cause of the contamination to be the continual overflow from New York City's antique sewer system, which would be hugely expensive to repair. Nor was Congress in the mood to evaluate alternatives. "There is no question," argued the chief engineer of the regional waste management agency, "that the New York City sewer system is the greatest cause of water pollution in the region. But a sewer system isn't sexy. It's expensive to fix, and nobody wants to hear about it. So people focused on what they understand . . . and they understand that sewage and the sea don't seem nice together."[23] Local representative Thomas J. Manton, D-Queens, initially opposed to the act, soon capitulated to political realities. "Nobody wanted to discuss the relative risks or merits," he later explained. "It had been a bad summer, and we all wanted to be able to say we did something. So we passed a law. I tried to have a debate. And it was like I was trying to destroy the planet."[24] As a result of the act, the city of New York will have spent at least $2 billion on facilities to convert sewage into fertilizer and $300 million annually for a decade thereafter to dispose of its sludge, although many experts believe an equally effective and much cheaper solution would have been possible if Congress had not ordained that ocean dumping be eliminated entirely but, instead, had renovated the existing sewer system to remove the harmful pollutants from the effluent before ocean release.

Environmental policies are seldom so poorly conceived, but this reactive policymaking ensures an environmental agenda in which place and priority among programs depend less on scientific logic than on political circumstance. Often, the losers are scientifically compelling environmental problems unblessed with political sex appeal. Moreover, once a program is legislatively attractive, it usually acquires a mandated budget that virtually ensures its survival. Most environmental scientists, for instance, consider indoor air pollution a more compelling health risk than abandoned hazardous waste sites or even some currently regulated forms of air pollution, but most of the EPA's air pollution budget is mandated for ambient air regulation, and Congress lacks enthusiasm to tackle indoor air pollution in the absence of a perceived crisis.[25]

Guidance: Too Much and Too Little

Behind the facade of high purpose and ambitious action of every major environmental law probably stretches a terrain mined with muddled language, troublesome silences, and inconsistent programs. Some of this is inevitable. Mistakes in statutory design occur because federal environmental regulations address problems of great scientific and administrative complexity with which legislators have had no prior experience. Moreover, members of Congress are typically lawyers, business executives, or other nonscientific professionals who depend on the expertise of administrators to clarify and interpret the law appropriately in regard to specialized environmental programs. The constant pressure of legislative affairs discourages most members of Congress from giving considerable attention to environmental issues or from developing an adequate understanding of them. "It's tough to get Congress to focus on bills with sufficient time to develop an adequate depth of understanding," observed John A. Moore, former acting deputy director for the EPA. "You've got 1 or 2 Congressmen who truly know it; there are 400 others that are going to vote on it."[26] Even conscientious legislators can be easily intimidated when they attempt to unravel the technical complexities of environmental legislation. During congressional debate over passage of the Safe Drinking Water Act (1974), for instance, proponents argued that twelve thousand contaminants existed with unknown causes. Debate raged within the EPA and Congress about whether the agency needed to regulate twenty to thirty, one hundred, or even thousands of water pollutants—even the Public Health Service's traditionally undisputed standard for selenium was made suspect. Finally, Congress had to give the EPA the final responsibility for identifying most of the appropriate pollutants for regulation.[27]

Environmental legislation is often vague and contradictory because Congress cannot or will not resolve major political conflicts entailed in the law. Instead, Congress often papers over the conflict with silence or deliberate obscurity in the statutory language, as illustrated by the WOTUS controversy introducing this chapter. This approach results in a steady flow of political hot potatoes to the bureaucracy, which must clarify this legal language—often to the accompaniment of political conflict and legislative criticism—or leave the job to the courts. The EPA becomes enmeshed in protracted litigation and political bargaining, program regulations essential to implementing the laws often become hostage to these procedures, and Congress frequently avoids a risky political bloodletting. "Congress outsources the rulemaking to the EPA," asserts regulatory critic David Schoenbrod, "so that the legislators can claim credit for protecting health while the agency bears the inevitable blame for delays, disappointments, and costs."[28]

Congressional frustration with the continual delay in implementing environmental laws has led to the habitual use of extravagant, extraordinarily detailed, and inflexible language in new environmental laws; to the constant mandating of precise deadlines for completing various programs; and to prescription, in excruciating detail, of how administrators are to carry out program activities—in effect, to a cure as bad as the disease.

Partisan Polarization and Political Stalemate

Beginning in the mid-1990s, party polarization in both congressional chambers has gradually intensified to the point where it has become extremely difficult, if not impossible, for Congress to respond incisively and expeditiously on a growing agenda of imperative environmental issues, including global climate change, the EPA's chronically underfunded regulatory responsibilities, energy conservation, long-overdue revisions of federal air and water pollution legislation, and much else. While partisan stalemate and deadlock now permeate virtually every agenda of legislative policy to an extent unprecedented for at least a century, no issue incites a more tenacious polarization than environmental regulation.[29] Congressional polarization, moreover, compounds the inherent political and institutional challenges to presidential leadership inherent in the constitutional checks and balances between Congress and the White House. Presidents of both parties have been thwarted by this chronic congressional incapacity to find consensus on the White House environmental policy agenda. Often, the solution has been to make an end run around Congress and to create policy by resorting to authority assumed to be inherent to the presidency—a predictably contentious strategy—as Barack Obama did in 2015 when he countered congressional failure to enact regulations to control climate change emissions by initiating his Clean Power Plan using the EPA's existing regulatory powers.

THE BUREAUCRACY: POWER THROUGH IMPLEMENTATION

Federal agencies concerned with environmental affairs and closely related matters such as energy, consumer protection, and worker health have grown explosively since 1970. More than 150 major new federal laws, most concerned with the broad regulation of business and the economy in the interest of public health and safety, have been enacted since then. More than twenty new regulatory agencies have been created to implement these programs, including the EPA, the Occupational Safety and Health Administration (OSHA), and the DOI's Office of Surface Mining. An understanding of such bureaucracies and especially the more environmentally important among them is essential to explaining the logic of federal environmental policymaking.

The Power to Choose

The Constitution appears to vest the power to formulate policy primarily in Congress, while leaving to the president and the executive branch the task of seeing that the laws are "faithfully executed." Although implemented and enforced principally in the bureaucracy, public policy actually develops in both branches of the government.

Delegated authority and administrative discretion are the wellsprings of bureaucratic power. Congress routinely invests administrators with responsibility for making a multitude of decisions it cannot or will not make itself about the implementation of policy; often, this becomes legislative power delegated to the executive branch. Even when delegation is not clearly intended, administrators assume the power to make public policy when they choose how to implement policies permitting different options—hence, the existence of administrative discretion.

Congress and the president, using a variety of constitutional and statutory powers, attempt to discipline the exercise of administrative discretion. Still, this oversight holds no certain rein on administrative discretion, particularly in light of the vast number and complexity of environmental programs, the elephantine size of the bureaucracy, and competing demands on presidential and congressional time.

Bureaucratic Competition

The bureaucracy is no monolith. Its powers in environmental affairs, although collectively vast, are dispersed and competitive. One source of this fragmentation is the federalizing of environmental administration. Many major environmental laws enacted in Washington, D.C., are administered partially or wholly through state governments; others give states an option to participate. Under the Federal Water Pollution Control Act, for instance, twenty-seven states currently administer their own water pollution permit systems; all but six states and the District of Columbia administer the Safe Drinking Water Act. The Clean Air Act (CAA) permits the states to participate in several major aspects of the program, including the control of pollutants and the establishment of emission standards for stationary sources.

Another cause of fragmented administrative authority is the chronic division of and overlapping responsibility for environmental programs among federal agencies. Twenty-seven separate federal agencies share major regulatory responsibility in environmental and occupational health. Regulating even a single pollutant often necessitates a bureaucratic convention. Toxic substances currently are regulated under twenty different federal statutes involving five agencies. To address all the problems in human exposure to vinyl chloride, for example, would require the collaboration of all five agencies working with fifteen different laws.[30]

Dispersed authority breeds conflict and competition among agencies and their political allies over program implementation, authority, and resources—the turf wars familiar to students of bureaucracy. And in environmental affairs, federal agencies are notoriously fitful collaborators. In this milieu of dispersed and competitive agency authority, policy implementation often becomes a continual process of collaboration and conflict between coalitions of agencies and their allies shaping and reshaping policy as the relative strengths of the conflicting alignments change. Moreover, administrative conflict crosses the institutional divisions of the federal government, spreading downward through the federal system to state and local governments and outward from government to organized private groups. Indeed, agencies failing to enlist diverse and active allies in their policy struggles may frustrate their own missions and leave their futures hostage to more politically skilled opponents.

The Environmental Protection Agency

The EPA, created by an executive order of President Nixon in 1970, is the largest federal regulatory agency in terms of budget and personnel. Its responsibilities embrace an extraordinarily large and technically complex set of programs ranging across the whole domain of environmental management. Asked if his job had been rewarding, a former administrator for the EPA replied that it was "like beating a train across a grade crossing—if you make it, it's a great rush. If you don't, you're dead."[31] Political controversy is the daily bread of the EPA's leadership. "The Administrator rarely goes to the President with good news and is more often the bearer of bad news," observed Lee Thomas, EPA administrator from 1985 to 1988. "You almost never have a decision where many people applaud it."[32] In such a politically charged setting, the EPA administrator's office has often been a revolving door through which a succession of executives pass, unwilling or unable to manage the inherited political turbulence.

Statutory Responsibilities. The size of the EPA's regulatory burden is suggested in Box 3.1, which summarizes the EPA's current statutory responsibilities. These regulatory programs represent the major environmental legislation of the past three decades. The EPA grew steadily in staff and budget until 1981, when the Reagan administration severely reduced both budget and personnel. The EPA has never fully recovered from the budgetary austerity that followed throughout the 1980s. While its administrative responsibilities have constantly increased and despite periods of occasional improvement, its budget measured in dollars (and not discounted for inflation) had increased relatively little through the end of 2015. Even though the Obama administration initially created a substantial increase in the EPA's resources during the president's first years in office, by the end of 2015, the continuing economic recession compelled Obama to propose a 13 percent reduction in the EPA's FY 2013 budget, reducing it to a level approaching its status in 2001.[33]

The agency presently has about fifteen thousand employees and an annual budget exceeding $8 billion, of which less than half supports its administrative activities (most of the money underwrites water treatment and Superfund grants).[34] EPA's proposed budget for FY 2019 equaled about 78 percent of its FY 2018 actual budget—a significant reduction widely criticized by environmental activists.[35] The agency, whose administrator is appointed by the president, consists of a Washington, D.C., headquarters and ten regional offices, each headed by a regional administrator. Unlike most regulatory agencies, the EPA administers both regulatory and distributive programs, such as the huge federal waste treatment grants, the Superfund program, and various research activities.

Notwithstanding some significant achievements, the EPA confronts a daunting array of problems in the early years of the twenty-first century: an unmanageable burden of continually growing regulatory responsibilities, a politically toxic inheritance of chronic congressional Republican antipathy toward much of EPA's regulatory programs compounded with legislative polarization thwarting congressional action on many overdue EPA reforms, a chronically inadequate budget, and the administrative complexities inherent in complicated environmental regulations.

BOX 3.1 MAJOR RESPONSIBILITIES OF THE EPA

The following are the major regulatory tasks assigned to the EPA in each important pollution control program.

Air quality

- Establishes national air-quality standards.
- Sets limits on the level of air pollutants emitted from stationary sources such as power plants, municipal incinerators, factories, and chemical plants.
- Establishes emission standards for new motor vehicles.
- Sets allowable levels for toxics, such as lead, benzene, and toluene in gasoline.
- Establishes emission standards for hazardous air pollutants, such as beryllium, mercury, and asbestos.
- Supervises states in their development of clean air plans.

Water quality and protection

- Issues permits for the discharge of any pollutant into navigable waters.
- Develops effluent guidelines to control discharge of specific water pollutants, including radiation.
- Develops criteria that enable states to set water quality standards.
- Administers grant programs to states to subsidize the cost of building sewage treatment plants.
- Regulates disposal of waste material, including sludge and low-level radioactive discards, into the oceans.
- Cooperates with the U.S. Army Corps of Engineers to issue permits for the dredging and filling of wetlands.
- Sets national drinking water standards to ensure that drinking water is safe.
- Regulates underground injection of wastes to protect purity of groundwater.
- With the U.S. Coast Guard, coordinates cleanup of oil and chemical spills into U.S. waterways.

Hazardous waste

- Maintains inventory of existing hazardous waste dump sites.
- Tracks more than 500 hazardous compounds from point of origin to final disposal site.

(Continued)

(Continued)

- Sets standards for generators and transporters of hazardous wastes.

- Issues permits for treatment, storage, and disposal facilities for hazardous wastes.

- Assists states in developing hazardous waste control programs.

- Maintains a multibillion-dollar fund (Superfund) from industry fees and general tax revenues to provide for emergency cleanup of hazardous dumps when no responsible party can immediately be found.

- Pursues identification of parties responsible for waste sites and eventual reimbursement of the federal government for Superfund money spent cleaning up these sites.

Chemical regulation, including pesticides and radioactive waste

- Maintains inventory of chemical substances now in commercial use.

- Regulates existing chemicals considered serious hazards to people and the environment, including fluorocarbons, polychlorinated biphenyls (PCBs), and asbestos.

- Issues procedures for the proper safety testing of chemicals and orders them tested when necessary.

- Requires the registration of insecticides, herbicides, or fungicides intended for sale in the United States.

- Requires pesticide manufacturers to provide scientific evidence that their products will not injure humans, livestock, crops, or wildlife when used as directed.

- Classifies pesticides for either general public use or restricted use by certified applicators.

- Sets standards for certification of applicators of restricted-use pesticides. (Individual states may certify applicators through their own programs based on the federal standards.)

- Cancels or suspends the registration of a product on the basis of actual or potential unreasonable risk to humans, animals, or the environment.

- Issues a "stop sale, use, and removal" order when a pesticide already in circulation is found to be in violation of the law.

- Requires registration of pesticide-producing establishments.

- Issues regulations concerning the labeling, storage, and disposal of pesticide containers.

- Issues permits for pesticide research.

- Monitors pesticide levels in the environment.

- Monitors and regulates the levels of radiation in drinking water, oceans, rainfall, and air.

- Conducts research on toxic substances, pesticides, air and water quality, hazardous wastes, radiation, and the causes and effects of acid rain.

- Provides overall guidance to other federal agencies on radiation protection matters that affect public health.

- Maintains inventory of chemical substances now in commercial use.

Other

- Sets acceptable noise levels for construction equipment, transportation equipment (except aircraft), all motors and engines, and electronic equipment.

Micromanaged and Overloaded. By the mid-1980s, it was already obvious, as the CEQ observed, that "the Environmental Protection Agency cannot possibly do all the things its various mandates tell it to do," and conditions have not improved.[36] More than three decades later, the agency is still years or decades behind in complying with important requirements in its ten major statutory programs, and new jobs are always ahead.

One reason for the agency's chronic compliance problems is the congressional penchant for packing legislation with a multitude of demanding deadlines, detailed management instructions, and hammer clauses that threaten dire consequences should the EPA fail to comply with various statutory deadlines. The EPA continues to experience what is probably the most relentless legislative oversight of any federal agency.

The cumulative result of this excessive congressional attention is written in the statistics of missed deadlines, lagging research, and impossibly distant completion dates for existing program responsibilities. The doleful litany includes the following two programs:

- The Federal Insecticide, Fungicide, and Rodenticide Act requires the EPA to evaluate more than fifty thousand individual pesticide products containing more than six hundred active ingredients and nine hundred inert ingredients. "If EPA has to prepare interim registration standards for all 600 active ingredients," the GAO concluded in 1986, "then the Agency may finish the first round reviews in about 2004."[37] In fact, by 2010 the EPA had not yet completed its first round of reviews.

- The Food Quality Protection Act (1996) requires the EPA to screen all commercial pesticides for estrogenic effects that may affect human health, to develop a screening and testing program by 1998, to implement the program by 1999, and to report to Congress on the program's accomplishments by August 2000. This requires the EPA to review data on six hundred pesticides in active commerce, 1,800 inert ingredients in twenty thousand pesticide products, and seventy-five thousand industrial chemicals, plus consumer products. None of this, including the report, had been accomplished by the end of 2016.

The CAA requires the EPA to review every five years its National Air Quality Standards for six pollutants named in the legislation, but the agency has never been able to complete these evaluations on time. One major reason for the delay: the massive accumulation of new scientific studies that continually require evaluation for each pollutant. In order to comply with a court-required review of its ozone standard by 2015, for example, EPA had to consider more than one thousand new studies since the last review in 2008.[38]

Needed: Clear Priorities. Like the man who mounted his horse and galloped off in all directions, the EPA lacks a constant course. With responsibility for administering ten separate statutes and parts of four others, the EPA has no clearly mandated priorities and thus no way of allocating scarce resources among different statutes or among programs within a single law. Nor does the EPA have a congressional charter, common to most federal departments and agencies, defining its broad organizational mission and priorities.

Congress has shown little inclination to provide the EPA with a charter or mandated priorities, in good part because the debate sure to arise on the relative merits and urgency of different environmental problems is an invitation to a political bloodletting most legislators would gladly avoid. Intense controversy over which problems to emphasize would be likely among states, partisans of different ecological issues, and regulated interests; the resulting political brawl would upset existing policy coalitions that themselves were fashioned with great difficulty.

EPA's Embattled Future: The Conflict Over Trump Regulatory Reform. Decades-long controversy within Congress and the White House over the scope of EPA's regulatory authority erupted during the 2016 presidential election in a relentless, unprecedented Republican attack led by Donald Trump on EPA's regulatory authority. "Environmental protection, what they do is a disgrace," Trump remarked shortly after his election. "Every week they come out with a new regulation," he complained.[39] Trump's threat to "get rid of EPA in every form" was fanciful—but not his determination to radically restructure EPA. Thus, the Trump election became the prelude to the most radical presidential plan to reorganize EPA and to reduce EPA's authority in the agency's history. Environmentalists and their allies, shocked by Trump's election and convinced his administration meant to massively degrade, not reform, the EPA's existing authority, mobilized nationally against the Trump regulatory agenda and Trump's newly appointed EPA administrator, Scott Pruitt, who enthusiastically embraced Trump's vision of a vastly diminished EPA in authority and resources.

Trump and Pruitt shared with congressional Republicans a conviction that EPA had collaborated with Democratic presidents and congressman for decades to progressively enlarge EPA's regulatory authority, usurping responsibilities that properly belonged to the states and imposing unreasonable, excessive environmental protection costs upon the American economy. Pruitt declared he would "refocus the Agency back to its core mission of protecting human health and the environment, restore power to the states through cooperative federalism, and improve processes by adhering to the rule of law"[40]—a prediction greeted with enthusiasm, especially among many regulated interests in the private sector.

By mid-2018, Trump and Pruitt had ordered sixty-seven major environmental policies revised or eliminated.[41] These included almost all of the most significant policies created by the Obama administration, such as the EPA's Clean Power Plan, the foundations for the federal government's recently created regulations to limited domestic climate-warming emissions, and the nation's commitment to the Paris Agreement, an international treaty among 195 nations to reduce their individual climate emissions. Off-shore energy exploration along the U.S. Atlantic Coast and in the Gulf of Mexico, opposed by the Obama administration, was again encouraged, while federal regulations controlling the environmental impacts of coal surface mining were scheduled for revision. Water and air pollution standards were to be critically reviewed. Virtually every major domain of federal environmental regulation was scheduled for eventual examination.

Plans to severely restructure the EPA itself were also rapidly implemented from the Trump administration's first day. A hiring freeze was ordered. EPA's scientific offices and advisory committees, frequently censured by Trump and Pruitt for alleged antibusiness bias and excessive regulatory zeal, were redesigned to create greater representation of regulated interests and their scientific experts on the panels. EPA's regulatory enforcement offices were rapidly reduced in size and scope. The administration's first budget proposed a 23 percent reduction in the agency's funding and radical, comprehensive staff reductions. Congress eventually approved a less severe but still substantial cutback in agency funding and personnel, thereby magnifying the mood of embattled competence growing among many staff accompanied by tension between the agency's new political leadership and its permanent professional staff.

The ultimate impact of these pervasive EPA reforms, like other items on the Trump environmental agenda, remains problematic. Environmental organizations have countered most major Trump-Pruitt initiatives with numerous legal challenges certain to delay the implementation of many intended reforms and to thrust upon the courts what may often become the ultimate responsibility for defining the scope of EPA's regulatory transformation. However, the early policy changes and staff reductions accomplished within EPA promote enough ambiguity and unpredictability about its regulatory decisions to impede its regulatory effectiveness. A certainty is that the EPA confronts an unusually problematic and contentious future under the Trump administration.

The Department of the Interior

Established as a cabinet-level department in 1845, the DOI is among the oldest and most important of all federal agencies. With a current budget of approximately $12.1 billion and 72,000 employees, the department's responsibilities leave few environmental issues untouched. These responsibilities include (1) protection and management of more than 549 million acres of public land—roughly 28 percent of the total U.S. land area—set aside by Congress for national parks, wilderness areas, forests, and other restricted uses; (2) administration of Native American lands and federal Native American programs, including authority over western tribal lands containing a large proportion of the coal, petroleum, uranium, and other largely unexploited energy resources in the western United States; (3) enforcement of federal surface mining regulations through its Office of Surface Mining; (4) conservation and management of wetlands and estuarine areas; and (5) protection and preservation of wildlife, including endangered species. Headed by a cabinet secretary appointed by the president, the department's programs historically have been a primary concern to environmentalists. The secretary of the Interior has traditionally been a westerner, a political concession to the western states, where most of the public lands are found. During the 1970s, the department secretaries appointed by presidents Nixon and Carter, although not necessarily outspoken environmentalists or even conservationists, were at least tolerable to the growing environmentalist movement. Since the 1980s, however, the relationship between the environmental community and DOI secretaries has often been combative.

The DOI has always been a battleground between interests seeking to conserve the resources in the public domain and those seeking generous access to them. The DOI's mandate to ensure "balanced use" of resources between conservation and development—a mandate that continually propels the department and its secretary into a storm of controversy concerning which use shall dominate—is a certain source of trouble for every secretary. Moreover, the department's programs serve a clientele including not only environmentalists but also the timber and cattle industries, mining companies, sports enthusiasts, a multitude of private corporations, and many other interests that expect the department to be solicitous of their viewpoints. Finally, the western states historically have maintained that they have not been given a sufficient voice in the administration of the federal properties that often constitute the vast majority of land within their boundaries. The desire of these states to assume greater control over the public domain within their jurisdictions and the resulting tensions with the federal government will outlive any administration.

The DOI, like the EPA, had been a major concern of the Trump reform plans. DOI's new secretary, Ryan Zinke, had announced a "huge" plan to restructure the agency and to reorganize the personnel because "30 percent of the agency's employees are not loyal to him or President Trump"[42]—a threat only partially fulfilled before Zinke's departure from Washington, and controversial proposals whose impact are examined in Chapter 9.

The Nuclear Regulatory Commission

The NRC was created by Congress in 1976 to assume the regulatory responsibilities originally vested in the Atomic Energy Commission. An independent agency with five commissioners appointed by the president, the NRC regulates most nonmilitary uses of nuclear facilities and materials. The commission's major activities related to the environment include (1) the regulation of the site choice, construction, operation, and security of all civilian nuclear reactors; (2) the designation and supervision of all nuclear waste repositories; (3) the regulation of uranium mining and milling facilities; and (4) the closing of civilian nuclear facilities after they discontinue production (called decommissioning). In 2018, the NRC included a staff of approximately 3,600 and a budget of $1 billion.

Environmental groups have been most concerned with the NRC's supervision of nuclear power plants and repositories for radioactive wastes. Although 104 nuclear plants were operating or approved for construction by 2015, the majority of these have been criticized by environmental groups for alleged deficiencies in structural safety, control of radioactive emissions, and waste storage.[43] In addition, environmental groups have often been aggressive in seeking NRC safety reviews of operating plants and personnel training procedures. The NRC has assumed a major responsibility for the review of site selection and the supervision of waste disposal at the nation's first permanent nuclear waste repository at Yucca Flats, Nevada. Environmental groups still regard the process of site construction and disposal as an issue likely to remain important for several decades.

The NRC and environmental groups have been both adversaries and allies. The environmental movement generally has supported the NRC's stricter enforcement and review of regulations for operating nuclear facilities and its increasingly rigorous standards for new facility licensing. Yet environmentalists also have criticized the NRC for allegedly siding too often with the nuclear power industry against its critics, for bureaucratic inertia and conservatism, and for ignoring technical criticism and data from sources not associated with the nuclear power industry or the commission. As with other regulatory agencies, the NRC is bound to its own clientele—the nuclear power industry—by professional associations, common technical and economic concerns, and historical sympathies; it is also committed to regulating the industry in the public interest while maintaining sufficient objectivity and disengagement from the nuclear power movement to do that job. These often-conflicting responsibilities lead the NRC into controversies with environmental interests. Nonetheless, the NRC and its mission remain among the most environmentally significant elements in the executive branch.

The Department of Energy

With a current budget exceeding $29.7 billion and more than 13,000 employees, the DOE and its programs and regulatory responsibilities continually involve a great diversity of environmentally related matters. Despite its size and importance, the DOE has been a stepchild of the executive branch. Widely criticized and often burdened with difficult, unpopular programs, the department has struggled especially with immense problems—legal, political, economic, and technical—created by its responsibility for management of the military nuclear weapons facilities under its jurisdiction since the late 1970s and the challenges in developing renewable energy technologies.

Under the DOE's jurisdiction are regulatory activities and energy programs strongly affecting the environment. The more important of these include (1) promotion of civilian nuclear power activities, (2) regulation of military nuclear facilities and radioactive wastes, (3) administration of the federal government's research and development programs in energy production and conservation, (4) regulation of price controls for domestic petroleum and natural gas, and (5) administration of federal research and development grants for commercial synthetic fuel production in the United States. The DOE is the principal executive agency involved in the regulation and production of many different energy technologies with significant environmental impacts. Also, by design, it is expected to undertake a volatile agenda of frequently contradictory and inconsistent missions destined to set it at odds with itself and with the environmental community: to promote environmentally risky energy technologies and to minimize the environmental risks, to promote energy use and energy conservation, to stimulate research and development of new energy-consuming and energy-saving technologies, to control energy prices in emergencies, and to avert energy shortages and stimulate long-range energy planning.

By far, the most politically and financially costly problem confronting the DOE remains the environmental contamination of the nation's nuclear weapons facilities. More than 122 nuclear weapons manufacturing and laboratory sites in thirty states, the Marshall Islands, and Puerto Rico have to be made safe. The cleanup program will probably exceed $250 billion and take perhaps a half century or more to accomplish, if it can be accomplished; no public or private agency previously has any prior experience in cleaning up radioactive contamination of such scale and complexity.[44] Spending for the cleanup of these nuclear weapons sites and for other related programs could involuntarily transform the DOE into the nation's largest environmental agency and launch it on the most expensive public works program in U.S. history.[45]

Barack Obama hoped to improve DOE's political karma by selecting Dr. Steven Chu, a Nobel laureate physicist, to be secretary of the Interior, who inaugurated what the administration expected to be a fresh, ambitious agenda of environmentally benign programs. These programs emphasized energy conservation, renewable energy, federal support for innovative energy technologies, and other initiatives that environmentalists generally perceived as a welcome change from the Bush administration's apparent preference for fossil fuels and nuclear power in national energy development.

THE COURTS: THE ROLE OF APPRAISAL

Federal judges actively participate in the environmental policy process in several ways. They continually interpret environmental law, an inevitable task in light of the ambiguities and silences common to environmental legislation. This statutory interpretation often amounts to policymaking by the judicial branch. Judges also attempt to ensure that agencies discharge their mandated responsibilities under environmental legislation and otherwise comply with administrative obligations. In addition, the federal courts enforce the Administrative Procedures Act (1946), the code of administrative procedures applicable to all federal agencies. Finally, the courts ensure that environmental laws and their administrative implementation comply with constitutional standards. As the volume of environmental litigation expands relentlessly, federal judges find themselves increasingly at the pulse points of environmental policymaking. Although critics have argued that federal judges are not prepared by a legal education for this pivotal role in adjudicating complex scientific and economic issues, the trend seems inexorable.

The Courts and Environmental Policy

The impact of the federal courts on environmental policy has changed over the decades since Earth Day 1970. In the 1970s, federal court decisions in both substantive and procedural issues generally worked to the advantage of environmental interests. During this period, environmentalists often saw the federal judiciary as the great equalizer, offsetting the previously enormous advantage enjoyed by regulated interests in administrative and judicial forums. Environmental organizations, aggressively exploiting the procedural advantages they had gained during the 1970s to compel federal enforcement of new regulatory programs, achieved some of their most significant judicial victories during this period. The federal courts greatly expanded opportunities for environmental groups to bring issues before the bench by a broadened definition of standing to sue, a legal status that authorized individuals or organizations to sue governmental agencies for failure to enforce environmental legislation.

By the 1990s, however, the federal judiciary was no longer a predictably friendly venue for environmentalism. Business and other regulated interests began to use the federal courts far more effectively than they had previously. The increased effectiveness of business interests also exemplified the great growth in number and activity of specialized not-for-profit legal foundations representing regulated industries in environmental litigation. Reasoning that the devil should not have all the good tunes, business patterned these associations after the successful public-interest legal foundations created in the 1970s to represent environmental interests. Like environmental public interest groups, these business associations maintain that they are suing the government in the public interest and enjoy tax-exempt status. However, business public-interest groups are financed principally by organizations, such as the Adolph Coors Company and the Scaife Foundation, that have fought vigorously against most of the major environmental regulatory programs passed since the 1970s. The benefit to business interests from this growing strength in environmental litigation does not depend solely on winning cases. Exhaustive and relentless challenges to federal regulation can delay the enforcement of environmental laws for many years and throw environmental groups on the defensive, compelling them to invest their resources in protracted legal battles. Often, battles are won not by the side with the best case but by the side with the most endurance.

Most federal environmental lawsuits begin and end in the lower federal courts (the Supreme Court hears fewer than one hundred cases a year; the circuit or appellate courts hear more than forty thousand appeals annually and often create most of the legal precedents that become the law of the land).[46] Federal judges in the Northwest, Midwest, and Far West have been especially critical of the administration's efforts to open up public lands to more energy exploration and its enthusiasm for increasing timber production on federal forests.[47]

The Supreme Court has been a very different matter. Beginning in the George W. Bush administration, the Court seemed receptive to much more restraint on environmental regulation, a trend predictably greeted with approval by many regulated industries and other related sectors of the economy.[48] This trend appeared to reflect the Court's increasingly conservative outlook resulting from the gradual appointment of new justices during the Bush administration and to project a problematic future for environmentalist litigation considered by the highest federal court.

However, the Supreme Court has seldom been wholly predictable about environmental issues. While most environmentalists still regard the Court as an unfriendly venue, the Court announced perhaps the most important of its decisions supporting environmental regulation, ironically, during the latter days of the G. W. Bush administration. A coalition of states, frustrated by congressional inability to pass legislation to regulate climate change CO_2 emissions and by the Bush EPA's refusal to use the CAA for the same purpose, sued the EPA, asserting the EPA was compelled to regulate CO_2 by the CAA. In a landmark decision, the Supreme Court ruled in *Massachusetts v. Environmental Protection*

Agency (2007) that CO_2 could potentially endanger human health or the environment as defined by the CAA. The Court then instructed the EPA to determine whether CO_2 was, in fact, a threat to humans or the environment (the *endangerment finding*) and, if so, to write appropriate regulations to control domestic CO_2 emissions. The Court's ruling became the basis for the Obama administration's first comprehensive regulations to control national CO_2 emissions, the Clean Air Plan, suspended later by the Trump EPA.

The Trump administration's sweeping rollback of environmental regulations immediately provoked a cascade of opposing environmentalist lawsuits. Less than a year after Trump's inauguration, practically every major EPA regulatory suspension was judicially contested. This rising tide of lawsuits, certain to prevail throughout the Trump presidency, is evidence of how important litigation has become for opponents of the Trump environmental agenda. The courts may become the venue where the ultimate fate for much of the Trump environmental agenda will be determined.[49]

Litigation as a Political Tactic

The impact of the courts on policy, as the previous discussion suggests, arises not only from the substance of court rulings but also from the use of litigation as a tactical weapon in policy conflict—a weapon used by all sides. Most environmental litigation arises from three sources: major environmental organizations (such as the Sierra Club or the Environmental Defense Fund); business and property interests, including public-interest law firms (such as the highly aggressive Western States Legal Foundation); and federal agencies (such as the EPA or the DOI) with major environmental responsibilities. Quite often, the courts become another political arena in which the losers in prior policy battles fought among Congress, the bureaucracy, and the White House can launch yet another campaign. Litigation is also a stall in the policy process, a frustration to the opposition. Litigation creates a bargaining chip to be bartered for concessions from the opposition. Both environmentalists and their opposition have used obstructive litigation to their advantage.

When Should Judges Become Involved?

The evolution of environmental politics increasingly embroils federal judges in resolving legal issues that have important policy consequences—in effect, implicating them in environmental policymaking. Moreover, many of these issues embrace highly technical or scientific disputes. Federal judges may, for instance, have to decide whether the EPA considered the proper animal tests in deciding that a chemical constituted a significant risk to human health. Judges are often reluctant participants in these affairs, so heavily weighted with policy or scientific implications. They may be compelled by law to adjudicate such matters but are acutely aware of their limitations as technical experts. Equally important, as

Supreme Court Justice Stephen Breyer observed, when the courts must substitute their judgment for an administrator's, the result is often politically unsatisfactory:

> Regulators must make "legislative-type" decisions, the merits of which depend upon finding, or prying out important general facts about the world; they work in a politically charged environment; they may need to seek compromise solutions acceptable to warring private groups. [But judges must make decisions,] the merits of which depend upon the relevant legal norm and a record . . . that need not contain all relevant facts about the world. . . . Given these differences, a compromise solution that a regulator considers reasonable, for practical administrative reasons, might not seem practical to a judge.[50]

Both critics and defenders of existing environmental policies have frequently proposed that some alternative venue to the traditional courts be created for resolving technical and scientific controversies arising from environmental regulation. One common suggestion is the creation of a science court in which technical experts would resolve the scientific and technical issues involved in environmental litigation, leaving the judges free to focus on the largely legal matters. Other proposals involve creating impartial technical advisers to judges when scientific issues confront the court. These and many other alternatives discussed among environmental law activists illuminate not only the evolving impact of environmentalism on U.S. legal institutions themselves but also the larger challenge entailed in integrating the judicial branch effectively and appropriately into the whole environmental policy process.

THE POLITICAL ENVIRONMENT OF ENVIRONMENTAL POLICYMAKING

Governmental institutions are fated to work in a political setting that is inconstant, influential, and fickle. Opportunities to make or change policy shift continually, often unpredictably, with changing political circumstances. At any given time, there is a difference between what policymakers want and what they can accomplish, between what they must do and what they prefer to do, between what is feasible and what is not. This ebb and flow of opportunity is created by different circumstances. The most important of these circumstances includes changes in the partisan control of governmental institutions, transient shifts of public mood, major economic change, and regulatory federalism. These can be called the changing seasons of policymaking.

Changing Party Majorities

The balance of party strength within Congress and between Congress and the White House powerfully shapes the substance and opportunities for environmental policymaking. In theory, opportunities to make or change policy are greatest when the White House and Congress are controlled by the same party. For example, the avalanche of environmental legislation originating in Washington, D.C., during the 1970s was largely the result of a broad bipartisan environmental coalition in both chambers that strongly supported innovative environmental programs proposed or accepted by both Republican and Democratic presidents. The political climate for environmentalists darkened dramatically with Reagan's 1980 election and remained unsettled during the 1980s and early 1990s, when shifting party majorities in Congress resulted in an environmental gridlock in which the Democratic House frustrated Senate Republican efforts to pass Reagan's sweeping agenda of change in existing environmental laws.

With a Republican in the White House in 1988, the environmentally important appointments of George Bush's administration generally went to individuals sympathetic to the Reagan–Bush regulatory reform agenda and thereby objectionable to most environmental organizations. The chill blowing toward the EPA from the White House was unmistakable; it became a continuing and effective obstacle to many environmental policy initiatives from Congress or the bureaucracy.

The Democrats' return to the White House with Clinton in 1992 turned out to be less the prelude to the bright future anticipated by environmentalists than a false dawn. Republicans regained control of both congressional chambers in 1994 and elevated to its leadership a cadre of Republicans outspokenly unsympathetic to most of the major environmental legislation created by Congress in the previous two decades. Thus began in Congress the progressive party polarization over environmental policy, which hardened through the years leading to the Trump presidency and practically precluded any significant collaboration between the White House and Congress except on those rare occasions when one party controlled both Congress and the White House.

The years from Republican George W. Bush's presidential election in 2000 through the end of Democrat Barack Obama's administration in 2016 demonstrated how shifting congressional majorities can profoundly—and sometimes abruptly—transform the course of environmental politics. Less than six months after Bush's election, Republicans lost their tenuous Senate majority. This in turn delivered the Senate majority to the Democrats, whose environmental policy agenda differed substantially from that favored by President Bush and Senate Republicans. Control of the Senate's policy agenda and all its committees now belonged to the Democrats. The White House no longer had the policy initiative in the Senate, and the president's whole environmental agenda, like the rest of his legislative program, would become more difficult to promote. Although Republicans temporarily recovered their Senate majority in the 2002 elections, Democrats reclaimed control of both chambers in the startling 2006 elections, much to the satisfaction of most environmentalists.

The election of Barack Obama and return of Democratic majorities to both congressional chambers in 2008 seemed to most environmentalists to imply, quite deceptively, greater collaboration between the White House and Congress in promoting environmentalist legislation. In fact, Republicans recaptured control of the House of Representatives in 2010 and the toxic deadlock over environmental policy returned. The significant environmental policy enactments of the Obama years depended mostly upon what Obama could accomplish through his executive authority, and those, as the Trump election quickly demonstrated, faced an uncertain future.

Shifting Public Moods

Presidents and Congress alike always feel enormous political pressure to respond when confronted by broad public majorities demonstrating a strong interest or apprehension about an environmental issue. The pressure to do something or to look as if one is doing something is almost irresistible when sudden spikes of public apprehension rise in the aftermath of a well-publicized environmental crisis. Many major environmental laws and regulations are direct responses to environmental disasters, real or threatened. The Three Mile Island nuclear reactor accident of 1979 begot new regulations from the NRC increasing the requirements for emergency planning at commercial nuclear power plants. The tragic 1984 chemical plant disaster at Bhopal, India, in which five thousand nearby residents and plant workers lost their lives, almost alone produced the community right-to-know provision of the Superfund Amendments and Reauthorization Act of 1986, which required industries using dangerous chemicals to disclose the type and amount of these chemicals to individuals living within an area likely to be affected by an accident on site. "The Bhopal train was leaving the station," observed one environmental lobbyist about Congress, "and we got the kind of legislation we could put on the train."[51] When California, in early 2001, suddenly experienced rolling power blackouts and steeply rising electric power costs, President Bush and congressional spokespeople of both political parties quickly proclaimed an energy crisis and produced competing prescriptions for a new national energy plan, even while experts debated whether such a crisis really existed. Opinion can also become an obstacle to environmental policymaking when the public mood is inhospitable to action. Advocates of environmental issues often must wait until the opinion climate is ripe to move the White House or Congress to action. Crisis or disaster may sometimes be the only force that moves the public will.

Economic Change

In all environmental policymaking, economics is the counterpoint to ecology. The impact of environmental policies on the economy is a continual preoccupation of environmental regulators and the regulated. Economic conditions, in turn, influence environmental policymaking.

The economic impact of environmental regulations is continually an issue in all discussions of environmental policy. Concern most often focuses on whether environmental regulation will inhibit the expansion of the gross national product, how regulations will affect business investments and the market positions of firms or industries, and whether regulatory costs are inflationary. Regulated interests frequently assert that specific policies will have most or all of these negative effects, whereas proponents of regulation usually claim no such negative effects will occur. Data wars erupt; each side summons its economists and econometrics to vindicate its position. Although the result of these conflicts is often inconclusive, the issues are vitally important. Policies that appear (or can be made to appear) to adversely affect economic growth, market positions, or business investment are likely to command greater and more critical attention from policymakers than those appearing more economically benign. In times of economic recession or depression, the economic impact of policies can become the major determinant of their survival.

Environmental regulations, in any case, do create major public and private costs. Between 1980 and 2000, about 60 percent of the cost of national pollution control was paid by the private sector.[52] In general, studies suggest that new capital spending for pollution control by the public and private sectors has not significantly deterred the growth of the gross national product or contributed much to inflation or to a rise in the consumer price index. For most industries, spending for pollution control has been a gradually diminishing portion of new capital investment since 1980. In 1990, business spending on pollution control was estimated at 2.8 percent of all capital investment but was expected to diminish to less than 2 percent by 2004, although final data are unavailable.[53]

Most theorists assume that a major economic recession, depression, or serious bout with inflation will profoundly affect environmental regulation. The United States experienced no major depression and only a few short recessions between 1970 and 2006.

The severe recession crippling the national economy starting in 2006 is widely expected to have a significant impact on environmental policymaking enduring well after 2016. Predictions include a growing public reluctance, shared by national political leaders, to support vigorous new environmental laws and regulations because they might inhibit economic recovery (a symptom of this malaise may be the growing public concern about the economic impact of environmental laws, discussed in Chapter 2).[54] The recession cut deeply into the Obama administration's environmental agenda, promoting increased emphasis on energy development, including new commercial nuclear power and carbon fuel production, cutbacks in the EPA's regulatory budget, and greater restraint in promoting new environmental regulations. The recession also produced a significant decline in major environmental group assets, leading to cutbacks in staff and programs until 2016 when the Trump presidential campaign inspired an unprecedented upsurge in membership and income growth for environmental organizations across the nation.

Regulatory Federalism

Despite the historical enlargement of federal powers, federalism remains a sturdy constitutional buttress supporting the edifice of authority—shared, independent, and countervailing—erected for the states within the federal system. An observer has said, "It is difficult to find any government activity which does not involve all three of the so-called 'levels' of the federal system." Yet no one level monopolizes power. "There has never been a time when it was possible to put neat labels on discrete 'federal,' 'state,' and 'local' functions."[55]

Environmental programs usually are federalized and sometimes regionalized in their implementation, thereby introducing another political dimension into the policy process. For instance, federal air and water pollution legislation is administered through the Washington, D.C., headquarters of the EPA, its ten regional offices, and the majority of state governments, which assume the responsibility for issuing to pollution dischargers permits specifying the acceptable control technologies and emission levels. This two- and three-tiered design ensures that state and regional interests take part in the regulatory process and that, consequently, state and local governments, together with their associated interests, actively pursue their individual, often competitive, objectives during program implementation. Even if the states are not formally included in the administration of federal environmental regulations, they are likely to insist on some voice in decisions affecting them. Federalism in environmental regulation guarantees voice and influence to the multitude of states involved, providing essential representation for various geographical interests affected politically and economically by federal environmental laws.

The most untiring watchdog over state environmental interests in Washington is the U.S. Senate. The status of the states has altered considerably since the 1970s. At the time of the first Earth Day, only a few progressive states such as California anticipated federal policymakers by initiating needed environmental regulations. Today, the states have often been well ahead of Washington in developing innovative and experimental environmental management and in attacking emerging environmental problems. Aggressive state pressure often forces the EPA's policy implementation and innovation. Thus, a coalition of northeastern states, collaborating in 2006 to sue the EPA for its failure to regulate national CO_2 emissions through the CAA, eventually forced the U.S. Supreme Court to review the scientific evidence for climate change despite the Bush administration's opposition.

Federalism can also complicate and delay program implementation. Few issues arouse state concern more than federal aid and administrative discretion for the states in program management. Federal aid comes in many forms: grants for program administration, staff training, salary supplements, program enforcement, and pollution control facilities; technical assistance in program development or enforcement; research cost sharing; and much more. The states understandably favor generous federal cost sharing in the administration of federally mandated environmental programs. Many proponents of environmental regulation believe that the amount of federal aid directly affects the quality of environmental protection, particularly in states lacking adequate staff and technical resources to implement programs on their own.

The amount of discretion permitted the states when interpreting and enforcing federal regulations within their own borders begets ceaseless controversy in U.S. environmental administration. In general, the states prefer the federal government to leave state administrators with enough discretion to adapt federal environmental regulations to unique local conditions and to be responsive to local economic and political interests. Assailing the federal government for imposing regulations on the states without respect for local interests is a political mantra among state officials, but the criticism has grown increasingly strident as the states' competence in and resources for pollution regulation improved throughout the 1990s.

Another fertile source of controversy in regulatory federalism is the existence of many regional conflicts deeply embedded in the nation's history. Disagreements between the western states, where most of the federal public lands reside, and Washington, D.C., over the management of the public domain west of the Mississippi—almost one third of the nation's land area—repeatedly erupt in the course of federal environmental regulation, as illustrated in Chapter 9.

CONCLUSION

In an important sense, all the nation's environmental problems can be solved. There are almost no contemporary environmental problems for which a technical or scientific solution does not exist or cannot readily be found. Even when ensuring environmental quality might require social action—perhaps a major shift of consumer spending away from gas-guzzler vehicles to highly fuel-efficient cars to reduce urban smog—what could solve the problem is usually much easier to imagine than how to accomplish it. With this perspective, perhaps the greatest challenge to environmental policymaking is finding the governmental, economic, and cultural arrangements—the institutional means—to achieve the environmental ends. To most Americans, the nation's environmental challenges are epitomized by polluted air, fouled water, dangerously unregulated hazardous and toxic wastes, and a multitude of other ecological derangements. This chapter illuminates the less-obvious dimension of the nation's environmental difficulties—the institutional and economic obstacles to implementing environmental policy effectively. Despite the numerous improvements in environmental quality since 1970, in many critical respects, the governmental institutions on which the nation now depends to reverse its ecological degradation are struggling and often failing at the task.

Difficulties with environmental policymaking often originate in the fundamental constitutional design of the political system or in deeply rooted political traditions. Among these problems are excessive congressional control of the agencies implementing environmental policy, legislative reluctance to create clear mandates and priorities within regulatory programs, the extreme fragmentation of committee control over environmental policy, and the resistance of entrenched bureaucracies to structural and policy reform. Although federalism is essential to the political architecture of any environmental regulatory program in the United States, it also complicates policy implementation by introducing competitive pluralistic interests. The institutions, moreover, must function in a volatile political climate of shifting party majorities, economic cycles, fluctuating public opinion, and contentious issues of policy implementation arising from tensions deeply embedded in a federalized regulatory process.

In essence, the quality of the nation's environmental policymaking is grounded in an institutional design that shapes and limits outcomes. To understand what policies are made, we inevitably must appreciate how they were created.

Suggested Readings

Kamieniecki, Sheldon, and Michael E. Kraft. *Business and Environmental Policy: Corporate Interests in the American System*. Cambridge, MA: MIT Press, 2007.

Keller, Ann Campbell. *Science in Environmental Policy: The Politics of Objective Advice*. Cambridge, MA: MIT Press, 2009.

Lindstrom, Matthew J., and Zachary A. Smith. *The National Environmental Policy Act: Judicial Misconstruction, Legislative Indifference, and Executive Neglect*. College Station: Texas A&M Press, 2001.

National Academy of Public Administration. *Setting Priorities, Getting Results: A New Direction for the U.S. Environmental Protection Agency*. Washington, DC: National Academy of Public Administration, 1995.

Scheberle, Denise. *Federalism and Environmental Policy: Trust and the Politics of Implementation*. Washington, DC: Georgetown University Press, 2004.

Notes

1. Jeremy P. Jacobs, "Supreme Court: Big Wins Elusive for EPA in Clean Water Act Showdowns," *E&E Reporter*, August 27, 2014, available at http://www.eenews.net/stories/1060004942.
2. Jonathan S. Wolff and Julie E. O'Keefe, "New Clean Water Act Rule Enlarges Regulatory Jurisdiction of EPA, Army Corps of Engineers, *National Law Review*, June 1, 2015, available at http://www.natlawreview.com/article/new-clean-water-act-rule-enlarges-regulatory-jurisdiction-epa-army-corps-engineers.

3. U.S. EPA, *Factsheet: Clean Water Rule,"* available at www.epa.gov/cleanwaterrule.

4. Jeremy P. Jacobs, "Supreme Court: Big Wins Elusive for EPA in Clean Water Act Showdowns."

5. Ron Farley, "EPA Issues Clean Water Rule Defining Waters of the United States," *Environmental Law Matters,* June 1, 2015, available at http://www.environmentallawmatters.com/epa-issues-clean-water-rule-defining-waters-of-the-united-states/.

6. Jenny Hopkinson, "Obama's Water War," *Politico,* May 28, 2015, available at www.politico.com/story/2015/05/epa-waterways-wetlands-rule-118319.

7. Ibid.

8. Carol Ryan Dumas, "Army Corps Memos Disparage EPA Over WOTUS," *Capital Press,* August 3, 2015, available at http://www.capitalpress.com/Nation_World/Nation/20150803/army-corps-memos-disparage-epa-over-wotus; "White House and EPA at Odds With U.S. Army Corps of Engineers Over New 'Waters of the U.S.' Rule," Great Lakes Legal Foundation, July 29, 2015, available at http://greatlakeslegalfoundation.org/2015/07/29/whitehouse-and-epa-at-odds-with-u-s-army-corps-of-engineers-over-new-%E2%80%9Cwaters-of-the-u-s-%E2%80%9D-rule/.

9. Timothy Cama, "Court Blocks Obama's Water Rule Nationwide," *The Hill,* October 9, 2015, available at http://thehill.com/policy/energy-environment/256493-court-blocks-obamas-water-rule-nationwide; Jonathan E. Adler, "Sixth Circuit Puts Controversial 'Waters of the United States' (WOTUS) Rule on Hold," *Washington Post,* October 9, 2015, available at https://www.washingtonpost.com/news/volokh-conspiracy/wp/2015/10/09/sixth-circuit-puts-controversial-waters-of-the-united-states-wotus-rule-on-hold/.

10. "Public's Policy Priorities Reflect Changing Conditions at Home and Abroad," Pew Research Center, Washington, DC (January, 2015) http://www.people-press.org/2015/01/15/publics-policy-priorities-reflect-changing-conditions-at-home-and-abroad/

11. Quoted by Nancy Pelosi, speaker of the House of Representatives, in Ken Root, "Agriculture Still Has Clout With Politicians," *High Plains Journal,* March 21, 2007, B12.

12. Useful illustrations of presidential activism in environmental policymaking are found in Dennis L. Soden, ed., *The Environmental Presidency* (Albany, NY: SUNY Press, 1999); Norman J. Vig, "Presidential Leadership and the Environment," in *Environmental Policy: New Directions for the Twenty-First Century,* ed. Norman J. Vig and Michael E. Kraft (Washington, DC: CQ Press, 2003), 103–125.

13. A useful summary of the EOP's development can be found in Harold C. Relyea, "The Executive Office of the President: An Historical Overview," Congressional Research Report to Congress, Order Code 98–606 GOV, Washington, DC, November 26, 2008.

14. National Environmental Policy Act, Title II, 42 U.S.C. § 4321 et seq. (1970).

15. Quoted in Russel E. Train, "The Environmental Record of the Nixon Administration," *Presidential Studies Quarterly* 26, no. 1 (1996): 191.

16. Christopher Schroeder, "The Evolution of Federal Regulation of Toxic Substances," in *Government and Environmental Politics: Essays on Historical Development Since World War II*, ed. Michael J. Lacey (Lanham, MD: University Press of America, 1990), 118.

17. Ralph Huitt, "Political Feasibility," in *Policy Analysis in Political Science*, ed. Ira Sharkansky (Chicago, IL: Markham, 1970), 414.

18. Barry G. Rabe, *Fragmentation and Integration in State Environmental Management* (Washington, DC: Conservation Foundation, 1986), 16–17. See also Michael E. Kraft, "Congress and Environmental Policy," in *Environmental Politics and Policy: Theories and Evidence*, ed. James P. Lester (Durham, NC: Duke University Press, 1989), 179–211.

19. "Mississippi 'Pork' Ranking," Official Trent Lott Press Release, May 2, 2002, available at www.lott.senate.gov/news/2000/502.pork.html.

20. Mark J. Landy and Mary Hague, "The Coalition for Waste: Private Interests and Superfund," in *Environmental Politics: Public Costs, Private Rewards*, ed. Michael S. Grave (New York: Praeger, 1992), 72.

21. Lawrence Mosher, "Clean Water Requirements Will Remain Even if the Federal Spigot Is Closed," *National Journal*, May 16, 1981, 874–878.

22. Quoted in Marcia Clemmitt, "Energy and Climate Change: Should Carbon-Based Fuels Be Phased Out?" *CQ Researcher*, July 24, 2009, available at http://library.cqpress.com/cqresearcher/search.php?PHPSESSID=207p8d 3i1ek2nbscahp1j5iad3&fulltext=climate+change&action=newsearch&sort= custom%3Asorthitsrank%2Cd&x=15&y=12.

23. Quoted in *New York Times*, March 22, 1993, B8.

24. Quoted in ibid.

25. GAO, "Indoor Air Pollution: Federal Efforts Are Not Effectively Addressing a Growing Problem," Report No. GAO/RCED 92–8, Washington, DC, October 1991, 6.

26. Quoted in Margaret E. Kriz, "Pesticidal Pressures," *National Journal*, December 12, 1988, 125.

27. Jared N. Day, "Safe Drinking Water-Safe Sites: Interaction Between the Safe Drinking Water Act and Superfund, 1968–1995," in *Improving Regulation: Cases in Environment, Health, and Safety*, ed. Paul S. Fischbeck and R. Scott Farrow (Washington, DC: Resources for the Future, 2000).

28. David Schoenbrod, "The EPA's Faustian Bargain," *Regulation* (Fall 2006): 41.

29. On American political polarization and its congressional implications, see: Pew Research Center for the People and the Press, *Partisan Polarization Surges in Bush, Obama Years* (Washington, DC: Pew Research Center, June 4, 2012), also available at www.people-press.org; Nolan McCarty, "Policy Consequences of Partisan Polarization in the United States," available at

bcep.haas.berkeley.edu/papers/McCarty.doc; Sean M. Theriault, "Party Polarization in Congress," available at www.ruf.rice.edu/~lmartin/Speakers/Theriault.pdf; and Sean M. Theriault, *Party Polarization in Congress* (New York: Cambridge University Press, 2008); William Galston, "Can a Polarized American Party System Be 'Healthy'?" *Issues in Governance Studies* (Washington, DC: Brookings Institution, 2010), available at http://www.brookings.edu/research/papers/2010/04/polarization-galston.

30. David D. Doniger, *The Law and Policy of Toxic Substances Control* (Baltimore, MD: Johns Hopkins University Press, 1978), 3.

31. Quoted in John H. Trattner, *The Prune Book: The 100 Toughest Management and Policy-Making Jobs in Washington* (Lanham, MD: Madison, 1988), 250.

32. Quoted in ibid., 249.

33. Green Energy News, "Obama Slashes EPA Funding By 13 Percent," February 21, 2011, available at www.renewable-energy-news.info/obama-budget-cuts-funding-for-epa-programs/?wpmp_switcher=mobile.

34. EPA, Office of the Chief Financial Officer, "FY 2008: Budget in Brief," Publication no. EPA-205-S-07-001, Washington, DC, February 2007, v.

35. Environmental Protection Agency, Office of the Chief Financial Officer, FY 2019 EPA Budget in Brief, "Overview, available at https://www.epa.gov/sites/production/files/2018-02/documents/fy-2019-epa-bib.pdf

36. CEQ, *Environmental Quality, 1985* (Washington, DC: Council on Environmental Quality, 1986), 14. See also Walter A. Rosenbaum, "Into the Nineties at EPA: Searching for the Clenched Fist and the Open Hand," in *Environmental Policy in the 1990s*, 2nd ed., ed. Norman J. Vig and Michael E. Kraft (Washington, DC: CQ Press, 1994), 121–143.

37. GAO, "Pesticides: EPA's Formidable Task to Assess and Regulate Their Risks," Report No. GAO/RCED 86–125, Washington, DC, April 1986, 35.

38. Patrick Ambrosio, "Groups Agree EPA Can't Meet Deadlines for Reviews, But No Consensus on Fix," Bloomberg *BNA Environmental Reporter*, available at http://news.bna.com/erln/display/batch_print_display.adp.

39. Coral Davenport, "Scott Pruitt Is Seen Cutting the EPA With a Scalpel, Not a Cleaver," *New York Times,* February 6, 2017, A12.

40. Talia Buford, ProPublica, "The Trump Administration's Regulatory Rollback at the EPA Stunned Longtime Staffers," *Business Insider*, December 27, 2017.

41. Eric Lipton, "Courts Thwart Administration's Effort to Rescind Obama-Era Environmental Regulations," *New York Times*, October 7, 2017, A1.

42. John Siciliano, "Ryan Zinke Plans Overhaul Because Interior Department Employees 'Not Loyal,'" *Washington Examiner*, November 5, 2017, available at www.washingtonexaminer.com/ryan-zinke-plans-overhaul-because-interior-department-employees-not-loyal.

43. Michelle Adato, James Mackenzie, Robert Pollard, and Ellyn Weiss, *Safety Second: The NRC and America's Nuclear Power Plants* (Bloomington: Indiana University Press, 1987), esp. chaps. 1, 5.

44. GAO, "Department of Energy: Cleaning Up Inactive Facilities Will Be Difficult," Report no. GAO/RCED 92–149, Washington, DC, June 1993; see also GAO, "Much Work Remains to Accelerate Facility Cleanups," Report no. GAO/RCED 93–15, Washington, DC, January 1993.

45. See Christopher Madison, "The Energy Department at Three—Still Trying to Establish Itself," *National Journal,* October 4, 1980, 16–19.

46. Werner J. Grunbaum, *Judicial Policy Making: The Supreme Court and Environmental Quality* (Morristown, NJ: General Learning Press, 1976), 31. See also Lettie McSpadden Wenner, "The Courts and Environmental Policy," in *Environmental Politics and Policy: Theories and Evidence,* ed. James P. Lester (Durham, NC: Duke University Press, 1989), 261–288.

47. Barton H. Thompson Jr., "Conservative Environmental Thought: The Bush Administration and Environmental Policy," *Ecology Law Quarterly,* 37 (2005): 307–348; John D. Graham, Paul R. Noe, and Elizabeth L. Branch, "Managing the Regulatory State: The Experience of the Bush Administration," *Fordham Urban Law Journal,* 33 (2006): 903–953; Blaine Harden, "Bush Policy Irks Judges in West; Rulings Criticize Agencies for Not Protecting the Environment," *Washington Post,* October 6, 2006, A3.

48. Jennifer Koons, "Supreme Court: A Rough Term for Environmentalists," *Environment and Energy Daily,* June 25, 2009, available at www.eenews.net/public/Greenwire/2009/06/25/3; Adam Liptak, "Environmental Groups Find Less Support in Court," *New York Times,* July 3, 2009, A10.

49. Tom DiChristopher, "Trump's EPA Hit With Lawsuit Over Suspension of Oil-and-Gas Drilling Rules," November 2, 2017, available at www.cnbc.com/2017/06/05/conservation-groups-sue-epa-over-stay-of-oil-and-gas-drilling-rules.html.

50. Stephen Breyer, *Breaking the Vicious Circle: Toward Effective Risk Regulation* (Cambridge, MA: Harvard University Press, 1993), 59.

51. Quoted in Margaret Kriz, "Fuming Over Fumes," *National Journal,* November 26, 1988, 3008.

52. U.S. Department of Commerce, Bureau of the Census, *Statistical Abstract of the United States, 1992* (Washington, DC: Government Printing Office, 1993), 217. Figures are given in 1982 dollar values, corrected for inflation.

53. EPA, "Environmental Investments: The Cost of a Clean Environment: A Summary," Washington, DC, 1990, vi.

54. W. K. Kellog Foundation, *The Quiet Crisis: The Impact of the Economic Downturn on the Nonprofit Sector* (Washington, DC: Kellog Foundation, March 2009).

55. Morton Grodzins, "The Federal System," in *American Federalism in Perspective,* ed. Aaron Wildavsky (Boston, MA: Little, Brown, 1967), 257.

COMMON POLICY
CHALLENGES

Risk Assessment and
Environmental Justice

Until 1998, few Americans knew about phthalates or cared about them. In November 1998, however, the environmental organization Greenpeace International released the first of its many reports demanding that the toy industry worldwide immediately abandon the use of the chemical diisononyl phthalate (DINP), an ingredient in vinyl, a material widely used throughout the industry in producing thousands of children's products as varied as pacifiers, rubber ducks, teddy bears, dolls, rattles, and teething rings. The report was another sortie in a militant campaign by environmentalists and public health officials against a large class of chemicals called phthalates or plasticizers, which make plastic products more flexible. In the United States, the announcement unleashed a relentless public controversy that has continued for more than twenty years, a conflict that quickly assumed a pattern common to the contemporary politics of environmental risk assessment.

A TOXIC NIGHTMARE
FROM TOYLAND?

First came a dramatic public condemnation of an important industrial chemical. Greenpeace International asserted a major domestic chemical manufacturer used the chemical DINP to manufacture products that children might chew, such as pacifiers and rattles, even though a similar compound caused liver damage in laboratory rats.[1] The accusation and accompanying information, quickly disseminated worldwide by the media, was alarming not only to the chemical producers and to parents whose children might be exposed to the products but also to the hundreds of manufacturers and consumers of other products using plasticizers—products such as medical equipment, food containers, consumer goods, packaging material, and much more—because plasticizers are a global commodity. A story on the popular ABC news program *20/20* in early 1998 repeated many of the Greenpeace International allegations, thus ensuring a huge domestic audience for the controversy. Within a few weeks, the plasticizer debate was a media event.[2]

Next, an acrimonious, highly technical dispute erupted in the public media, abetted by technical publications and professional spokespeople caught up in the controversy, over the extent of the health risks resulting from exposure to the plasticizers. At the same time, the controversy was quickly politicized. Organized groups representing environmentalists, consumers, public health interests, the chemical and toy manufacturers, governmental agencies, parents, political think tanks, and many others rapidly aligned on sides of the issue. Conflict approached the surreal, as exquisitely technical and publicly confounding arguments raged over baby bottle nipples, animal fetuses, Teletubbies, squeeze toys, liver biopsies, monkey testicles, and other exotica. Even Barbie was implicated. At stake were possibly a billion dollars in worldwide product sales, the ethical and economic stature of the chlorine chemical industry, markets for hundreds of manufacturers using the embattled chemicals, and perhaps the health of uncounted children worldwide.

The Political Front

Within a week of the Greenpeace International announcement, twelve consumer, environmental, and religious groups demanded that the U.S. Consumer Product Safety Commission (CPSC), the federal regulatory agency responsible for ensuring the safety of children's products sold in the United States, ban vinyl toys for small children. The National Environmental Trust, a coalition of environmental organizations, urged the U.S. government to ban all vinyl baby products. In November 1998, the CPSC also stated that it was uncertain about the risks to babies from DINP but nonetheless advised parents to throw away nipples and pacifiers made with vinyl and asked manufacturers not to use DINP in products children might put in their mouths.

Meanwhile, the manufacturer of DINP and many industrial consumers were rising to DINP's defense. Major toy manufacturers, such as Mattel; large toy retailers, including Toys R Us; and the industry's trade association, the Toy Manufacturers of America, all publicly defended the safety of the plasticizers used for decades in children's products.

A Scientific Enigma

The actual risk to children from exposure to plasticizers seemed anything but clear. One problem was the absence of a standard procedure to determine how much of the suspect chemical a child could realistically be expected to absorb. In addition, toy components vary considerably in their plasticizer content.

Another major problem involved the reliability of the animal tests indicating that DINP and its predecessor could cause liver damage in humans. Critics of these tests noted that similar damage did not occur in other experimental animals, including guinea pigs, hamsters, and monkeys. Other issues, such as the age of the test animals, might matter.[3]

Finally, there was the unsettling enigma about how long it could take before any health problems might appear among children exposed to plasticizers. The damaging effects of such exposure might be latent for many years and, as a consequence, the current incidence of any suspected damage might greatly underestimate the long-term damage to humans. Thus, it might seem prudent to ban the plasticizers even in the absence of convincing, current evidence of their danger.

Barbie Gets a Green Makeover

With the controversy public, the Toy Manufacturers of America reluctantly advised its members to voluntarily eliminate DINP-based vinyl products even while it maintained their safety.[4] The industry's capitulation was ensured when Mattel, the world's largest toy manufacturer, announced in December 1999 that it would substitute plant- and vegetable-based plastics for chlorine-based vinyls. Barbie was destined for a complete chemical makeover, along with a multitude of other familiar toys.

In 2003, to the considerable satisfaction of the Chlorine Chemistry Council and toy manufacturers, the CPSC voted unanimously to deny the petition to ban phthalates from products for children younger than five years old, because there appeared to be "no demonstrable health risk."[5] The CPSC also knew how to defend itself. This decision, it noted, was supported by numerous scientific studies, including a meticulous inquiry concerning "mouthing habits" among infants.[6] Average daily mouthing time, however, was not the science that satisfied most public health and environmental advocates, who continued to demand the elimination of phthalates from toys.

The Controversy Continues . . .

By 2006, phthalate opponents had rearmed with a new wave of highly publicized scientific studies once again implying that phthalates might be a human toxic. One university study suggested that mothers exposed during pregnancy to high levels of phthalates found in cosmetics, plastics, and detergents might have "less masculine" boys; another investigation noted that plastic food containers might "contribute" to breast cancer.[7] Public health and environmental advocates persisted, determined to skewer high-profile industries, such as nail polish manufacturers, with apparently damning scientific research. Phthalates opponents also put pressure on the federal government from other venues, such as California, where the legislature, San Francisco, and several other cities banned baby toys containing phthalates.

By 2010, continuing scientific evidence raised such substantial doubt about phthalate safety that parents and other consumers of phthalate-containing products were no longer left to decide which side—if any—should be trusted. A 2008 report of the National Academy of Sciences urged Congress and the EPA to promote new studies about the effects of cumulative human exposure to all phthalates.[8] In September 2008, Congress passed the Consumer Product Safety Reform Act (CPSRA), mandating that the CPSC prohibit DINP and certain other phthalates in children's toys and care products and requiring manufacturers of children's products to test and certify their safety.

The American Chemistry Council still expressed the industry's dissatisfaction with the CPSRA, arguing that "after all this study and review, no reliable scientific evidence has found phthalates to cause adverse human health effects."[9] In mid-2012, the plasticizer controversy revived on yet another front when the Food and Drug Administration, the federal agency responsible for assuring the safety of ingredients in domestic food products, proposed to ban a plasticizer in infant feeding products. By 2013, the phthalate conflict had spread across a regulatory battlefront embracing a multitude of other phthalates. The CPSC, confronting a swelling volume of risk assessment studies by phthalate critics, was compelled to parse out of the data further decisions concerning additional phthalates to regulate, in what children's products, and what exposure levels to prohibit.

In 2015, the CPSC vastly enlarged the scope of federal phthalate regulation. A new rule prohibited the phthalate DINP in all children's toys, expanded the list of phthalates permanently banned from child care products, and ratcheted down the level of phthalates permitted in specified children's products.[10] But the new rule assured further phthalate controversy, because it also removed several plasticizers from existing regulation and failed to extend regulation to other children's products, such as rainwear, footwear, backpacks, and rubber ducks.

However, a new, improved rubber duck and other children's toys free of banned plasticizers still contained other unregulated plasticizers.

By 2018, it was clear that the phthalate controversy would persist, despite evidence of some regulatory success, because phthalates are so diverse and widely used in consumer products that they defy rapid evaluation. In late 2017, for instance, scientists reported encouraging news that exposure to some phthalates, especially those now regulated in children's toys, was declining. But in mid-2017, research by a major public health advocacy group also identified phthalates in almost 30 cheese products, including string cheese, cottage cheese, and macaroni and cheese powder, suggesting that an expanding list of food products is likely to become a matter of regulatory concern.[11]

In a broader perspective, the conflict also introduces the common policymaking pathway for most risk assessments required by federal law and the focus of this chapter—a path littered with protracted litigation, sustained political infighting, disputed science, and multiple government venues.

RISK ASSESSMENT AND THE LIMITS OF SCIENCE

The EPA alone writes thousands of risk assessments annually in various forms to carry out its regulatory responsibilities.[12] In 1993, President Clinton further elevated the importance of risk assessment by requiring in Executive Order 12866 that all regulatory agencies, not only environmental ones, "consider, to the extent reasonable, the degree and nature of risks posed by various substances or activities within its jurisdiction" and mandating that each proposed regulatory action explain how the action will reduce risks "as well as how the magnitude of risk addressed by the action relates to other risks within the jurisdiction of the agency."[13]

Traditional risk assessment associated with environmental regulation creates a flow of decisions that starts, as Figure 4.1 indicates, when the EPA or another regulatory agency is required to determine whether a substance—a commercial chemical, for example—constitutes a sufficient hazard to humans or to the environment to require regulation under one of many current environmental regulatory laws. The process begins with research that assembles currently available information about the possible adverse health or environmental effects of a suspected hazard, such as a chemical. If the research suggests possibly adverse effects to humans or the environment, the regulatory agency proceeds to risk assessment, during which additional information is obtained or experiments are conducted concerning the current levels of exposure to a suspected chemical, and an estimate is made of the likely adverse consequences. If this risk assessment indicates that a chemical is sufficiently hazardous to meet the requirements for regulation, the agency proceeds to risk management, during which regulators consider alternative strategies for the chemical's regulation and then propose a regulatory plan. Figure 4.1 may imply a dependably neat, deliberate, and timely sequence of decisions, but the reality is often many contested decisions and years or decades of elapsed time.

Risk assessment now incites the impassioned policy conflicts once confined to holy wars, such as the benefit–cost debate. A major reason is that risk assessment lies in the treacherous zone between science and politics, where practically all environmental policies reside and where collaboration between public officials and scientists is both essential and difficult. What public officials and scientists involved in policymaking want from each other is often unobtainable. Public officials seek from scientists information accurate enough to indicate precisely where they should establish environmental standards and credible enough to defend in the inevitable conflicts to follow. Scientists want government to act quickly and forcefully on ecological issues they believe to be critical.[14] Yet science often cannot produce technical information in the form and within the time desired by public officials. Indeed, science often cannot provide the information at all, leaving officials to make crucial decisions from fragmentary and disputable information.

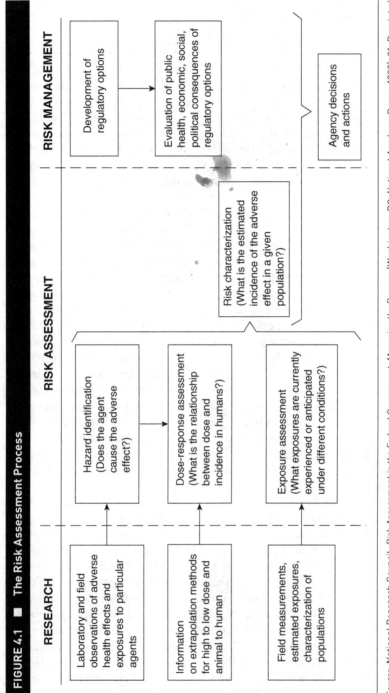

FIGURE 4.1 ■ The Risk Assessment Process

RESEARCH

RISK ASSESSMENT

RISK MANAGEMENT

Laboratory and field observations of adverse health effects and exposures to particular agents

Hazard identification (Does the agent cause the adverse effect?)

Development of regulatory options

Evaluation of public health, economic, social, political consequences of regulatory options

Information on extrapolation methods for high to low dose and animal to human

Dose-response assessment (What is the relationship between dose and incidence in humans?)

Risk characterization (What is the estimated incidence of the adverse effect in a given population?)

Field measurements, estimated exposures, characterization of populations

Exposure assessment (What exposures are currently experienced or anticipated under different conditions?)

Agency decisions and actions

Source: National Research Council, *Risk Assessment in the Federal Government: Managing the Process* (Washington, DC: National Academy Press, 1983), 21. Reprinted with permission from National Research Council. Courtesy of the National Academies Press, Washington, DC.

In short, risk assessment frequently compels public officials to make scientific judgments and scientists to resolve policy issues for which neither may be trained. The almost inevitable need to resolve scientific questions through the political process and the problems that arise in making scientific and political judgments compatible are two of the most troublesome characteristics of environmental politics.

Derelict Data and Embattled Expertise

Controversy among experts commonly arises in environmental policymaking. Contending battalions of experts, garlanded with degrees and publications and primed to dispute each other's judgment, populate congressional and administrative hearings about risk assessment. Policymakers are often left to judge not only the wisdom of policies but also the quality of the science supporting the policies.

Missing Data. Why is controversy so predictable? Frequently, there is a void of useful data about the distribution and severity of environmental problems or possible pollutants. Many problems are so recent that public and private agencies have only just begun to study them. Many pollutants—hazardous chemicals, for instance—have existed for only a few decades; their ecological impacts cannot yet be measured reliably. The EPA alone receives about 1,500 petitions annually requesting the approval of new chemicals or new uses of existing chemicals for which tests may be required.[15] Quite often, the result is that nobody has the information that somebody should have. For instance, the EPA and the U.S. Department of Health and Human Services together have data reporting the degree of exposure among the general population for less than 15 percent of more than 1,400 chemicals considered to pose a threat to human health.[16] Lacking high-quality data, experts often extrapolate answers from fragmentary information, and plausible disputes over the reliability of such procedures are inevitable.

Late and Latent Effects. Disagreement over the severity of environmental problems also arises because the effects of many substances thought to be hazardous to humans or the environment may not become evident for decades or generations. The latency and diffusion of these impacts also may make it difficult to establish causality between the suspected substances or events and the consequences. Asbestos, a hazardous chemical whose malignancy has been documented since 1979, illustrates these problems.[17] Since World War II, approximately eight million to eleven million U.S. workers have been exposed to asbestos, a mineral fiber with more than two thousand uses; its heat resistance, electrical properties, immunity to chemical deterioration, and other characteristics made it appear to be ideal to a multitude of major industries. In the past, it was used widely to manufacture brake and clutch linings, plastics, plumbing, roofing tile, wall insulation, paint, paper, and much else. Asbestos is highly carcinogenic. Among those exposed to significant levels of asbestos, 20 to 25 percent died of lung cancer, 7 to 10 percent perished from mesothelioma (cancer of the chest lining or stomach), and another

8 to 9 percent died from gastrointestinal cancer.[18] The toxicity of asbestos became apparent only decades after workers were exposed, because the cancers associated with it do not become clinically evident until fifteen to forty years after exposure, and severe illness may appear two to fifty years after the cancers first appear in humans. Added to the incalculable cost of human suffering is the immense economic impact of these delayed effects. More than two thousand new cases of incurable asbestos-related cancer now appear each year in the United States. Presently, three hundred thousand lawsuits arising from human exposure to asbestos are pending in the nation's courts, and twenty thousand to fifty thousand lawsuits are predicted annually for several decades. U.S. corporations and insurers have spent more than $30 billion to defend and settle asbestos lawsuits. The total cost of these suits, according to several professional estimates, may exceed $200 billion.[19]

Many other substances used in U.S. commerce, science, and domestic life are suspected of producing adverse impacts on humans or the environment. Yet conclusive evidence might not appear for decades, whereas government officials must decide whether to regulate these substances now. Difficult as such decisions are, a failure to act, as in the case of asbestos, eventually may prove so costly in human suffering and economic loss that many scientists may be reluctant to wait for conclusive data. These issues are illustrated by the federal government's continuing problems with the chemical dioxin.

The Case of Dioxin. Early in the 1990s, the EPA was persuaded by growing scientific evidence to initiate a searching reevaluation of its twenty-year-old exposure standards for the chemical dioxin, which it had characterized earlier as one of the most lethal substances on Earth.[20] The most dangerous among the seventy-five varieties of dioxin was thought to be 2,3,7,8-tetrachlorodibenzodioxin (TCDD), considered so harmful that the EPA's maximum exposure standards had limited human ingestion of TCDD to 0.006 trillionth of a gram per day for every kilogram (2.2 pounds) of body weight over an average lifetime—in other words, an average-size man was limited daily to an amount equal to a grain of sand sliced one billion times.

The EPA's original exposure standard for dioxin, as with most risk assessments made by federal agencies, was extrapolated largely from animal experiments. In the late 1970s, the EPA ordered an end to the production of the weed killer 2,4,5-T, also a dioxin, on the basis of its own earlier studies and additional, if circumstantial, evidence of great harm to individuals exposed to high concentrations of the herbicide. When concentrations of dioxin far exceeding levels considered safe were discovered during 1981 in the soil of Times Beach, Missouri—the result of illegal toxic waste disposals—the EPA decided that public safety required the permanent evacuation of the entire Missouri community. All 2,240 residents were removed to new residences and reimbursed for their property at a cost exceeding $37 million, while an additional $100 million was spent to clean up other nearby contaminated sites. During the 1980s, hundreds of lawsuits were filed against the federal government by Vietnam War veterans for alleged health impairment from exposure to dioxin in the defoliant Agent Orange. Meanwhile, the EPA's strict standards were expected to cost the paper and pulp industry about $2 billion for pollution control.

But a growing number of scientific experts questioned not only the EPA's exposure standards for dioxin but also the reliability of all the animal studies for determining the safe levels of human exposure to hazardous substances.[21] A particularly damning public indictment of the EPA's own standard appeared in 1991 when the federal scientist who had ordered the evacuation of Times Beach admitted to a congressional committee that he made the wrong decision. "Given what we know now about this chemical's toxicity," then assistant surgeon general Vernon N. Houk stated, "it looks as if the evacuation was unnecessary."[22] Additional complications arose in the 1990s. A panel of experts convened by the EPA concluded that, although dioxin was a significant cancer threat to people only when they were exposed to unusually high levels in chemical factories, it wreaked biological havoc among fish, birds, and other wild animals even in minute doses.[23] Shortly thereafter, the agency supervising all federal animal studies used in toxics regulation released another report suggesting that animal studies alone were not reliable for judging the exposure risks to human beings in toxics research.[24] The Clinton administration and EPA officials were extremely uneasy with the existing exposure standards, and a thorough restudy of the issue was ordered.

In mid-2000, the EPA released the results of its long-awaited restudy. To the surprise of the White House and most EPA officials, the agency for the first time concluded that dioxin TCDD was a "human carcinogen" and that one hundred related chemicals were "likely" human carcinogens. The result was all the more startling because domestic emissions of dioxin had declined by 87 percent since 1984.[25] Some environmental organizations then deduced from the EPA's risk estimates that about one hundred of the 1,400 cancer deaths occurring in the United States daily were attributable to dioxin. Predictably, the EPA's decision was assailed from both sides of the controversy. Major chemical producers asserted the EPA was "out of sync" with dioxin regulation in the rest of the world and the report was "counterintuitive to what the facts are." The U.S. Chamber of Commerce suggested the decision wasn't based on "sound science." Greenpeace International, like some other environmental groups, lacerated the EPA for failing to control aggressively the remaining dioxin emissions; "That suggests that [the EPA] can't walk and chew gum at the same time," it sniffed.[26]

Still, the dioxin controversy will not go away. In July 2006, the National Academy of Sciences review concluded that the EPA should reassess the risks of dioxin exposure, especially exposure to very low dioxin doses, and issue a revised risk assessment explaining more clearly "how it selects both the data upon which the reassessment is based and the methods used to analyze them."[27] Meanwhile, the existing EPA risk standards would be enforced. In December 2009, the EPA initiated a comprehensive restudy of dioxin health risks. By 2012, the EPA had concluded that "generally, over a person's lifetime, current exposure to dioxins does not pose a significant [non-cancer] health risk," but the agency had not completed its study by 2018.[28]

Animal and Epidemiological Experiments. Having rejected most controlled human studies, scientists are left with the only alternative: controlled animal experiments in which test animals are exposed to substances, the effects monitored, and the risks to human beings extrapolated from the findings.

These animal studies are particularly controversial when used to estimate the effects of low levels of chemical exposure on humans—for instance, a dose of a few parts per million or billion of a pesticide or heavy metal in drinking water over thirty years. The human risks of cancer or other serious illnesses will be small, but how small?[29] And how reliable is the estimate? Animal studies do not and cannot use enough animals to eliminate all possibilities of error in estimating the effects of low-level exposure on humans. To demonstrate conclusively with 95 percent confidence that a certain low-level dose of one substance causes fewer than one case of cancer per million individuals would require a "mega mouse" experiment involving six million animals.[30] Instead, researchers use high doses of a substance with relatively few animals and then extrapolate through statistical models the effect on humans from low-level exposure to the tested substance. But these models can differ by a factor of as much as one hundred thousand in estimating the size of the dose that could produce one cancer per million individuals. A litany of other problems is associated with small-animal studies. Various animals, for example, differ greatly in their sensitivity to substances; dioxin is 5,000 times more toxic to guinea pigs than to hamsters.[31]

The Limited Neutrality of Scientific Judgment

Perhaps fifty opportunities exist in a normal risk assessment procedure for scientists to make discretionary judgments. Although scientists are presumed to bring to this task an expertise untainted by social values to bias their judgments, they are not immune to social prejudice, especially when their expertise is embroiled in a public controversy. According to physicist Harvey Brooks, a veteran of many public controversies,

> The more an issue is in the public eye, the more expert judgments are likely to be influenced unconsciously by pre-existing policy preferences or by supposedly unrelated factors such as media presentations, the opinions of colleagues or friends, or even the emotional overtones of certain words used in the debate.[32]

Scientific judgment on environmental issues can be influenced by one's beliefs about how government should regulate the economy, by one's institutional affiliation, or by other social and political attributes.[33] A study of several hundred risk professionals involved in federal environmental policymaking suggests that, once risk professionals become involved in policymaking, there is "a weakening of disciplinary perspectives and a strengthening of viewpoints based on politics and ideology."[34] Yet no barrier can be contrived to wholly insulate science from the contagion of social or economic bias. This is a strong argument for keeping scientific and technical determinations open to examination and challenge by other experts and laypersons.

WHAT RISKS ARE ACCEPTABLE?

Risk assessment for environmental policymaking is also difficult because no clear and consistent definition of "acceptable risk" exists in federal law. Acceptable risk is usually defined in environmental regulation by statutory criteria—that is, by standards written into law to guide regulators in determining when to regulate a substance. Despite repeated congressional efforts at clarification, the only consistency in these statutory standards is their inconsistency.[35] Determining acceptable risk often remains an intensely discretionary—and often political—affair, however much the language of the law may conceal it.

A Multitude of Risk Criteria

A multitude of different congressional standards guide regulatory agencies in making determinations of acceptable risk. Different substances often are regulated according to different standards. The same substance may be subject to one regulatory standard when dumped into a river and another when mixed into processed food. Statutory risk standards are commonly vague and sometimes confusing; congressional intent may be muddled, often deliberately.

In general, regulatory agencies encounter one or more of the following statutory formulas in determining the permissible exposure levels to various substances.[36] The examples are drawn from existing legislation.

- *Health-based criteria.* Regulatory agencies are to set standards based on risks to human health from exposure to a hazard. These standards are usually "cost oblivious," because they seldom permit agencies to use the cost of regulation as a consideration in standard settings. The CAA (1970) mandates that national primary ambient air-quality standards "shall be . . . in the judgment of the Administrator, based on [air-quality] criteria and allowing an adequate margin of safety . . . requisite to protect human health." The EPA is also left to determine the magnitude of this "margin of safety" and to whom it applies.[37]

- *Technology-based criteria.* The EPA is instructed to ensure that pollution sources will use the best available or the maximum achievable technology or some other specified technology criteria to control their hazardous emissions. In effect, acceptable risks are defined by whatever residual risks to public health may exist after the prescribed control technologies are applied to a pollution source.

- *Balancing criteria.* Congress mandates that an agency consider, to varying extents, the costs of regulation or the magnitude of threat to human health alongside the benefits in setting a standard for human or environmental exposure. Or Congress may permit cost considerations to be among other criteria that an agency may consider. These statutes define how various considerations, such as cost and risk, are to be balanced in determining acceptable risk.

Congress often packs regulatory laws with so many criteria for risk determination—lest any important consideration be ignored—that regulatory decisions become enormously complicated. Consider, for instance, the multitude of criteria the EPA was ordered to use under TSCA (1976) when deciding whether the risks from exposure to a substance are unreasonable:

The type of effect (chronic or acute, reversible or irreversible); degree of risk; characteristics and number of humans, plants and animals, or ecosystems, at risk; amount of knowledge about the effects; available or alternative substances and their expected effects; magnitude of the social and economic costs and benefits of possible control actions; and appropriateness and effectiveness of TSCA as the legal instrument for controlling the risk.[38]

Agencies spend considerable time working out detailed internal regulations to translate these complexities into workable procedures. But agencies often face imperious deadlines for making regulatory decisions, fragmentary information relevant to many criteria for standard setting, and disputes among interest groups concerning the validity of information and the priorities for criteria in policymaking. In the first years of a new regulatory program, an agency can expect virtually every major decision to be challenged through litigation, usually by an interest alleging the agency has failed to interpret its statutory responsibilities properly.[39]

How Much Risk Reduction Is Enough?

Extremely sophisticated technologies now enable scientists to detect hazardous substances in increasingly small concentrations, currently as small as parts per billion or trillion. It is usually impossible to assert scientifically that such low concentrations are wholly innocent of adverse risk, however slight, to humans or the environment. In addition, the cost of controlling hazardous substances often rises steeply as progressively higher standards are enforced; for instance, after reducing 85 percent of a substance in a waterway, it may cost half as much or more to remove an additional 5 to 10 percent. When regulatory agencies confront a trade-off between the costs and benefits of risk prevention, what criteria should govern the choice? Advocates for vigorous regulation assert that regulators should err on the side of caution by insisting on extremely high standards for controlling risks and without sensitivity to the economic burden imposed on regulated inter-ests.[40] This may leave the public with unrealistic expectations about the benefits, which in most cases will be extremely small, if not undiscoverable, when regu-lators insist on eliminating even minuscule risks from hazardous substances.[41] Often, advocates of strict regulation are indignant at the suggestion that human lives may be endangered if the cost of protection is deemed excessive—an asser-tion, skillfully delivered, that implies that officials are venal or inhumane for imperiling lives to save money for a regulated interest.

RISK ASSESSMENT RECONSIDERED: THE PRECAUTIONARY PRINCIPLE

Considering the challenges involved with traditional risk assessment, is there a better way to deal with environmental risks? Environmentalists, together with many scientists, public health authorities, and policy professionals, have vigor-ously promoted the precautionary principle as an approach to risk management as quite different and, they believe, less complicated and more environmentally protective than the current federal method of risk assessment.[42] The "precaution-ary principle," in one widely accepted interpretation, declares, "when an activity raises threats of harm to human health or the environment, precautionary mea-sures should be taken even if some cause and effect relationships are not fully established scientifically."[43]

The principle has been widely adopted and implemented in European Union environmental legislation and important international environmental agree-ments. It is the premise undergirding the global movement to control greenhouse gas emissions. Proponents of the precautionary principle assert that it has several advantages over traditional risk assessment:

- It mandates preventive action in the face of uncertainty rather than waiting for the determination of acceptable risk and the resolution of all the many scientific controversies often involved in regulating possible hazards.

- It shifts the burden of proof to the proponents of an activity or chemical, who assume the obligation to establish the safety or acceptability of the suspected hazard.

- It promotes the exploration of a wide range of alternatives to possibly harmful actions, including the possibility of not creating the potential hazard.

- It encourages public participation in decision-making by requiring transparency and stakeholder participation.[44]

Proponents of the precautionary principle would contend, for example, that if these principles had been invoked in the regulation of dioxin, much of the previously described political controversy, enormous consumption of time, seemingly interminable litigation, and perhaps unsolvable scientific disputes about acceptable risk could have been avoided, while the human and environmental danger from dioxin exposure would have been more rapidly reduced.

The precautionary principle, however, also entails potentially significant risks that prompt others to caution against its widespread adoption. The most fundamental concern is that "it seeks to stop innovation before it starts."[45] It may stifle important commercial, scientific, or economic initiatives whose possibly substantial benefits will be lost—what economists call the opportunity costs—because real or suspected hazards may also be involved. In addition, some urgent problems may be unsolvable without accepting significant real or anticipated risk in the solution.

The principle may also be applied prematurely. Consider the widely reported appearance of Colony Collapse Disorder (CCD) among honeybees and related pollinators worldwide. Beginning in 2006, domestic beekeepers reported hive losses of 25 to 36 percent, most in hives where the symptoms were unrelated to known reasons for bee deaths. Some scientists and food experts warned of an ominous threat to the national food system.[46] During the succeeding years, the national media widely disseminated the CCD story, often citing suggestions by some apparently reliable sources about a possible catastrophic collapse of the national food supply—a 2013 *Time* cover story, for example, ominously titled "A World Without Bees," warned about "the price we'll pay if we don't figure out what's killing the honeybee."[47] The *Time* article, like many other CCD stories, suggested that the bee killer was probably a class of common agricultural pesticides called neonicotinoids. Some fragmentary, seemingly credible evidence did imply that neonicotinoids *might* be the hive destroyer.[48]

Based on the available, if tentative, evidence, by 2014 a well-organized campaign had been organized by pesticide critics to convince the EPA to immediately prohibit the application of neonicotinoids to agricultural food crops. If EPA's regulatory authority had been based on the precautionary principle, the agency might have had sufficient evidence to suspend application of neonicotinoids to food crops, at least temporarily. However, this would probably have been unwise. Continuing research available by 2016 suggested that neonicotinoids were only one among many plausible causes of CCD, including bee mites, poor management practices, newly emergent diseases, and food crop change. Some scientific journals, popular news media, and respected researchers have proposed that no CCD epidemic exists or that the evidence is more speculative than had been assumed.[49]

The precautionary principle, at the very least, would require policymakers and regulators to learn an unfamiliar way of thinking about risk management. "Teaching ourselves and our leaders a persistent precautionary approach," observes one scientist, "is like learning to tie shoes by following instructions. It's hard to do at first and may require justification, repetition and reassurance."[50]

The Value of Science in Environmental Policymaking

Despite the scientific disputes attending environmental policymaking, it remains important to recognize how often science provides useful and highly reliable guidance to policymakers. Often, the scientific data relevant to an issue clearly point to the adverse effects of substances and define the magnitude of their risks. This was certainly evident in the data leading to the federal government's decision to ban most domestic agricultural uses of the pesticides dichlorodiphenyl-trichloroethane (DDT), aldrin, and dieldrin, for instance. Furthermore, even when one set of data does not alone provide definitive evidence of human risks from exposure to chemicals, numerous studies pointing to the same conclusion taken together can provide almost irrefutable evidence; such was the case in the epidemiological evidence indicting asbestos as a human carcinogen. Often, the reliability of data will be routinely challenged by those opposed to the regulation of some substance, regardless of the ultimate merit—or lack thereof—of their case. In the end, public officials must make decisions on the basis of the best evidence available. For all their limitations, scientific data often enable officials to define more carefully and clearly the range of options, risks, and benefits involved in regulating a substance, even when the data cannot answer all the questions of risk conclusively.

Even if indisputable data were available on the risks of human exposure to all levels of a substance, scientific controversy over the acceptable level would continue. It is asserted sometimes that science should be responsible for determining the magnitudes of risk from exposure to chemicals and that government should define the acceptability. Such a division of labor is rarely possible. Scientists, too, are often drawn into the nettlesome problem of determining what levels of exposure to substances ultimately will be acceptable.

RISK AND DISCRIMINATION: THE PROBLEM OF ENVIRONMENTAL JUSTICE

In October 1997, a jury in New Orleans in a landmark decision awarded $3.4 billion in damages to eight thousand people who had been evacuated a decade previously from their community near a major train route after a tank car filled with the chemical butadiene had caught fire. This award was the largest liability ever assessed in federal court on the basis of environmental discrimination. The fact that most of the plaintiffs lived in a poor, underprivileged neighborhood and thus were exposed to "environmental racism" appeared to have been a major consideration in the jury's generous damage award, even though the plaintiffs' attorneys had only alluded to such racism during the trial. "No one said this is racism," explained one of the lawyers for the neighborhood, "but the facts were such that any commonsense appraisal would tell you that the poorer, underprivileged neighborhood was discriminated against."[51]

It is testimony to the present political potency of the environmental justice movement in the United States that a decade previously the idea of environmental racism had been virtually unknown in public discourse and legal language, let alone as a cause for civil damage claims. Now, issues of environmental justice—or environmental equity—are raised in so many different political and judicial venues that the language has become almost a staple in political discussions involving minorities and health risks. During the Obama presidency, environmental justice was declared an EPA priority. "This is not an issue we can afford to relegate to the margins," asserted EPA Administrator Lisa Jackson. "It has to be part of our thinking in every decision we make."[52]

What Is Environmental Justice?

No consensus exists in law or political debate on the meaning of "environmental justice" or about "environmental equity" and "environmental racism"—two terms often used interchangeably with environmental justice. After considerable difficulty, the EPA in 1994 decided that environmental justice should mean "the fair treatment and meaningful involvement of all people regardless of race, color, national origin, or income with respect to the development, implementation or enforcement of environmental laws, regulations, and policies."[53] In February 1994, President Clinton issued Executive Order 12898, Federal Actions to Address Environmental Justice in Minority Populations and Low-Income Populations, which identified environmental injustice as "disproportionately high and adverse human health or environmental effects created by [executive agency] programs, policies, and activities on minority populations and low-income populations . . ." In contrast, Robert D. Bullard, an environmental justice scholar and leading national advocate for the environmental justice movement, equates environmental justice with the elimination of environmental inequity, which he suggests has at least three implications:[54]

- *Procedural inequity.* The extent to which governing rules, regulations, and evaluation criteria are not applied uniformly. Examples of procedural inequity are holding hearings in remote locations to minimize public participation, stacking boards and commissions with pro-business interests, and using English-only material to communicate to non-English-speaking communities.

- *Geographical inequity.* A situation in which the direct benefits, such as jobs and tax revenues, from industrial production are received by some neighborhoods, communities, and regions, but the costs, such as the burdens of waste disposal, are fixed elsewhere.

- *Social inequity.* The extent to which environmental decisions mirror the power arrangements of the larger society and reflect the still-existing racial bias in the United States. Institutional racism, for instance, influences the siting of noxious facilities, placing many black communities in so-called sacrifice zones.

The concept of environmental justice is commonly evoked in situations in which identifiable minorities have been exposed, deliberately or not, to disproportionate health or safety risks from a known hazard, such as a chemical waste dump or an environment-polluting industrial site. Still, practically every definition of environmental justice or related terms abounds in ambiguities—what, for instance, constitutes a "disproportionate" health risk, and how is "minority" defined?

As these definitions demonstrate, the advocates of environmental justice now use the term or its close relations to embrace an enormous diversity of political and economic practices far surpassing the human health and safety issues traditionally associated with environmental risk. Here are two examples:

- In 2012, the North Carolina Environmental Justice Network collaborated with state water conservation organizations to initiate a lawsuit against a Jones County hog farm that discharged into the Trent and Neuse Rivers the animal wastes from a ten thousand-hog concentrated feeding operation and, the alliance asserted, exposed local residents and river recreationists to excessive and disproportionate risk from waterborne health hazards.[55]

- In Texas, where research suggests Hispanics living near coal-fired electric utilities are disproportionately exposed to hazardous air pollutants, Hispanic environmental justice advocates have joined other state environmental organizations in initiating a vigorous campaign to inform and to mobilize Hispanics for political action, demanding more vigorous state and federal regulatory control over such exposures.[56]

More important than its precise definition, however, is the concept's social impact. The movement has gradually become a potent political force. Its most important impacts have been to compel government attention at all levels to issues of environmental discrimination, to motivate grassroots political movements nationwide that mobilize minorities against apparent environmental discrimination, and to bring environmental discrimination within the scope of judicial concern and remedy.

A Growing Movement

The environmental justice movement achieved major national attention in 1991 when six hundred delegates met in Washington, D.C., at the first National People of Color Environmental Leadership Summit. From its inception, the movement's relationship to mainstream environmental advocacy groups has been ambivalent. The movement assumes a very different social and economic aspect from the predominantly middle-class, white, and relatively affluent organizations dominating U.S. environmental politics. Moreover, the movement's agenda focuses primarily on local communities, toxic and hazardous waste sites, and new organizational identities. At the same time, environmental justice generates a political gravity that can draw minority advocates into a closer political orbit with organized environmentalism. Mainstream environmental organizations have been quick to recognize that environmental justice offers an opportunity to attract economic and racial minorities to the environmental movement and to overcome persistent criticism that environmentalism is or appears to be a "white thing." The Sierra Club's National Environmental Justice and Community Partnerships and the National Resources Defense Council's environmental justice website are two among many illustrations of this strategy. Environmental justice organizations, for their part, often create strategic partnerships with mainstream environmental advocacy groups when this works to their political advantage, yet the movement insists on maintaining an identity apart from mainstream environmentalism.

The Federal Government and Environmental Justice

The environmental justice movement has relied primarily upon three federal enactments to provide a basis for administrative or legal action against governmental or private entities alleged to be responsible for environmental injustice. Two of these measures have been President Clinton's Executive Order 12898, noted earlier, and the EPA's 1994 guidelines for environmental justice (currently called Plan EJ 2014). The executive order requires federal executive agencies to identify and eliminate environmental injustice as part of their mission. While the executive order compels federal administrators to implement a policy of environmental justice, it is also limited because it is not enforceable in court and does not create any rights or remedies.[57] The EPA's Office of Environmental Justice, created also in 1994, has been responsible for promoting the EPA's environmental justice guidelines throughout the agency's organization and programs, although like Executive Order 12898 it neither creates judicially recognizable rights nor authorizes the courts to enforce it. The third foundation for political and legal action, Title VI of the Civil Rights Act (1964), has been interpreted by the federal courts to include a substantive and enforceable right to environmental justice, although Title VI does not mention environmental justice explicitly.

The movement's fundamental conviction that cultural, racial, and ethnic minorities have been exposed disproportionately to health and safety risks throughout the United States has inspired an aggressive campaign to identify and mobilize these minorities, to demand various forms of compensation for those afflicted by such discrimination, and to demand that governmental policymaking be redesigned to weigh issues of environmental equity in environmental policy-making. The movement has been aided powerfully by active support from numerous social action organizations affiliated with many of the nation's major religious denominations. The movement has also been alert to the environmental justice implications of the global climate change issue, and in mid-2000, a new climate justice movement emerged from the organizational base. "Climate change is the most significant social and political challenge of the 21st Century," a leadership manifesto declares, "and the time to act is now." This new climate agenda "must be just, fair, sustainable, and equitable" and should, among other goals, "protect all of America's people regardless of race, gender, nationality, or socioeconomic status and their communities equally from the environmental health, and social impacts, of climate change.[58]

Environmental Justice Organizations and Institutions

The environmental justice movement has grown in size, organizational skill, and political influence. By 2010, one directory listed more than 800 groups (many of these are small and transitory, however).[59] This may, however, greatly underestimate the strength of the movement because it does not include a number of other organizations that have actively adopted environmental justice as a part of their larger agendas in recent years. "The last decade has seen some positive change in the way environmental groups in the United States relate to each other around health, environment, economic, and racial justice," notes a 2011 survey of national environmental justice activism. "An increasing number of community-based groups, networks, university-based centers, environmental and conservation groups, legal groups, faith-based groups, labor, and youth organizations have formed partnerships and collaboratives to address environmental and health issues that differentially impact poor people, people of color, and children. The number of people of color environmental groups has grown from 300 groups in 1992 to more than 3,000 groups and a dozen networks after 2011."[60] The internet has provided a highly congenial and virtually costless venue for network development. Especially significant in enlarging the resource base and intellectual breadth of the environmental justice movement has been the rapid expansion of college- and university-based environmental justice research, teaching, and advocacy centers. Among the earliest of these were the Clark Atlanta University's Environmental Justice Resource Center and the University of Michigan's Environmental Justice Program and Multicultural Environmental Leadership Initiative. By 2011, there were "13 university-based environmental justice centers, four of which are located in Historical Black Colleges and Universities . . . 22 legal clinics that list environmental justice as a core area, and six academic programs that grant degrees in environmental justice, including one legal program."[61] Other professionally related programs include the Energy Justice Network; advocacy specialists in the American Bar Association, the Environmental Law Institute, and other professional legal associations; and a multitude of independent legal and paralegal entities at all government levels. The EPA has maintained a very substantial environmental justice website. Another website creates an environmental justice scorecard for communities, based on federal toxic emissions reports, that "profiles environmental burdens in every community in the U.S., identifying which groups experience disproportionate toxic chemical releases, cancer risks from hazardous air pollutants, or proximity to Superfund sites and polluting facilities emitting smog and particulates."[62] In addition, specialized environmental justice media are increasing, such as the Inner City Press's *Environmental Justice Reporter*. The movement's leadership now embraces virtually all people of color and all the economically disadvantaged within its mission, so that Native Americans, Latinos, and Asians, among other important domestic minorities, are being recruited.

This growing coalition committed to social equity in environmental regulation illustrates why the creation and solution of environmental risks are often inherently a political issue. Since the EPA created its Office of Environmental Justice in 1992, numerous state and local governments have also declared a commitment to environmental justice by law or executive order.

Environmental Justice and the Courts

State and local courts, where such litigation typically originates, have not proven to be a major venue for the environmental justice movement. A major reason is that most states lack appropriate statutory or administrative enactments creating a basis for legally enforceable rights, claims to damage, or other awards based upon evidence of environmental injustice. Only six states, for example, have enacted legislation creating a judicially enforceable right to environmental justice. Nineteen states have not yet enacted any measures to address environmental justice, while the remaining states have taken a variety of actions, such as creating study commissions or state boards to identify issues of environmental injustice and to promote their resolution.[63]

The federal courts, however, have been more receptive to litigation based on claims of environmental injustice, based primarily upon Title VI of the Civil Rights Act (1964), which prohibits major forms of discrimination against racial, ethnic, national, and religious minorities and women.[64] Using Title VI for leverage, environmental justice advocates have achieved modest but important progress in enforcing civil rights, criminal penalties, and civil financial awards against public and private institutions based upon claims of discrimination based upon environmental evidence. The EPA, for instance, is among many federal agencies that have used the Civil Rights Act as well as President Clinton's executive order to initiate environmental justice activities.

Administrative Challenges

Administering laws that mandate environmental justice has been labored and controversial from its inception. Stakeholders may agree on its necessity, yet translating environmental justice into public policy—like implementing other public laws—can manufacture formidable obstacles between the word and the deed.

Laggard Federal Initiative. One major obstacle has been the frequent lack of resources and irresolution among federal agencies to implement their environmental justice mandates. The EPA, in particular, has constantly struggled with impediments, not all of its own creation, in enforcing its environmental justice regulations and Executive Order 12898. At the beginning of the Obama administration, eighteen years after Clinton's Executive Order, a very careful review of EPA's implementation concluded that the EPA had "repeatedly and systematically failed to incorporate environmental justice considerations into core programs and decision-making."[65] These problems promoted Obama's Administrator Lisa Jackson's promise of "a full-scale revitalization" of the environmental justice program.[66] Some of these problems arose from White House failures to fund generously the agency's environmental justice activists and from the meager data sometimes available to characterize environmental justice conditions.

By 2015, the prospects for implementation of Executive Order 12898 seemed to improve significantly. For the first time in two decades, the EPA was taking significant new steps to translate Clinton's Executive Order 12898 into future routines. If consistently implemented, a number of new agency policies and guidance directives "could together create real momentum toward improving environmental conditions in minority and low-income communities."[67] Often, however, continual pressure by environmental justice organizations has been required to compel careful attention to environmental justice issues at the EPA and other federal agencies. Moreover, the vigor of EPA's environmental justice program seemed problematic after the Trump administration initially proposed to eliminate the program and subsequently reduced its staff and budget substantially.[68]

The Challenge of Data Quality. Scientific data relevant to environmental justice problems has been improving significantly since the mid-1990s. Demographic data now demonstrate clearly enough that many millions of Americans live dangerously close to toxic facilities and that "the people who live in 'fence-line zones' closest to such facilities are disproportionately African American and Latino and are also more likely to be of low income."[69] Nonetheless, almost all discourse about environmental justice—whatever the venue—is still likely to ignite controversy over the scientific basis of claims to environmental injustice.[70]

Fragmentary evidence accumulating for decades and more deliberate studies in recent years often seem to demonstrate that minorities and poor individuals are disproportionately exposed to health risks from environmental pollutants because of their residence.[71] Several studies have suggested as much; for example, one Detroit, Michigan, survey, cited by sociologists Paul Mohai and Bunyan Bryant, indicated that "minority residents in the metropolitan area are four times more likely than white residents to live within a mile of a commercial hazardous waste facility."[72]

Still, having a hazardous facility as a neighbor does not preclude challenging problems in assembling and interpreting the social, economic, and scientific data essential as evidence of environmental injustice. One problem is the frequent difficulty of obtaining basic information about population exposures to environmental risks that is sufficiently rich in detail and covering long-enough periods to satisfy the requirements of common risk assessment methods. With the exception of lead exposure, little reliable evidence existed before 2000 about the specific relationship of race or class to environmental health measures. Moreover, even when considerable evidence exists that disadvantaged populations have frequently experienced higher levels of exposure and risk from environmental hazards when compared to more advantaged groups, the data concerning the long-term health impacts are often meager or missing.

Additionally, it is difficult with existing data to demonstrate that adverse health impacts among disadvantaged populations exposed to environmental hazards are caused primarily or in significant measure from these exposures among the many other plausible causes of ill health.[73] Especially when there is a possibility of population exposure to multiple environmental hazards—a situation quite common in minority communities—the appropriate scientific protocols for estimating individual or population exposure have seldom existed. An additional obstacle is demonstrating that economic or racial minorities have been exposed deliberately to disproportionate environmental risks or that risk exposures were assumed involuntarily. It may be argued in political debate and courtrooms that individuals exposed to environmental risks often move to their residences deliberately and with knowledge of the environmental risks so that the environmental exposures were voluntary.

Finally, difficulties arise over the appropriate strategies for identifying how risks may be distributed unfairly in environmental regulation and how this inequity can be solved. Over how long a period, for example, should risk estimates be made? Which populations qualify as disadvantaged? To what extent should the ability of individuals to protect themselves from such risks be taken into account? What sort of environmental risks should be included? How can such issues be introduced early enough in the regulatory decision-making process to influence the outcomes?

For environmental justice advocates, however, the available evidence of injustice seems convincing if not overwhelming. For example, a policy paper by one major advocacy group begins, "Although communities of color, tribes and indigenous peoples, and the poor have been heavily and disproportionately affected by noxious risk producing environmental practices for decades," as if stating common knowledge.[74] At the other extreme, Christopher H. Foreman Jr. of the Brookings Institution completed an extensive study of claims made by environmental justice advocates and concluded that

> [W]hen you clear away all the smoke blown over risk and racism in recent years, there turns out to be remarkably little good evidence indicating that low-income and minority citizens regularly bear a disproportionate share of society's environmental risk, much less that they develop pollution related illnesses more often than other citizens.[75]

Environmental Justice and Politics:
The Case of Flint, Michigan

Surveying these difficulties, critics have argued that the environmental justice agenda is ultimately a means to much broader political ends. The movement's political potency, so the argument runs, is grounded less on scientific credibility than on the capacity of its grassroots organizers to mobilize minorities and to articulate deeply rooted historical social grievances for which environmental issues are often symbolic. "It effectively speaks to the fear and anger among local communities feeling overwhelmed by forces beyond their control, and outraged by what they perceive to be assaults on their collective quality of life," Foreman concludes.[76] To the movement's leadership, such assertions are likely to appear to be an effort to deflect attention from the evidence of environmental injustice by implicitly attacking the motivation of its leaders.

A municipal water pollution crisis beginning in 2014 in Flint, Michigan, a city 57 percent black, quickly enlarged into a national media drama illustrating the complex crosscurrents of political, scientific, and governmental conflict frequently complicating environmental justice issues. From the beginning, the problem was embedded with disputes about the scientific credibility of the evidence, about which government entities were responsible for the problem and its solution, and about the political motives of the civic activists who asserted that environmental injustice had been created.[77]

The crisis began when Flint's city managers switched the city's municipal water supply in 2014 from the Detroit River to the Flint River to save millions of dollars and avert a municipal financial collapse. Almost immediately, complaints appeared among Flint households, and soon reached local media, about health problems associated with exposure to the water: rashes, hair loss, nausea, offensive odors, and more. Most of the health problems involved black residents.

Local and state officials, including environmental and health administrators, initially discounted the complaints, citing cold weather, aging pipes, population decline, and public misunderstanding of Flint's apparent water quality problems. Some state environmental regulators implied that local black civic activists were turning the lead exposure into a "political football" by claiming environmental injustice to create broader political support and by distorting the scientific facts. Other officials claimed the problem was exaggerated by an "anti-everything group."[78]

When bacterial water contamination appeared in some neighborhoods in October 2014, public health officials recommended that residents temporarily boil water while the infestation was removed. Still, water quality declined and national media attention increased. When Flint's General Motors plant refused in October to use municipal water because it corroded car parts, local civic activists brought increasing pressure on city and state public officials to analyze Flint's water quality thoroughly and to eliminate its water pollutants rapidly.

Throughout 2015, the magnitude of Flint's water pollution became increasingly evident and alarming. Dangerous concentrations of lead were discovered in several neighborhood water systems and then in blood samples drawn from Flint schoolchildren. The pollution issue was compounded by disagreement between state and local environmental officials over the credibility of the evidence and responsibility for the problem, even as independent scientific experts warned that the lead pollution was a serious public health issue. By September 2015, local physicians recommended that the city immediately end consumption of Flint River water, and in October 2015 the city water system reconnected to the Detroit River. Two months later, Flint officials declared a health emergency, and in January 2016, President Obama declared a state of emergency in Flint and enabled federal aid for the city and surrounding county. Local civic activists continue to seek health care and compensation for residents who were chronically exposed to Flint's contaminated municipal drinking water.

Despite its critics, the environmental justice movement now claims a salience on the agenda of national environmental policy that is unlikely to decline in the near future. For the nation's governments, one of the most daunting challenges is to find a way to effectively translate lofty goals, such as environmental equity or environmental justice, into specific policy procedures and specific governmental actions. How to bring environmental justice to the desktop and conference table of routine governmental regulation? It seems evident that a successful policy translation will require, at least, the rapid development of a science base, which means acquiring and disseminating information about the exposure of minority populations to specific environmental hazards and developing reliable methodologies for estimating individual and population risks from such exposure. Administrative law and procedure must be modified in detail and depth so that considerations of inequitable environmental risk can be considered in a timely and explicit manner in regulatory decision-making. Converting prescription into practice will be arduous, however, in light of the current disagreement on appropriate metrics for measuring discrimination and equity and on the degree of difference among populations that constitutes inequity.

CONCLUSION

The complex new problems of risk assessment in environmental regulation confirm that we live in a historically unique era of technocratic power. U.S. science and industry, in common with those of other advanced industrial nations, now possess the capacity to alter in profound but often unpredictable ways the biochemical basis of future human life and thus to change future ecosystems radically. In its extreme form, represented by nuclear weapons, modern technology has the power to eradicate human society, if not humanity itself. But modern technologies also can alter the future ecosphere in a multitude of less dramatic but significant ways: through the deliberate redesign of genetic materials in human reproduction, through the depletion of irreplaceable energy resources such as petroleum or natural gas, through the multiplication of long-lived hazardous substances whose biological impacts on humans and the ecosystem may magnify through hundreds of years, and many more. We are practically the first generation in the world's history with the certain technical capacity to alter and even to destroy the fundamental biochemical and geophysical conditions for societies living centuries after ours. It is, as one social prophet noted, a power that people of the Middle Ages did not even credit to devils.

With this new technocratic power comes the ability to develop technologies, to manufacture new substances, and to deplete finite resources so that the benefits are largely distributed in the present and the risks, for the most part, are displaced into the future. Future societies may inherit most of the burden to create the social, economic, and political institutions necessary for managing the risks inherent in this generational cost transfer. Such technical capacity can become an exercise of power undisciplined by responsibility for the consequences.

This transfer of risk raises fundamental ethical and social questions for government. Should public institutions be compelled in some formal and explicit way to exercise regard for the future impact of decisions concerning environmental management today? And if so, how much regard? When deciding whether to develop dangerous technologies, should government be forced, if necessary, to consider not only the future ecological implications of these technologies but also the ability of future societies to create institutions capable of controlling them?

This issue is significant, because government and economic institutions have a tendency to discount the future impacts of new technologies or newly developed chemicals when compared with the immediate impacts. In economic terms, this is done in formal cost–benefit analysis by discounting future benefits and costs rather substantially. In political terms, it amounts to adopting a strategy that favors taking environmental actions on the basis of short-term political advantage rather than long-term consequences. (Elected officials, especially, often treat as gospel the legendary advice of a former House speaker to a new colleague: Remember that when it comes time to vote, most folks want to know, "What have you done for me lately?") It is particularly difficult for public officials to develop a sensitive regard for the distant future when there are no apparent political rewards for doing so. At some time, the political cynic in practically all public officials whispers, "What has posterity done for you lately?"

Suggested Readings

Foreman, Christopher H. *The Promise and Peril of Environmental Justice.* Washington, DC: Brookings Institution Press, 1998.

Hanna-Attisha, Mona. *What the Eyes Don't See.* New York: One World Publishers, 2018.

Keller, Ann Campbell. *Science in Environmental Policy: The Politics of Objective Advice.* Cambridge, MA: MIT Press, 2009.

Konisky, David M., ed. *Failed Promises: Evaluating the Federal Government's Response to Environmental Justice.* Cambridge, MA: MIT Press, 2015.

Margolis, Howard. *Dealing With Risk: Why the Public and the Experts Disagree on Environmental Issues.* Chicago: University of Chicago Press, 1997.

Mitchell, Sandra D. *Unsimple Truths: Science, Complexity, and Policy.* Chicago: University of Chicago Press, 2009.

National Research Council. *Science and Decisions: Advancing Risk Assessment.* Washington, DC: National Academies Press, 2009.

Smith, Rick, and Bruce Lourie. *Slow Death by Rubber Duck.* Knopf Canada, 2019.

Notes

1. Matthew L. Wald, "Chemical Element of Vinyl Toys Causes Liver Damage in Lab Rats," *New York Times,* November 13, 1998, A20.
2. Matthew L. Wald, "Citing Possible Dangers, Groups Seek Ban on Vinyl Toys," *New York Times,* November 20, 1998, A24; Scott Allen, "IV Bag Hazards Are Alleged; Trace Toxins Found, Interest Groups Say," *Boston Globe,* February 22, 1999, A3.
3. Andrea Foster and Peter Fairley, "Phthalates Pay the Price for Uncertainty," *Chemical Week,* February 17, 1999, 54.
4. Ibid.
5. David Kohn, "New Questions About Common Chemicals," *Newsday,* March 3, 2003, available at www.ourstolenfuture.org/Commentary/News/2003/2003-0304-Newsday-phthalates.htm.
6. Steven Milloy, "A Toy Story," *Tech Central Station,* February 25, 2003, available at www.techcentralstation.com/022503C.html.
7. Seth Borenstein, "Study Links Chemical to Changes in the Womb," *Albany Times-Union,* May 27, 2005, A1; "Plastics," *Houston Chronicle,* June 3, 2005, B10.
8. National Academy of Sciences, Committee on Health Risks, *Phthalates and Cumulative Risk Assessment: The Task Ahead, Report in Brief* (Washington, DC: National Academy Press, 2008).
9. American Chemistry Council, "ACC Believes Amendment to Consumer Products Safety Commission Reform Act Will Not Produce Benefits Envisioned by Authors," March 5, 2008, available at http://phthalates.americanchemistry.com/Media-Room/News/Consumer-Products-Safety-Commission-Reform-Act.

10. Brandan P. Mueller, Robert Stang, and Glennon Fogarty, "New Federal Safety Standard Proposed for Phthalates in Children's Toys and Certain Child Care Products," *Technology, Manufacturing and Transportation Industry Insider*, available at http://www.tmtindustryinsider.com/2015/02/new-fed eral-safety-standard-proposed-for-phthalates-in-childrens-toys-and-cer tain-child-care-articles/.

11. David Oliver, "Health Buzz: Controversial Chemicals Found in Macaroni and Cheese Products, Report Says," *U.S. News & World Report*, available at https:// health.usnews.com/wellness/health-buzz/articles/2017-07-13/report -controversial-chemicals-found-in-macaroni-and-cheese-products.

12. National Academy of Public Administration, *Setting Priorities, Getting Results: A New Direction for EPA* (Washington, DC: Author, 1995), chap. 3.

13. "Executive Order 12866—Regulatory Planning and Review," *Federal Register*, October 4, 1993.

14. For a general discussion of the political and administrative setting of risk assessment, see Committee on Risk Assessment of Hazardous Air Pollutants, National Research Council, *Science and Judgment in Risk Assessment* (Washington, DC: National Academies Press, 1994), chap. 2.

15. GAO, "Chemical Risk Assessment: Selected Federal Agencies' Procedures, Assumptions and Policies," Report no. GAO-01-810, Washington, DC, August 2001, 14.

16. Ibid.

17. See CEQ, *Environmental Quality, 1979* (Washington, DC: CEQ, 1980), esp. 194.

18. Ibid.

19. Gregory Zuckerman, "Specter of Costly Asbestos Litigation Haunts Old Economy Companies," *Wall Street Journal*, December 27, 2000, A3; Alex Berenson, "A Surge of Asbestos Suits, Many by Healthy Plaintiffs," *New York Times*, April 10, 2002, A1.

20. On the controversy over dioxin, see John A. Moore, Renate D. Kimbrough, and Michael Gough, "The Dioxin TCDD: A Selective Study of Science and Policy Interaction," in *Keeping Pace With Science and Engineering: Case Studies in Environmental Regulation*, ed. Myron F. Ulman (Washington, DC: National Academies Press, 1993), 221–242.

21. Ibid.

22. Quoted in Keith Schneider, "Times Beach Warning: Regrets a Decade Later," *New York Times*, August 15, 1991, D23.

23. Keith Schneider, "Panel of Scientists Finds Dioxin Does Not Pose Widespread Cancer Threat," *New York Times*, September 26, 1992, D20.

24. Joel Brinkley, "Many Say Lab-Animal Tests Fail to Measure Human Risk," *New York Times*, March 23, 1993, D20.

25. Cindy Skrzycki and Joby Warrick, "EPA Links Dioxin to Cancer; Risk Estimate Raised Tenfold," *Washington Post*, May 17, 2000, A1.

26. Ibid.

27. National Research Council, *Health Risks from Dioxin and Related Compounds: Evaluation of the EPA Assessment* (Washington, DC: National Academies Press, 2006). See also "EPA Assessment of Dioxin Understates Uncertainty About Health Risks and May Overstate Human Cancer Risk," *National Academies News*, July 11, 2006, available at www.nationalacademies.org/onpinews/newsitem.aspx?RecordID=11688.

28. "EPA Administrator Pledges Strong Federal Cleanup Presence at Dow Dioxin Site in Michigan and Accelerated Assessment of Dioxins' Human Health Impacts," May 26, 2009, available at https://archive.epa.gov/epa pages/newsroom_archive/newsreleases/3ffa6e8e70763f28852575c20064b 26b.html.

29. On the general problems of animal experiments, see David D. Doniger, *The Law and Policy of Toxic Substances Control* (Baltimore: Johns Hopkins University Press, 1978), pt. I.

30. Animal data are cited in Philip M. Boffey, "The Debate over Dioxin," *New York Times*, June 25, 1983, A10.

31. Ibid.

32. Harvey Brooks, "The Resolution of Technically Intensive Public Policy Disputes," *Science, Technology, and Human Values* 9 (Winter 1984): 40. For estimates of discretionary judgments in risk assessment, see National Research Council, Commission on Life Sciences, Committee on the Institutional Means for Assessment of Risks to Public Health, *Risk Assessment in the Federal Government: Managing the Process* (Washington, DC: National Academies Press, 1983), chap. 1.

33. Frances M. Lynn, "The Interplay of Science and Values in Assessing and Regulating Environmental Risks," *Science, Technology, and Human Values* 11 (Spring 1986): 40–50.

34. Thomas M. Dietz and Robert W. Rycroft, *The Risk Professionals* (New York: Russell Sage, 1987), 111.

35. A comprehensive review of the various statutory standards for risk in federal law is found in John J. Cohrssen and Vincent T. Covello, *Risk Analysis: A Guide to Principles and Methods for Analyzing Health and Environmental Risks* (Washington, DC: Council on Environmental Quality, 1989), 14–15; see also Walter A. Rosenbaum, "Regulation at Risk: The Controversial Politics and Science of Comparative Risk Assessment," in *Flashpoints in Environmental Policymaking: Controversies in Achieving Sustainability*, ed. Sheldon Kamieniecki, George A. Gonzalez, and Robert O. Vos (Albany, NY: SUNY Press, 1997), 31–62.

36. This analysis is based on National Academy of Public Administration, *Setting Priorities, Getting Results*, chap. 3.

37. In contrast, the Food Quality Protection Act (1996) requires, very precisely, that the EPA must set the standard to protect infants and children from allowable pesticide residues in food at ten times the safety factor for adults unless reliable data show that a different factor would be safe.

38. CEQ, *Environmental Quality, 1979*, 218.
39. An agency sometimes invites litigation. By interpreting the manner in which risk determinations should be made by agencies, judges often dissipate the fog of uncertainty about congressional intent and provide agencies with firm guidelines for future determinations.
40. A sampling of this literature may be found in the collection of articles by Peter Lewin, Gerald L. Sauer, Bernard L. Cohen, Richard N. Langlois, and Aaron Wildavsky in *Cato Symposium on Pollution*, special issue of *Cato Journal* 2 (Spring 1982).
41. Ibid.
42. The CPSRA—the 2008 legislation that Congress intended to resolve the phthalate controversy mentioned at the beginning of this chapter—does contain a rare example of the precautionary principle in national environmental legislation.
43. Science and Environmental Health Network, "Wingspread Conference on the Precautionary Principle," January 26, 1998, available at www.sehn.org/wing.html.
44. Stephen G. Wood, Stephen Q. Wood, and Rachel A. Wood, "Whither the Precautionary Principle? An American Assessment From an Administrative Law Perspective," *American Journal of Comparative Law* 54, suppl. (Fall 2006): 581–610.
45. Ronald Bailey, "Precautionary Tale," *Reason Magazine*, April 1999, available at http://reason.com/archives/1999/04/01/precautionary-tale.
46. Heather Pilatic, *Pesticides and Honey Bees: State of the Science* (San Francisco, CA: Pesticide Action Network of North America, 2012), available at www.panna.org; and U.S. EPA, "Colony Collapse Disorder," available at http://www2.epa.gov/pollinator-protection/colony-collapse-disorder.
47. Bryan Walsh, "The Price We'll Pay If We Don't Figure Out What's Killing the Honeybee," *Time*, August 19, 2013, available at http://time.com/559/the-plight-of-the-honeybee/.
48. EPA, *Pesticides and Honey Bees.*
49. EPA, *Pesticides and Honey Bees*: Genetic Literacy Project, "There's No Wild Bee Colony Collapse Either," *Science 2.0*, available at http://www.science20.com/genetic_literacy_project/theres_no_wild_bee_colony_collapse_either-156960; Jon Entine, "Neonicotinoids and the Beepocalypse That Never Was," *Science 2.0*, available at http://www.science20.com/jon_entine/neonicotinoids_and_the_beepocalypse_that_never_was-156551; Patterson Clark, "We All Get Stung By Bee Colony Collapse," *Washington Post*, May 18, 2015, available at https://www.washingtonpost.com/apps/g/page/national/we-all-get-stung-by-bee-colony-collapse/1108.
50. Nancy Myers, "Introduction," in *Precautionary Tools for Reshaping Environmental Policy*, ed. Nancy Myers and Carolyn Raffensperger (Cambridge, MA: MIT Press, 2004), 12.
51. Quoted in *Wall Street Journal*, October 29, 1997, B3.

52. Lisa P. Jackson, "Remarks to the National Environmental Justice Advisory Council, as Prepared 07/21/2009," available at http://yosemite.epa.gov/opa/admpress.nsf/dff15a5d01abdfb1852573590040b7f7/313ec9a2bc80d6778525 75fa007b3c42!OpenDocument.

53. EPA, "Environmental Justice," available at. https://www3.epa.gov/environmentaljustice/.

54. Robert D. Bullard, "Waste and Racism: A Stacked Deck?" *Forum for Applied Research and Public Policy* 8 (Spring 1993): 29–35. On the general problems of defining environmental justice, see Evan J. Rinquist, "Environmental Justice: Normative Concerns and Empirical Evidence," in *Environmental Policy in the 1990s,* 3rd ed., ed. Norman J. Vig and Michael E. Kraft (Washington, DC: CQ Press, 1997), 231–254; EPA, Office of Policy, Planning, and Evaluation, *Environmental Equity: Reducing Risk for All Communities, Vol. 1: Workgroup Report to the Administrator* (Washington, DC: Author, June 1992), 1.

55. Anne Blythe, "Environmental Groups Say 10,000-Hog Farm Pollutes Waterways," *Charlotte News & Observer,* August 6, 2012, available at https://www.organicconsumers.org/news/environmental-groups-say -10000-hog-farm-pollutes-waterways.

56. "Air Pollution: An Environmental Justice Issue for Hispanics," *Texas Vox,* June 29, 2011, available at http://www.texasvox.org/air-pollution-an -environmental-justice-issue-for-hispanics/.

57. EPA, Office of Civil Rights, "Title VI and Environmental Justice at EPA," available at http://www.epa.gov/ocr/t6andej.htm.

58. Environmental Justice Leadership Forum on Climate Change, "Principles of Climate Justice," November 2009, available at http://www.ejleadershipfo rum.org/ej-forum-principles-of-climate-change/.

59. Environmental Justice Resource Center, "People of Color in the United States and Puerto Rico," *People of Color Environmental Groups Directory* (Flint, MI: C. W. Mott Foundation, 2000), chap. 4; Multicultural Environmental Leadership Development Initiative, "Directory of Environmental Justice Organizations," available at http://meldi.snre.umich.edu/ej_orgs.

60. Robert D. Bullard, Glenn S. Johnson, and Angel O. Torres, *The State of Environmental Justice in the United States Since Summit II: Timeline-Milestones 2002–2011* (April 2011): 5, available at https://www.greenbiz.com/news/2000/07/05/people-color-environmental-groups-directory.

61. Ibid, 5.

62. Scorecard, the Pollution Information Site, available at http://scorecard.org/.

63. Patricia A. Robert, "The State of the States: Progress in Environmental Justice Law and Policy?" presented at The State of Environmental Justice in America 2007 Conference, Washington, DC, March 29–31, 2007; and Julie Sze, "The State of the States: Environmental Justice Programs," University of California (2004), commissioned by the Ford Foundation, available at ej.ucdavis.edu/includes/docs/Sze_WhitePaper.pdf.

64. Uma Outka, "NEPA and Environmental Justice: Integration, Implementation and Judicial Review," *Boston College Environmental Affairs Law Review* vol. 33, no. 3 (2006): 601–625.

65. David M. Konisky, *The Challenge of Achieving Environmental Protection for All*, Scholars Strategy Network, May 2015, available at http://thesocietypages .org/ssn/2015/07/01/environmental-protection-for-all/.

66. See, for example, GAO, "Environmental Justice: EPA Should Devote More Attention to Environmental Justice When Developing Clean Air Rules," Report no. GAO 05-289, Washington, DC, July 5, 2005, 10.

67. Ibid.

68. David Konisky, "Will We Reverse the Little Progress We've Made on Environmental Justice?" *The Conversation*, April 16, 2017, available at http:// theconversation.com/will-we-reverse-the-little-progress-weve-made-on -environmental-justice-76120.

69. Derrick Z. Jackson, *Environmental Justice? Unjust Coverage of the Flint Water Crisis* (Cambridge, MA: Shorenstein Center on Media, Politics and Public Policy, 2017), p. 4.

70. See, for example, Anita Milman, "Geographic Pollution Mapping of Power Plant Emissions to Inform Ex-Ante Environmental Justice Analyses," *Journal of Environmental Planning and Management* 49 (July 2006): 587–604; Paul Mohai and Robin Saha, "Reassessing Racial and Socioeconomic Disparities in Environmental Justice Research," *Demography,* 43 (May 2006): 383–399.

71. Ivette Perfecto and Baldemar Valazquez, "Farm Workers: Among the Least Protected," *EPA Journal,* 18 (March–April 1992): 13–14; Dee R. Wernette and Leslie A. Nieves, "Breathing Polluted Air," *EPA Journal* 18 (March–April 1992): 16–17.

72. Paul Mohai and Bunyan Bryant, "Race, Poverty, and the Environment," *EPA Journal* 18 (March–April 1992): 8.

73. See, for example, Robert J. Brulle and David N. Pellow, "Environmental Justice: Human Health and Environmental Inequalities," *Annual Review of Public Health* 2006, 103–124; Jean D. Brender, Juliana A. Maantay, and Jayajit Chakraborty, "Residential Proximity to Environmental Hazards and Adverse Health Outcomes," *American Journal of Public Health* 101, no. S1 (2011): S37–S52; and Onyemaechi C. Nweke, Devon Payne-Sturges, Lisa Garcia, et al., "Symposium on Integrating the Science of Environmental Justice Into Decision-Making at the Environmental Protection Agency: An Overview," *American Journal of Public Health* vol. 102, no. S1 (September 2011): S19–S26.

74. Eileen Gauna, Sheila Foster, Carmen Gonzalez, Lisa Heinzerling, Catherine O'Neill, Clifford Rechtschaffen, and Robert R. M. Verchick, "CPR Perspective: Environmental Justice at Stake," Center for Progressive Reform, available at www.progressiveregulation.org/perspectives/environjustice.cfm.

75. Christopher H. Foreman Jr., "The Clash of Purposes: Environmental Justice and Risk Assessment," Brookings Institution: Social Policy, March 20,

1988, available at http://www.brookings.edu/research/articles/1998/03/20 environment-foreman.

76. Foreman, "Clash of Purposes."

77. "Events That Led to Flint's Water Crisis," *New York Times*, January 21, 2016, available at https://www.nytimes.com/interactive/2016/01/21/us/flint-lead -water-timeline.html.

78. John Eligon, "A Question of Environmental Racism in Flint," *New York Times*, January 22, 2016, A1.

MORE CHOICE

The Battle Over Regulatory Economics

Donald Trump had been president only ten days when he dramatized his new domestic policy agenda before the national media by signing with theatrical gesture an executive order "On Reducing Regulation and Controlling Regulatory Costs."[1] Trump's assault upon the costs of governmental regulation had been unceasing throughout his presidential campaign. He had condemned what he called the "ever-growing maze of regulations, rules, restrictions [that have] cost our country trillions and trillions of dollars, millions of jobs, countless American factories, and devastated many industries."[2] And no federal agency was more often denounced for this regulatory cost inflation than the EPA. Trump's promised regulatory rollback at EPA had been the political capital that secured massive support for his presidency from the nation's business sector and demonstrated how firmly economic controversy has become inevitable in any discussion of national environmental policymaking. Debate over the economic rationality of environmental regulation has not ceased since the first Earth Day. Critics, including many economists, assert that both the process and the objectives of current environmental regulation have been flawed by economic inefficiency, irrationality, and contradiction. Environmentalists and many other economists, among others, believe that economic arguments are often inappropriate, if not deliberately deceptive, when used by critics to evaluate environmental policies.

Although some environmental regulations are very costly, the total public cost of regulation to the United States appears reasonable. Spending for environmental programs, including regulation, constituted about 1 percent of the total federal budget in FY 2017, less than expenditures for Housing and Communities, Transportation, Education, and Food and Agriculture, and much less than the massive allocations for Medicare, Health, Social Security, Unemployment and Labor—these latter entitlement programs altogether accounted for more than 60 percent of all federal spending.[3] However, controversy about the compliance costs and public benefit from environmental regulation is one of the great holy wars of environmental politics, unceasing since the first Earth Day.

Most federal government estimates of the economic impact from environmental regulation conclude that the collective benefits far exceed the costs. A White House Office of Management and Budget (OMB) review of environmental regulatory benefits and costs between 2006 and 2016, for instance, estimated environmental regulatory costs conservatively of $54 billion and benefits at $196 billion.[4] Regulated interests, including not only the private sector but often state and local governments, frequently dispute the accuracy of these and other favorable estimates of regulations' economic impact. Regulated private interests, especially the manufacturing and electric utility sectors, have been vehement critics of EPA's environmental regulations. Compliance costs for such regulated sectors can often be substantial. For example, EPA's own estimate of the annual cost to regulated business for compliance with its 2011 national emission standards for hazardous air pollutants from coal- and oil-fired electric utilities are $8.2 billion.[5]

While proponents of environmental regulation argue that the long-term economic and social benefits—especially for public health—more than offset such imposed costs, troubling problems arise. Could the same or better results— perhaps far better—be achieved much less expensively? Could regulated business also save considerable money and invest it in more socially productive activities? Might better results be had by switching to a different form of regulation? As regulatory costs and dissatisfaction over regulatory achievements mount, even the environmental movement, traditionally hostile to proposals for economic reform, has felt compelled to examine critically the economic basis of current environmental laws. The debate can whirl into mind-numbing complexity that only an economist could love, but the answers may powerfully shape future environmental regulation, and the major issues, at least, are clear.

Controversy has traditionally focused on two issues: the use of BCA (benefit–cost analysis) as a major criterion in writing environmental regulations and the effectiveness of marketplace incentives rather than the current command-and-control methods for securing compliance with environmental standards. This chapter looks at these issues, beginning with a discussion of the BCA controversy, followed by a brief description of the command-and-control approach to regulation and a comparison with some proposed alternatives.

THE BENEFIT–COST DEBATE

In theory, BCA seems simple and straightforward. Essentially, it is a process by which federal agencies (usually regulators such as the EPA) compare the net benefits and costs of a proposed action—usually a regulatory law—to determine whether the benefits exceed the costs. Using this procedure, they can also compare alternative proposals to determine which is the more economically desirable. BCA is a constant issue in environmental regulation, because a common complaint about almost all environmental regulations written since 1970 is that the congressionally mandated procedures for setting environmental standards are too often insensitive to costs. "Cost-oblivious" laws, such as portions of the CAA or the Occupational Safety and Health Act, in which benefit–cost considerations are explicitly forbidden as regulatory criteria, are cited as examples of legislatively ordained disregard for the economic consequences of regulation. Other laws, such as the RCRA (Resource Conservation and Recovery Act of 1976), have been criticized for failing to require specifically that regulatory agencies consider costs, among other factors, in setting environmental standards. In the view of critics, this mandated indifference toward BCA breeds a carelessness about costs among regulators that inflicts economic penalties on regulated interests. Even when Congress has permitted or required some kind of BCA in regulatory decision making, critics assert that, too often, agencies can ignore the results or treat them as a formality.[6]

A Long and Contentious History

The conflict over BCA resonates throughout U.S. regulatory history. Every administration since John F. Kennedy's has attempted to use some institutional arrangement to promote sensitivity to economic costs and benefits in regulatory policymaking by federal agencies.

The Battle Over Regulatory Impact Analyses. Ronald Reagan, whose administration was viewed by environmentalists with nearly unanimous disfavor, initiated the most aggressive effort to promote BCA in environmental policymaking with Executive Order 12291. The executive order, issued practically the day Reagan was inaugurated, required all federal agencies to prepare a type of BCA, called a Regulatory Impact Analysis (RIA), for any major, new regulatory proposals to demonstrate that the benefit of such proposals would exceed the anticipated costs. Reagan's order unleashed a prolonged, bitter conflict among ideological supporters of Reagan's so-called regulatory reform in Congress, the executive agencies, and the business community on one side and environmentalists, most congressional members, and other White House critics on the other.

Bill Clinton's administration appeared to put the BCA controversy to rest, at least temporarily, when Clinton issued Executive Order 12866 in September 1993, significantly relaxing the requirements for the preparation and review of RIAs in federal agencies and greatly diminishing the OMB's role in the process, much to the satisfaction of environmentalists. Nonetheless, the new order still required federal agencies to prepare and review BCAs frequently, insisting that they remain a formal part of regulatory procedure.

The Second Generation of Benefit–Cost Analysis. By the time of George W. Bush's inauguration in 2000, BCA in the form of RIAs had come to stay in environmental regulation. The White House and Congress now accepted the idea that RIAs (or another form of BCA) should be considered frequently, if not routinely, when the EPA or other regulatory agencies proposed new environmental regulations. As Cass Sunstein notes, the second-generation debate raises

> difficult questions about how (not whether) to engage in cost–benefit analysis—how to value life and health, how to deal with the interests of future generations, how to generate rules of thumb to simplify complex inquiries . . . how and when to diverge from the conclusion recommended by cost–benefit analysis. . . .[7]

In his second term, George W. Bush refueled the BCA controversy with Executive Order 13422, which mandated the most substantial and (critics claimed) most aggressive benefit–cost assault on environmental regulations since Ronald Reagan ordained RIAs. Environmentalists charged that Bush's revised benefit–cost mandate amounted to a White House power grab at environmental regulation. The new RIA makeover, however, gained little traction, because the Obama administration quickly nullified its impact with the new Executive Order 13422 in February 2009, largely restoring the earlier Clinton rules and mandating another review of the RIA process.

Many Varieties of Benefit–Cost Analysis. If calculate they must, what kind of BCA should environmental agencies use? Every federal environmental law currently requires or permits a somewhat different approach to BCA. The one certainty is that no current federal law compels the EPA or any other environmental regulator to adopt or reject a proposed regulation solely on the basis of a benefit–cost calculation. One federal law, the CAA, prohibits the EPA from basing any air-quality standards on a consideration of cost. Some federal laws, such as the Safe Drinking Water Act (1974), require the EPA to "consider" benefits and costs when contemplating new regulations; other statutes, such as the Occupational Safety and Health Act, may instruct regulators to consider only regulations that are "economically feasible"; and still others may allow the regulatory agency to consider benefits and costs among other factors when writing regulations, without specifying how much importance the economic considerations ought to assume.[8] It is hardly surprising, then, that environmental regulatory agencies approach BCA in different ways. Sometimes, the same agency must use a different approach to BCA depending on which law is being enforced. Most economists and other regulatory experts believe that, at the very least, the current jumble of procedures for BCA requires radical simplification.

Despite all the differences, a few important common issues arise in virtually all approaches to BCA. These issues concern the general merits of BCA and the procedures by which benefits and costs are calculated.

The Case for Benefit–Cost Analysis

A number of advantages are claimed for BCA. Many regulatory experts believe that BCA can greatly assist Congress and regulatory agencies in setting priorities for pollution control by identifying which regulations are the most economically desirable. "By drawing attention to costs and benefits," argues Sunstein, "it should be possible to spur the most obviously desirable regulations, to deter the most obviously undesirable ones, to encourage a broader view of consequences, and to promote a search for least-cost methods of achieving regulatory goals."[9]

Economists point to transparency as another advantage of BCA, in the sense that "the results of a well-executed BCA analysis can be clearly linked to the assumptions, theory, methods, and procedures used in it. This transparency can add to the accountability of public decisions by indicating where the decisions are at variance with the analysis."[10] Thus, an argument over the economic impact of a proposed environmental regulation would presumably be clarified considerably because a competent BCA would enable all sides to understand what went into the economic evaluation and to examine the validity of the components of that valuation. In addition, proponents believe that a competent BCA can reveal where important information is lacking about the costs of and benefits from a policy—what has been called "ignorance revelation." Moreover, it is also argued, BCA gives policymakers a common metric for comparing policies and choosing among them.[11]

Proponents of BCA argue that, at the very least, it can point decision-makers to the most economically desirable or cost-effective policies for achieving a regulatory goal. "Even if one objects . . . to basing environmental policy on benefit–cost analysis," argues economist A. Myrick Freeman III, "it still makes good sense to be in favor of cost-effective environmental policies. Cost-effectiveness means controlling pollution to achieve the stated environmental quality standards at the lowest possible total cost."[12] Moreover, proponents add, critics of BCA are really objecting to incompetent analysis, especially when created deliberately to produce a desired outcome. Competent BCA sometimes can identify policies that are both economically and environmentally wiser than those currently implemented. According to Freeman, a well-conceived BCA would probably have revealed better alternatives to many federally financed water resource developments, such as dams, stream channelization, and flood-control projects, that were justified originally by questionable BCAs. Freeman notes that these analyses used techniques that systematically overstated the benefits of water resource development, understated the economic costs, and ignored environmental costs. The result was the construction of a number of economically wasteful and environmentally damaging projects as well as serious consideration of misguided proposals, such as the one to build a dam in the Grand Canyon.[13]

When all the regulated sectors of the U.S. economy are considered, the critics reason, a huge inflationary diversion of capital from more economically desirable uses results. Critics frequently allege that excessive regulatory costs and complexity will drive some firms out of business or out of the country. Spokespeople for major national business associations, such as the Business Roundtable and the U.S. Chamber of Commerce, have alleged that excessive regulatory costs have depressed significantly the growth rate of the gross national product. Virtually all critics of environmental regulations complain of "green tape"—the paperwork and related expense required for regulatory compliance. Critics are skilled at reciting a dismal inventory of the rules, pages of the Federal Register, and volume of paper generated by regulation: According to such estimates, for instance, in 2012, federal environmental regulations amounted to forty-seven rules, $16.3 billion in compliance costs, and 1,743,944 hours of paperwork for the regulated interests.[14]

Few proponents of BCA argue, however, that it should be the sole criterion for regulatory strategies. Still, they believe that the routine use of the procedure would make regulators more sensitive to the costs of their regulatory decisions and more likely to select regulatory procedures with net benefits or with the least cost among alternatives. Many supporters also believe that BCA leads to a better quality of decision-making. As economist Paul Johnson observes, "The value is that it injects rational calculation into a highly emotional subject. . . . It offers you a range of alternatives. Without stringent analysis, nobody knows whether costs imposed by regulatory programs are money well spent."[15] And, although it is seldom admitted, many advocates hope the publicity given to regulatory costs, especially when net benefits are lacking, will deter agencies from choosing such regulations.

The Case Against Benefit–Cost Analysis

Environmentalists traditionally have opposed the routine use of BCA in setting environmental standards. Some still regard it as a categorical evil, wholly inappropriate for the selection of environmental regulations. Others recognize that economic considerations may sometimes merit attention in writing environmental laws but believe benefit–cost calculations are easily distorted to the advantage of regulated interests. Environmentalists assert that BCA often distorts economic reality by exaggerating the regulatory costs and underestimating the benefits. Regulated interests, the argument continues, often deliberately magnify their compliance costs; it is difficult, in any case, to obtain accurate economic data from them. In addition, regulated interests give little attention to the economic "learning curve," which often yields a substantial savings over the full period of regulation as they gain experience and expertise in controlling their pollutants. Benefits from regulation, in contrast, are often underestimated because they are not easily calculated. For instance, how are the health benefits from significantly cleaner air over the next several decades to be calculated? What value is to be placed on rivers, streams, and lakes made fishable and swimmable again?

Some benefits almost defy monetizing. For instance, an agency may consider regulatory alternatives involving different levels of risk to populations from exposure to hazardous or toxic substances. What is the appropriate value to be placed on a life saved? A variation of BCA sometimes advocated in such a situation is to compare the costs of regulation with estimates of the lives saved from the different strategies. Such a comparison implicitly requires regulators to decide how much an individual human life is worth.

As a practical example, in 2006, a BCA study conducted by the EPA examined the impact of reducing its recommended air-quality threshold for soot from fifteen micrograms per cubic meter to fourteen micrograms. This apparently minor reduction would create an estimated $1.9 billion in additional annual control costs among the regulated industries but would also prevent an estimated twenty-four thousand premature deaths. "It's pretty darn obvious," asserted the president of the environmental advocacy group Clean Air Watch, "that better standards would mean fewer premature deaths."[16] Not all experts agree with this regulatory arithmetic. But a metric that measures lives against dollars spent on pollution controls appears to confront decision-makers with a choice that will seem arbitrary, if not morally repugnant: saving dollars or lives.

Critics note, moreover, that BCA traditionally ignores equity considerations, an increasingly potent argument as the environmental justice movement expands (see Chapter 4). In a sense, this is correct; common BCA lacks a social conscience, because it is unconcerned with the social distribution of benefits and costs—that is, with which groups are winners and losers in the distribution.[17] "It is often argued," explains economists Raymond J. Kopp, Alan J. Krupnick, and Michael A. Toman, "that [BCA] takes the existing distribution of income as given and does not consider the equity implications of the policies it seeks to evaluate."[18] It is possible, however, to factor at least some equity considerations into BCA, but such an exercise is uncommon and fraught with difficulties for regulatory agencies that must decide whose equities are to be considered and how to compare equity among different groups.

Perhaps the most persuasive reason for resisting BCA, in the environmentalist's view, is that reducing an environmental value, such as clean air or water, to a monetary figure makes it appear to be just another commodity that can be priced, bought, and sold. According to Stephen Kelman,

> Many environmentalists fear that subjecting decisions about clean air or water to the cost–benefit tests that determine the general run of decisions removes those matters from the realm of specially valued things. . . . The very statement that something is not for sale enhances and protects the thing's value in a number of ways. . . . [It] is a way of showing that a thing is valued for its own sake, whereas selling a thing for money demonstrates that it was valued only instrumentally.[19]

Environmentalists often believe they stand apart from regulated business through a profound ethical disagreement over the intrinsic worth of wild places, uncontaminated air and water, and other environmental amenities. This conviction of moral purpose imparts to the movement much of its passion and persistence. It also elevates arguments over BCA to the level of ethical principles, making compromise especially difficult.

Reality and Rhetoric

In practice, BCA has often been more paper tiger than bulldog in regulatory affairs. Several major environmental programs, such as the CAA and the Occupational Safety and Health Act, prohibit BCA or severely limit its application in the regulations implementing them (although the EPA spent $2 million preparing an unused BCA for an air-quality standard anyway).[20] Many other regulatory proposals escape Executive Order 12291 because their impacts did not exceed $100 million. Currently, agencies often prepare BCAs but, lacking confidence in the results, turn to other criteria in writing regulations. Sometimes, perhaps often, agencies do not, despite formal requirements, diligently explore alternatives to their proposed regulations. At the end of a comprehensive, independent 2008 survey of RIA writing at the EPA, Richard Morgenstern, a former high-level EPA economist, concluded that

> One of the things that we found in actually reviewing specific regulations was that despite the mandate that exists and the guidelines that agencies consider alternatives . . . in many instances they do not consider alternatives. So if you think about it, what's the point of doing what's probably a million dollar study in looking into a lot of aspects of regulation if you're not going to give serious consideration to an alternative?[21]

And agencies showed little consistency in how they prepared their analyses, notwithstanding OMB guidelines. Experience demonstrated at the EPA, as in many other agencies, the severe limitations and inherent bias implicit in data deficiencies.[22]

In some instances, however, the White House has used—or has attempted to use—BCA to stifle environmental regulations objectionable to the president. This was perhaps the most potent impact of Reagan's RIAs.[23] The OMB's review of regulatory agency RIAs, however, was far less aggressive under Reagan's successor, George H.W. Bush.

By 2012, it was apparent that Barack Obama had largely continued the approach to BCA of the Clinton administration in requiring quantification of costs and benefits when evaluating proposed regulation—with one significant difference. In May 2012, Obama issued Executive Order 13563, which requires the additional consideration of benefits difficult to quantify such as "equity, human dignity, fairness, and distributive impacts" and strongly emphasizes public participation in the process—thus, it appears to require, when possible, considerations of environmental justice as potential regulatory costs and benefits. The impact of this requirement, however, remains uncertain since the election of Donald Trump, who has largely ignored issues of equity and environmental justice in his EPA reform agenda.

Benefit–Cost Analysis's Continuing Problems

By now, thousands of regulatory economic analyses have been prepared by federal administrators. Yet they continue to struggle when attempting to estimate realistically the benefits or costs of the regulatory programs they implement. Whatever the reason—incompetence, inexperience, creative bookkeeping, or something else—regulatory cost estimates frequently prove to be inaccurate. For example, the EPA's Superfund cost estimates have been unreliably low, and the situation is no better for hazardous waste site remediation required by the RCRA.[24] Often, EPA officials, like other regulatory officials, appear nonchalant about guidelines, or perhaps confounded by them, even when guidance is explicit.

Regulatory officials, environmental or otherwise, still frequently discount their own agency analyses when making regulatory decisions. This is not necessarily administrative malfeasance—federal agencies are usually required only to consider the benefits and costs in the course of policymaking—but the situation bespeaks the considerable practical difficulty in using RIAs and the substantial official uneasiness about the situation. Nonetheless, estimates about policy benefits and costs, some grievously flawed, continue to pack policy debates.[25]

At least one agency, the U.S. Army Corps of Engineers, seems almost incapable of conquering an addiction to "cooked" BCAs.[26] Environmentalists are especially critical of these dubious BCAs because of the Corps' enormous impact on the nation's environmental management. The Corps' FY 2018 budget exceeded $4.8 billion for civil works, including, especially, local public works, such as levees, dams, and drainage canals, dear to all congressional members, even though these projects often become environmental disasters. For almost a century, these projects have frequently been justified by dubious BCAs, which Congress uncritically accepts because doing so works to the advantage of local constituencies. Every president from Jimmy Carter through Barack Obama has vigorously opposed these questionable projects, with mixed success. "On Capitol Hill," writes a veteran political reporter, "it is still considered almost bad form to oppose a water project in another member's district. . . . Corps authorizations have long been viewed as congressional prerogatives, nearly as automatic as the franking privilege or special license plates."[27] Despite repeated promises to swear off "cooked" economics, the Corps still invites suspicion of its BCA math. Few verdicts about the Corps' BCA process have been as blistering as the GAO evaluation, toward the end of the George W. Bush administration, which had virtually nothing good to report. "The cost and benefit analyses performed by the Corps to support decisions on Civil Works projects or actions were generally inadequate to provide a reasonable basis for deciding whether to proceed with the project or action," stated the GAO. For example, for the Delaware Deepening Project, the GAO found credible support for only about $13.3 million per year in project benefits compared with the $40.1 million per year claimed in the Corps' analysis; and for the Oregon Inlet Jetty Project, the GAO analysis determined that, if the

Corps had incorporated more current data into its analysis, the reported benefits would have been reduced by about 90 percent.[28]

In reality, the Corps' resolve to improve its BCAs has often been smothered by the incessant congressional pressure to justify coveted projects. Consider, for example, Louisiana's congressional delegation, the undisputed national champion at harvesting Corps projects. During George W. Bush's first administration, before Hurricane Katrina, Louisiana reaped $1.6 billion in Corps-funded projects and, in the years following Katrina, an additional $14 billion, mostly to reconstruct the New Orleans levees. "We live and die by what the Corps of Engineers does or doesn't do, literally," observed John Breaux, Louisiana's Democratic U.S. senator for eighteen years. "The Corps are us."[29] Louisiana's congressional delegation is distinguished only by its proficiency in collecting Corps projects. Few congressional delegations can long resist the temptation to press the Corps for benefit–cost calculations that justify attractive, local projects.[30]

BCA is not, however, necessarily an administrative charade. Impressive examples of improved economic efficiency and substantial savings due to BCA at the EPA, for instance, exist. Nonetheless, and despite confidence among many economists that BCA quality and influence are improving among regulatory agencies, the evidence still is not convincing. More persuasive is the conclusion from a meticulous study of forty-eight major federal health, safety, and environmental regulations between 1996 and 1999: "We find that economic analyses prepared by regulatory agencies do not provide enough information to make decisions that will maximize the efficiency and effectiveness of a rule." Moreover, the findings "strongly suggest that agencies failed to comply with the executive order and adhere to the OMB guidelines."[31]

Some Lessons

Much can yet be learned from the experiences since 1980. The blizzard of econometric data normally accompanying arguments over the cost of regulation should be at least initially considered suspect—by all sides. Willfully or not, regulated businesses will often overestimate the costs of regulation and the proponents of regulation will often underestimate them. Also, as experience with the Reagan and George W. Bush administrations illustrates, BCA is so vulnerable to partisan manipulation that it is often discounted by officials even when they are allowed to consider the economics of regulation. As a former adviser to President Richard Nixon recalls, "In executive branch meetings, the EPA staff repeatedly seemed to minimize pollution costs, while other agencies weighed in with high costs to meet the identical pollution standard. Often, we halved the difference. . . ."[32] Many regulatory decisions made on the basis of political, administrative, or other considerations are sanctified later by economics for the sake of credibility. Sometimes, costs are inflated grossly, not so much by individual regulations as by the multiplicity and unpredictability of regulatory procedures.

This discussion should clarify at least a few aspects of the benefit–cost controversy. First, there is no substantial evidence that regulatory costs have become so excessive that BCA must be routinely imposed on all environmental regulation programs. Second, there are doubtless instances, perhaps a substantial number of them, in which BCA might suggest better solutions to environmental regulation than would otherwise be selected. For this reason, such analysis should not be excluded categorically from consideration unless Congress specifically mandates an exclusion. Third, it matters a great deal who does the calculating. All BCAs should be open to review and challenge during administrative deliberations. Fourth, Congress should indicate explicitly in the text of environmental legislation or in the accompanying legislative history how it expects regulatory agencies to weight economic criteria alongside other statutory guidelines to be observed in writing regulations to implement such legislation. Fifth, regulatory costs might be diminished significantly not by using BCA but by using economic incentives in securing the compliance of regulated interests with environmental programs.

The Emerging Problem of Environmental Valuation

The BCA controversy illuminates an especially vexing problem inherent to most debates about environmental policy: How can environmental amenities be valued accurately if some metric must be devised? This issue is at the core of traditional economic theory, because it raises profound questions about the assumptions implicit in placing value on nonmarket goods, such as clean air or pristine wilderness. In recent years, this problem has stimulated considerable debate among economists and others concerned with environmental valuation, which has led to several significant proposals for a radical change in the way environmental amenities are evaluated and, as a consequence, in how environmental policymaking transpires.

Environmental Accounting. Many economists, recognizing that the continuing development of environmental policymaking increasingly confronts policymakers with problems of environmental valuation not addressed by traditional economics, propose the development of environmental accounting as an alternative. In effect, environmental accounting attempts to broaden enormously the scope of environmental amenities to which society attaches significant value and to devise a metric appropriate for comparing these values with other, usually monetary, values involved in policy evaluation. In this perspective, environmental amenities with obvious and immediate human benefits would be valued—clean air and water, for instance—but so would habitats essential to the preservation or proliferation of species, ecological sites essential for biosphere preservation or improvement, environments of unusual beauty, flora and fauna of biological significance, or other aspects of the human environment important for ecological reasons. Identifying these distinctively valued ecological elements will be difficult and challenging but no less so than assigning an appropriate value to them.

Environmental accounting is especially difficult because it requires both economists and ecologists to work at the intellectual margins of their disciplines, where theory and evidence are often tenuous. Ecologists, for instance, may strongly suspect that the eradication of certain species will create a long-term economic disruption of human environments without being able to prove it or to estimate the scope of the disturbance. Because many environmental amenities are neither bought nor sold in markets, economists would have to construct shadow prices—best estimates of real market value—by a tortuous, inevitably contentious logic. "Demand and supply curves must be constructed," explains economist Roefie Hueting; however, "constructing a complete demand curve is difficult because the intensity of individual preferences for environmental functions cannot be expressed in market behavior or translated into market terms. This is further complicated by the fact that the consequences of today's actions will often only be manifest in future damage."[33]

Many economists assert, in rebuttal, that a procedure called *revealed preferences* is a reasonable substitute for a market in valuing environmental amenities. Economists Kopp, Krupnick, and Toman offer an example:

> It would be wrong . . . to think of economic values as dollar-denominated values in one's brain to be downloaded when a person is asked the worth of a beautiful sunset; rather, such a value might be inferred from the things that one gives up to see the sunset (e.g., the cost of travel to the ocean). . . . To economists . . . the importance of things (tangible or intangible) is revealed by what a person will give to obtain them. . . . If the thing given up was money, the value can be expressed in monetary units; otherwise, it is expressed in the natural units of the thing given.[34]

Contingent Valuation. One approach to environmental valuation currently proposed for federal policymakers is a methodology called *contingent valuation*, meaning that a monetary value is to be assigned to an environmental amenity whose use or destruction would deprive others of its future availability. Contingent valuation could be used, for example, to estimate the monetary cost to the public created by haze over the Grand Canyon, by widespread pollution of Alaskan waters caused by oil tanker spills, or by any other event that deprives the public of the passive value in an environmental amenity. In a typical case, a representative segment of the relevant public would be asked how much it would be willing to pay to prevent haze over a national park or to avoid an oil spill. Through statistical procedures, a monetary value would then be assigned to an environmental amenity based on these public valuations. Alaska's state government used contingent valuation in the early 1990s to discover what value Americans who might never visit Prince William Sound would assign to preventing a catastrophic oil spill there—a strategy used to estimate the monetary damages for which the Exxon Corporation would be held liable for the devastating oil spill by the tanker Exxon Valdez in 1989. Based on an average response of $30 per person, Alaskan officials estimated that Americans would collectively pay $2.8 billion to avoid such a disaster.[35]

Contingent valuation remains controversial among economists and other policymakers. Many economists dismiss the methodology as "junk economics" because, they assert, the public cannot accurately assess the value in the passive use of an environmental amenity. Critics argue that the public is overly generous with hypothetical statements about personal outlays, tends to exaggerate the value of an amenity, and is often influenced by the wording of questions. To support these contentions, critics cite studies showing enormous variability in public environmental valuations: Saving an old-growth forest in the Pacific Northwest was valued between $119 billion and $359 billion, and sparing the whooping crane from extinction was valued between $51 billion and $715 billion.[36] Understandably, some of the most aggressive opponents of contingent valuation in federal policymaking are corporations, such as Exxon, which feel at considerable financial risk.

REGULATION STRATEGIES: COMMAND AND CONTROL VERSUS THE MARKETPLACE

The CAA was the first in a long succession of federal environmental laws based on the command-and-control approach to environmental regulation (see the next section). Chapters 6 and 7 illustrate well how this approach has been translated into specific statutes to control air and water pollution, toxic and abandoned waste, drinking water quality, and practically every other environmental hazard currently regulated by Washington, D.C. Many economists, regulatory scholars, and policy practitioners, including some environmental leaders, now consider command-and-control regulations to be a policy antique, too economically flawed and administratively clumsy to cope effectively with many current environmental problems. At the very least, they suggest, command-and-control laws often require refitting with newer economic approaches. The most commonly proposed reform for the command-and-control approach is to substitute or add market-based approaches that rely fundamentally on economic incentives and markets to accomplish the environmental improvements intended.

Market-based regulation, in fact, has become a fundamental standard by which critics judge almost all aspects of command-and-control regulation. Thus, it is helpful to compare briefly the philosophy of command-and-control with market-based regulation before discussing current environmental regulations in greater detail.

Command-and-Control Regulation

The foundation of federal pollution regulation is the command-and-control approach, also called "standards and enforcement." This approach creates many of the characteristic processes and problems familiar from current governmental management of the environment. Regulatory horror stories abound, convincing believers that a better approach lies in less direct governmental involvement and more economic incentives to encourage pollution abatement. In fact, both approaches have virtues and liabilities, and a combination of both approaches often seems more effective than one alone.[37] The command-and-control approach can best be understood as a set of five phases through which pollution policy evolves: goals, criteria, quality standards, emission standards, and enforcement.

Goals. In theory, the first step in pollution abatement begins with a determination by Congress of the ultimate objectives to be accomplished through pollution regulation. In practice, these goals are often broadly and vaguely worded. Sometimes, as when Congress decides to press technology by setting pollution standards that it hopes will force industry to develop control technologies not currently available, the goals are deliberately made extremely ambitious as an incentive for vigorous regulatory measures by regulated interests. The principal goals of the CAA are, for example, to protect public health and safety. Vague goals are not as important in defining the operational character of a regulatory program as are the more detailed specifications for the setting of pollution standards, emission controls, and enforcement—the real cutting edges of regulation. Statements of goals, however, may be politically significant as signals to the interests involved in regulation about which pollutants and sources will be given priority and how vigorously Congress intends to implement programs. The CAA goal of establishing national air-quality standards for major pollutants, for instance, was an unmistakable signal that Congress would no longer tolerate the continual delays in controlling air pollution caused by past legislative willingness to let the states create their own air-quality standards.

Criteria. Criteria are the technical data, commonly provided by research scientists, indicating which pollutants are associated with environmental damage and how such pollutants, in varying combinations, affect the environment. Criteria are essential to give public officials some idea of what pollutant levels they must achieve to ensure various standards of air and water quality. If regulators intend to protect public health from the effects of air pollution, they must know what levels of pollution—sulfur oxides, for instance—create public health risks. In a similar vein, restoring game fish to a dying lake requires information about the levels of organic waste such fish can tolerate. Criteria must be established for each regulated pollutant and sometimes for combinations of pollutants.

Obtaining criteria frequently is difficult because data on the environmental effects of many pollutants still may be fragmentary or absent. Even when data are available, there is often as much art as science in specifying relationships between specific levels of a pollutant and its environmental effects, because precise correlations may not be obtainable. The reliability of criteria data also may vary depending on whether they are obtained from animal studies, epidemiological statistics, or human studies. Criteria are likely to be controversial, especially to those convinced that a set of data works to their disadvantage. Given the limitations in the criteria data, regulatory agencies often have had to set pollution standards with information that was open to scientific criticism but was still the best available.

Quality Standards. Goals and criteria are preludes to the critical business of establishing air-quality and water-quality standards—the maximum levels of various pollutants to be permitted in air, soil, workplaces, or other locations. As a practical matter, defining standards is equivalent to declaring what the public, acting through governmental regulators, will consider to be pollution. An adequate set of quality standards should specify which contaminants will be regulated and what levels and combinations will be accepted in different pollutant categories.

Creating quality standards—another way of defining acceptable risk—is ultimately a political decision. Criteria documents rarely provide public officials with a single number that defines unambiguously what specific concentration of a pollutant produces precisely what effects. A rather broad range of possible figures associated more or less closely with predictable effects is available; which one is accepted may be the result of prolonged struggle and negotiation among the interests involved in regulation. This battle over numbers is a matter of economics as much as science or philosophy. The difference between two possible pollution standards, only a few units apart, may seem trivial. But the higher standard may involve millions or billions of additional dollars in pollution-control technologies for the regulated interests and possibly many additional years before standards are achieved. Sometimes, Congress establishes a standard based on a number's political "sex appeal." The original requirements in the CAA that automobile emissions of hydrocarbons and carbon monoxide be reduced by 90 percent of the 1970 levels by no later than 1975 were accepted largely because the 90 percent figure sounded strict and spurred the auto industry into action. In practical terms, the figure might have been set at 88 percent or 85 percent or some other number in this range, with about the same results. Air-quality standards created by the EPA for the major criteria pollutants—that is, pollutants that the CAA specifically designates for regulation because of their well-known, pervasive threat to public health—are identified in Table 5.1.

Emission Standards. Standards for clean air or water are only aspirations unless emission standards exist to prescribe the acceptable pollutant discharges from important sources of air or water contamination. If emission standards are to be effective, they must indicate clearly the acceptable emission levels from all important pollution sources and should be related to the pollution-control standards established by policymakers.

Congress has used two different methods of determining how emission standards should be set. In regulating existing air pollution sources under the CAA, Congress requires that emissions be limited to the extent necessary to meet the relevant air-quality standards; determining what emission controls are necessary

TABLE 5.1 ■ National Ambient Air-Quality Standards

Pollutant	Standard value[a]		Standard type[b]
Carbon monoxide (CO)			
8-hour average	9 ppm	10 mg/m³	Primary
1-hour average	35 ppm	40 mg/m³	Primary
Nitrogen dioxide (NO₂)			
Annual arithmetic mean	0.053 ppm	100 µg/m³	Primary and secondary
Ozone (O₃)			
1-hour average	0.12 ppm	235 µg/m³	Primary and secondary
8-hour average[b]	0.08 ppm	157 µg/m³	Primary and secondary
Lead (Pb)			
Quarterly average		1.5 µg/m³	Primary and secondary
Particulate (PM₁₀) *Particles with diameters of 10 µm or less*			
Annual arithmetic mean		50 µg/m³	Primary and secondary
24-hour average		150 µg/m³	Primary and secondary
Particulate (PM₂.₅) *Particles with diameters of 2.5 µm or less*			
Annual arithmetic mean[b]		15 µg/m³	Primary and secondary
24-hour average[b]		65 µg/m³	Primary and secondary
Sulfur dioxide (SO₂)			
Annual arithmetic mean	0.03 ppm	80 µg/m³	Primary
24-hour average	0.14 ppm	365 µg/m³	Primary
3-hour average	0.50 ppm	1,300 µg/m³	Secondary

Source: U.S. EPA, Office of Air Quality Planning and Standards, available at https://www3.epa.gov/ttn/naaqs/criteria.html.

[a]The two values are approximately equivalent concentrations.

[b]The ozone 8-hour standard and the PM₂.₅ standards are included for information only. A 1999 federal court ruling blocked implementation of these standards, which the EPA proposed in 1997.

depends on where the quality standards are set. In controlling new air pollution sources and most water polluters, the emission controls are based on the available technologies. This technology-based approach sets the emission levels largely according to the performance of available technologies. A direct and critical relationship exists between air-quality standards and emission controls. For example, once the EPA declares national ambient air-quality standards, each state is required in its State Implementation Plan to calculate the total emissions of that pollutant within an air shed and then to assign emission controls to each source of that pollutant sufficient to ensure that total emissions will meet air-quality standards. In effect, this approach calls for the states to decide how much of the total pollution "load" within an air shed is the responsibility of each polluter and how much emission control the polluter must achieve. This process has become bitterly controversial. Experts often have difficulty determining precisely how much of a pollution load within a given body of water or air can be attributed to a specific source; this difficulty compounds the problem of assigning responsibility for pollution abatement equitably among a large number of polluters.[38]

Regulated interests, aware of the relationship between air-quality standards and emission controls, will attack both standards and controls in an effort to avoid or relax their assigned emission controls. Regulated industries also chronically complain that insufficient attention is given to the cost of emission controls when government regulators prescribe the acceptable technology. The backlash against emission controls often falls on state government officials who, under existing federal law, usually are responsible for setting specific emission levels, prescribing the proper technologies, and enforcing emission restraints on specific sources. Enforcing emission controls is accomplished largely through issuing a permit to individual dischargers specifying the permissible emission levels and technological controls for their facilities. The political and economic influence of regulated interests is often far more formidable in state capitals than in Washington, D.C., and state regulators often feel especially vulnerable to these local pressures.

Enforcement. A great diversity of enforcement procedures might be used to ensure that pollution standards are achieved; adequate enforcement must carry enough force to command the respect of those subject to regulation. Satisfactory enforcement schemes have several characteristics: They enable public officials to act with reasonable speed (very rapidly in the case of emergencies) to curb pollution, they carry sufficient penalties to encourage compliance, and they do not enable officials to evade a responsibility to act against violations when action is essential. It is desirable that officials have a range of enforcement options that might extend from gentle prodding to secure compliance at one end, all the way to litigation and criminal penalties for severe, chronic, or reckless violations at the other. In reality, when it comes to enforcement, administrative authority is often the power to make a deal. Armed with a flexible variety of enforcement options, administrators are in a position to bargain with polluters that are not in compliance with the law, selecting those enforcement options they believe will best achieve their purposes. This bargaining, a common occurrence in environmental regulation, illustrates how political pressure and administrative discretion concurrently shape environmental policy (enforcement is examined in greater detail in the next section). In the end, an effective pollution abatement program depends largely on voluntary compliance by regulated interests. No regulatory agency has enough personnel, money, and time to engage in continual litigation or other actions to force compliance with pollution standards. Furthermore, litigation usually remains among the slowest, most inflexible, and inefficient means of achieving environmental protection. Administrative agencies prefer to negotiate and maneuver to avoid litigation as a primary regulatory device whenever possible.

What's Wrong With Command-and-Control?

Economists have been the most outspoken critics of command-and-control regulation. However, they are now joined by an increasing number of other critics, including some leading environmental organizations such as Environmental Defense, whose experience with command-and-control regulation since 1970 has demonstrated that it has some severe deficiencies. First, critics assert, it offers regulated interests few economic incentives to comply rapidly and efficiently with mandated pollution standards. In the economist's perspective, the standards-and-enforcement approach lacks an appeal to the economic self-interest of the regulated. Even severe penalties for noncompliance with the law often fail to motivate polluters to meet required pollution control deadlines. Penalties are often not assessed or are severely weakened by negotiation with regulatory agencies. Some firms find it more profitable to pay penalties and to continue polluting in violation of the law than to assume the often far-steeper costs of compliance. In addition, polluters have no economic incentive to reduce their emissions below the regulatory requirements.

Second, traditional regulatory approaches require the federal government to specify the appropriate technologies and methods for their use in practically every instance in which pollutants are technologically controlled. Highly complicated, exquisitely detailed specifications that make poor scientific or economic sense for particular industries or firms can result. One reason for this situation is that neither Congress nor administrators may have sufficient scientific training or experience to make correct judgments about the appropriate technologies for pollution abatement in a specific firm or industry. Also, regulators sometimes lack sufficient information about the economics of firms or industries to know which technologies are economically efficient—that is, which achieve the desired control standards the least expensively.

Third, proponents assert that incentive approaches can be simply and economically administered. As a National Academy of Public Administration report notes,

> Incentive-based systems are administratively simple because . . . they require much of the regulatory energy to be expended up front in the

design state of the regulatory program. If the design is correct, less burdensome administration may be facilitated. Further, once the program is in place, regulators can rely on the energies of the private sector to drive pollution downward.[39]

The alternative seems to require bureaucratic legions toiling endlessly in the regulatory vineyards. "Command-and-control regulation," continues the report, "may impose a never-ending requirement on regulators to develop new and more stringent industry-specific regulations on smaller and smaller discharge points."[40]

Fourth, proponents point out that a market incentive approach is easier for the public to understand and presumably easier to approve. Economic incentives focus on a pollution-reduction goal that the public would presumably find much more comprehensible—hence, easier for government to defend politically—than technology specifications with all the mystifying technical disputation about their appropriateness and efficiency.

Regulation Goes to the Market

Economic incentives are not new to U.S. environmental management. Many familiar forms of environmental control, such as sewage treatment charges, taxes on leaded gasoline, and deposit-refund systems for disposable beer and soft drink containers, use the pulling power of economic incentives to encourage pollution control. Table 5.2 provides a brief summary of the different methods used in the United States.

Not until a decade after Earth Day 1970 did the EPA first experiment warily with economic regulatory incentives. This set in motion a succession of additional economic innovations at the EPA, culminating in the current emissions trading program in the CAA.

Cap and Trade: The Gamble on Sulfur Dioxide Emissions Trading. The most innovative provision of the 1990 amendments to the CAA is the emissions trading scheme created by Title IV. These provisions, sometimes called the Acid Rain Program, aim specifically at emissions of sulfur dioxides associated with human health risks, environmental degradation, and especially acid precipitation. The regulatory approach, known as "cap and trade," was intended to reduce by the year 2010 the nation's total emissions of sulfur dioxide to 8.5 million tons below the level of 1980 emissions. To accomplish this overall goal, a mandatory cap was established on the total sulfur dioxide emissions annually from the nation's utilities. The program was implemented in two phases.

Phase I began in 1995 and regulated 110 of the nation's electric utilities with the largest sulfur dioxide emissions, primarily coal-burning facilities, and 182 smaller units, all in the East and Midwest:

- A mandatory cap is set on the total sulfur dioxide emissions permitted annually from these sources.

TABLE 5.2 ■ Economic Incentives Used in Environmental Regulation		
Incentives	**Examples**	**Pros and cons**
Pollution charges and taxes	Emission charges Effluent charges Solid waste charges Sewage charges	*Pros:* Stimulates new technology; useful when damage per unit of pollution varies little with the quantity of pollution *Cons:* Potentially large distributional effects; uncertain environmental effects; generally requires monitoring data
Input or output taxes and charges	Leaded gasoline tax Carbon tax Fertilizer tax Pesticide tax Virgin material tax Water user charges Chlorofluorocarbon taxes	*Pros:* Administratively simple; does not require monitoring data; raises revenue; effective when sources are numerous and damage per unit of pollution varies little with the quantity of pollution *Cons:* Often weak link to pollution; uncertain environmental effects
Subsidies	Municipal sewage plants Land use by farmers Industrial pollution	*Pros:* Politically popular; targets specific activities *Cons:* Financial impact on government budgets; may stimulate too much activity; uncertain effects
Deposit-refund systems	Lead-acid batteries Beverage containers Automobile bodies	*Pros:* Deters littering; stimulates recycling *Cons:* Potentially high transaction costs; product must be reusable or recyclable
Marketable permits	Emissions Effluents Fisheries access	*Pros:* Provides limits to pollution; effective when damage per unit of pollution varies with the amount of pollution; provides stimulus to technological change

Incentives	Examples	Pros and cons
		Cons: Potentially high transaction costs; requires variation in marginal control costs
Reporting requirements	Proposition 65	*Pros:* Flexible, low cost
	Superfund Amendments and Reauthorization Act	*Cons:* Impacts may be hard to predict; applicable only when damage per unit of pollution does not depend on the quantity of pollution
Liability	Natural resource damage assessment	*Pros:* Provides strong incentive
	Nuisance, trespass	*Cons:* Assessment and litigation costs can be high; burden of proof large; few applications
Voluntary programs	Project XL 33/50 Energy Star	*Pros:* Low cost; flexible; many possible applications; way to test new approaches
		Cons: Uncertain participation

Source: U.S. EPA, Office of Policy, Economics, and Innovation, "The United States Experience With Economic Incentives for Protecting the Environment," Document no. EPA-240-R-01-001, Washington, DC, January 2001, ix.

- Each source is granted by the EPA an annual allowance—each allowance equals one ton of sulfur dioxide emissions—based on its current emission levels and the overall emission cap.

- At the end of each year, each source must have allowances equal to its emissions for that year.

- Each utility is permitted to bank, sell, or carry over to the following year any emission allowances in excess of its actual emissions.

- Each utility must carefully measure and report its annual emissions and submit to an annual EPA emission audit.

- Each utility is free to select whatever method it chooses to control its emissions and to meet its annual emission cap.

Phase II began in 2000 and regulated electric utilities and other sources of sulfur dioxide emissions nationally. Altogether, more than 2,000 units were affected by this phase by the beginning of 2001. All units are regulated in the same manner as in Phase I.

The early results of cap and trade were keenly scrutinized. The critical tests: Would a market in tradable emission permits develop among the regulated utilities, and would it produce the economic and environmental benefits predicted by its proponents?

By the beginning of Barack Obama's administration, most economic experts had agreed that Title IV had been a success—but not completely. Using three measures for evaluation—environmental quality, the performance of the market, and economic assessment, such as cost savings, innovation, and economic efficiency—one careful summary concluded that Title IV "generally . . . has worked well in achieving its stated goals of achieving emissions targets, resulting in substantial environmental and public health benefits," and a later thorough review concluded optimistically that "the SO_2 allowance trading system had come to be seen as both innovative and successful. It has become exceptionally influential, leading to a series of policy innovations in the United States and abroad to address a range of environmental challenges, including the threat of global climate change."[41] However, the trading program significantly reduced ambient SO_2 concentrations associated with acid rain but had not eliminated them.

CONCLUSION

To most Americans, the nation's environmental troubles are epitomized by polluted air, fouled water, dangerously unregulated hazardous and toxic wastes, and a multitude of other ecological derangements. This chapter illuminates a less-obvious dimension of the environmental crisis that is equally dangerous in its ecological implications—the economic problems in implementing environmental policy effectively. In many critical respects, the institutions and policies the nation now depends on to reverse its ecological degradation are failing, sometimes badly. Equally as imperative as new technological solutions are to ecological ills are new economic and institutional solutions. Finding these solutions will require critical, difficult debate within the environmental movement and among public policymakers at all governmental levels concerned with ecological restoration.

These problems are especially refractory, because they often originate in the fundamental constitutional design of the political system or in deeply rooted political traditions. Among these is a historical dependence on traditional policy approaches to environmental problems, particularly the command-and-control method of regulation and the single-media approach to controlling specific pollutants. Although other approaches often seem more appropriate and in some cases have been tried experimentally, they are strongly resisted by a multitude of institutional, professional, and economic interests with a stake in the status quo.

Often, the environmental movement itself has been excessively conservative in resisting policy innovation.

Among the significant economic problems arising from environmental regulation, none is debated more often than the high cost of environmental regulation. As costs continually rise well above expectations, the need to find cost-effective, cost-saving approaches to policymaking grows more apparent. Although BCA is sometimes a useful strategy for reducing regulatory costs, its serious political and economic deficiencies suggest that other approaches, involving more economic incentives for pollution abatement in the private sector, are likely to be more broadly effective. None of the problems now associated with regulatory incapacity is likely to be solved easily or quickly.

Suggested Readings

Ackerman, Frank, and Lisa Heinzerling. *Priceless: On Knowing the Price of Everything and the Value of Nothing.* New York: The New Press, 2004.

Harrington, Winston, Richard D. Morgenstern, and Thomas Sterner, eds. *Choosing Environmental Policy: Comparing Instruments and Outcomes in the United States and Europe.* Washington, DC: Resources for the Future, 2004.

Heal, Geoffrey. *Nature and the Marketplace: Capturing the Value of Ecosystem Services.* Washington, DC: Island Press, 2001.

Portney, Paul R., and Robert N. Stavins, eds. *Public Policies for Environmental Protection.* 2nd ed. Washington, DC: Resources for the Future, 2000.

Revesz, Richard, and Paul Livermore. *Retaking Rationality: How Cost Benefit Analysis Can Better Protect the Environment and Our Health.* New York: Cambridge University Press, 2008.

Tietenberg, Tom, and Lynne Lewis. *Environmental & Natural Resources Economics.* 9th ed. Saddle River, NJ: Prentice Hall, 2011.

Notes

1. Danny Vinik, "Trump's War on Regulation Is Real, But Is It Working?" *Politico*, January 20, 2018, available at https://www.politico.com/agenda/story/2018/01/20/trumps-regulatory-experiment-year-one-000620.
2. Associated Press, "Trump Relishes Progress On Rolling Back Federal Rules,"*Fox News*, December 14, 2017, available at https://www.foxnews.com/politics/trump-relishes-progress-on-rolling-back-federal-rules.

3. Jasmine Tucker and Lindsay Koshgarian, "President Obama Proposes 2017 Budget," *National Priorities Project*, available at https://www.nationalpriorities.org/analysis/2016/president-obamas-2017-budget/.

4. Executive Office of the President, Office of Management and Budget, *20173 Draft Report to Congress on the Benefits and Costs of Federal Regulations and Agency Compliance With the Unfunded Mandates Reform Act* (Washington, DC: Government Printing Office, 2017), 10.

5. Ibid, p. 70.

6. The arguments for considering costs in environmental regulation are usefully summarized in Allen V. Kneese and Charles L. Schultze, *Pollution, Prices and Public Policy* (Washington, DC: Brookings Institution Press, 1975); see also A. Myrick Freeman III, "Economics, Incentives, and Environmental Regulation," in *Environmental Policy in the 1990s*, 2nd ed., ed. Norman J. Vig and Michael E. Kraft (Washington, DC: CQ Press, 1997), 189–208.

7. Cass Sunstein, "Cost–Benefit Default Principles," AEI-Brookings Joint Center Working Paper no. 00–07/University of Chicago, Law and Economics Working Paper no. 104, Washington, DC, October 2000, 5, available at http://papers.ssrn.com/s013/papers.cfm?abstract_id=247884; see also John D. Graham, Paul R. Noe, and Elizabeth L. Branch, "Managing the Regulatory State: The Experience of the Bush Administration," *Fordham Urban Law Journal* 33 (May 1, 2006): 953–1001.

8. Ibid., 10–14.

9. Quoted in ibid., 10.

10. Raymond J. Kopp, Alan J. Krupnick, and Michael A. Toman, "Cost–Benefit Analysis and Regulatory Reform: An Assessment of the Science and Art," Discussion Paper no. 97–19, Resources for the Future, Washington, DC, 1997, 14.

11. Ibid.

12. Freeman, "Economics, Incentives, and Environmental Regulation," 150, 153.

13. Ibid.

14. Sam Batkins, "Piling On: The Year in Regulation," *American Action Forum* (January 2013), available at http://americanactionforum.org/research/piling-on-the-year-in-regulation; see also Clyde Wayne Crews Jr., *Ten Thousand Commandments* (Washington, DC: Competitive Enterprise Institute, 2015), 1–2.

15. Paul Johnson, "The Perils of Risk Avoidance," *Regulation* (May–June 1980): 17.

16. Brian Hansen, "New Soot Rules to Cost Power Sector $400 Million Annually, EPA Reckons," *Inside Energy*, October 16, 2006, 6.

17. Kopp, Krupnick, and Toman, "Cost-Benefit Analysis and Regulatory Reform."

18. Ibid.

19. Stephen Kelman, "Cost–Benefit Analysis: An Ethical Critique," *Regulation* (January–February 1981): 39.

20. U.S. GAO, "Cost–Benefit Analysis Can Be Useful in Assessing Regulations, Despite Limitations," Report no. GAO/RCED 84–62, Washington, DC, April 1984, iii.

21. E&E News PM, "RFF's Morgenstern Discusses Cost-Benefit Analysis Reform," *E&ETV's OnPoint* 10, no. 9 (April 2, 2009), available at www.eenews .net/tv/transcript/969.

22. See, for example, Ruth Greenspan Bell, "For EPA Regulations, Cost Predictions Are Overstated," World Resources Institute, available at www .wri.org/stories/2010/11epa-regulations-cost-predictions-are-overstated.

23. On the history of the OMB's use of BCA under the Reagan administration, see W. Norton Grubb, Dale Whittington, and Michael Humphries, "The Ambiguities of Cost–Benefit Analysis: An Evaluation of Regulatory Impact Analysis Under Executive Order 12,291," in *Environmental Policy Under Reagan's Executive Order,* ed. V. Kerry Smith (Chapel Hill: University of North Carolina Press, 1984), 121–166; GAO, "Cost–Benefit Analysis Can Be Useful," 7; Edward Paul Fuchs, *Presidents, Managers, and Regulation* (Englewood Cliffs, NJ: Prentice-Hall, 1988), esp. 124; Joseph Cooper and William F. West, "Presidential Power and Republican Government: The Theory and Practice of OMB Review," *Journal of Politics,* 50 (November 1988): 864–895.

24. GAO, "Much Work Remains to Accelerate Facility Cleanups," Report no. GAO/RCED 93–15, Washington, DC, January 1993, 17.

25. Traci Watson, "Clean Air: EPA Report Hails Law as Success," *USA Today,* October 21, 1997.

26. The Corps is not required to use an RIA, but it must still produce a BCA for proposed projects.

27. Michael Grunwald, "An Agency of Unchecked Clout: Water Projects Roll Past Economics, Environmental Concerns," *Washington Post,* September 10, 2000, available at www.washingtonpost.com/wp-dyn/content/article/2006/05/12/ AR2006051201550.html.

28. GAO, "Corps of Engineers: Observations on Planning and Project Management Processes for the Civil Works Program," Report no. GAO 06–529T, Washington, DC, March 15, 2006, 1.

29. Quoted in Gerard Shields, "Congress and the Corps—Politics, Provincialism, Sometimes Interfere With Priorities, Plans," (Baton Rouge) *Advocate,* November 9, 2008, A01.

30. See, for example, the comprehensive report National Academy of Public Administration, "Background: Adapting to Changing Missions and Demands," *Prioritizing America's Water Resources: Budget Reform for Civil Works Construction Projects at the U.S. Army Corps of Engineers* (Washington, DC: National Academy of Public Administration, 2007), chap. 2.

31. Robert W. Hahn, Jason K. Burnett, and Yee-Ho I. Chan, "Assessing the Quality of Regulatory Impact Analyses," Working Paper no. 001, AEI–Brookings Joint Center for Regulatory Studies, Washington, DC, January 2000,

executive summary. For similar conclusions, see also Winston Harrington, Richard D. Morgenstern, and Peter Nelson, "On the Accuracy of Regulatory Cost Estimates," Working Paper no. 99–18, Resources for the Future, Washington, DC, January 1999.

32. John C. Whitaker, "Earth Day Recollections: What It Was Like When the Movement Took Off," *EPA Journal*, 14 (July–August 1988): 11.

33. Roefie Hueting, "Correcting National Income for Environmental Losses: A Practical Solution for a Theoretical Dilemma," in *A Survey of Ecological Economics*, ed. Rajaram Krishnan, Jonathan M. Harris, and Neva R. Goodwin (Washington, DC: Island Press, 1995), 248.

34. Kopp, Krupnick, and Toman, "Cost–Benefit Analysis and Regulatory Reform," 30.

35. *New York Times*, September 6, 1993.

36. Ibid.

37. Winston Harrington, Richard D. Morgenstern, and Thomas Sterner, eds., "Overview," in *Choosing Environmental Policy: Comparing Instruments and Outcomes in the United States and Europe* (Washington, DC: Resources for the Future, 2004), 1–22; National Academy of Public Administration, *The Environment Goes to Market* (Washington, DC: National Academy of Public Administration, 1994), chap. 1; Paul R. Portney, ed., *Current Issues in U.S. Environmental Policy* (Baltimore, MD: Johns Hopkins University Press, 1978), esp. chap. 1; Erica L. Dolgin and Thomas G. P. Guilbert, eds., *Federal Environmental Law* (St. Paul, MN: West, 1974), esp. the articles by Robert Zener, "The Federal Law of Water Pollution Control," 682–791, and Thomas Jorling, "The Federal Law of Air Pollution Control," 1058–1148.

38. On the problem generally, see Kneese and Schulze, *Pollution, Prices, and Public Policy*, chap. 2.

39. National Academy of Public Administration, *Environment Goes to Market*, 12.

40. Ibid.

41. Dallas Burtraw and Sarah Jo Szambelan, *U.S. Emissions Trading Markets for SO_2 and NO_x*, RFF Research Paper RFF DP 09–40 (Washington DC: Resources for the Future, October 2009, 1, available at http://www.rff.org/Publications/Pages/PublicationDetails.aspx?PublicationID=20925; and Richard Schmalensee and Robert N. Stavins, "The S02 Allowance Trading System: The Ironic History of a Grand Policy Experiment," Joint Center of the Department of Economics, MIT Energy Initiative and MIT Sloan School Management, Paper CEEPR 2012–12, August 2012, available at http://dspace.mit.edu/handle/1721.1/72007.

6

COMMAND AND CONTROL IN ACTION

Air and Water Pollution Regulation

Clean air and clean water are powerful public images. Leaders of the environmental movement regard the CAA of 1970 and the Federal Water Pollution Control Act Amendments (FWPCAA) of 1972 as the foundations of the environmental era. Public opinion polls show that Americans almost universally recognized on the first Earth Day that the nation's degraded air and waters were major ecological problems. Clean air and water acquired political chic. Politicians so routinely assured constituents of their unceasing regard for clean air and clean water that both quickly become clichés instead of realities.

After more than four decades of sustained effort by government and the private sector to eliminate air and water pollution, with a cumulative public expenditure between 2000 and 2012 exceeding $80 billion and an additional industrial expenditure of $46 billion, the nation's air and water remain seriously polluted.[1] Some dramatic achievements, many lesser but impressive gains, and a multitude of marginal improvements make up the veneer that brightens reports about implementation of the CAA and the FWPCAA with cosmetic success. But air and water quality remain seriously degraded throughout much of the United States. By 2017, the EPA estimated that more than 110.9 million Americans, mostly urbanites, lived in counties where pollution levels exceed at least one national air quality standard.[2] The water quality in almost two thirds of the nation's river and stream miles has never been assessed because of deficient state monitoring.[3] The water quality in approximately half of the nation's surveyed river and stream miles is still considered by the EPA to be significantly impaired.[4]

Why aren't there truly impressive results from so massive a national investment? To many observers (as noted in the discussion of market approaches to regulation in Chapter 5), the problem is the policy itself, the command-and-control logic so firmly embedded in the two earliest and most important national pollution laws of the first environmental era. Other difficulties result from new or unexpected scientific discoveries that complicate pollution control. But all these difficulties are compounded by political problems. Federal, state, and local governments have not invested the enormous resources and have not made the politically difficult decisions needed to deal effectively with air and water pollution on a national scale. Public belief about the intensity of pollution and the urgency of further new air and water quality regulation has often wavered and fragmented into partisan polarization in the last several decades.

THE POLITICS OF COMMAND-AND-CONTROL REGULATION

The language and logic of command-and-control regulation is politically innocent. Formally, environmental regulators are supposed to follow a legislatively prescribed pathway to pollution control generally described in Chapter 5. In reality, each command-and-control element is a distinctive decision-making arena rich with political implications behind the statutory language and shaping the impact of regulation as much as the formal language of the law. The technicality of pollution regulation, however, creates a language and style of action that conceal the extent to which political forces operate behind the facade of prescribed regulatory procedures. In fact, regulation is fundamentally a political enterprise, involving considerable negotiation and sometimes conflict magnified by the number and diversity of the actors and institutions involved. (See Figure 6.1.)

Policymaking Beyond Public View

The implementation of most environmental regulatory programs does not routinely involve the public or public opinion. Unlike the White House and Congress, the federal bureaucracy is neither highly visible nor readily understood by the public; regulation operates, in the words of political scientist Francis E. Rourke, behind an "opaque exterior"[5] that the public seldom cares to penetrate. This dearth of dependable public interest means that the constellation of political forces and actors involved in regulatory politics ordinarily is confined to organized interests, governmental officials, scientists, technicians, and other insiders. Given the complexity and technicality of environmental issues, this situation is not surprising. But it emphasizes the extent to which regulatory politics tends to involve a process that is highly specialized and commonly closed to public involvement.

FIGURE 6.1 ■ Key Players in Enforcement of Pollution Control Laws

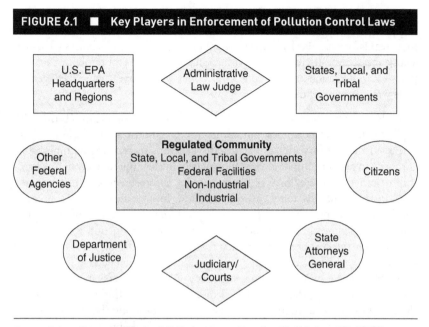

Source: Robert Esworthy, "Federal Pollution Laws: How Are They Enforced?" CRS Report to Congress, Report No. 7-5700-RL34384 (Washington, DC: Congressional Research Service, 2012), available at www.fas.org/sgp/crs/misc/RL34384.pdf.

Political Pressure Points

Political pressure and conflict will flow to wherever administrative discretion exists in the regulatory process. Such administrative discretion ordinarily is found at several points in pollution regulation:

- *When words, phrases, or policy objectives are unclear.* Congress may deliberately shift responsibility to administrators for settling disputes between interests that are in conflict over how a law should be phrased. Tossing this political hot potato to administrators ensures that partisans on all sides of an issue with something to gain or lose by the law's interpretation will scramble to influence whichever officials or bureaucracies resolve such obscurities. Sometimes, this lack of legislative clarity results from congressional confusion or ignorance.

- *When technical standards must be created or revised.* Existing legislation regulating air pollution, water pollution, and hazardous substances ordinarily requires the EPA to define the standards and prescribe the appropriate control technologies necessary to meet mandated standards. Often, regulatory agencies also are required by such legislation to review periodically and, if appropriate, revise such standards or technology requirements. Legitimate disagreement often exists (as noted in Chapter 5) over the technical and economic justifications for most regulatory standards. In the presence of expert dissension about such issues, a large measure of discretion rests with regulatory agencies for resolving such disputes. This discretion and the conflict it invites will reappear whenever agencies review regulatory standards.

• *When compliance deadlines are flexible.* Pollution legislation may bristle with explicit compliance deadlines, but administrators almost always have authority to extend them. Legislation is particularly generous in granting administrators authority to extend compliance deadlines when, in their opinion, economic hardship or other inequities may result from strict enforcement. For instance, the CAA instructs the EPA to set emission standards for new air pollution sources by considering, among other things, "the degree of emission limitation achievable through the application of the best system of emission reduction which (taking into account the cost of achieving such reduction) the administrator determines has been adequately demonstrated." Such a fistful of discretionary authority in effect permits the EPA to extend compliance deadlines for specific air pollution sources by increasing the time allowed to search for pollution controls meeting these multiple criteria. In many cases, a compliance deadline also may be relaxed if an agency determines that it is beyond the technical ability of a polluter to install the proper controls in the required time.

The Politics of Enforcement

Few provisions in current pollution legislation compel federal officials to stop a polluting activity. Most often, enforcement actions are discretionary, as in Section 111 of the CAA, which instructs the EPA administrator to regulate any pollutant from a stationary source when, in the judgment of the administrator, it may cause or contribute to "air pollution which may reasonably be anticipated to endanger public health or welfare." Even when enforcement action is initiated, officials are usually given optional methods for securing compliance.

Typically, air and water pollution laws are enforced through state or local agencies with considerable discretion to decide what level of emission controls will be required of an air or water polluter and when emission controls must be achieved. These become conditions for the permits that all air- and water-polluting firms must obtain from state, federal, and local authorities to operate. In air pollution regulation, for instance, regulators can decide which emission controls are technically and economically feasible and can issue variances that temporarily waive emissions control deadlines or technology specifications.[6] Regulators seek voluntary compliance. They want to avoid imposing penalties as a means of ensuring compliance if possible, because they know that resorting to administrative or judicial tribunals very likely will involve a protracted, inflexible process with no assurances that the polluter will be compelled to control emissions speedily and efficiently at the conclusion.

Regulated firms often balk at a regulatory agency's initial specification of acceptable control technologies and deadline dates for compliance with emission standards. The usual solution is bargaining between regulator and regulated, particularly when regulatory agencies confront an economically and politically influential firm or group of firms that is capable of creating political pressures on the regulatory agency to reach some accommodation over required control technologies or compliance deadlines. Regulatory agencies typically will make some concession to firms concerning the required control technologies or compliance deadlines. One form of these concessions is the frequently used variance that allows a firm some delay in achieving emission controls that are otherwise required under the law.

Agencies also depend heavily on firms to monitor and report their own pollution emissions, in part because of the sheer volume of regulated entities. Under the CAA, for instance, more than thirty-five thousand major and 350,000 minor facilities are regulated.[7] Most regulatory agencies still lack the personnel and other resources to inspect routinely and monitor all emission controls within their jurisdictions. Voluntary compliance is almost a necessity. Quite often, regulatory agencies monitor only the larger sources of pollution emissions within their jurisdiction, leaving smaller sources to report their own compliance with permit conditions under all but exceptional circumstances. Even monitoring the largest pollution sources does not necessarily ensure that air or water pollutants are satisfactorily regulated.

Often, the administrative ability to make a deal allows a regulatory agency to achieve more pollution abatement than would be the case if it insisted on extremely stringent emission standards in full and immediate compliance with the law. This is true particularly when the regulated firm either is unable to comply fully and immediately with a strict interpretation of the law or is willing to fight indefinitely in the courts or administrative hearing rooms to prevent any regulation. Many regulatory agencies, limited by staff and funding that are inadequate for their mandated responsibilities, have no practical alternative to relying on voluntary compliance and accommodation. Agencies may logically conclude that it is better to bargain with the regulated interests in the hope of achieving some limited goals than to adopt what may become an ultimately futile strategy of insisting on stringent compliance with the law.

REGULATING AIR QUALITY

The CAA, together with its important 1977 and 1990 amendments, constitutes one of the longest, most complex, and most technically detailed federal regulatory programs ever enacted. The CAA creates a standards-and-enforcement program in which the federal government establishes national ambient air-quality standards for major pollutants, the states and local government agencies assume primary responsibility for implementing the program within federal guidelines, and the various levels of government share enforcement responsibilities. However, the states may enact more stringent standards for airsheds in their jurisdictions.

Overall, national air quality has undoubtedly improved—in a few instances, dramatically—since the CAA's enactment in 1970. By 2018, the EPA was regulating more than two hundred air pollutants—most of them toxic air pollutants identified by Congress or the EPA since 1990. However, the most important of these pollutants in terms of public health and political significance are the so-called criteria pollutants—carbon monoxide, nitrogen oxides, ozone, particulate matter, sulfur dioxide, and lead—whose regulation was mandated in 1970 by the original CAA and whose health effects are summarized in Box 6.1. The improvement in both air quality and pollution emissions associated with these six pollutants between 1980 and 2016 has been, in most cases, significant and, in the case of lead, dramatic. Airborne lead, which is especially hazardous to children, has been virtually eliminated through the abolition of leaded automobile fuels. Since 1980, sulfur dioxide emissions decreased by more than 90 percent and carbon monoxide emissions by 73 percent.[8] The data understate the significance of these achievements, because they do not estimate what pollution emissions would have been in the absence of regulation during a period from 1990 to 2016, when the U.S. population increased by 24 percent and vehicle miles traveled increased by 40 percent. Additional improvement is predicted as new regulatory programs are implemented. Here are two examples:

- Recent EPA diesel regulations for trucks are expected to remove 90 percent of the soot from present diesel motor emissions.

- The EPA 2006 Clean Air Mercury Rule is expected to significantly reduce mercury emissions from coal-fired power plants—the largest remaining sources of mercury emissions in the country—from 48 to 15 tons per year, a reduction of nearly 70 percent.

Despite this improvement, the nation's air remains seriously degraded in several respects. First, ground-level ozone, a primary component of urban smog, remains a pervasive problem. This low-level ozone poses significant human health risks and produces more than $1 billion in agricultural crop damage annually. Currently, more than 116 million Americans, mostly urbanites, live in areas that are not in compliance with the ozone standard. Second, emissions of nitrogen oxides, a precursor of acid precipitation and a greenhouse gas contributing to urban smog, have increased since 1970. Third, U.S. releases of greenhouse gases, especially carbon dioxide (CO_2), is predicted to increase by more than 42 percent between 2000 and 2020 under present U.S. air-quality policies—a surge in climate-change emissions considered highly undesirable by most climate scientists, unacceptable by environmentalists, and threatening internationally (as discussed fully in Chapter 10).[9] In addition, the control of small particulates, identified as an important public health problem in the early 1990s, has just begun. Finally, air toxics have yet to be adequately regulated.

BOX 6.1 HUMAN HEALTH AND ENVIRONMENTAL EFFECTS OF COMMON AIR POLLUTANTS

Ozone (ground-level ozone is the principal component of smog)

- *Source.* Ozone is produced by a chemical reaction involving volatile organic compounds (VOCs) and nitrogen oxides.

- *Health effects.* Ozone causes breathing problems, reduced lung function, asthma, irritated eyes, stuffy nose, and reduced resistance to colds and other infections and may speed up aging of lung tissue.

- *Environmental effects.* Ozone can damage plants and trees; smog can cause reduced visibility.

- *Property damage.* Ozone damages rubber, fabrics, and other materials.

Volatile organic compounds (smog formers)[a]

- *Source.* VOCs are released from burning fuel (e.g., gasoline, oil, wood, coal, and natural gas) and from solvents, paints, glues, and other products used at work or at home. Cars are a common source of VOCs. VOCs include chemicals such as benzene, toluene, methylene chloride, and methyl chloroform.

- *Health effects.* In addition to ozone (smog) effects, many VOCs can cause serious health problems such as cancer.

- *Environmental effects.* In addition to ozone (smog) effects, some VOCs, such as formaldehyde and ethylene, may harm plants.

Nitrogen dioxide (one of the nitrogen oxides, a smog-forming chemical)

- *Source.* Nitrogen dioxide is produced in the burning of gasoline, natural gas, coal, oil, and other fuels. Cars are a common source of nitrogen dioxide.

- *Health effects.* Nitrogen dioxide causes lung damage and illnesses of the breathing passages and lungs (the respiratory system).

- *Environmental effects.* Nitrogen dioxide is an ingredient of acid rain (acid aerosols), which can damage trees and lakes. Acid aerosols reduce visibility.

- *Property damage.* Acid aerosols can eat away stone used in buildings, statues, and monuments.

Carbon monoxide

- *Source.* Carbon monoxide is produced in the burning of gasoline, natural gas, coal, oil, and other fuels.

- *Health effects.* Carbon monoxide reduces the ability of blood to bring oxygen to body cells and tissues; the cells and tissues need oxygen to work. Carbon

(Continued)

(Continued)

monoxide may be particularly hazardous to people who have heart or circulatory (blood vessel) problems and to people who have damaged lungs or breathing passages.

Particulate matter (dust, smoke, soot)

- *Source.* Particulate matter is produced in the burning of wood, diesel, and other fuels; by industrial plants; through agriculture (e.g., plowing and burning off fields); and from driving on unpaved roads.

- *Health effects.* Particulate matter causes nose and throat irritation, lung damage, bronchitis, and early death.

- *Environmental effects.* Particulate matter is the main source of haze that reduces visibility.

- *Property damage.* Ash, soot, smoke, and dust can dirty and discolor structures and other property, including clothes and furniture.

Sulfur dioxide

- *Source.* Sulfur dioxide is produced in the burning of coal and oil (especially high-sulfur coal from the eastern United States) and through industrial processes (e.g., those involving paper and metal).

- *Health effects.* Sulfur dioxide causes breathing problems and may cause permanent damage to lungs.

- *Environmental effects.* Sulfur dioxide is an ingredient in acid rain (acid aerosols), which can damage trees and lakes. Acid aerosols reduce visibility.

- *Property damage.* Acid aerosols can eat away stone used in buildings, statues, and monuments.

Lead

- *Source.* Lead is found in leaded gasoline (being phased out), paint (used, for example, on houses and cars), and smelters (metal refineries); it is used in the manufacture of lead storage batteries.

- *Health effects.* Lead causes brain and other nervous system damage; children are especially at risk. Some lead-containing chemicals cause cancer in animals. Lead causes digestive and other health problems.

- *Environmental effects.* Lead can harm wildlife.

Source: Adapted from EPA, Office of Air Quality Planning and Standards, The Plain English Guide to the Clean Air Act, available at www.epa.gov/oar/oaqps/peg_caa/pegcaa11.html (accessed March 6, 2001).

[a]All VOCs contain carbon, the basic chemical element found in living things. Carbon-containing chemicals are called organic. Volatile chemicals escape into the air easily. Many VOCs are also hazardous air pollutants, which can cause serious illnesses. The EPA does not list VOCs as criteria air pollutants, but they are included here because efforts to control smog also target VOCs for reduction.

The Clean Air Act and the 1977 Amendments

In broad outline, the CAA, including the 1977 amendments, mandates the following programs:

1. *National air-quality standards.* The act directs the EPA to determine the maximum permissible ambient air concentrations for pollutants that it found to be harmful to human health or the environment. The EPA was instructed to establish such standards for at least seven pollutants: carbon monoxide, hydrocarbons, lead, nitrogen oxide, particulates, ozone, and sulfur oxides. The agency was to set two types of national ambient air-quality standards without considering the cost of compliance:

   a. *Primary standards.* Primary standards were supposed to protect human health with an adequate margin of safety for particularly vulnerable segments of the population, such as the elderly and infants.

   b. *Secondary standards.* Secondary standards were intended to maintain visibility and to protect buildings, crops, and water.

2. *Stationary source regulations.* The EPA was to set maximum emission standards for new stationary sources, called "new source performance standards."

3. *State implementation plans.* Each state was required to create a plan indicating how it would achieve federal standards and guidelines to implement the act fully by 1982. The plans were to contain information relating to several important elements:

   a. The nation was divided into 247 air-quality control regions for which states were made responsible. The regions were classified as either attainment or nonattainment regions for each of the regulated pollutants.

   b. States were also made responsible for enforcing special air-quality standards in areas with especially clean air. These regions were called prevention of significant deterioration (PSD) regions.

   c. States were required to order existing factories in nonattainment areas to retrofit their plants with control technologies representing "reasonably available control technology."

4. *Mobile source emission standards (for automobiles and trucks).* Title II of the CAA created a detailed but flexible timetable for achieving auto and truck emission controls.

With the exception of lead, by 1990, reductions in other pollutants still seemed unsatisfactorily slow, and urban air pollution—especially concentrations of nitrogen oxide, ozone, and VOCs—continued to be a major concern. After almost a decade of bitter impasse, the White House, environmentalists, and Congress collaborated to rewrite comprehensively the 1970 legislation by passing the Clean Air Act Amendments of 1990, the most important and imaginative regulatory reform in more than a decade.

The Clean Air Act Amendments of 1990

The new amendments are a curious mélange of hammer clauses, multitudinous deadlines, and other tread-worn approaches combined with a timely sensitivity to emerging problems and an aggressive new approach to global climate protection based on an innovative, market-inspired scheme for emissions trading. This mix of tradition, invention, and desperation represents what may be the last, best hope for fortifying the original CAA sufficiently to achieve its purpose. The major features are outlined in the sections that follow.[10]

Title I: Nonattainment Areas. The amendments established a new classification of areas that failed to meet national air-quality standards for ozone, carbon monoxide, and particulates and created deadlines of from three to twenty years for attaining these standards. They also created a graded set of regulatory requirements for each area, depending on the severity of the pollution.

Title II: Mobile Sources. The new amendments set more than ninety new emission standards for autos and trucks.

Title III: Hazardous Air Pollutants. The amendments required the EPA to create national emission standards for hazardous air pollutants for all major sources of hazardous or toxic air pollutants and specified 189 chemicals to be regulated immediately. They established a multitude of specific deadlines by which the EPA was ordered to list categories of industrial processes that emit dangerous air pollutants, to establish health-based standards for each hazardous chemical emission, and to ensure that sources of hazardous emission have established safety controls at their facilities.

Title IV: Control of Acid Deposition. The amendments created a new emissions trading program for sulfur oxides, a major precursor of acid precipitation. Under this new approach, the EPA was "to allocate to each major coal-fired power plant an allowance for each ton of emission permitted; sources cannot release emissions beyond the number of allowances they are given. Allowances may be traded, bought, or sold among allowance holders . . ."[11] The 110 largest sulfur oxide sources in the utility industry were required to meet stricter emission standards. In addition, emissions of nitrogen oxides were to be reduced by two million tons annually.

Title VI: Stratospheric Ozone Protection. Title VI listed specific ozone-depleting chemicals and created a schedule for phasing out their production or use. It also pledged the United States to an accelerated phaseout of ozone-depleting chemicals that exceeded the schedule to which the United States had agreed in the 1987 Montreal Protocol on Substances That Deplete the Ozone Layer.

CURRENT CONTROVERSIES IN AIR-QUALITY REGULATION

The CAA is the nation's longest, most complex regulatory law. Its legal and technical intricacy seems to ensure employment for lawyers and judges unborn and unrelenting partisan debate about its wisdom and implications among politicians and economists. At the same time, it is among the most revolutionary and ambitious environmental laws in U.S. history, the foundation of U.S. environmental regulation. Major issues involved with the CAA include the impact of federalism, regulatory science, and partisan change in the presidency. Current controversies over small-particulate regulation and controls for climate-warming air emissions illustrate these issues.

Science and Regulatory Change: Small Particulates

Improved scientific research can complicate pollution control. Regulation strives for predictability, consistency in interpreting and applying the law, and stability in established norms for decision-making. Science breeds discovery, embraces change, promotes experimentation, and challenges tradition. Science is a constant troubler to regulatory order. Since 1970, the CAA has regulated airborne particulates as one of the original criteria pollutants. But the continuing enrichment of scientific data since 1970 is forcing EPA to change its understanding of which particulates should be regulated and which levels can be tolerated.

EPA Revises a Regulation. In 1971, the EPA issued air-quality standards for particulates without distinction regarding size. Particulates (extremely small, solid particles of matter found in the air and produced by dust, smoke, fuel combustion, agriculture, and forest cultivation, among other sources) have been known for many decades to pose health hazards. Initially, however, the EPA's standards on particulates assumed that size was not a significant factor in the health risks posed. By 1987, accumulating scientific research had demonstrated conclusively that small particulates, those smaller than ten microns (one micron or micrometer equals 1/25,000 inch), are especially hazardous to humans because they can be inhaled into lung tissue, unlike larger particulates, which are trapped in air passages to the lungs.[12] These smaller particulates are commonly found in cigarette smoke, diesel engine emissions, and windblown dust, among other sources. They are also dangerous because they can carry carcinogenic chemicals into the lungs.

In 1987, the EPA issued new air-quality standards for small particulates. However, existing emission controls for particulates were not designed specifically to control small particulates, and many sources of small particulates were not regulated at all.

About 250 air-quality control regions failed the new ambient air-quality standards for fine particulates. In the West, a major problem was windblown dust, not easily controlled by any existing technology. The EPA established tailpipe standards for emissions from diesel trucks and buses, beginning with the 1988 model year, that became increasingly stringent for models beginning in 1991. But monitoring data about the origin and distribution of fine particulates was inadequate, and states were slow to identify the magnitude of their problems and the sources to be regulated. Control technologies for stationary sources of small particulates were not well tested, and the control costs were not accurately known. In effect, small particulates had become a separate emission-control problem, and the states spent much of the 1990s acquiring a capability to regulate them. The EPA's most recent particulate standards, enacted concurrently with the 1997 revised smog rules, created new regulations specifically for particulates smaller than 2.5 microns, because scientific research had demonstrated that these posed a distinct human health risk.

Regulated Interests Resist. Automobile manufacturers, fossil-fuel-burning facilities, and the trucking industry were predictably concerned about the additional compliance costs to meet the proposed new standards. And they were angered by this "regulatory ratcheting"—the appearance of new, progressively more stringent regulatory rules with which they must comply—creating the third different particulate standard within a decade. Proponents of the new standards argued that they were protecting the elderly, children, and people with chronic lung disease from a new, scientifically verified health risk. For regulated interests, the real problem seemed to be the economically disruptive impact of regulatory science on their existing environmental control strategies.

Predictably, the disaffected truckers, utilities, and other regulated industries took their case to court, all the way to the Supreme Court, challenging the EPA's authority to promulgate the new regulatory rules in what turned out to be one of the most significant environmental regulatory cases since the 1970s. Essentially, the dissidents challenged the EPA's discretionary authority, granted by Congress in the CAA, to set ambient air-quality standards solely on the basis of public health considerations. The EPA, they argued, had interpreted this authority too broadly, and Congress had been negligent in permitting the agency too much discretion in interpreting such authority. Had the Supreme Court agreed with this argument, the logic could well have overturned a huge array of other environmental regulations across the whole domain of federal environmental regulation and left a chaos of regulatory confusion. The Supreme Court, however, rejected the assault on the EPA's congressionally delegated authority and in a landmark ruling (*Whitman v. American Trucking Associations,* 531 U.S. 457) affirmed in 2001 both the delegated authority and the EPA's latitude in interpreting that authority.

The Federal Courts Intervene. What followed was a splendid example of EPA decision-making driven by the judicial lash. With Supreme Court approval, the EPA began to issue regulations in 2002 to implement its small-particulate standards. But the agency was sued again in 2002, this time by environmental groups, for failing to review its standards for small and large particulates by a 2002 deadline set by the CAA (which required an EPA review of all air-quality standards every five years). After further negotiation, the EPA reached a settlement with the environmental groups in which it agreed to review again its particulate standards. In 2006, the EPA decided to implement its new small-particulate standard and also to abandon its earlier standard for large particulates—another instance of regulatory ratcheting driven by ongoing scientific research. Meanwhile, the EPA estimated in 2005 that at least 129 counties with more than 68 million people appeared to exceed the standard for small particulates established in 1997 and that almost four hundred additional counties with a population exceeding ninety-one million people had provided insufficient data to even determine whether they had met particulate standards.[13] Thus, a substantial proportion of the national population, most of them urban dwellers, appeared to be living in areas that might be subjected in the near future to increasingly stringent air pollution controls that could significantly affect economic development.

In November 2009, EPA Administrator Lisa Jackson announced that the EPA would begin reviewing and if necessary revising existing standards for particulates and all criteria pollutants regulated by the CAA. But the EPA was too slow to satisfy eleven states that joined health and environmental groups in suing the agency in federal court for its delay. Finally, in June 2012, the EPA proposed revised regulations that would reduce the amount of fine particulates in the air by 17 percent below currently permitted levels. The EPA was required to issue its final version of the new regulations by December 2012, thus the Obama administration inherited more contention over CAA regulations for this second term.[14] In March 2015, the EPA finally issued a proposed rule concerning how the states were to implement the new particulate emission standards. State air quality control officials complained that the new rule was two years late and certain to create unnecessary delay and expense for the fourteen urban areas in six states required to upgrade their particulate emission controls. The most optimistic estimates were that the emission controls would not take effect until at least 2021.[15]

Clean Power and Partisan Politics: The Clean Power Plan

The Clean Power Plan is the first comprehensive federal government strategy to regulate the nation's climate-warming emissions. Controversy over the Clean Power Plan (CPP) began in 2007 when the Supreme Court ruled in *Massachusetts v. EPA* that EPA was required by the Clean Air Act to regulate national air emissions of carbon monoxide (CO_2), which scientists declared to be a major cause of global climate warming. After his 2008 election, Barack Obama vigorously supported the

EPA's multiyear endeavor to draft a technically and economically complex strategy for national CO_2 regulation, whose final version became the CPP.[16]

The plan incited a ferocious partisan battle once it was proposed by the EPA in August 2015. Barack Obama intended the plan to be the most significant and enduring legacy among his environmental policies. It also became ground zero for President Donald Trump's fierce assault on EPA environmental policymaking, the very model of all that Trump and congressional Republicans believed was wrong with EPA's regulations and climate policies. Trump had promised to reject the plan, and less than a year after Trump's election, new EPA administrator, Scott Pruitt, redeemed Trump's promise and repealed the plan, much to the satisfaction of congressional Republicans. "Boom, it's gone,"[17] the president had predicted. However, the Clean Power Plan did not go 'boom.' Instead it remains, contested and unresolved, on a battleground within Congress and the federal courts.

Proposed: Strict National CO_2 Emissions Controls. In early August 2015, the Obama administration released the final, toughest, most controversial version of EPA's proposed Clean Power Plan. The proposed rule, all 1,560 pages, was EPA's most aggressive strategy for using the Clean Air Act to control the nation's climate-change emissions.[18] The legal and political conflict unleashed by the plan magnified the bitter partisan political conflict between the Obama administration and Congressional Republicans over climate regulation that prevailed throughout Obama's two presidential terms. Opponents of an earlier plan version, armed with all the weapons and strategies of skilled political infighting, were fully prepared to fight the plan through the 2016 presidential election. Every candidate for the 2016 Republican nomination was already a declared opponent.

In essence, a major goal of the plan was to reduce U.S. emissions of CO_2 in 2030 by 10 percent compared to emissions in 2005. The electric power industry was a critical regulatory target for the plan because this sector is responsible for about 31 percent of national carbon emissions. Equally important, in Obama's perspective, adoption of the plan would greatly enhance U.S. influence in its effort to hasten global action to abate climate change at the 2015 Paris global climate conference and assure credibility to the nation's own commitments to future global climate agreements. The plan set goals for each state to reduce its CO_2 emissions from the electric power sector based on its existing emissions and the 2030 reduction national target. States were given several alternative strategies for meeting these new emission goals and additional options within each strategy. States could concentrate regulation primarily on the power plants and apply emission standards for each unit. Alternatively, states could create statewide or regional emission targets for the whole power sector and adopt a variety of strategies for achieving that goal, including emissions trading, carbon taxes, or various combinations of fuel-switching, new nuclear plants, or renewable energy development. EPA estimated that the plan would cost $8.4 billion by 2030 but create $45 billion in benefits, mostly through improved public health. EPA also calculated that the cost of compliance for the regulated industries was neither excessive nor damaging to the national economy.

If all state goals were achieved, the most significant impact would be to alter the mix of fuels used by the utility sector: Coal, the largest source of utility fuel, would diminish to 27 percent, renewables would grow from 12 percent to 20 percent, while natural gas and nuclear power would remain largely unchanged. All states were required to submit compliance plans by September 2016 and to achieve compliance by 2022. States without compliance plans would be subject by default to federal rules.

The Controversy Enlarges. The proposed plan would not burden all states equally; some states, anticipating the need for CO_2 emission regulation, had already initiated reduction plans or were planning to do so. However, numerous states had incentive to oppose the plan. Regulatory work and cost would fall most heavily upon states with a high proportion of coal-generated electric power, such as Kentucky and West Virginia. Some of these were also among sixteen states already displeased with more stringent reduction targets in the plan's earlier version. Announcement of the final proposal unleashed the expected onslaught of litigation, corporate condemnation through the media, and congressional (mostly Republican) criticism. A coalition of coal companies and fourteen coal-reliant states had already attempted unsuccessfully through the courts to halt an earlier version of the plan. The final version produced what one opponent predicted would be "a tsunami of litigation."

Critics, led by Trump, repeated throughout the 2016 presidential campaign a trinity of indictments against the campaign. First, Trump gained considerable political traction among coal miners, the coal industry, and coal-producing states by joining congressional Republicans in declaring that the plan constituted a "war on coal" and was certain to weaken further an already economically depressed coal industry while accelerating unemployment among coal miners. Moreover, Trump and his congressional allies charged that EPA's plan exceeded its regulatory powers created by the CAA. Finally, the plan's opponents predicted it would escalate energy prices, deflate the shale gas boom, and damage the consumer economy—an accusation EPA's new administrator echoed when he celebrated his repeal of the plan by asserting he had saved Americans $33 billion.[19]

The tsunami of litigation promised by opponents rolled into the courts almost immediately following EPA's announcement of the final plan, the roster of contenders on both sides illustrating the enormous political and economic scale of the conflict. Four different groups initiating legal opposition to the plan included twenty-four attorneys general of Republican states, a coalition of business groups headed by the U.S. Chamber of Commerce, coal industry giant Murray Energy, and electric utilities from South Carolina, North Dakota, and Oklahoma. Petitioners urging the courts to uphold the plan included the states of California and New York and the cities of Washington, D.C., Chicago, Philadelphia, and New York City.[20] As the presidential election campaign gained momentum in early 2016, hostile litigation was slowly working through the federal courts.

EPA's repeal of the plan in October 2017 provoked a fresh wave of litigation, initiated by environmental and scientific organizations, joined by several states and some industries, to compel EPA to enforce its final version of the plan. Whatever the outcome of this new litigation, the EPA will still be compelled by the Supreme Court's verdict in *Massachusetts v. EPA* (2007) to create *some* regulatory plan to control national CO_2 emissions.

REGULATING WATER QUALITY

The nation's aquatic inheritance is not just water but different water systems, each essential to modern U.S. society and each currently threatened or already severely polluted by different combinations of pollutants.

Surface Water

The nation's surface waters—streams, rivers, lakes, wetlands, and coastal areas—are the nation's most visible water resources. Almost 99 percent of the population lives within fifty miles of a publicly owned lake. Streams, rivers, and lakes account for a high proportion of all recreational activities, commercial fishing grounds, and industrial water resources. Because surface waters are so intensively used and so highly visible, their rapidly accelerating degradation became the most immediate cause for congressional action in the 1960s and 1970s; arresting water pollution and restoring the nation's once-high water quality became a focal point for environmental legislation. In 1972, Congress enacted the nation's most important water pollution control legislation, the Federal Water Pollution Control Act, also called the Clean Water Act. The legislation created a national water pollution regulatory program intended to achieve "zero discharge of pollutants into waters of the United States by 1985" and "fishable and swimmable waters" by 1983. These ambitious goals were more inspirational than achievable, but they did signal the onset of a determined federal and state government initiative to reclaim degraded waters, protect endangered watersheds, and preserve pristine rivers, streams, and lakes.

Most of the fragmentary data available on national water quality since 1970 has come from monitoring surface-water conditions. Surprisingly little reliable information exists about the quality of most U.S. surface waters. Even after the turn of the twenty-first century, estimates of surface-water quality continue to be ambiguous and uncertain, largely because comprehensive, reliable monitoring data remain unavailable. Federal agencies such as the EPA and the CEQ have traditionally based their surface-water-quality indexes on only six pollutants, excluding common sources of water degradation, such as heavy metals, synthetic organic compounds, and dissolved solids. In general, surface-water quality seems, despite some spectacular achievements, to have remained in about the same condition since the late 1980s. It is often difficult, in any case, to know what significance to impute to available statistics, because EPA's last comprehensive survey

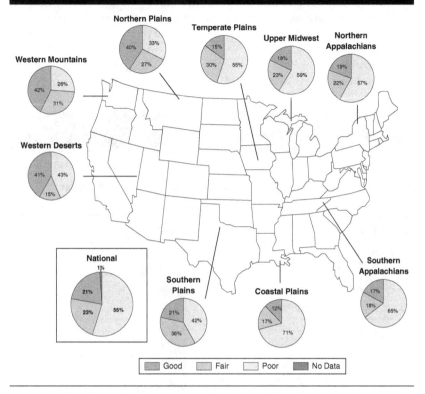

FIGURE 6.2 ■ Biological Condition of U.S. Rivers and Streams, 2009

Good   Fair   Poor   No Data

Source: U.S. EPA, Office of Wetlands, Oceans and Watersheds, Office of Research and Development, *National Rivers and Streams Assessment, 2008–2009* (Washington, DC: EPA, 2013). Document No. EPA/841/D-13/001, 63.

Note: Percentages may not add up to 100% due to rounding.

on national stream quality based on 2016 data reported that only 30 percent of national river and stream miles had been assessed.[21] Among the streams that were assessed, more than half were judged to be in poor condition and, as Figure 6.2 indicates, some regional waters were in worse shape. Wetlands are still largely terra incognita; little more than 8 percent of wetlands acreage has been evaluated for water quality.

Just how problematic is state monitoring is suggested by a GAO description of the evaluated data used by many states. "Evaluated data," explains the GAO report, "include site-specific monitoring data more than 5 years old and information that serves as an indicator of water quality conditions, such as anecdotal evidence or reports on wildlife or habitat conditions"[22]—in short, sophisticated guesswork.

Considering the nation's population growth and economic expansion since 1980, the stability of water quality must be considered an achievement of sorts—it could have been much worse. Nevertheless, the quality of the nation's surface water apparently is not greatly improved. And so things will remain as long as the dull but essential task of data collection remains politically unattractive and underfunded.

The leading causes of surface-water pollution, along with the data limitations, can be identified readily (see Figure 6.3). By far, the largest contributor

FIGURE 6.3 ■ Probable Sources of Impairment of Assessed U.S. Rivers and Streams, 2009

National Summary

Probable Sources of Impairments in Assessed Rivers and Streams

Probable Source Group	Miles Threatened or Impaired
Agriculture	131,149
Unknown	103,292
Atmospheric Deposition	99,930
Hydromodification	61,088
Urban-Related Runoff/Stormwater	60,849
Municipal Discharges/Sewage	58,558
Natural/Wildlife	51,588
Unspecified Nonpoint Source	49,007
Habitat Alterations (Not Directly Related to Hydromodification)	34,990
Resource Extraction	29,289
Silviculture (Forestry)	19,381
Industrial	17,920
Construction	12,903
Other	10,176
Land Application/Waste Sites/Tanks	9,409
Legacy/Historical Pollutants	5,991
Spills/Dumping	3,351
Recreation and Tourism (Non-Boating)	1,808
Aquaculture	317
Groundwater Loading/Withdrawals	270
Recreational Boating and Marinas	142
Commercial Harbor and Port Activities	52
Military Bases	20

Source: U.S. EPA, "National Summary of State Information," available at http://ofmpub.epa.gov/waters10/attains_nation_cy.control.

to this pollution is agricultural runoff. Other significant sources of nonpoint pollution (i.e., pollution arising from diffuse, multiple sources rather than from a pipe or other point source) include urban runoff and atmospheric deposition; these are the most technologically and politically formidable pollutants yet to be controlled.

The Federal Water Pollution Control Amendments

The 1972 amendments to the Clean Water Act completely changed the substance of the earlier legislation and established the regulatory framework that now prevails. Among the most important provisions were the following:

1. *Goals.* The amendments established two broad goals whose achievement, if possible, assumed an unprecedented regulatory structure and unusually rapid technological innovation:

   a. That "the discharge of pollutants into navigable waters of the United States be eliminated by 1985."

   b. That "wherever attainable, an interim goal of water quality which provides for the protection and propagation of fish, shellfish and wildlife and provides for recreation in and on the water be achieved by 1 July 1983."

2. *Regulating pollution dischargers.* The legislation required that all direct dischargers of pollution into navigable waterways satisfy two different standards:

   a. *Discharge limits for existing nonmunicipal sources.* States were to designate the use of a water body (recreation, fishing, boating, etc.) and establish limits of pollution discharges into each water body. The EPA would identify what technologies each pollution source must adopt to control its discharges. A different set of standards was established for municipal wastewater treatment facilities.

   b. *Discharge limits for municipal treatment plants.* All facilities, regardless of age, were required to have "the best practicable treatment technology" by July 1, 1983.

   c. *Discharge limits for new nonmunicipal sources.* All new sources of discharge, except municipal treatment plants, were required to use control technologies based on "the best available demonstrated control technology, operating methods or other alternatives."

   d. *Toxic discharge standards.* The EPA was required to establish special standards for any discharge determined to be toxic.

3. *Federal and state enforcement.* The EPA was authorized to delegate responsibility for enforcing most regulatory provisions to qualified states, which would issue permits to all polluters specifying the conditions for their effluent discharges.

4. *Nonpoint pollution regulation.* Amendments added in 1987 required each state to have a plan approved by the EPA for controlling pollution from nonpoint sources. Such plans must include "best management practices," but states are permitted to decide whether to require owners and managers to use such practices or to make their use voluntary.

Even the most ardent advocates of the legislation recognized that the rigorous compliance deadlines for effluent treatment and wastewater facility construction would not be attained. They were convinced that pressing technology ultimately worked—eliminating all pollutants from the nation's waters hardly seemed impossible to a people who could launch a satellite carrying their language a billion light-years into space.

The Political Setting

The political struggle over implementation of the FWPCAA has been shaped by several factors. First, the implementation of the legislation is federalized. The 1972 law permitted the states to decide on the designated use for a body of water. In general, state regulatory agencies are more vulnerable than is Washington, D.C., to pressure from local water polluters to designate uses for bodies of water that will permit moderate to heavy pollution. This propensity of local regulatory agencies to accommodate regulated interests also extends to enforcement of designated water uses and the associated emission controls. Regulated interests often are likely to press vigorously for a major state role in the administration and enforcement of water-quality standards, believing that this works to their advantage more than implementation through the EPA's regional and national offices. State enforcement of pollution controls on major dischargers has improved significantly since 1972, but many violators still go undetected or unpunished.

Forty-six states have assumed major implementation responsibilities, such as issuing and enforcing permits for effluent dischargers, initiating requests for federal grants to build new local waste treatment facilities, and supervising the administration of the grant programs in their jurisdictions.[23] The states thus exercise considerable influence on program implementation directly through their own participation—and the pursuit of their own interests in the program—and through their congressional delegations, which remain ever vigilant in protecting the interests of the folks back home. Control standards vary greatly among the states for the same pollutant, often provoking states with strict standards to complain that more lenient states enjoy an unfair advantage in the competition for new business. Among six major states, for instance, the same five toxic pollutants were treated very differently:

In some states, the permitting authorities consistently established numeric limits on the discharges, while in other states, the authorities consistently required monitoring. In some states, no controls were imposed. In addition, the numeric discharge limits for specific pollutants differed from state to state and even within the same state for facilities of similar capacity.[24]

The political character of the program also depends on the enormous administrative discretion left to the EPA in prescribing the multitude of technologies that must be used by effluent dischargers to meet the many different standards established in the law. In 1972, when the Clean Water Act was amended, for instance, about twenty thousand industrial dischargers were pouring pollutants into more than 2,500 municipal waste treatment facilities.

The EPA was charged with identifying the pretreatment standards to be used by each major class of industrial discharger. This might eventually require standards for several hundred different classes and modified standards for subclasses. The final standards issued by the EPA in 1976 for industries producing "canned and preserved fruits and vegetables" alone contained specifications for fifty-one subcategories. Administrators also are limited by the state of the art in treatment technologies and by dependence on the regulated interests for information concerning the character of the discharger's production processes and technical capacities. Finally, the program's implementation has been affected continually by the active, if not always welcome, intervention of the White House, Congress, and the federal courts in the program's development. Federal and state regulatory agencies have had to conduct the program in a highly political environment, in which all major actions have been subject to continual scrutiny, debate, and assessment by elective public officials and judges. This is hardly surprising for a program involving so many billions of dollars and so many politically and economically sensitive interests.

A Stubborn Problem: Nonpoint Pollution

The most common source of surface-water pollution remains virtually uncontrolled in every state since the 1972 passage of the FWPCAA. Nonpoint pollution—pollution that does not originate from a specific source, such as a sewage pipeline, smokestack, or auto exhaust—is estimated to be the major cause of pollution in 65 percent of the stream miles not meeting state standards for their designated use.[25] Overall, more than one third of the stream miles in the United States appear to be affected by nonpoint pollution. Nonpoint pollution also affects groundwater quality. Figure 6.4, which portrays the proportion of nitrogen in major streams across the United States originating from nonpoint sources, illustrates the geographical breadth of this pollution.

Nonpoint pollution is especially troublesome. Its origin is often elusive. Almost all states lack enough information to identify most of the nonpoint sources polluting their surface waters.[26] It is not easily controlled technically or economically. Many different sources require many different control strategies.

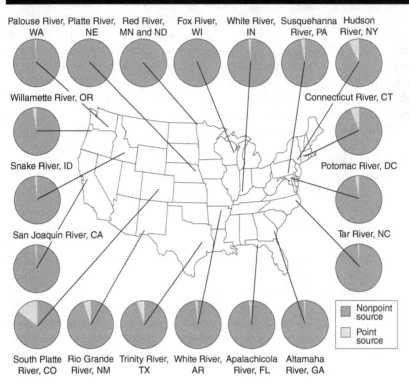

FIGURE 6.4 ■ Point and Nonpoint Sources of Nitrogen in Watersheds of the Continental United States

Proportions of nonpoint and point sources of nitrogen vary in watersheds across the continental United States. Commercial fertilizer and manure typically constitute the major sources of nitrogen to the first NAWQA study units. Atmospheric nitrogen is significant in most study units except in the far West and the Northern Great Plains. Point sources are an important source of nutrients to watersheds near large urban areas, such as Denver in the South Platte River Basin and Hartford in the Connecticut, Housatonic, and Thames River Basins.

Source: U.S. Department of the Interior, U.S. Geological Survey, "The Quality of Our Nation's Water—Nutrients and Pesticides," Circular No. 1225 (November 2000), 29.

The largest source of nonpoint pollution is agriculture; croplands, pasture, and rangelands together pollute about one third of the nation's stream miles with metabolic wastes from animals, sediment, fertilizers, pesticides, dissolved solids, and other materials. Agricultural runoff and urban storm water runoff are the major causes of the eutrophication of lakes, whereby dissolved organic substances create such a high level of oxygen demand in the waters that higher forms of plants and animals die from oxygen deprivation. Eutrophication eventually leaves most lakes lifeless.

Control Is Politically and Technically Difficult

Reducing agricultural pollution requires several difficult strategies, because technological solutions are rarely available. Most often, production practices must be altered. Farmers might be encouraged or required to reduce the volume of fertilizer, pesticides, and other chemicals used in crop production. Animal populations might be limited or dispersed. New crop and land management techniques might reduce soil runoff. In many instances, land-use planning might be used to prevent or reduce agricultural activities. But powerful agricultural groups and members of Congress for whom they are a major constituency believe such strategies will have adverse economic impacts and have opposed most measures intended to reduce agricultural runoff by most of these methods. Many state governments, fearful of damaging a major component of the state economy, are reluctant to do more than encourage farmers to voluntarily seek ways to limit their pollution runoff.

The current strategy for controlling nonpoint pollution has set regulators on a collision course not only with agricultural organizations but also with the commercial timber industry, the commercial and residential construction industry, meat packers and shippers, coal-mining firms, and a multitude of trades and professions associated with each. Since the early 1990s, the EPA has required states to identify all their waters that fail water-quality standards and, for each impaired water, to identify the amount by which each nonpoint pollutant must be reduced to meet these water-quality standards. Specifically, each state is required to specify for each nonpoint pollutant a total maximum daily load (TMDL), the maximum amount of each pollutant permitted in each water body over a twenty-four-hour period. This calculation has proved to be enormously difficult and controversial. The scale of the undertaking is staggering. The National Academy of Sciences reported in 2000 that

> given the most recent lists of impaired waters submitted by EPA, there are about 21,000 polluted river segments, lakes, and estuaries making up over 300,000 river and shore miles and 5 million lake acres. The number of TMDLs required for these impaired waters is greater than 40,000 [and] most states are required to meet an 8- to 13-year deadline for completion of the TMDLs.[27]

Nonetheless, most states have created some TMDLs or have attempted to do so. Perhaps the most nationally visible conflict over these calculations has arisen from efforts by the state of Florida and the federal government to create TMDLs for dissolved phosphorous in runoff degrading the Everglades from the vast sugarcane-growing region north of Lake Okeechobee. In this instance, as in most others involving the creation of TMDLs, scientific and legal controversy abounds and litigation proliferates. The TMDL calculation remains inherently problematic, and state regulators complain that the process is so adversarial that TMDL should mean "too many damn lawyers."

"This State's Gone Hog Wild": The Battle Over Concentrated Animal Farms

In mid-1997, corporate animal farms first made national news in the worst possible way. In eastern North Carolina, one corporate hog farm, home to twelve thousand pigs, was flooded by runoff from heavy rain. The swirling runoff flushed twenty-five million gallons of feces and urine from the farm's eight-acre waste lagoon into a knee-deep tide that inundated surrounding cotton and tobacco fields and then poured into the New River. The spill killed ten million fish along a seventeen-mile stretch of the river between Richlands and Jacksonville, closed 364,000 acres of wetlands to shell fishing for months, and prompted Rep. Charlie Rose, D-NC, to demand that the EPA declare a moratorium on new factory farms until their environmental contamination could be controlled. The following year, North Carolina's largely corporate hog farms produced more than sixteen million hogs—the nation's second-largest state hog production. "This state's gone hog wild," Rose complained. "We have a wonderful quality of life here, but a greedy, unregulated hog industry will ruin it overnight if we're not careful."[28]

Concentrated Animal Farms Are Increasing. The North Carolina spectacle was among the first of an increasing number of highly publicized incidents to thrust the problem of concentrated animal farming into national visibility and frame an ongoing political struggle in almost every agricultural state. The issue is a tangle of surface water, groundwater, and drinking water regulatory problems often falling between the margins of state and federal water pollution laws and provoking the jurisdictional problems common to regulatory federalism.

Concentrated animal feeding operations (CAFOs) are quickly transforming virtually all sectors of major animal production in the United States—cattle, hogs, poultry, turkeys, and dairy. The EPA describes these farms as

> facilities that confine animal feeding activities, thereby concentrating animal populations, animal manure, and animal mortality. AFO [animal feeding operation] activities can cause a range of environmental and public health problems, including oxygen depletion and disease transmission in surface water, pathogens and nutrient contamination in surface and ground water, methane emissions to the air, and excessive buildup of toxins, metals, and nutrients in soil.[29]

CAFO farming has expanded rapidly until, currently, more than 77 percent of the beef cattle and 72 percent of hogs and (egg-) layers in the United States are raised and managed on large farms. Due to their large size, CAFOs can increase meat production efficiency and lower the cost of related animal products and, in some instances, stimulate local economies. Ten large companies in 2014 produced more than 90 percent of the nation's poultry. CAFOs also produce prodigious quantities of waste that must be managed. A large farm with eight hundred thousand hogs, for example, produces more than 1.6 million tons of manure per year, which is one and a half times more than the annual sanitary waste produced by the city of Philadelphia.[30] The production of small, family-owned animal feeding operations is diminishing rapidly in the wake of increasing CAFOs. In North Carolina, several decades ago, two million pigs were raised on twenty-two thousand mostly family farms; by 2017, there were 2,300 farms raising more than nine million hogs mostly on CAFOs.[31] More than seven thousand very large CAFOs currently operate in the United States, most owned by large food production corporations and housing from one thousand to more than one hundred thousand animals each. In Oklahoma, North Carolina, Missouri, Georgia, Colorado, Texas, and Utah, to cite but a few examples, corporate animal production has become a major agricultural industry and the provocation for bitter political conflict. The EPA estimates that groundwater in seventeen states has been impaired by fecal streptococci and fecal coliform bacteria originating on animal feedlots. In these states, CAFOs are more than an environmentalist matter; they set smaller family farmers against corporate farms, rural legislators against urban ones, and economic boomers against proponents of slow growth.

Regulatory Problems. At least four major laws, including the Clean Water Act and the CAA, provide the EPA with authority to regulate some aspects of CAFO waste, but no single federal law currently creates an integrated regulatory approach.[32] Although the EPA has initiated since 2008 an increasing number of regulatory actions to control CAFO air and water pollution, it still lacks such essential information as an accurate inventory of the size and location of CAFOs in the United States.[33] The states vary enormously in the extent to which their existing water pollution laws control CAFOs. Intense disputes have become common concerning how strictly CAFOs should be regulated and whether their continued proliferation should be encouraged. Congressional members from every state experiencing a growth surge in large CAFOs have introduced legislation calling for a comprehensive federal regulatory program affecting all states and thereby eliminating the possibility that some states might create so-called pollution havens for large CAFOs. But Congress has yet to enact comprehensive CAFO regulatory legislation, an impasse due largely to conflicts between Washington and the states over their respective roles in a new regulatory regime and to disagreement among major corporate animal producers over acceptable regulations.

The CAFO wastes also create a variety of potentially hazardous and unregulated air emissions because the human and environmental health effects have not been characterized sufficiently to determine their relevance to the CAA. Among these emissions are methane, nitrous oxide, hydrogen sulfide, ammonia, and possibly the products from decomposition of animal manure and urea as well as particulate matter from dry manure, bedding and feed materials, biological matter (animal dander and feathers), and unpaved dirt lots.[34]

Although EPA expected to have relevant data available about the location and type of pollutants associated with CAFOs nationally by 2013, it was still incomplete by 2018. However, in early 2015, EPA was sued by a coalition of environmental groups asserting that the agency had been too slow to initiate regulatory action against CAFO air and water pollution.[35] Responding to this litigation and growing pressure from environmental and public health groups, the EPA has increased its regulatory activities and other measures to promote greater control of CAFO's adverse environmental impacts and to encourage more vigorous state regulation as well.

Groundwater

During the 1980s, the nation's groundwater became a major concern. Lying below Earth's upper porous surface and a lower layer of impermeable rock, groundwater percolates through the upper layer and collects until it eventually saturates subsurface soil and rock. Much of this water flows slowly to the sea through permeable layers of sand or gravel called aquifers. These aquifers sustain the life and vitality of communities throughout much of the United States. Groundwater is as essential as surface water to the nation's existence, and it is far more abundant—the annual flow of groundwater is fifty times the volume of surface flows, and most lies within a half mile of Earth's surface. Almost 50 percent of the U.S. population and 95 percent of its rural residents depend on groundwater for domestic uses. More than 40 percent of all agricultural irrigation originates from groundwater. Perhaps most important, more than 100 million Americans receive their drinking water from public water systems whose source is groundwater.[36] Because groundwater filters slowly through many levels of fine soil as it percolates downward and flows onward through the aquifers, it traditionally has been virtually free of harmful pollutants. Today, however, groundwater is seriously degraded in many areas of the United States.

Although groundwater monitoring has improved since Earth Day 1970, the complexity of groundwater systems and the expense of monitoring have convinced the EPA that "we may never have a complete picture of the nature and extent of the problem."[37] But the EPA has identified an enormous number of actual or potential sources of groundwater contamination:

- About 13,000 hazardous waste sites that are now potential candidates for the Superfund National Priority List (an inventory of the most dangerous sites)

- Millions of septic systems

- More than 180,000 surface impoundments, such as pits, ponds, and lagoons

- An estimated 500 hazardous-waste land disposal facilities and about 16,000 municipal and other landfills

- Millions of underground storage tanks (USTs)

- Thousands of underground injection wells, used to dispose of hazardous and solid wastes by flushing them into deep aquifers

- Millions of tons of pesticides and fertilizers spread on the ground, mostly in rural areas

Many Programs, Many Governments, Many Agencies. The 1977 discovery of massive groundwater contamination caused by the abandoned hazardous waste site at New York's Love Canal became the nation's first groundwater crisis. Groundwater contamination has been a crisis-driven issue, thrust on governmental agendas by waves of public apprehension following revelations of widespread groundwater contamination from hazardous waste dumps, agricultural chemicals, and industrial and governmental chemical accidents. Improved monitoring also has added urgency to the groundwater issue by revealing previously unknown chemical contamination (although often in only trace amounts). But the quality of most underground waters remains unknown.

Traditionally, groundwater management has been considered a state and local governmental responsibility. Although the federal government has no comprehensive groundwater management program, approximately forty-five different federal programs affect groundwater in some manner.[38] The primary federal responsibility for implementing many of the major programs affecting groundwater rests with the EPA. However, many other agencies and programs are also involved. The mélange of federal agencies and programs involved in groundwater management ensure incoherence, inconsistency, and competing authority in the federal government's approach to groundwater problems.

The states' considerable responsibility for groundwater management has been acquired through federal legislation and their own initiative. Forty-one states currently have their own groundwater-quality standards, although little consistency exists among them. The number of groundwater contaminants regulated varies from fourteen in one state to 190 in another. In addition, almost all states have assumed responsibility for implementing federal drinking water standards established under the Safe Drinking Water Act (SDWA) in 1974.

Controlling subsurface pollution is troublesome because groundwater filters very slowly as it flows. An aquifer may move no more than ten to one hundred feet annually. In any case, many toxic contaminants are not captured or neutralized by filtering. Moreover, the extent of groundwater pollution may be impossible to estimate adequately, because the pollution plume radiating outward through an aquifer from a pollution source can take a number of unpredictable directions. Often, plumes will contaminate millions or billions of gallons of water.

Many sources of groundwater contamination are still being identified. The nation's estimated 1.2 million abandoned oil and gas wells, of which perhaps two hundred thousand are not properly plugged, are examples. Abandoned wells, often drilled to a depth of more than one mile, can contaminate groundwater with brine, which is four times more saline than seawater and contains heavy metals, radioactivity, and other possible toxic substances (toxics). In Texas, perhaps forty thousand to fifty thousand abandoned wells may still pose pollution problems, and an estimated 386,000 wells have never been registered. A Texas health official recalls, "We've found leaking wells from the old days that were rock-plugged, bucket-plugged, tree-stump plugged and even one plugged with nothing more than a glass jug."

Continuing Chemical Contamination. The many substances known or suspected to contaminate groundwater defy concise enumeration. One survey indicated that the states collectively have set standards for approximately thirty-five inorganic compounds, thirty-nine volatile organic compounds, 125 nonvolatile organic compounds, and fifty-six pesticides, among other substances.[39] These chemicals represent only a small portion of those used in the U.S. economy and found in groundwater. These contaminants originate from many sources. States now regulate many of these sources, such as USTs, underground injection wells, and abandoned waste sites. Although most states have at least some standards for groundwater quality, it is unclear how well the standards are enforced. Among groundwater contaminants, synthetic chemicals and nutrients, particularly nitrates and phosphates, remain especially difficult to regulate because of their great number and wide diffusion in the ecosystem. Most states set standards for and monitor only a fraction of the chemicals likely to be present in groundwater. Almost all states identify toxics as a major source of water-quality problems. These toxics can originate in thousands of abandoned and poorly regulated hazardous waste sites or from agricultural activity, injection wells, municipal landfills, and sludges.

Federal and state regulators made three chemical groundwater contaminants a priority: nutrients, pesticides, and USTs. Nutrients, such as nitrates, are found most often in groundwater affected by agricultural production, including both crops and livestock. Pesticides and USTs are especially troublesome. In the 1990s, at least 143 pesticides and twenty-one of their transformation products were detected in the groundwater of forty-three states. These pesticide concentrations usually do not exceed state water-quality standards for agricultural areas. However, pesticides may be a more serious problem in nonagricultural areas, particularly around golf courses, commercial and residential areas, rights-of-way, timber production and processing areas, and public gardens. In any case, pesticides are ubiquitous in all U.S. waters. A major concern is the limited information available about the health effects associated with exposure to most pesticides, even in trace amounts. Federal groundwater standards, called maximum contaminant limits (MCLs), have yet to be established for most of these pesticides. Existing MCLs are often based on incomplete information. The U.S. Geological Survey has cautioned that

> MCLs and other criteria are currently based on individual pesticides and do not account for possible cumulative effects if several different pesticides are present in the same well [and] many pesticides and most transformation products have not been widely sampled for in ground water and very little sampling has been done in urban and suburban areas, where pesticide use is often high.[40]

Governmental concern about USTs has grown steadily with the increasing number of discovered sites. Currently, about 566,000 USTs are regulated by the federal and state governments, with an estimated one hundred thousand or more under active federal cleanup. Perhaps as many as two hundred thousand additional USTs are unregistered and pose a threat of groundwater contamination if they are leaking.[41] These leaks contaminate the groundwater, damage sewer lines and buried cables, poison crops, and ignite fires and explosions. More than 80 percent of the tanks in use were constructed of bare steel, are easily corroded, and had to be replaced or severely modified to meet new federal standards mandated in the mid-1990s. Unfortunately, abandoned USTs are often located under active or deserted gasoline stations, airports, large trucking firms, farms, golf courses, and manufacturing plants and may never be discovered.

Half of the abandoned USTs known to regulators have been orphaned (that is, no identifiable owner can be found).[42]

Drinking Water

All ecosystems are intricately and subtly interrelated. The negligent dumping of contaminants into surface water and groundwater eventually follows a circle of causality, delivering the danger back to its source. Flint, Michigan's, water crisis described in Chapter 4 is a reminder that the nation's drinking water can also deliver these unwelcome contaminants into American homes.

The average American uses 100 gallons of water daily (most of it to water lawns and wash motor vehicles). More than 80 percent of the nation's 52,110 community water systems depend on groundwater for domestic use, and the remainder use surface water to provide Americans with over one billion glasses of drinking water consumed daily. Recognizing that community drinking water was threatened by the rising volume of pollutants entering surface and groundwater, Congress passed the SDWA in 1974 to ensure that public water supplies achieved minimum health standards. In 1977, the EPA, following the SDWA's mandate, began to set national primary drinking water standards that established maximum levels in drinking water for microbiological contaminants, turbidity, and chemical agents, and by 1985, standards existed for approximately thirty substances. Standard setting lagged badly at the EPA, however, and in another demonstration of excessive congressional control, the 1986 amendments to the SDWA required the EPA to adopt standards for sixty-one more contaminants by mid-1989, create twenty-five more standards from a new list by 1991, and set standards for twenty-five additional chemicals every three years thereafter. Once standards are established, the states are given primary responsibility for enforcing them and other provisions of the act on more than seventy-nine thousand public water systems. Since the 1986 amendments were written, the number of regulated contaminants expanded to seventy-two and reached 288 by 2013.[43]

By 1996, it was apparent that this excursion into legislative micromanagement was ill conceived, and in an enlightened moment rare to its oversight of the EPA, Congress relaxed its grip on the EPA's regulatory process with the 1996 amendments to the SDWA. The amendments instructed the EPA to focus its efforts on the highest-risk drinking water contaminants, with special attention to those particularly dangerous to the elderly and children—a more manageable and productive task. Equally important, the 1996 amendments contained right-to-know provisions that required all community drinking water systems to provide consumers with periodic information about the quality of their drinking water, about compliance with existing federal and state quality controls, and about opportunities for public involvement in local drinking water regulation. The states welcomed other provisions of the amendments that offered federal financial assistance to upgrade local water systems because a great many states lacked the financial, technical, and staff resources to enforce even the SDWA's minimum standards, and many small and large water systems were virtually ignored.

In many respects, the SDWA has been a success. By the end of 2011, about 90 percent of the U.S. population was served by community water systems with no reported violations of existing health-based standards, and almost one hundred contaminants were regulated under the act.[44] Unfortunately, almost 21 million Americans still drink from community water systems that violate one or more health-based standard,[45] and many water systems, including some of the largest, are still infiltrated by dangerous concentrations of chemical and biological contaminants which have no set standards and, as a consequence, have no regulatory controls.

Injection wells continue to be a major significant cause of drinking water contamination. More than 700,000 active or abandoned injection wells exist in the United States. About one half of all liquid hazardous waste generated in the United States is pumped into these injection wells, the largest portion from oil and gas production and refining facilities. Although liquid hazardous wastes are subject to federal regulation, no detailed national standards exist for the solid waste eliminated through the injection wells. Rural water supplies seem especially vulnerable to contamination from injection wells and abandoned hazardous waste sites. A 1984 EPA assessment of rural water quality reported unsafe levels of cadmium in about one sixth of the nation's rural wells, mercury concentrations above safe levels in about one quarter of the wells, and lead at dangerous levels in one tenth of these wells.

CONCLUSION

Air and water are the primary issues on the environmental agenda. They are the first, most essential, most politically visible, and most important tasks of environmental restoration and regulation. The condition of the nation's air and water has been examined in considerable detail in this chapter to emphasize the daunting scope and complexity of the challenge of ecological restoration and to illustrate how short a distance the United States has traveled toward that goal since environmentalism emerged as a major political force in the country in the 1970s.

This chapter illustrates that the difficulties encountered in cleaning up the nation's air and water cannot be blamed solely on political incompetence, policy deficiencies, administrative failures, or scientific bungling. Rather, scientific and technological development continually pose new challenges to regulation by creating new chemicals and new technologies with unanticipated environmental effects. In addition, scientific research continually redefines and elaborates the nature of environmental degradation and its consequences—as shown in the study of airborne particulates and toxics, for instance—forcing continual rethinking of and change in regulatory strategies. And even so unexciting and obscure an activity as environmental monitoring leads to new definitions of environmental degradation, as the study of groundwater contamination reveals. The United States, as with all other nations now committed to environmental restoration, must suffer a learning curve. It must acquire experience in a policy domain with which no government on Earth was involved a scant few decades ago. Those who govern can learn, but it takes time.

This review of the nation's current air and water pollution control programs is a sobering reminder that it will take a very long time and require an enormous amount of money, scientific resources, and administrative skill to give us back the healthful air and water we once had and hope to have again. So formidable a goal will not be easily realized. It may not happen in the lifetime of any American living today.

Suggested Readings

Bryner, Gary C. *Blue Skies, Green Politics: The Clean Air Act and Its Implementation.* 2nd ed. Washington, DC: CQ Press, 1995.

Cohen, Richard E. *Washington at Work: Back Rooms and Clean Air.* New York: Macmillan, 1992.

Morag-Levine, Noga. *Chasing the Wind: Regulating Air Pollution in the Common Law State.* Princeton, NJ: Princeton University Press, 2003.

Rogers, Peter. *America's Water: Federal Role and Responsibilities.* Cambridge, MA: MIT Press, 1999.

Sharpstein, Bill. *Dirty Water: One Man's Fight to Clean Up One of the World's Most Polluted Bays.* Berkeley: University of California Press, 2010.

Thornton, Joe. *Pandora's Poison: Chlorine, Health, and a New Environmental Strategy.* Cambridge, MA: MIT Press, 2000.

Notes

1. Industry estimates based on U.S. Department of Commerce, *Pollution Abatement Costs and Expenditures, 2005* (Washington, DC: Government Printing Office, 2008), v; and Robert Esworthy, "Federal Pollution Control Laws: How Are They Enforced?" *Congressional Research Service Report to Congress* (Washington, DC: Congressional Research Service, 2012, Summary, available at www.fas.org/sgp/crs/misc/RL34384.pdf; public spending estimated from EOP, OMB "Outlays Function and Subfunction: 1962–2113, The Budget for Fiscal Year 2009, Historical Tables," Table 3.2, available at http://www.gpo.gov/fdsys/browse/collection.action?collection Code=BUDGET&browsePath=Fiscal+Year+2009&searchPath=Fiscal+Year+2009&leafLevelBrowse=false&isCollapsed=false&isOpen=true&packageid=BUDGET-2009-TAB&ycord=397.
2. U.S. EPA, *Air Quality: National Summary,* "Air Quality Trends," Report EPA 841-R-16-011, 2, available at https://www.epa.gov/air-trends/air-quality -national-summary.
3. U.S. EPA, "Summary of Water Quality Assessments for Each Waterbody for Reporting Year 2012," available at http://ofmpub.epa.gov/waters10/ attains_nation_cy.control#total_assessed_waters.
4. Ibid.
5. Francis E. Rourke, *Bureaucracy, Politics, and Public Policy* (Boston: Little, Brown, 1969), 103.
6. Paul B. Downing and James N. Kimball, "Enforcing Pollution Laws in the U.S.," *Policy Studies Journal* 11 (September 1982): 55–65.
7. GAO, "EPA Cannot Ensure the Accuracy of Self-Reported Compliance Monitoring Data," Report no. GAO/RCED 93-21, Washington, DC, March 1993, 4; GAO, "Air Pollution: Difficulties in Implementing a National Air Permit Program," Report no. GAO/RCED 93-59, Washington, DC, February 1993, 2.
8. EPA, Air Trends, "Air Quality—National Summary," available at https://www .epa.gov/air-trends/air-quality-national-summary.

9. EPA, "Climate Change-Greenhouse Gas Emissions," March 12, 2007, available at www.epa.gov/climatechange/emissions/index.html#proj, based on data from U.S. Department of State, "U.S. Climate Action Report—2002," Washington, DC, 2002. For other U.S. projections, see EPA, "Inventory of U.S. Greenhouse Gas Emissions and Sinks: 1990–2004," Report no. USEPA-430-R-06-002, Washington, DC, April 2006; Juliet Eilperin, "Ex-EPA Chiefs Agree on Greenhouse Gas Lid," *Washington Post,* January 19, 2006, A04.

10. These summaries are adapted from Gary C. Bryner, *Blue Skies, Green Politics: The Clean Air Act of 1990 and Its Implementation,* 2nd ed. (Washington, DC: CQ Press, 1995), chap. 4.

11. Ibid., 126.

12. EPA, Office of Air and Radiation, "1995 National Air Quality Trends Brochure: Particulate Matter (PM-10)," Washington, DC, 1997.

13. EPA, "Air Trends," available at www.epa.gov/air/airtrends/sixpoll.html.

14. Leslie Kaufman, "Pressured, E.P.A. Proposes Soot Limit," *New York Times,* June 15, 2012, A29.

15. Patrick Ambrosio, "EPA Proposes Implementation Rule for Fine Particulate Standards," *Bloomberg BNA News,* March 13, 2015, available at http://www .bna.com/epa-proposes-implementation-n17179923978/.

16. The plan is briefly summarized at Simon Evans, "A Detailed Q&A on Obama's Clean Power Plan," *Carbon Brief,* available at http://www.carbonbrief .org/blog/2015/08/q-and-a-obamas-clean-power-plan/; see also Nathan Richardson, "A Quick Legal FAQ on EPA's Clean Power Plan," *Resources for the Future Common Resources,* available at http://common-resources.org/ blog/2015/quick-legal-faq-epa-s-clean-power-plan#sthash.ps6Kljyn.dpuf; and US EPA, *Clean Power Plan for Existing Power Plants,* available at http:// www.epa.gov/cleanpowerplan/clean-power-plan-existing-power-plants.

17. Justin Worland, "Energy Companies Don't Like the Clean Power Plan—or President Trump's Plan to Kill It," *Time,* October 19, 2017, http://time.com/ 4976455/clean-power-plan-repeal-scott-pruitt-trump/.

18. The plan is briefly summarized at Simon Evans, "A Detailed Q&A on Obama's Clean Power Plan," *Carbon Brief,* available at http://www.carbonbrief .org/blog/2015/08/q-and-a-obamas-clean-power-plan/; see also Nathan Richardson, "A Quick Legal FAQ on EPA's Clean Power Plan," *Resources for the Future Common Resources,* available at http://common-resources.org/ blog/2015/quick-legal-faq-epa-s-clean-power-plan#sthash.ps6Kljyn.dpuf; and US EPA, *Clean Power Plan for Existing Power Plants,* available at http:// www.epa.gov/cleanpowerplan/clean-power-plan-existing-power-plants.

19. "'The War on Coal Is Over': EPA Boss to Roll Back Obama's Clean Power Rules," *The Guardian,* October 9, 2017, available at www.theguardian .com/environment/2017/oct/09/epa-scott-pruitt-abandon-clean-power -plan-obama.

20. Ben Adler, "Can Polluters Block Obama's Clean Power Plan in Court?" *Grist*, November 5, 2015, available at http://grist.org/climate-energy/can-polluters-block-obamas-clean-power-plan-in-court/.

21. U.S. EPA, Office of Wetlands, Oceans and Watersheds, Office of Research and Development, *National Rivers and Streams Assessment, 2008–2009* (Washington, DC: EPA, 2013). Document No. EPA/841/D-13/001.

22. GAO, "Water Quality: Identification and Remediation of Polluted Waters Impeded by Data Gaps," Report no. GAO/T-RCED 00–88, Washington, DC, February 2000, 5. See also GAO, "The Nation's Waters: Key Unanswered Questions About the Quality of Rivers and Streams," Report no. GAO/PEMD 86–6, Washington, DC, September 1986, 3.

23. Robert Esworthy, *Federal Pollution Control Laws: How Are They Enforced?* (Washington, DC: Congressional Research Service, 2014), Report No. RL34834, 10.

24. GAO, "Drinking Water Quality," Report no. GAO/RCED 97–123, Washington, DC, July 29, 1997, 3–4.

25. EPA, "Environmental Progress and Challenges: EPA's Update," Washington, DC, 1996, 49.

26. GAO, "National Water Quality Inventory Does Not Accurately Represent Water Quality Conditions Nationwide," Report no. GAO/RCED 00–54, Washington, DC, March 22, 2000, 27.

27. National Academy of Sciences, Commission on Geosciences, Environment and Resources, *Assessing the TMDL Approach to Water Quality Management: Executive Summary* (Washington, DC: National Academies Press, 2000), 2.

28. Quoted in Michael Satchell, "Hog Heaven—and Hell," *U.S. News & World Report*, January 22, 1996, 55, 57–59. See also Natural Resources Defense Council, "America's Animal Factories: How States Fail to Prevent Pollution From Livestock Waste," December 1998, available at www.nrdc.org/water/pollution/factor/aafinx.asp.

29. National Pollution Discharge Elimination System, "Animal Feeding Operations (AFOs) Regulations, Guidance, Policy and Funding," available at https://www.epa.gov/npdes/animal-feeding-operations-afos-regulations-guidance-policy-and-funding.

30. GAO, "Concentrated Animal Feeding Operations: EPA Needs More Information and a Clearly Defined Strategy to More Effectively Protect Air and Water Quality," Report no. GAO 08–1177T, Washington, DC, September 24, 2008, 14.

31. Adam Skolnick, "The CAFO Industry's Impact on the Environment and Public Health," *Sierra*, February 23, 2017, available at https://www.sierraclub.org/sierra/2017-2-march-april/feature/cafo-industrys-impact-environment-and-public-health.

32. Ibid., "Summary."

33. John Devine, "EPA Chickens Out by Dropping Industrial Livestock Information Collection Effort," *NRDC Switchboard*, July 24, 2012, available at http://switchboard.nrdc.org/blogs/jdevine/epa_chickens_out_by_dropping_i.html.

34. National Academy of Sciences, "Air Emissions from Animal Feeding Operations: Current Knowledge, Future Need," Washington, DC, 2003.

35. Kate Valentine, "Groups Sue EPA Over Failure to Regulate Emissions From Factory Farms," *Climate Progress*, January 30, 2015, available at http://thinkprogress.org/climate/2015/01/30/3617172/epa-cafos-lawsuit/.

36. Peakwater, "Quality of Water From Public-Supply Wells in the United States," available at http://peakwater.org/2010/05/quality-of-water-from-public-supply-wells-in-the-united-states.

37. EPA, "Environmental Progress and Challenges," 52.

38. GAO, "Groundwater Quality: State Activities to Guard Against Contaminants," Report no. GAO/PEMD 88–5, Washington, DC, February 1988, 13.

39. GAO, "Groundwater Quality," 38–39.

40. U.S. Geological Survey, "Pesticides in Ground Water," USGS Fact Sheet FS-255–95, Washington, DC, 1995.

41. Sierra Club, *Leaking Underground Storage Tanks: A Threat to Public Health & Environment*, available at https://www.csu.edu/cerc/documents/LUST ThreattoPublicHealth.pdf.

42. EPA, Office of Underground Storage Tanks, "The UST Corrective Action Program," Washington, DC, 1997. See also EPA, Office of Underground Storage Tanks, "Report to Congress on a Compliance Plan for the Underground Storage Tank Program," Report no. EPA-510-R-00-001, Washington, DC, June 2000.

43. EPA, Office of Water, *2012 Edition of the Drinking Water Standards and Health Advisories*, available at water.epa.gov/action/advisories/drinking/. . . / dwstandards2012.pdf.

44. EPA, Office of Water, "Drinking Water: Past, Present, and Future," Report no. EPA-816-F-00–002, Washington, DC, February 2000.

45. Maura Allaire, Haowei Wu, and Upmanu Lall, "National Trends in Drinking Water Quality Violations," Abstract, Proceedings of the National Academy of Sciences of the United States of America, February 12, 2018, available at http://www.pnas.org/content/early/2018/02/06/1719805115/tab-article-info.

A REGULATORY THICKET

Toxic and Hazardous Substances

If legal historians should choose a top ten in toxic litigation, a place surely will be reserved for the small community of Jurupa Valley, California. There, in early 1993, a legal spectacle began that demanded superlatives. "It's got to be among the top five civil cases in the history of American jurisprudence," one defense lawyer burbled as the proceedings began. Indeed, everything seemed dramatically oversized, like a production from some Hollywood of hazardous waste.[1]

TOXIC AND EXPENSIVE: THE STRINGFELLOW WASTE SITE

After eight years of planning and the screening of two thousand jurors, the trial began with 3,700 plaintiffs (all Jurupa Valley residents); thirteen defendants, including the state of California and major corporations such as Rockwell International, Northrop, McDonnell Douglas, and Montrose Chemicals; and injury claims exceeding $800 million. At issue was liability for injuries alleged to have been inflicted on Jurupa Valley from exposure to more than two hundred chemicals in thirty-four million gallons of waste dumped into the Stringfellow Canyon between 1956 and 1972. The legal battle over financial responsibility for the Stringfellow disaster ended—or seemed to end—in late 2012, almost two decades after litigation began and shortly before the community abandoned the name "Avon Springs" and its unsavory association with the Stringfellow site. Jurupa Springs residents had already received more than $50 million in damages from one hundred companies that had used the site for dumping, but $22 million had been spent to initiate the new trial. The thirty lawyers and twenty-four jurors would eventually review more than three hundred thousand pages of court documents and thirteen thousand defense and 3,600 plaintiff exhibits for the initial proceeding. By then, Stringfellow had graduated from top billing on the EPA list of the nation's worst abandoned waste sites to "one of the most contaminated sites on the planet."[2]

The trial has been held in installments. The first trial, involving seventeen plaintiffs, ended on September 17, 1993, when the jury found the state of California responsible for allowing toxic releases from the Stringfellow site but awarded the plaintiffs only $159,000 of the $3.1 million they had claimed in damages. In 1994, most of the plaintiffs settled out of court and the number of plaintiffs was reduced to only 763. The next year, the federal court ruled that the state of California was liable for all the site cleanup costs. After three more years of litigation, California agreed to assume the cleanup costs if seventeen private plaintiffs dropped their demands for $90 million in reimbursement for their own cleanup costs.

In early 2000, estimates suggested that the site may require four hundred years of remediation at a cost of $740 million. In 2000, California also initiated lawsuits against thirty-five of its own insurers for refusing to compensate the state for the Stringfellow cleanup costs. In early 2005, sixteen insurers finally settled with the state for $93 million in cleanup costs (which made the list of "The 100 Top Insurance Verdicts of 2005" in one legal publication).[3] Trials began in 2006 for the first of the remaining nineteen insurers who claimed that they were not compelled to pay the full amount of all the policies they had issued to California for the Stringfellow property; meanwhile, California was spending more than $10 million annually to clean up and monitor the waste site. Years of contention seemed to end in August 2012, when the California courts ruled that the state's insurers would have to pay the full amount on all the policies they had each issued for the waste site.[4] The box score: more than forty years from site closure to last litigation, $180 million spent on cleanup, $100 million in current settlement costs, seventeen acres of contaminated ground, and thirty-four million gallons of toxic waste for which to account.[5] But new pollution still appears and escalating costs persist. In 2002, plumes of the chemical perchlorate were discovered contaminating drinking water wells near the site. In 2016, a new $52 million treatment plant was dedicated to clean up all the known chemicals at the site, a cost of $8.8 million annually in addition to $1.2 million yearly to test water samples.[6]

It may also take decades to dissipate the emotional pain associated from Jurupa Spring's civic life. In 2013, the local school board voted to name a new $60 million school "Glen Avon High School" only after months of bitter contention within the community. Opponents of the new name contended that it perpetuated the Stringfellow stigma. "Glen Avon," explained one civic activist, suggests to many people a community that is "nothing but white trash, toxic waste and toothless women."[7]

THE GROWTH OF FEDERAL TOXICS REGULATION

The Stringfellow Canyon site is considered among the worst toxic site cleanups ever attempted. Even so, many legal experts believe that the Stringfellow litigation is a signpost along a sprawling road of expansive and expensive future litigation as hazardous waste regulations multiply and government seeks more aggressively to satisfy public apprehension about toxic and hazardous substances. An ironic counterpoint to this growing litigation with its burgeoning liability awards has been the mounting disagreement among scientific experts about the extent of public risk from exposure to manufactured, stored, and abandoned chemical substances. Indeed, in no other area of environmental regulation has scientific uncertainty about the extent of the risk and identity of hazardous substances been greater or more public.

Currently, more than twenty-four federal laws and a dozen federal agencies are concerned with regulating the manufacture, distribution, and disposal of carcinogenic substances and other toxic or hazardous chemicals. The chapter focuses upon the EPA's implementation of five of these laws concerned with chemical risks to public health. Congress once predicted that three of these laws—the Toxic Substances Control Act (TSCA, 1976), the Resource Conservation and Recovery Act (RCRA, 1976), and the Comprehensive Environmental Response, Cleanup and Liability Act (known as Superfund, 1980)—would amount to "cradle-to-grave" regulation of toxic and hazardous substances. The fourth law, the Emergency Planning and Community Right-to-Know Act (EPCRA, 1988), created perhaps the most widely publicized of all toxic chemical laws, the Toxics Release Inventory (TRI). The final law, the Food Quality Protection Act (1996), is an effort to improve regulation as a result of new concerns about public exposure to hazardous and toxic substances arising since the earlier laws were enacted.

Implementing these laws has proved enormously challenging, not only because the scope and expense of regulation were vastly underestimated but also because new scientific controversies arise concerning the extent to which existing hazardous and toxic substances—or others continually being created—constitute significant risks to humans or to the environment. To illustrate why these conflicts often defy satisfactory resolution, the chapter describes the ongoing scientific and political controversies associated with continuing efforts to clean up the most famous of all existing abandoned waste sites at Love Canal, New York, and the challenges involved in proving that a group of recently identified chemicals, called "endocrine disruptors," are a public health menace requiring regulation and not, as critics claim, a scientific fiction.

Chemicals: The Safe, Untested, and Toxic

The environmentalists' hell is a firmament of compacted pesticide awash in toxic sludge. Environmentalists are not alone in attributing to chemicals a special menace.

Most Americans apparently believe that the air, water, and earth are suffused with real or potential toxic menaces. The Gallup Organization polled a sample of Americans in mid-2015 concerning environmental risks about which they "worried a great deal" and discovered that Americans worried most about (1) drinking water; (2) pollution of rivers, lakes, and reservoirs; and (3) air pollution—all more or less associated with chemical substances.[8] Americans are often misinformed about the extent of environmental risks and frequently exaggerate the danger from the environmental pollutants they most fear. But widespread media coverage of hazardous chemical spills, newly discovered abandoned toxic waste sites, and other real or alleged chemical crises have forced attention on toxic and hazardous substances and imparted a sense of urgency to resolving the problems.

A World of Chemicals

Most toxic and hazardous substances are an inheritance of the worldwide chemical revolution following World War II. The creation of synthetic chemicals continued at such a prolific pace after 1945 that, by the mid-1960s, the American Chemical Society had registered more than four million chemicals, an increasing proportion of which were synthetics created by U.S. chemists since 1945. Today, more than eighty-four thousand chemicals are used daily in U.S. industry; between five hundred and one thousand new chemicals are created annually.

About 98 percent of chemical substances used commercially in the United States are considered harmless to humans and the ecosystem. However, more than one hundred twenty thousand establishments in the United States create and distribute chemicals, and the industry's capacity to produce and distribute still more new substances is growing. TSCA does not require chemical companies to test the approximately seven hundred new chemicals now annually introduced into commerce for toxicity, and companies generally do not voluntarily perform such testing.[9]

Toxic and Hazardous Chemicals

Many chemicals have been tested to determine their hazardousness, but few have been tested rigorously to determine their toxicity or risk to human or environmental health. Testing is particularly difficult and expensive when the long-term effects of a chemical are being investigated. Studies may require decades.[10]

Cancer is the gravest and most widely feared of all toxic impacts from chemical exposures. By 2015, perhaps 1,500 to two thousand of all chemical substances, a small proportion of all suspected carcinogenic chemicals produced in the United States, had been tested sufficiently by federal agencies to determine their carcinogenicity. In 2014, for instance, the federal government's annual *Report on Carcinogens* contained profiles of only 243 substances that federal agencies had identified as "known to be human carcinogens" or "reasonably anticipated to be human carcinogens."[11]

In recent years, the EPA has improved the speed and efficiency of its own risk assessments. But the EPA's risk assessing is hobbled by an inadequate budget, limited staff, a huge burden of different regulatory programs, and the constant tide of newly manufactured chemicals added to a catalog of many thousand existing and newly manufactured chemicals. Thus, TSCA requires the EPA to demonstrate that certain chemicals may constitute a potential health risk before it can require industrial manufacturers or users to test such chemicals, but the EPA examines only a very small portion of chemicals currently used or newly manufactured for their possible health risks.[12] Persuasive scientific evidence that environmental chemicals, such as pesticides and toxic industrial air emissions, are causing widespread cancer is quite often insufficient or nonexistent. The National Cancer Institute and the U.S. Centers for Disease Control and Prevention have usually reported a lack of confirmed evidence to support these accusations.

Pesticides are a substantial component of proven or suspected toxic chemicals and chemical wastes. Pesticides are so widely and routinely used in U.S. agriculture that many farmers believe productivity cannot be sustained without them. Common foods, such as vegetables and fruits, are treated with dozens of possible carcinogens among the 20,700 pesticides currently available in the United States. Annual pesticide use in the United States has declined slightly since 2010 but still exceeds eight hundred million pounds annually.[13] These products contain more than 890 active ingredients.[14] Most of the pesticide products used in the United States since 1947 were registered before their long-term effects were understood. Federal legislation in 1972 required the EPA to reevaluate all existing pesticides in light of new information about their effects on humans and the environment. The EPA has prohibited or limited severely the use of many pesticides, including DDT, aldrin, dieldrin, toxaphene, and ethylene dibromide, and as a result, the levels of persistent pesticides in human fatty tissue has declined. Even if a chemical product is restricted or prohibited, the EPA often lacks the resources to implement controls quickly. One striking example is that the EPA estimated before 1980 that more than half a million office buildings, apartment houses, stores, and other public or commercial buildings contained potentially dangerous loose asbestos, but the agency decided by 1988 to take no action because the federal government, the states, and the private sector lacked the money and personnel to remove safely the deteriorating asbestos.[15]

Two Chemical Risk Controversies

The regulatory risk assessment discussed in Chapter 4 arises continually with toxics management. Chemical testing of any sort is time consuming and costly, but when the long-term effects of a chemical are involved, studies may require decades. Moreover, substances currently suspected of having toxic effects often have not existed long enough for long-term impacts to be apparent. If testing deals with chronic effects of exposure to small quantities of chemicals—doses as small as parts per billion or trillion—difficulties in identifying the presence of the substance and the rate of exposure among affected populations may be formidable. Even repeated testing may not produce conclusive evidence concerning the human health and environmental impact, as exemplified by two continuing toxic chemical controversies. The first, concerning Love Canal, the signature site that dramatized the nation's dangerous abandoned toxic waste problem, illustrates some of the practical challenges in determining when toxic waste is sufficiently regulated. The second matter, the controversy over endocrine disruptors, reveals some common difficulties in proving that a chemical should be a regulated toxic.

Love Canal: How Much Regulation Is Enough? Love Canal is now infamous, the chemical dump that produced the Superfund legislation and achieved fame sufficient to have its own web page on Google Sightseeing. It is also an excellent showcase for some practical challenges involved in deciding how and when to control known toxic wastes in an imperfect regulatory world of limited data, inevitable political controversy, and potentially dangerous public health hazards.[16]

In 1975, federal and state government officials determined that the huge, abandoned industrial chemical dump known as Love Canal, near Niagara Falls, New York, appeared to constitute such a health menace to the surrounding residential communities that hundreds of nearby residents were urged to sell their homes to the federal government and leave the neighborhood. In 1978, President Jimmy Carter ordered 259 families living nearest the site to be evacuated; subsequently, between 1978 and 1980, a total of more than 950 families were ordered to leave by federal and state agencies. The deserted homes were boarded up and abandoned at a public cost of more than $17 million. Later in 1982, the EPA and the U.S. Public Health Service released the results of their massive investigation concerning the health effects of the Love Canal site upon the families in the nearby residential community. Contrary to earlier studies by New York State, the EPA asserted that it had found the neighborhood near Love Canal no more dangerous for residents than any other part of nearby Niagara Falls.

The evidence seemed formidable. More than six thousand samples of human and environmental materials near the site were collected and subjected to one hundred fifty thousand analytical measurements to determine what contaminants they contained. This data suggested that only a ring of houses a block from the waste site or closer had been affected significantly. But the study was challenged immediately because 90 percent of the samples were free of any chemicals. This result, asserted experts, could mean either an absence of chemicals or insufficient sensitivity in the measuring procedures. Other critics charged that the massive evacuation had been politically motivated.[17]

Although New York health officials later asserted that the undetected chemicals could not be present in more than minute quantities, the Environmental Defense Fund's own scientific expert asserted that so much variance existed in the competence of the many laboratories conducting the tests and that so many sources of error could exist in some tests that chemicals could indeed have been present. Officials at the National Bureau of Standards also questioned the sensitivity of the test procedures. That same year, the federal Centers for Disease Control released its own study of former Love Canal area residents, indicating that they were no more likely to suffer chromosomal damage than residents elsewhere in Niagara Falls. Even if such damage were present, noted the study, it was impossible to know if it was linked to the later occurrence of illnesses.[18]

In mid-2004, the EPA appeared to write the last chapter in the Love Canal saga by declaring that the dump, now a Superfund project, was "clean" and thus no longer menacing for nearby residents.[19] However, in mid-2012, numerous former students who attended public school near Love Canal when it was discovered claimed they had experienced serious health problems in later years from exposure to the dump's toxics, asserted that uncontrolled toxic chemical wastes were seeping again from the site, and pledged to revive investigation into the Canal's long-term health impacts.[20] A year later, six families who purchased houses on the Love Canal restoration site, after assurance that the area was safe, sued EPA and New York State, charging that the site continued to leak hazardous chemicals and they had experienced illness linked to these uncontrolled chemical exposures. "We're stuck here. We want to get out," said one home owner, adding that he'd been plagued by mysterious rashes and other ailments since he moved into the four-bedroom home purchased a decade ago for $39,900."[21]

Endocrine Disruptors: Toxic Enough to Regulate? The list of worrisome chemicals lengthened in the latter 1990s when scientific and governmental attention turned suddenly to a potentially huge inventory of chemicals called endocrine disruptors. Scientific research has suggested that certain externally produced chemicals, especially many human-made synthetic compounds, may sometimes mimic naturally produced hormones in humans and animals and may interfere, perhaps disastrously, with the normal functioning of the endocrine system. Many of these disruptors, according to some scientific theories, gain their potency from the bioaccumulation of extremely small doses in human and animal tissue over long periods of time. The possible human health effects could include cancers of the reproductive system, reduced sperm counts in males, abnormalities of fetal development leading to learning and behavioral disorders, and many other pathologies associated with hormonal malfunctions. Some scientists believe that disruptors have been responsible for sexual abnormalities and deformities in gulls, terns, eagles, and fish.[22]

If endocrine disruptors exist, apprehension seems prudent. The number of substances which have been suggested as possibly contributing to perturbation of the endocrine system is "vast," explained one careful study of the issue:

Man-made or generated substances include broad classes of chlorinated and non-chlorinated compounds and heavy metals widely used in industrial and household products such as paints, detergents, lubricants, cosmetics, textiles, pesticides, and plastics, as well as by products of sewage treatment and waste incineration and other forms of combustion. Many pharmaceutical products, including contraceptives, have hormonal activity. There are also large amounts of plant hormones (mainly phytoestrogens) commonly ingested in human (and animal) diets—especially vegetarian products. . . .[23]

In short, here is something to unnerve everybody. Yet the disruptor issue emerges from a fog of uncertainty and scientific controversy. The effect of disruptors on humans and animals, the identity of truly dangerous substances, the results of long- and short-term exposures, the relative dangers to adults and fetuses, and much more are largely unknown. Scientists themselves disagree about the danger. [24]

The public history of endocrine disruptors is the very model of how environmental issues acquire political clout. Expert meetings held in the United States in 1991 and 1993 first called major scientific attention to the possible danger of endocrine disruptors. However, the issue's political momentum mounted when, in 1993, the BBC broadcast the documentary *Assault on the Male,* which suggested that human and animal reproductive problems might arise from endocrine disruptors. The issue rose to national attention with the publication in 1996 of *Our Stolen Future,* written by a team of U.S. scientific interpreters, who vividly described the menace presumably posed by disruptors:

> Hormone-disrupting chemicals are not classical poisons or typical carcinogens. They play by different rules. They defy the linear logic of current testing protocols built on the assumption that higher doses do more damage. For this reason, contrary to our long-held assumptions, screening chemicals for cancer risk has not always protected us from other kinds of harm. Some hormonally active chemicals appear to pose little if any risk of cancer. . . . [S]uch chemicals are typically not poisons in the normal sense. Until we recognize this, we will be looking in the wrong places, asking the wrong questions.[25]

This aura of mystery, dread, and imminence proved to be a powerful political catalyst, creating additional media attention, provoking public concern, and compelling a response from government officials. In 1996, Congress passed the Food Quality Protection Act to require that the EPA create and then implement an endocrine disruptor screening program, thus adding one more to the growing list of federal laws intended to regulate toxic and hazardous chemicals from the cradle to the grave.

FEDERAL LAW: TOXICS REGULATION FROM THE CRADLE TO THE GRAVE?

Among the two dozen federal laws relating to toxic and hazardous substances, five of them, three passed in the 1970s, define the fundamental framework for regulating the disposal of these substances: the TSCA, the EPCRA, the RCRA, the Superfund legislation, and the Food Quality Protection Act (1996). These laws represent a congressional effort to create a comprehensive regulatory program for all chemical substances from their initial development to final disposal—the cradle-to-grave control that seemed essential to achieving, for the first time, the responsible public management of chemical products. Few laws, even by the standard of recent environmental legislation, mandate a more complex and technically formidable administrative process than do these programs. A brief review of their major provisions suggests the immense regulatory tasks involved.

Regulating Chemical Manufacture and Distribution: The Toxic Substances Control Act

The major purpose of TSCA is to regulate the creation, manufacture, and distribution of chemical substances so that substances hazardous to humans and the environment can be identified early and then controlled properly before they become fugitive throughout the ecosystem. TSCA requires the EPA to achieve five broad objectives:

1. *Information gathering.* The EPA is required to issue rules asking chemical manufacturers and processors to submit to the administrator information about their newly developed chemicals, including the formula, data on adverse health and environmental effects; and the number of workers exposed to the chemical. In achieving these goals, the administrator is also to:

   a. publish a list of all existing chemicals; and

   b. assure that all sources manufacturing, processing, or distributing chemicals in commerce keep records on adverse health reactions and submit related health and safety studies.

2. *Screening of new chemicals.* Manufacturers of new chemicals are to notify the EPA at least ninety days before producing the new chemical commercially. Information similar to that required for existing chemicals is also required for new chemicals. The EPA is allowed to suspend temporarily the manufacture of any new chemical in the absence of required information and to suspend production of a new chemical permanently if it finds a "reasonable basis to conclude that the chemical presents or will present an unreasonable risk of injury to health or the environment."[26]

3. *Chemical testing.* The EPA is given the authority to require manufacturers or processors of potentially harmful chemicals to test them.

4. *Control of chemicals.* The EPA is required to take action against chemical substances or mixtures for which a reasonable basis exists to conclude that their manufacture, processing, distribution, use, or disposal presents

an unreasonable risk of injury to health or the environment. The control requirements are not to "place an undue burden on industry" yet provide an adequate margin of protection against unreasonable risk.

5. *Control of asbestos.* The EPA is required to develop a strategy to inspect all schools for asbestos-containing material and to develop and implement plans to control the threat of any asbestos discovered.

How TSCA Regulates. EPA follows a procedure known as IRIS (Integrated Risk Information System) when assessing any chemical that may qualify for its evaluation. Figure 7.1 illustrates why IRIS's extensive data and review requirements often move assessments at a glacial pace frustrating for advocates of prompt, economically efficient, effective toxics regulation.

FIGURE 7.1 ■ The Integrated Risk Information System (IRIS)

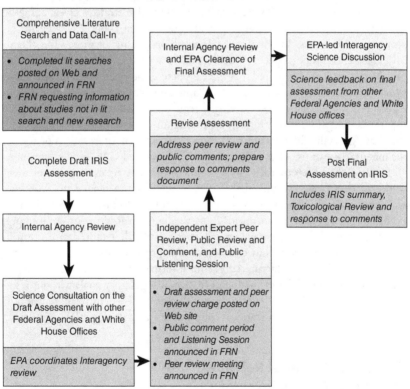

Assessment Development Process for New IRIS

Source: U.S. EPA, *Integrated Risk Information System: IRISTrack,* available at http://cfpub.epa.gov/ncea/iristrac/. (accessed September 20, 2012)

Considering the cumbersome IRIS process, the EPA's record for having so far identified more than 550 chemicals as human health risks among more than eighty-four thousand commercial chemicals now used in the United States should be considered at least an important achievement in light of the public health risks it has reduced or eliminated.[27]

The Regulatory Burden. One formidable problem posed by TSCA is that it loads upon EPA a regulatory task for which the agency has never been provided with adequate resources in professional staff, budget, or congressional support.[28] TSCA requires the EPA to assume the initiative for creating and interpreting a vast volume of integrated technical information. Obtaining the data often requires that chemical manufacturers, processors, consumers, and waste depositors provide timely, accurate information—information they previously guarded jealously. With this heavy burden of initiative, the agency would have been hard-pressed to meet all its program obligations under TSCA with even the most benevolent funding and generous personnel levels.

By 2009, the EPA had been able to test fewer than two hundred of more than sixty-two thousand commercial chemicals on its original TSCA agenda. To lighten its testing overload, the EPA resorted to an alternative strategy of encouraging chemical companies to voluntarily provide test data on about 2,800 chemicals produced or imported in amounts of one million pounds or more. The chemical industry would not agree to provide data on several hundred of these chemicals. Moreover, TSCA required that the EPA determine whether a chemical about which it has received data will pose an "unreasonable risk" before the EPA can regulate its production or use—a virtual regulatory dead end. "EPA officials say that the act's legal standards for demonstrating unreasonable risk are so high that they have generally discouraged EPA from using its authorities to ban or restrict the manufacture or use of existing chemicals," concluded GAO's investigators.[29]

By 2017, the EPA was still so overwhelmed with TSCA's chemical assessment workload that Congress amended TSCA in an effort to reduce the workload and simplify the regulatory process.[30,31] Among other reforms, the new legislation simplified the selection of chemicals to be regulated, placed responsibility upon manufacturers to demonstrate chemical safety, explicitly required protection of vulnerable populations such as children and pregnant women, and reduced the ability of chemical manufacturers to claim information as confidential. Despite these improvements, EPA cannot achieve its new regulatory goals without a significant increase in the required funding and personnel—an unlikely prospect in light of the Trump administration's commitment to reducing EPA's regulatory authority and budget.[32]

Publicizing Chemical Releases: The Toxics Release Inventory

The EPCRA created the national Toxics Release Inventory, among the most publicized, effective, and publicly accessible of all current federal toxics regulations. The TRI creates a database containing information collected since 1988 on the disposal or other releases of more than 650 toxic chemicals by thousands of U.S. facilities together with information about how these facilities manage those chemicals through recycling, energy recovery, and treatment. One of TRI's primary purposes is to inform communities about toxic chemical releases to the environment. Since its creation, it has been directly and indirectly responsible for encouraging thousands of organized community and interest-group initiatives to identify and regulate exposures to air toxics, many previously unknown.

TRI records a steady decrease in chemical releases since 1988. As Figure 7.2 illustrates, in the decade between 2006 and 2016, total chemical releases into air, water, and land decreased about 21 percent. Equally important, toxic releases directly into air diminished by a very significant 58 percent, most of this improvement due to the electric utilities shift from coal to other fuel sources and improved control technologies for coal emissions.[33]

Regulating Solid Waste: The Resource Conservation and Recovery Act

The major purposes of RCRA and its 1980 and 1984 amendments are to control solid waste management practices that could endanger public health or the environment and to promote resource conservation and recovery. Solid wastes are defined in the act to include waste solids, sludges, liquids, and contained

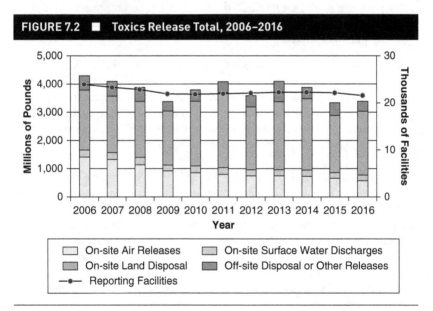

FIGURE 7.2 ■   Toxics Release Total, 2006–2016

Source: U.S, EPA, *Toxics Release Inventory 2016 National Analysis: Executive Summary*, available at https://www.epa.gov/trinationalanalysis/report-sections-2016-tri-national-analysis

gases—all forms in which discarded toxic and hazardous substances might be found. In addition to providing federal assistance to state and local governments in developing comprehensive solid waste management programs, RCRA also mandates the following:

1. *Criteria for environmentally safe disposal sites.* The EPA is required to issue regulations defining the minimum criteria for solid waste disposal sites considered environmentally safe. It is also required to publish an inventory of all U.S. facilities failing to meet these criteria.

2. *Regulation of hazardous waste.* The EPA is required to develop criteria for identifying hazardous waste, to publish the characteristics of hazardous wastes and lists of particular hazardous wastes, and to create a manifest system that tracks hazardous wastes from their points of origin to their final disposal sites. The EPA also is to create a permit system that would require all individuals or industries generating hazardous waste to obtain a permit before managing such waste.

3. *Resource recovery and waste reduction.* The act requires the Commerce Department to promote the commercialization of waste recovery, to encourage markets for recovered wastes, and to promote waste recovery technologies and research into waste conservation.

4. *State implementation.* The act provides for state implementation of regulations affecting solid waste management and disposal if state programs meet federal standards. The EPA will enforce these provisions in states that do not or cannot comply with federal regulations for the program's enforcement.

5. *Mandated deadlines and waste-by-waste review.* The 1984 RCRA amendments create deadlines for the EPA to set standards for the disposal of specific wastes. If the EPA fails to do so, congressionally mandated standards will be applied. The EPA is also ordered to evaluate nineteen specific substances, and deadlines are established for the agency to regulate new kinds of waste disposal activity.

Congress was determined to drive the EPA hard. It instructed the EPA in exquisite detail concerning how to implement virtually every aspect of RCRA, from the allowable permeability of liners for surface impoundments to the concentrations at which many different chemical wastes must be banned from land disposal. Twenty-nine different deadlines for specific program activities were listed—for example, a ban on land disposal of bulk liquid in landfills within six months, new regulations for small-quantity waste generators within seventeen months, and interim construction standards for underground storage tanks within four months.[34]

It is also becoming evident that the number of potential waste storage and treatment facilities in the United States requiring corrective actions under RCRA is likely to exceed vastly the initial estimates. The EPA has estimated that perhaps 3,700 waste treatment and storage facilities will require cleanup under RCRA rules.[35] Moreover, the current list of twenty thousand facilities subject to RCRA inspections is likely to grow as more facilities are discovered. If the estimates are accurate, the size and scope of the cleanup program would be as large as the expected Superfund cleanup and may cost more than $22.7 billion. The cleanup of all sites may not be completed until the year 2025.

The impediments to the RCRA program are those common to most federal regulatory efforts: cost and complexity, foot-dragging by regulated waste managers, insufficient money for needed oversight, and wrangling about cleanup terms. "The agency, the states, and companies often disagree on how cleanup should be pursued," explained a GAO report. "These disagreements prolong the cleanup process because more time is needed [to define] the cleanup terms, and companies must sometimes meet the duplicate requirements of both federal and state regulators."[36]

Cleaning Up Abandoned Waste: Superfund

The discovery of Love Canal in 1978 escalated rapidly into a national media event dramatizing to Americans the danger of abandoned toxic wastes within the United States. In the crisis-driven style characteristic of the 1970s, Congress reacted by passing in 1980 the Comprehensive Environmental Response, Compensation, and Liability Act (CERCLA), commonly called "Superfund." The Superfund legislation included an appropriation of $1.6 billion—which became only the down payment—to clean up the nation's worst abandoned toxic and hazardous waste sites.

When the first Superfund legislation was enacted, the nation's abandoned and uncontrolled hazardous waste dumps were uncharted territory. Collaboration among the nation's governments seemed essential to identify abandoned sites, assess their health hazards, create standards for cleanup, and, if possible, assign to site creators the financial liability for the cleanup. Congress attempted to address these and other major abandoned waste problems through four major Superfund programs:

1. *Information gathering and analysis.* Owners of hazardous waste sites were required to notify the EPA by June 1981 about the character of buried wastes. Using this information, the EPA would create a list of national sites.

2. *Federal response to emergencies.* The act authorized the EPA to respond to hazardous substance emergencies and to clean up leaking chemical dump sites if the responsible parties failed to take appropriate action or could not be located.

3. *The Hazardous Substance Response Fund.* The act created an initial trust fund of $1.6 billion to finance the removal, cleanup, or remedy of hazardous waste sites. About 86 percent of the fund was to be financed from a tax on manufacturers of petrochemical feedstocks and organic chemicals and on crude-oil importers.

4. *Liability for cleanup.* The act placed liability for cleaning up waste sites and for other restitution on those responsible for release of the hazardous substances.

The National Priority List. One important result of the Superfund legislation is that EPA is required to create an inventory of the nation's dangerous hazardous waste sites and to identify the most dangerous sites on a National Priority List (NPL). EPA is required to initiate action to clean up the NPL sites. In 2017, the NPL included 1,392 sites in U.S. states and territories (Table 7.1). The EPA has estimated that there are at least fifty thousand eligible sites, and many experts believe the actual number may exceed this estimate by at least twenty thousand.[37] Thus, the program continually confronts a huge backlog of contaminated sites, some posing massive cleanup costs, all involving technical complexity, potential political squabbles, and perhaps time-consuming litigation.

"The Largest, Most Complicated, and Most Disliked." The Superfund program has been a consensus choice as the most controversial, expensive, and problematic of all environmentalism's showcase legislation. By George W. Bush's second term, EPA officials, increasingly testy at the continued criticism of Superfund, were pointing to significant improvements in the speed and economy of site cleanups.

The EPA's annual Superfund reports remain relentlessly optimistic, but the total Superfund costs cast a more pessimistic aspect. Superfund long ago exhausted its originally authorized funding of $15.4 billion and will greatly exceed the $26.4 billion that the EPA estimated in the early 1990s would be necessary to complete the entire program. Since 1981, Superfund appropriations have totaled more than $32 billion in nominal dollars or about $1.2 billion annually.[38] Superfund costs during the decade of 2000 to 2010 alone are estimated to have been approximately $14 billion to 16.4 billion.[39] Since the late 1990s, moreover, a diminishing congressional interest in Superfund has been evident in the gradual decline of annual funding for new projects and a decrease in the number of new projects undertaken.[40] Superfund's unquestionable improvements have not pacified program critics, especially congressional Republicans, who seldom find much to like about Superfund.

Completed cleanups have averaged about $2.1 million each, but many troublesome sites create enormous cost escalations. One hundred fifty-four Superfund projects costing more than $50 million—such as California's Stringfellow

TABLE 7.1 ■ Hazardous Waste Sites on the National Priority List by State and Outlying Area, 2016				
State and outlying areas	Total sites	Rank	Percentage distribution	Federal	Nonfederal
Total[1]................................	1,392	(X)	(X)	160	1,232
United States..................	1,371	(X)	(X)	158	1,213
Alabama.............................	14	32	1.0	3	11
Alaska................................	6	45	0.4	5	1
Arizona..............................	9	43	0.7	2	7
Arkansas...........................	9	43	0.7	–	9
California...........................	99	2	7.2	24	75
Colorado............................	21	20	1.5	3	18
Connecticut......................	15	30	1.1	1	14
Delaware...........................	15	30	1.1	1	14
Dist. of Columbia..............	1	50	0.1	1	–
Florida...............................	55	6	4.0	6	49
Georgia..............................	17	26	1.2	2	15
Hawaii................................	3	46	0.2	2	1
Idaho..................................	9	43	0.7	2	7
Illinois...............................	49	9	3.6	5	44
Indiana...............................	40	11	2.9	–	40
Iowa...................................	13	35	0.9	1	12
Kansas...............................	13	35	0.9	1	12
Kentucky............................	13	35	0.9	1	12
Louisiana...........................	16	28	1.2	1	15
Maine.................................	13	35	0.9	4	9
Maryland............................	21	20	1.5	10	11
Massachusetts..................	34	14	2.5	6	28
Michigan............................	67	5	4.9	–	67
Minnesota..........................	25	18	1.8	2	23
Mississippi........................	10	40	0.7	–	10
Missouri.............................	33	15	2.4	3	30
Montana.............................	18	23	1.3	–	18
Nebraska...........................	17	26	1.2	1	16
Nevada...............................	2	48	0.1	–	2

(Continued)

TABLE 7.1 ■ (Continued)

State and outlying areas	Total sites	Rank	Percentage distribution	Federal	Nonfederal
New Hampshire...............	21	20	1.5	1	20
New Jersey......................	115	1	8.4	6	109
New Mexico......................	16	28	1.2	1	15
New York..........................	87	4	6.3	4	83
North Carolina................	39	12	2.8	2	37
North Dakota...................	–	51	–	–	–
Ohio.................................	43	10	3.1	4	39
Oklahoma........................	9	43	0.7	1	8
Oregon............................	14	32	1.0	2	12
Pennsylvania...................	97	3	7.1	6	91
Rhode Island...................	12	38	0.9	2	10
South Carolina................	25	18	1.8	2	23
South Dakota...................	2	48	0.1	1	1
Tennessee.......................	18	23	1.3	3	15
Texas...............................	54	7	3.9	4	50
Utah.................................	18	23	1.3	5	13
Vermont...........................	12	38	0.9	–	12
Virginia............................	31	16	2.3	11	20
Washington......................	51	8	3.7	13	38
West Virginia...................	10	40	0.7	2	8
Wisconsin........................	38	13	2.8	–	38
Wyoming..........................	2	48	0.1	1	1
Puerto Rico......................	18	(X)	(X)	1	17

[1]Total includes areas not shown separately.

Source: Statistical Abstract of the United States, *Geography and Environment: ProQuest Statistical Abstract of the U.S. 2018,* Table 420, available at https://statabs.proquest.com/sa/search .html?&sec=C7095-1.6&y=current

Notes: (–) indicates zero; (X) indicates not applicable.

dump—have achieved "megasite" status because of the time, technical complexity, and legal difficulties they entail.[41] About 20 to 33 percent of each Superfund site expenditure has been absorbed in litigation and negotiation. One estimate suggests that approximately twenty thousand lawyers were engaged in Superfund litigation by 2000.[42]

The reasons for Superfund's plodding pace and high costs are clear. The enormous legal costs generated by Superfund are largely the result of the complexities involved in establishing liability for abandoned hazardous waste dumps and the difficulty in recovering damages from private parties. Another inducement to delay and expense has been disagreement between regulatory officials and communities affected by Superfund over the appropriate amount of cleanup required to make sites safe. Superfund officials endure intense community pressure to achieve the most stringent and costly standards at a site restoration. When officials and communities disagree about the matter, litigation often results even before cleanup begins.

While EPA continues to struggle with CERCLA's implementation, its accomplishments since 1980 are significant, if often ignored or deprecated. "In many ways, CERCLA has been wildly successful," concluded one careful review of CERCLA's first thirty years. "The EPA has investigated over forty-seven thousand sites suspected of releasing hazardous substances into the environment. Many of these sites have been addressed by removal actions, state authorities, or by private parties. Just over 1,600 sites have been placed on the NPL, and cleanups have been fully implemented at more than two thirds of these sites.[43] Additionally, the nation's hazardous waste exposures and resulting health risks would doubtless be more severe if CERCLA did not exist.

A Continuing Challenge: Underground Disposal. More than half of the nation's liquid waste is flushed into deep underground cavities or water systems by many industries and municipalities, where it is presumed to disperse too deeply to contaminate water or soil used by humans. Much of this waste is known to contain toxic chemicals. However, such disposal is seldom carefully monitored or regulated. Experts suspect that many hazardous materials buried in this way will migrate through subsurface water flows until they contaminate drinking water wells and aquifers used for irrigation, lakes, rivers, or soil. For these reasons, the National Academy of Sciences has recommended that the federal government promote incineration, chemical processing, or other more modern procedures for waste disposal. Although federal and state water-quality regulators have succeeded in diminishing underground disposal, more than twelve million gallons of waste materials are still injected underground annually.[44]

Chemical Threat or Chemiphobia?

Although experts agree that the public should be concerned about the health risks associated with exposure to chemical substances and chemical wastes, they cannot easily determine which kinds of exposure and how much exposure are unacceptably risky. A related issue is that the elimination of all risk from exposure to toxic and hazardous substances is often impossible or unacceptably expensive, yet federal regulations such as the Superfund legislation do not clearly define how much cleanup is enough. According to political scientists Marc Landy and Mary Hague,

> In principle, one would want to clean until [an abandoned hazardous waste] site is called perfectly "safe." However . . . there is no scientifically identifiable point at which an "unsafe" site becomes "safe." No matter how much cleanup has been performed at a site, it can always be argued that more cleanup would reduce risk even further.[45]

A second issue involves political chemistry. When public fear about hazardous substances blends with official eagerness to appear tough on pollution, the resulting risk-averse political climate often spawns hasty, severe regulatory policies. A political synergy between public fear and governmental overreaction often results, as we have observed previously, in targeting for greatest attention those pollutants exciting the greatest public apprehension rather than those posing the most scientifically documented health risks.

Finally, regulatory costs have been especially controversial in toxic and hazardous substance regulation because of the rapid and severe escalation in the number of regulations and the growing recognition that future regulations will cost enormously more. Federal regulations, for instance, require all municipal landfills to be built with plastic and clay liners, liquid collectors, and treatment systems to prevent leaking toxic waste. These regulations have drastically raised the cost of opening a new municipal landfill and forced most of the country's existing 6,500 landfills to close when retrofitting became too expensive. And future landfill costs may be far greater still as the variety of waste-dump toxics and their health risks are better documented.[46]

To many critics, all these problems have produced public chemiphobia, while impelling governmental regulators to appease public opinion through excessively harsh chemical controls at enormous economic, scientific, and political cost to the nation. To many conservative critics, these regulations are too often "animated by a quasi-religious mind-set that combines an aversion to even minimal risks with a strong preference for governmental intervention in markets and a fierce hostility toward corporations."[47] Even the many experts who disagree with these conclusions often recognize that toxic and hazardous substance regulation is the most difficult, least satisfactory, domain of contemporary environmental policymaking.

The Food Quality Protection Act: Improved Pesticide Regulation

The Food Quality Protection Act is a constructive congressional effort to eliminate the regulatory morass created by fifty years of different statutory standards for pesticide residues on food. The act simplified regulatory standards for an extremely widespread, diverse, and politically contentious group of chemicals. Equally important, it abolished the zero-tolerance provisions for pesticide residues required by the Delaney clause of the Federal Food, Drug and Cosmetic Act (1949), which were widely regarded as unreasonably stringent scientifically and economically. The most important provisions of the act include the following:

1. *A single, health-based standard.* All pesticide residues must demonstrate "a reasonable certainty of no harm" if they are to be permitted in food products.

2. *Tightened risk standards.* Risk calculations must consider all nonoccupational sources of exposure, including drinking water, and exposure to other pesticides with a common mechanism of toxicity when setting tolerances. This provision allows regulators to consider not only the effect of the residue itself but also the impact of other kinds of exposure to the same or similar pesticides outside a workplace.

3. *Provisions for children.* This provision requires an explicit determination of safe exposures for children and, if necessary, a tenfold increase in the adult safety standards to be used for children when the relevant children's data are uncertain.

4. *Endocrine testing.* The EPA is required to establish a comprehensive screening program for chemical endocrine effects on humans, to implement the program, and to report on its progress to Congress.

5. *Consumer right to know.* This provision requires distribution of brochures in grocery stores on the health effects of pesticides, how to avoid risks, and which foods have tolerances for pesticide residues based on benefit considerations.

Leading national environmental advocacy groups generally accepted the new legislation warily, recognizing reluctantly that zero tolerance for pesticide residues probably had become an indefensible cancer-exposure standard economically and even scientifically. Still, many environmental leaders feared the new legislation might have breached irreparably a high wall of resistance to cancer risk they had legally erected over fifty years, inviting a flood of other legislation eroding the zero-tolerance standard for other ingredients in food.

The NIMBY Problem

NIMBYs are a common presence at proposed toxic waste and hazardous facility sites. The NIMBYs (shorthand for Not In My Backyard) may be white-collar professionals, executives, or articulate, well-educated, and politically sophisticated individuals. They can be housewives, teachers, perhaps salespeople, or public officials. They personify members of a well-recognized, potent citizen resistance movement.[48] NIMBY is

> a reaction or attitude towards any project, such as the siting of a hazardous enterprise or affordable housing projects, that is perceived to pose a threat to health or safety, status or reputation of a neighborhood or geographical area. NIMBYism can take the form of a protest against authorities or industry by the formation of action groups comprised by local residents. This response by the local population derives from a variety of reasons, including: a sense that they are being overrun by the authorities or industry to a genuine concern for the health and safety of residents of the community.[49]

NIMBYism is all too familiar to federal, state, and local officials attempting to implement state programs for issuing permits for hazardous waste sites as required by RCRA or trying to plan for the designation or cleanup of a Superfund site. It poses a formidable obstacle to waste-site management under RCRA and Superfund. It is the environmental movement's problem, too.

Federal and State Law Can Encourage NIMBYism. NIMBYism thrives because of numerous and still increasing state and federal laws that empower citizen activism in the implementation of many different environmental laws and regulations. Most states now have legislation in which citizens are given some role in the writing, implementation, and enforcement of environmental laws. Seventeen states require the appropriate agencies to prepare environmental impact statements for their activities and mandate public notice and involvement in the process.[50]

Federal law provides many opportunities for citizen participation in environmental regulation. Major environmental laws, such as the CAA, the Clean Water Act, RCRA, and Superfund, grant citizens the standing to sue federal agencies to compel their enforcement of environmental regulations. The Surface Mining Control and Reclamation Act (1977), the 1984 RCRA amendments, and the 1972 Clean Water Act amendments, among many others, require the responsible federal and state agencies to involve the public in writing and implementing regulations. Several federal environmental laws also permit citizens or citizen organizations to sue private firms for failure to comply with the terms of their pollution-discharge permits and to recover the costs involved in the suits. Public notice and hearings are routinely required of environmental agencies before major regulations are promulgated or permits are issued for pollution discharges or hazardous waste sites. These statutory provisions have set in motion political forces powerfully abetting NIMBYism. There also has been an explosion of ad hoc state and local groups that have organized to deal with specific hazardous waste issues, ranging from the closing of city waste dumps to state policies for hazardous waste transportation.

Many existing state and national environmental organizations now give major attention to hazardous waste issues and provide technical assistance and education for concerned citizens. These groups believe they are ultimately contributing to better implementation of RCRA and Superfund by ensuring greater citizen understanding and acceptance of waste policy decisions made by government officials. Often, however, this activism arouses or emboldens citizen opposition to providing permits for local hazardous waste sites. State governments are not innocent of NIMBYism. Almost any hazardous waste proposal can arouse it. Public hearings on siting hazardous facilities, as political scientist Michael E. Kraft observed, can become "a perfect forum for elected officials and the general public to give vent to fears and concerns, and to denounce decision-making on the siting question."

Distrust of Information Encourages NIMBYism. NIMBYism is rarely routed by better information, more-qualified experts, improved risk communication techniques, and other palliative actions premised on the assumption that the public will be more reasonable about a hazardous facility siting if it is better educated about the issues. All this belies the widespread belief among scientific experts and risk professionals that NIMBYism is rooted in the public's scientific illiteracy.[51]

Why is better risk communication not enough? Because NIMBYs usually distrust the source of governmental risk information: public officials and their scientific spokespeople. In addition, the critics of governmental hazardous waste management often have their own experts and information sources. The conflicting sides, notes Harvard physicist and science policy expert Harvey Brooks, tend to become "noncommunicating publics that each rely on different sources and talk to different experts. Thus, many public policy discussions become dialogues of the deaf. . . ."[52] Often, the true wellsprings of public anxiety about waste siting are not understood by technical experts; people worry about "potentially catastrophic effects, lack of familiarity and understanding, involuntariness, scientific uncertainty, lack of personal control by the individuals exposed, risks to future generations," and more.[53]

Critics often hold environmentalists responsible for NIMBYism. They assert that the environmentalist rhetoric favored by NIMBYs is little more than deceptive but respectable packaging for middle-class selfishness. In reality, argue the critics, most NIMBYs want somebody else to bear whatever risks are associated with hazardous waste sites, while they continue to benefit from the products and economic activities that produce the waste. Even if NIMBYism is well intentioned, critics also note, it fails to solve waste problems. Eventually, waste has to go someplace. It is unfortunate, the critics conclude, that the waste often ends up at whatever sites are the least well defended politically, not at the most appropriate places. Thus, many environmental justice problems (as observed in Chapter 4) and numerous controversies between the states over high-level nuclear waste disposal (see Chapter 8) are created or intensified by NIMBYism.

Whatever its merits, the certain continuation of NIMBYism poses difficult problems for environmental regulation. Is it possible to secure informed public consent to the siting and management of hazardous waste facilities? Must solutions be imposed by judicial, administrative, or political means? Is there danger that continuing the promotion of public involvement in making these decisions will enshrine procedural democracy at the expense of social equity—in effect, will citizen participation gradually result in selectively exposing the least economically and politically advantaged sectors of the public to the most risks from hazardous waste? These questions can only grow in importance as the hazardous waste problem magnifies in the twenty-first century.

CONCLUSION

In no other major area of environmental policy is progress measured in such modest increments as the regulation of toxic and hazardous wastes. Hazardous waste in abandoned or deliberately uncontrolled landfills numbering in the thousands has yet to be controlled properly. Federal and state governments have yet to approve and implement on the appropriate scale the strategies required to ameliorate hazardous waste problems. The risks already associated with hazardous substances and the many others that will become apparent with continuing research in the twenty-first century are unlikely to diminish without a massive and continuing federal commitment of resources to implementing the programs as intended by Congress—a commitment of resources and will on a scale that has been lacking so far.

Implementation of TSCA, RCRA, and Superfund is likely to be slow, because these laws raise technical, legal, and political problems on an order seldom matched in other environmental policy domains. First, no other environmental programs attempt to regulate so many discrete, pervasive substances; we have observed that the hazardous substances that may lie within the scope of these laws number in the tens of thousands. Second, regulation is delayed by the need to acquire technical information never previously obtained by government, to conduct research on the hazardousness of new chemicals, or to secure from corporations highly guarded trade secrets. Third, almost every major regulatory action intended to limit the production, distribution, or disposal of chemical substances deemed toxic or hazardous by government is open to technical controversy, litigation, and other challenges concerning the degree of risk associated with such substances and their suitability for regulation under the laws. Fourth, opponents of regulatory actions under TSCA, RCRA, and Superfund have been able to use to good advantage all the opportunities provided by requirements for administrative due process and the federalized structure of regulation to challenge administrative acts politically and judicially. Fifth, in many instances, the states responsible for implementing the programs have been slow to provide from their own resources the means necessary to ensure proper implementation.

From a broader perspective, the enormous difficulties in controlling hazardous substances once they are released into the ecosystem, together with the problems of controlling their disposal, emphasize the crucial role that production controls must play in hazardous substance management. Indeed, it may be that the human and environmental risks from hazardous chemicals may never be constrained satisfactorily once these substances are let loose in the environment. U.S. technology development has proceeded largely with an implicit confidence that whatever human or environmental risks may be engendered in the process can be contained adequately by the same genius that inspired technology's development—a faith, in effect, that science always will cure whatever ills it creates. Toxic and hazardous substances pose for the nation a formidable technological challenge: how to reckon the human and environmental costs of technology development while technologies are yet evolving, and then, how to prudently control dangerous technologies without depriving the nation of their benefits.

Suggested Readings

Foster, Kenneth R., David E. Bernstein, and Peter W. Huber. *Phantom Risk: Scientific Inference and the Law.* Cambridge, MA: MIT Press, 1999.

Gerrard, Michael B. *Whose Backyard, Whose Risk?* Cambridge, MA: MIT Press, 1999.

Rabe, Barry G. *Beyond NIMBY: Hazardous Waste Siting in Canada and the United States.* Washington, DC: Brookings Institution Press, 1994.

Raffensberger, Carolyn, and Joel Tickner, eds. *Protecting Public Health and the Environment.* Washington, DC: Island Press, 1999.

Rahm, Dianne, ed. *Toxic Waste and Environmental Policy in the 21st Century United States.* Jefferson, NC: McFarland, 2002.

Wilson, Duff. *Fateful Harvest: The True Story of a Small Town, a Global Industry, and a Toxic Secret.* New York: Harper Collins, 2002.

Notes

1. Quoted in Nick Madigan, "Largest-Ever Toxic Waste Suit Opens in California," *New York Times,* February 5, 1993, A17.
2. U.S. EPA, "Superfund Success Stories," available at www.epa.gov/superfund/randomize/thumbs3.htm.
3. "Top 100 Verdicts of 2005," Verdictsearch, available at www.verdictsearch.com.

4. "Insurers Must Pay for Hazardous Waste Site Cleanup, Court Rules," *Los Angeles Times*, August 9, 2012, available at http://latimesblogs.latimes.com/lanow/2012/08/insurance-companies-hazardous-waste-cleanup.html.

5. Ibid.

6. David Danelski, "Stringfellow Acid Pits: How State Spent $52 Million in Latest Cleanup Effort," *Press-Enterprise*, July 22, 2016, available at https://www.pe.com/2016/07/22/stringfellow-acid-pits-how-state-spent-52-million-in-latest-cleanup-effort/.

7. Quoted in Will Matthews, "Stringfellow Retains Reputation: 'Glen Avon' Backlash Underscores Lasting Stigma," *Inland Valley Daily Bulletin* (Ontario, CA), January 11, 2003, 1A.

8. Jeffrey M. Jones, "U.S. Concern About Environmental Threats Eases," *Gallup Politics*, March 25, 2015, available at http://www.gallup.com/poll/182105/concern-environmental-threats-eases.aspx.

9. GAO, "Observations on Improving the Toxic Substances Control Act: Statement of John Stephenson, Director, National Resources and Environment," Report no. GAO 10–292, Washington, DC, December 2, 2009, "Highlights."

10. GAO, *Chemical Assessments: Challenges Remain With EPA's Integrated Risk Information System Program*, GAO-12-41, December 2011, 14, available at htttp://www.gao.gov/assets/590/586620.pdf.

11. Some listed chemicals consist of a class of related substances that are not listed separately. See U.S. Department of Health and Human Services, Public Health Service, National Toxicology Program, *Report on Carcinogens*, 13th ed. (Washington, DC: National Toxicology Program, 2014), 5.

12. GAO, *Transforming EPA's Process for Assessing and Controlling Toxic Chemicals* (Washington, DC: Author, 2012), available at www.gao.gov/highrisk/risks/safety-security/epa_and_toxic_chemicals.php#found.

13. Estimate based upon pesticide data found in Arthur Grube, David Donaldson, Timothy Kiely, and La Wu, *Pesticides Industry Sales and Usage, 2006 and 2007 Market Estimates* (Washington, DC: US EPA, Office of Chemical Safety and Pollution, Prevention, 2011), 4.

14. National Research Council, Committee on the Future Role of Pesticides in U.S. Agriculture, *The Future Role of Pesticides in U.S. Agriculture* (Washington, DC: National Academies Press, 2000), 33.

15. Philip Shabecoff, "EPA Pulls Back on Asbestos Rules," *New York Times*, March 9, 1985, 1, 48.

16. Google Sightseeing, "Why See the World for Real?: Love Canal," available at http://googlesightseeing.com/2009/05/love-canal/.

17. An accurate and informative summary of the Love Canal issue can be found in Lois Gibbs, "History of Love Canal," *The Encyclopedia of the Earth*, available at http://www.eoearth.org/article/History_of_Love_Canal#gen2.

18. U.S. Centers for Disease Control, "Cytogenetic Patterns in Persons Living Near Love Canal—New York," May 27, 1983, available at http://www.cdc.gov/mmwr/preview/mmwrhtml/00000084.htm.

19. Anthony dePalma, "Love Canal Declared Clean, Ending Toxic Horror," *New York Times*, March 18, 2004, available at http://www.nytimes.com/2004/03/18/nyregion/love-canal-declared-clean-ending-toxic-horror.html.

20. Rick Pfeiffer, "Former Love Canal Students Seek Answers," *Niagara-Gazette*, August 21, 2012, available at http://niagara-gazette.com/local/x1088167343/Former-Love-Canal-students-seek-answers.

21. Carolyn Thompson, "Lawsuits: Love Canal Still Oozes 35 Years Later," *USA Today*, November 2, 2013, available at http://www.usatoday.com/story/money/business/2013/11/02/suits-claim-love-canal-still-oozing-35-years-later/3384259/; see also Andrew Revkin, "Love Canal and Its Mixed Legacy," *New York Times*, November 25, 2013, available at http://www.nytimes.com/2013/11/25/booming/love-canal-and-its-mixed-legacy.html.

22. Center for Bioenvironmental Research, Tulane and Xavier Universities, "Environmental Estrogens: What Does the Evidence Mean?" New Orleans, LA, 1996; Center for the Study of Environmental Endocrine Disruptors, "Significant Government Policy Developments," Washington, DC, 1996; Center for the Study of Environmental Endocrine Disruptors, "Effects: State of Science Paper," Washington, DC, 1995.

23. Center for the Study of Environmental Endocrine Disruptors, "Effects," 12.

24. Center for the Study of Environmental Endocrine Disruptors, "Significant Government Policy Developments," 17.

25. Theo Colborn, Dianne Dumanoski, and John Peter Meyers, *Our Stolen Future: Are We Threatening Our Fertility, Intelligence, and Survival?* (New York: Penguin, 1996), 7.

26. Linda Schierow, "Summaries of Environmental Laws Administered by the EPA: The Toxic Substances Control Act," Congressional Research Service Report no. RL30022, Washington, DC, 2006, 2.

27. National Research Council, Committee on Improving Risk Analysis Approaches Used by the U.S. EPA, Science and Decisions: Advancing Risk Assessment, "Summary" (Washington, DC: National Academies Press, 2009). See also GAO, *Chemical Assessments: Challenges Remain With EPA's Integrated Risk Information System Program*, "Highlights," GAO-12-41, December 2011.

28. GAO, *High Risk Series: An Update*, Document GAO-15-290 (Washington, DC, 2015), 280.

29. GAO, "Chemical Regulation: Actions Are Needed to Improve the Effectiveness of EPA's Chemical Review Program," Report no. GAO-06–1032T, Washington, DC, August 2, 2006, 1; see also Mary Cole, "When Superfund Expenses Go Mega," *Los Angeles Times*, January 26, 2007, 1A.

30. GAO, *High Risk Series: An Update*, Document GAO-15-290 (Washington, DC: 2015), 280.

31. The amendments were enacted as the Frank R. Lautenberg Chemical Safety for the 21st Century Act.

32. Sheldon Krimsky, "The Unsteady State and Inertia of Chemical Regulation Under the US Toxic Substances Control Act," *PLOS*, December 18, 2017, available at https://doi.org/10.1371/journal.pbio.2002404.

33. U.S. EPA, "Toxics Release Inventory 2016 National Analysis: Executive Summary," available at https://www.epa.gov/trinationalanalysis/report-sections-2016-tri-national-analysis.

34. Ibid., 90–91.

35. GAO, "RCRA Corrective Action Program," Report no. GAO/RCED 97–3, Washington, DC, 1997; GAO, "Hazardous Waste: EPA Has Removed Some Barriers to Cleanups," Report no. GAO/RCED 00–2000, Washington, DC, August 2000, 10–11. See also EPA, Office of Solid Waste, Economics, Methods, and Risk Analysis Division, "A Study of the Implementation of the RCRA Corrective Action Program," September 25, 2000, available at http://yosemite1.epa.gov/ee/epa/ria.nsf/vwTD/723E3A531445993085256C60006A69E9.

36. GAO, "RCRA Corrective Action Program," 2.

37. GAO, "Superfund: Estimates of Number of Future Sites Vary," Report no. GAO/RCED 95–18, Washington, DC, November 1994, 14. See also CEQ, *Environmental Quality, 1992* (Washington, DC: U.S. Government Printing Office, 1993), 127.

38. GAO, "Superfund Funding and Cost," Report no. GAO-08-841R, Washington, DC, July 18, 2008, 4.

39. Robert Hersh, Michael B. Batz, and Katherine D. Walker, *Superfund's Future: What Will It Cost?* (Washington, DC: Resources for the Future), 131.

40. GAO, Superfund: Trends in Federal Funding and Cleanup of EPA's Nonfederal National Priorities List Sites, Report GAO-15-812, Washington, DC. GAO, 2015, "Highlights."

41. GAO, "Superfund Program: Current Superfund Program and Future Challenges," Report No. GAO-04-475R, Washington, DC, February 18, 2004.

42. Landy and Hague, "Coalition for Waste." On the general problems with Superfund, see, for example, Steven Cohen and Sheldon Kamieniecki, *Environmental Regulation Through Strategic Planning* (Boulder, CO: Westview Press, 1991); Daniel Mazmanian and David Morell, *Beyond Superfailure: America's Toxics Policy for the 1990s* (Boulder, CO: Westview Press, 1992).

43. Martha L. Judy and Katherine N. Probst, "Superfund at 30," *Vermont Journal of Environmental Law* 11, no. 1 (2009): 241.

44. EPA, "2007 Toxics Release Inventory (TRI), Public Data Release Reports," Report no. EPA 260-R-09-001, Washington, DC, April 2009, 6.

45. Marc Landy and Mary Hague, "The Coalition for Waste: Private Interests and Superfund," in *Environmental Politics: Public Costs, Private Rewards*, eds. Michael S. Greve and Fred L. Smith (New York: Praeger, 1992), 70.

46. Keith Schneider, "Rule Forcing Towns to Pick Big New Dumps or Big Costs," *New York Times*, January 6, 1992, A1.

47. Michael S. Greve, "Introduction," in *Environmental Politics: Public Costs, Private Rewards,* eds. Michael S. Greve and Fred L. Smith (New York: Praeger, 1992), 5–6.

48. On the sources and impact of NIMBYism generally, see Luther J. Carter, *Nuclear Imperatives and Public Trust: Dealing with Radioactive Waste* (Washington, DC: Resources for the Future, 1987); Clarence Davies, Vincent T. Covello, and Frederick W. Allen, eds., *Risk Communication* (Washington, DC: Conservation Foundation, 1987); Roger E. Kasperson, "Six Propositions on Public Participation and Their Relevance for Risk Communication," *Risk Analysis,* 6 (September 1986): 275–281; Patrick G. Marshall, "Not in My Backyard," *CQ Editorial Research Reports,* June 1989, 311.

49. Olurominiyi Ibitayo and Misse Herber, "NIMBYism," *The Encyclopedia of the Earth,* November 18, 2008, available at http://www.eoearth.org/article/NIMBYism.

50. Michael S. Greve, "Environmentalism and Bounty Hunting," *Public Interest,* 97 (Fall 1989): 15–29.

51. Thomas M. Dietz and Robert W. Rycroft, *The Risk Professionals* (New York: Russell Sage Foundation, 1987), 60.

52. Harvey Brooks, "The Resolution of Technically Intensive Public Policy Disputes," *Science, Technology and Human Values* 9 (Winter 1984): 48.

53. Kraft, "Risk Perception," 7.

ENERGY

America's Energy Politics in Transformation

In mid-2018, *Forbes*, a major publication for the American business sector, noted almost casually that something remarkable was evolving in America's energy sector, something almost unimaginable only a decade earlier. "America," the magazine predicted, "is on the cusp of taking the throne as the world's leading energy powerhouse."[1] Moreover, many energy experts had already concluded that this unprecedented surge of energy production could propel the United States toward a plausible future of energy independence in less than a decade.

When Donald Trump entered the White House in 2016, this was a radically different reality from what Barack Obama had confronted beginning his second term only four years previously. Petroleum imports were now falling, domestic petroleum production and exports were rising. Many experts were speculating that the continuing domestic natural gas "boom" and innovative production of "fracked" petroleum could stifle the economically fragile U.S. coal industry. The often-predicted revival of commercial nuclear power once again seemed illusory. And in the West, vast wind farms and sprawling, thousand-acre solar arrays were emerging in grasslands and deserts.

Donald Trump promised that his presidency would drive the pace of this energy transformation even further and faster. If successful, the Trump energy agenda would also create the most radical revision of national energy regulation since the first Earth Day. This new agenda included major relaxation of the Obama administration's regulations limiting national carbon emissions, expansion of oil and gas exploration on public lands and the Outer Continental Shelf (OCS), and promotion of greater energy production. This chapter concerns these rapid transformations in the U.S. energy economy, the Trump administration's new energy agenda, and its impact upon national environmental policy and politics.

THE FOUNDATION: A FOSSIL FUEL NATION

The United States has a ravenous energy appetite, and most of the consumption has been fossil fuel, as Figure 8.1 illustrates. Collectively, Americans constitute approximately 4.5 percent of the world's population and consume about 25 percent of the world's energy production. Many of the nation's major pollution problems are caused directly by current methods of producing and consuming this energy. Consider the environmental impact of fossil fuels. About 80 percent of all energy currently consumed in the United States comes from petroleum, natural gas, and coal.[2] The ecological consequences of this combustion are numerous:

- Transportation accounts for more than a third of air-polluting nitrogen oxide emissions and almost 40 percent of carbon monoxide emissions.[3]

- Electric power generation, primarily from coal, produces more than 80 percent of sulfur dioxide air pollution.[4]

- About half the U.S.-generated climate-warming CO_2 emissions come from petroleum, 28 percent from coal, and 29 percent from natural gas.[5]

FIGURE 8.1 ■ U.S. Energy Consumption by Energy Source, 2017

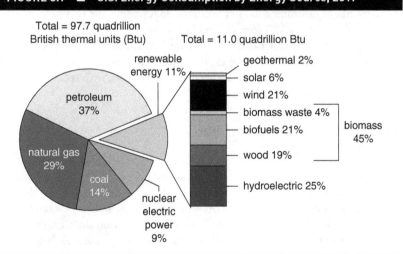

Total = 97.7 quadrillion British thermal units (Btu)   Total = 11.0 quadrillion Btu

petroleum 37%
natural gas 29%
coal 14%
nuclear electric power 9%
renewable energy 11%

geothermal 2%
solar 6%
wind 21%
biomass waste 4%
biofuels 21%
wood 19%
hydroelectric 25%
biomass 45%

Source: Energy Information Administration, "U.S. Energy Facts Explained," available at https://www.eia.gov/energyexplained/?page=us_energy_home

Note: Sum of components may not equal 100% because of independent rounding.

So intimate is the association between energy and environmental quality that the nation's energy agenda in the second decade of the twenty-first century will become environmental policy by another name.

Petroleum: A Revived Economy

One of the most important emerging transformations in the U.S. energy economy has been the decline of imported petroleum beginning in 2010: At the beginning of the Trump administration, petroleum imports declined from almost 55 percent of total consumption in 2008 to 19 percent in 2017.[6] The growing U.S. oil production is primarily the result of the improvement and rapid national dispersion of fracking technology, the technology introduced in Chapter 1 and further explored when natural gas is next considered.

The World's Leading Oil Exporter

The rapid reversal of U.S. imported oil consumption has been accompanied by an equally significant increase in domestic petroleum refining, again reversing a trend of declining domestic oil production that prevailed since the early 1970s. Together, these dual transitions have rapidly created a new petroleum market quite unlike that which prevailed as late as 2009. If these trends were to continue, as many experts had predicted, the United States would replace Saudi Arabia as the world's leading oil producer in less than a decade.

At the same time, the International Energy Agency (IEA) also cautions, the United States is not an "energy island" invulnerable to the global energy economy and its environmental implications. For example, the IEA predicts that both mainland China and Europe's rapid economic growth will create growing competition with the United States for world petroleum production.[7] This is an important reason many energy experts join environmentalists in advocating increased domestic energy conservation as a national security issue to protect against future imported oil blockades.

Oil, the Outer Continental Shelf, and the Environment

While a revival of domestic petroleum production and exports has an almost irresistible economic and political allure for U.S. policymakers, it is also loaded with long-standing, controversial environmental issues as well as new ones, such as fracking technology. The history of petroleum production since Earth Day is inseparable from environmental conflicts incited by the political and economic pressure to expand traditional production from existing petroleum reserves despite the environmental risks.

Petroleum production from oil reserves on federal lands has been one traditional source of impassioned conflict between proponents of accelerated petroleum production and environmentalists. The long and fierce conflict over petroleum drilling on the huge continental area constituting the Alaskan National Wildlife Refuge introduces the next chapter concerning public lands. Another major flashpoint for these controversies in recent years has been the ecological impact of oil production from submerged public lands on the OCS. These conflicts have further intensified by the Trump administration's commitment to accelerating energy exploration in all these geographic areas.

The Outer Continental Shelf. The OCS consists of the land submerged between a continent and the deep ocean. America's OCS encompasses 1.76 billion acres of submerged, taxpayer-owned lands. Generally, the OCS begins three to nine nautical miles from shore (depending on the state) and extends two hundred nautical miles outward—or farther if the continental shelf extends beyond that limit. The federal government administers the submerged lands, subsoil, and seabed of the OCS. Jurisdiction over OCS lands is divided between the coastal states, whose authority extends three miles from their ocean borders (except for Texas and the west coast of Florida, where state jurisdiction extends to nine nautical miles), and the federal government, which controls OCS lands for two miles beyond the state three-mile limit. Altogether, production from existing state and federal energy leases accounts for about 30 percent of domestic petroleum production and 25 percent of natural gas.

The OCS and Environmental Controversy. The Department of the Interior (DOI) has estimated that federally controlled OCS lands contain vast reserves of oil and natural gas.[8] The DOI regulates energy exploration in the OCS by determining the location of OCS land open to exploration, issuing permits for exploration, and enforcing safety and environmental regulations for energy production from oil and gas wells. Environmentalists have been especially vigilant about federal leasing and supervision of energy production on the OCS. They have persistently criticized federal regulators for insufficient oversight of environmental laws governing OCS energy development and have resisted pressure on the federal government by international energy producers to open vast new OCS tracts to exploration.

The ongoing battle over OCS energy development escalated to international attention following the catastrophic incineration and collapse of British Petroleum's *Deepwater Horizon* drilling platform into the Gulf of Mexico in April 2010. The platform's destruction on April 22 constituted the largest accidental marine oil spill in U.S. history, releasing 4.9 million barrels of crude oil into the Gulf and creating the largest oil spill in U.S. history. What followed was an ecological disaster whose long-range environmental impacts will take decades to assess. Environmentalists angrily asserted that the Gulf disaster demonstrated both the inherent risks of increased energy exploration in the OCS and the federal government's lax regulatory oversight of OCS petroleum production.

Investigation by the DOI's own inspector general, a bipartisan congressional committee, and numerous other official and unofficial entities between 2010 and 2011 revealed that the Minerals Management Service (MMS) responsible for regulatory supervision of Gulf energy production had failed to enforce rigorously its regulatory oversight, which could have prevented the spill. In the aftermath of further DOI and congressional investigations, the secretary of the interior promised radical reform at the MMS.[9] The MMS became a classic example of the problem created when federal agencies are responsible for both regulating and promoting the same industry.

Renewed Pressure for OCS Energy Production. Despite the Gulf oil spill, the White House and Congress continue to share a keen and increasingly partisan interest in the future of OCS lands. While congressional Republicans have pressed for accelerated OCS energy development and Democrats have usually advocated restraint, political and economic cross-pressures often blur partisan differences, particularly concerning the OCS lands under state jurisdiction. For example, Florida's Senate and House delegations of both parties are usually together in opposing any OCS development likely to create environmental damage to the state's coast. In the aftermath of *Deepwater Horizon*, President Obama was compelled in the presence of the country's persistently deep economic recession to modify his resistance to OCS exploration and to advocate "safe and responsible" oil production. On January 15, 2015, Obama announced his intention to open parts of the Atlantic Coast OCS lands, excluding Maryland, Delaware, and Florida, for oil leasing and also to block access to most oil deposits in the Beaufort and Chukchi Seas off Alaska's North Slope—a trade-off meant to simultaneously hasten economic recovery and please environmentalists—which proved unacceptable to environmentalists who wanted no increased OCS exploration.[10]

The 2016 presidential election, however, swiftly and radically redefined the controversy over OCS leasing. In early 2018, the DOI, following the Trump energy agenda, announced its intention to allow energy exploration in nearly all U.S. coastal waters, the single largest expansion of oil and gas leasing in American history and a rejection of the Obama administration's restriction of exploration along the Atlantic seaboard and in the Arctic.[11] This new proposal further inflamed the political controversy over the OCS lands when the governors of nine coastal states immediately opposed the prospective new energy exploration off their coasts. This ongoing state–federal controversy is destined to unfold in both Congress and assuredly in the federal courts, which often become the final arbiter in such regulatory conflicts.

NATURAL GAS AND THE GAS "BOOM"

Natural gas in its several different forms is often considered the most attractive and versatile of all the fossil fuels in the nation's near future. Natural gas is commercially produced primarily from oil fields and natural gas fields, although the industry is now aggressively extracting natural gas from unconventional sources, such as shale gas and coal-bed methane. U.S. proven reserves are steadily increasing as new extraction technologies develop. To many U.S. energy sectors, natural gas is increasingly important, economically and environmentally, as an alternative to petroleum and coal if the entailed risks of increasing gas production prove acceptable. And like all projections about future domestic energy use, predictions of future gas supply depend upon numerous assumptions or scenarios—such as continued economic growth and absence of major political crises—that caution against treating predictions as if they are destiny.

Domestic Resources: Increasing Supply and Demand

Natural gas now provides a significant portion of energy to several important U.S. economic sectors, especially electric power and industrial production. Proven reserves of domestic onshore and offshore natural gas have grown annually since 1999, accelerated by the development of economically practical extraction from shale.[12] According to the U.S. Energy Information Administration (EIA), the United States possesses enough natural gas reserves to supply more than one hundred years of use at 2010 consumption levels.[13] Domestic production of natural gas is expected to increase significantly in the future, but so is total U.S. energy demand; the EIA has predicted that by 2030, natural gas will provide about 25 percent of domestic energy consumption, about the proportion of current consumption.

Natural Gas Is Replacing Coal

Much of the expected change in future natural gas production and consumption is expected to result not only from increased fracking but also from changes in fossil fuel consumption by the electric power and industrial sections, which together consume almost two thirds of current natural gas production. Both electric utilities and industry have responded to tougher air pollution regulations and the decreasing price of natural gas by substituting gas for coal-fired facilities in existing or planned installations. Progress Energy, for example, one of the nation's largest electric utilities, has announced plans to shut down eleven North Carolina coal plants by 2017 and to substitute natural gas in two of them.[14]

Natural gas exploration and production has traditionally entailed environmental hazards. Exploration and drilling for natural gas disturbs surface vegetation and soil as well as subsurface geology; pipelines can pose air and water pollution problems. Natural gas wells and pipelines require infrastructure, such as engines and drilling rigs, also environmentally hazardous when unregulated. Some natural gas, mostly methane, also leaks from drilling sites and pipelines.

The oil and gas industry has made an effort to avoid gas leaks, and where natural gas is produced but can't be transported economically, it is "flared" or burned at well sites. One new environmental issue now inseparable from all discourse about a coming boom in natural gas production is the environmental risks associated with fracking technology.[15]

Fracking: "Almost a Miracle" or an Environmental Danger? Fracking technology has rapidly spread across the United States. Map 8.1 illustrates the domestic shale deposits most important for fracked petroleum and natural gas production.[16] At the outset of the Obama administration, the new drilling boom involving fracking seemed to many industry leaders the assured path toward a bright future. "It's almost divine intervention," burbled Aubrey K. McClendon, chairman and chief executive of the Chesapeake Energy Corporation, one of the nation's largest natural gas producers. "Right at the time oil prices are skyrocketing, we're struggling with the economy, we're concerned about global warming, and national security threats remain intense, we wake up and we've got this abundance of natural gas around us."[17]

By 2018, the *New York Times* reported optimistically that fracking technology "had led to a drilling frenzy enabling a doubling of output in a decade,

MAP 8.1 ■ Major Oil Shale Deposits in the United States

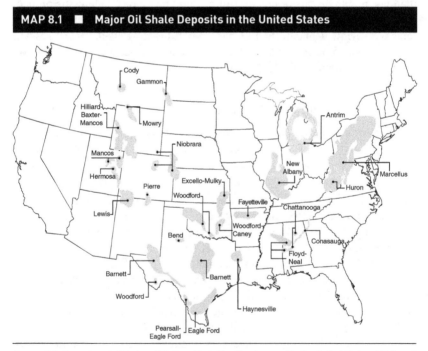

Source: U.S. Department of Energy, "Modern Shale Gas Development in the United States: A Primer," available at http://energy.gov/fe/downloads/modern-shale-gas-development-united-states-primer.

transforming unlikely places like North Dakota and New Mexico into world class petroleum hubs."[18] Many industry experts, aware that energy production and prices can be highly volatile, still remain cautious about fracking's future. A collapse of crude oil prices beginning in mid-2014, for example, forced a shutdown of numerous drilling sites across the United States, devastating many fracking boomtowns. Still, the well-financed, large fracking operations survived and increased production, encouraging most energy experts and financial markets to view the industry's future with increasing optimism as the technology continues rapidly to redefine America's future petroleum and natural gas economy.

A Disputed Environmental Impact. Hydrologic fracturing "involves pumping liquids under high pressure into a well to fracture the rock and allow gas to escape from tiny pockets in the rock."[19] Millions of gallons of chemically treated water, called brine, is mixed with sand and blasted down a drilling hole to shatter petroleum shale and release the embedded gas. The return water, called flowback, is a cocktail of water, chemical toxins, carcinogens, and other chemical wastes, sometimes including radioactive components and inert substances that must be purified before the flowback is suitable for other uses. Most of the return water, however, is pumped back underground into shale sites for containment. Almost all natural gas and petroleum exploration and production from federal lands use fracking technology regulated by the DOI. More than fifty-seven thousand wells are located on private land at the major geologic sites identified on Map 8.1. These private sites are presently regulated by the states.

Chapter 1 illustrated the ambivalence with which environmentalists and many residents near fracking operations regard hydrologic fracturing. Despite environmentalist criticism, many gas production companies, contending their brine formulas are trade secrets, refuse to publicly disclose their composition and deny that brine can contaminate underground water. The industry contends, moreover, that proven technologies are available for distilling an environmentally safe liquid from flowback when needed. The CEO of Halliburton Co., a major energy consulting firm, was so convinced of brine's safety that he invited (or compelled) an associate to drink some fracking fluid during a meeting of the Colorado Oil and Gas Association, and the media reported that his associate consumed a "bit of the liquid" without harm.[20]

Contested Environmental Regulations. Under considerable political pressure from oil shale states, environmentalists, Congress, and communities near fracking operations, the EPA initiated studies to characterize the content and dispersion of flowback. In early 2015, the EPA released results of its first investigation. While the EPA acknowledged that hydraulic fracturing had the potential to impact drinking water resources, it concluded: "We did not find evidence that these mechanisms have led to widespread, systemic impacts on drinking water resources in the United States. Of the potential mechanisms identified in this report, we found specific instances where one or more mechanisms led to impacts on drinking water resources, including contamination of drinking water wells. The number of identified cases, however, was small compared to the number of hydraulically fractured wells."[21] EPA's conclusions were too tentative, the case studies too few, to satisfy fracking's environmental critics or to provide scientific evidence sufficient to describe accurately fracking's broader ecological impact.

The rapid expansion of fracking across the country has also confronted many state and local governments with difficult and controversial regulatory problems, frequently leading to conflicts between governments over regulatory rules and authority. The Obama administration in 2017 proposed the first federal regulations to control fracking on federal lands. The regulations would have set environmentally protective standards for fracking brine, disposal of fracking waste, and site restoration. Many western governors, corporate energy developers, and other economic interests, concerned that the proposed regulations would inhibit new fracking sites, vigorously opposed this initiative and stalled its implementation with litigation until 2018. Following his election, Donald Trump redeemed a campaign promise and repealed the Obama regulatory proposal.[22] Predictably, environmentalists and other proponents of stringent national fracking regulations challenged the Trump regulatory reversal in the federal courts, creating at least a temporary regulatory stalemate while fracking proceeds on federal lands.

COAL: THE PROMISE AND PERILS OF ABUNDANCE

Although the United States has coal reserves sufficient for 250 years at current consumption rates, persistent economic and environmental problems have plagued the coal industry, steadily shrinking its domestic market and workforce. When Donald Trump entered the White House, the coal industry, whose abundance once seemed a secure and certain foundation of the national electric power production, was in a second decade of decline. In 2000, coal generated more than half the nation's electric power. By 2016,[23] coal produced only a third of America's electricity as natural gas gradually replaced coal as electric utility fuel. Coal miners faced an increasingly precarious future: coalfield employment had declined more than 20 percent in ten years. By 2000, climate change had become the most recent among many global signatures for coal's environmental risks, another ominous offset to the attractions of coal energy in a nation extravagantly endowed with what was once called "black gold."

The Trump Administration's New Regulatory Agenda

The environmental regulation of coal and its impact upon the coal industry became a centerpiece for the Trump presidential campaign. Trump's assault on federal coal regulations—what he called Obama's "war on coal"—powerfully attracted voters in coal-producing states and dominated the Trump administration's early environmental agenda. Trump's principal target was the Obama administration's Clean Power Plan (CPP), which proposed rigorous regulation of national climate-warming emissions, primarily from coal-fired electric power generation. Speaking to pro-coal audiences in Pennsylvania and West Virginia, for example, Trump declared that miners were the major casualties from the war on coal and promised that he would quickly end the war and restore prosperity to the coalfields. "We will start winning, winning, winning, and you are going to be very proud," he told an audience in Charleston, West Virginia, "[a]nd for those miners, get ready, because you are going to be working your asses off . . ."[24]

Within a year of its inauguration, the Trump administration revoked or suspended many federal environmental regulations and executive orders constituting the foundation of the Obama administration's coal policies. The major changes included

- suspending the CPP to regulate climate-warming emissions from coal-fired electric utilities,

- reversing a moratorium on new coal leases on federal lands,

- reducing EPA staff and funding for research on climate-warming impact of coal combustion,

- terminating DOI research on the health effects of coal mine mountain-top removal, and

- reducing staff and funding for regulation of surface mining environmental impacts and site restoration.

If implemented, the cumulative effect of these and numerous other coal-related Trump initiatives would constitute the most radical revocation and revision of federal coal regulation since Earth Day 1970. The Trump administration's coal policy has incited intense opposition among environmentalists and their allies, creating a volatile political conflict extending across all the major venues of federal coal policymaking, especially the EPA, the DOI, and the federal courts.

The battle over coal regulation has also invested the federal courts with great importance as a strategic weapon in the environmentalist counterattack on the Trump antiregulatory initiatives. Many of the regulations targeted for revocation or revision cannot be modified without a legislatively required, prolonged process of administrative and public review, which may include judicial oversight. These requirements create time and opportunity for opponents to stall deregulation and to rally political opposition while creating the possibility that the federal courts may reject proposed regulatory changes. Nonetheless, coal deregulation had become so crucial to the administration's entire environmental agenda that the coalfields merited recognition in Trump's first State of the Union address.

"We have ended the war on American energy—and we have ended the war on beautiful, clean coal," he announced.[25] The political fortune of Trump and the deregulation of coal have become inexorably intertwined and continue to dominate much of Trump's environmental agenda.

Coal and Climate Change

Every aspect of the nation's coal utilization—mining, transportation, combustion, waste disposal—entails environmental hazards unless diligently and continually regulated. Until mid-1990, federal coal regulations focused primarily upon the environmental damage created by coal mining and the air pollutants emitted by coal combustion, primarily sulfur oxides, nitrogen oxides, and methane. However, scientific research has gradually revealed the magnitude of global climate warming and identified CO_2 emissions from coal combustion as a primary source. Since 2000, no issue about coal regulation has become more disruptive and contentious in discourse than the control of CO_2 emissions associated with climate change.

The Obama Clean Power Plan. When Barack Obama entered the White House, research had established that anthropomorphic (human) activity was the primary cause of this climate warming and that fossil fuels combustion, particularly coal emissions, were a principal source of climate-warming gas ("greenhouse gases" or GHG). Following the 2008 presidential election, Obama declared climate legislation a priority and vigorously championed federal government policies, creating a comprehensive domestic regulatory regime to limit domestic GHG. Obama relied principally upon the Clean Air Act for the authority to limit emissions from coal combustion, especially CO_2, the major GHG. The EPA, responsible for implementing the Clean Air Act, became the focus of the fierce regulatory conflict over limiting domestic GHG emissions, a controversy persisting throughout the Obama presidency and into the Trump administration.

Advocates of CO_2 regulation had won a major judicial victory in 2007 when the Supreme Court ruled in *Massachusetts v. Environmental Protection Agency* that the Clean Air Act authorized the EPA to regulate CO_2 emissions if the EPA determined that the emissions endangered human health or the environment. In 2011, the EPA announced that sufficient scientific evidence supported a decision that CO_2 did endanger human health and the environment; the agency began drafting the Obama administration's CPP, a comprehensive, complex regulatory proposal to limit all national CO_2 emissions from both existing and new electric utilities.

EPA announced the final version of the CPP in August 2015. The important elements of the plan included

- the first national standards for carbon emissions for power plants,

- state-by-state emission targets and flexible requirements that states and utilities create plans for implementing the mandated pollution controls by specified deadlines,

- requirements that EPA create an implementation plan for any state failing to create a plan by a specified date,

- encouragement for states to create a "cap and trade" method for achieving emission controls based on economic market principals, and

- provisions to encourage greater renewable energy production through alternatives to carbon fuels.[26]

EPA's analysis of CPP included substantial estimated health and economic benefits from its full implementation: total benefits, estimated to be $26 to $45 billion, were predicted to include prevention of 3,600 premature deaths, 1,700 heart attacks, and 90,000 asthma attacks.

The CPP Opposed and Suspended. The CPP's opponents, including most congressional Republicans, numerous electric utilities, conservative think tanks, the mining industry, and many other large corporate interests, disputed all the EPA's estimated CPP benefits and produced foreboding counterestimates. For instance, one major conservative think tank, the Heritage Foundation, predicted that CPP's economic damage would include 300,000 lost jobs, $2.5 trillion in lost domestic product, and $7,500 income loss per person.[27] The Obama White House had barely released the final CPP proposal before it was stalled. Opponents of the CPP adopted two strategies to frustrate its enforcement. The attorneys general of 27 states immediately challenged in federal court the Obama EPA's authority to create the CPP, compelling EPA to delay the plan's implementation while the Court considered the case. Also, the president quickly ordered EPA to revoke the plan following his election, thus erecting a second barrier to its implementation—a decision then contested by environmentalists in the federal courts. The impact of these judicial engagements was to suspend indefinitely a national plan for CO_2 emissions control, to entangle in litigation any determination about the scope and substance of EPA's future regulatory powers, and to leave electric utilities in a pall of uncertainty about how, and when, to plan for future regulatory impacts. Meanwhile, the Trump administration, expecting the courts to reject the Obama CPP, instructed EPA to draft a new, more limited national CO_2 regulatory plan that Trump asserted would be more economically efficient, less costly, and more generous in granting the states freedom to determine how to regulate than the Obama proposal. This alternative strategy, strongly supported by most utilities, mining interests, and congressional Republicans, is expected to materialize only after the 2018 elections and a prolonged drafting period.

The Difficult Search for Clean Coal

The coal industry may have welcomed a blockade of the CPP, but the industry has long realized that some kind of CO_2 emission regulations were inevitable and that coal faced a bleak economic future without a new technology to reduce significantly CO_2 emissions from power generation. Thus began the search for a "clean coal" technology that would be environmentally protective, affordable enough to sustain the industry economically, and politically popular to preclude regulations as stringent as the much disliked CPP.

The quest for a clean coal technology, however, has been both costly and disappointing. The technology (or CCS) involves "separating CO_2 from coal and capturing the gas either before or after coal combustion. It is then compressed to a super critical liquid, transported by pipeline to an injection well and then pumped underground to depths sufficient to maintain critical pressures."[28] If the technology works, the CO_2 "seeps into the pore spaces in the surrounding rocks and its escape to the surface is blocked by a caprock, or overlaying impermeable layer." The underground storage capacity in the United States is believed to be ample and widespread, and leakage of CO_2 from properly situated storage sites is predicted to be negligible.

The Obama administration had budgeted $3.4 billion for CCS development, but the earliest pilot project, at the American Electric Power Company's site near New Haven, West Virginia, was cancelled by the company less than a year after its initiation for economic reasons.[29] A second Mississippi project, a widely publicized industry effort to demonstrate the viability of CSS technology, was abandoned in 2017, three years behind schedule and $4 billion over budget at a total cost of $7.5 billion. The Mississippi debacle foreshadowed a very problematic future for CCS and its contribution to the industry's economic revival.[30]

Without the prospect of this substantial federal research and development support, public and private electric power companies were unlikely to invest alone the estimated $1 billion required to create an operational electric power facility equipped with a new and largely unproven CCS technology.[31] The coal industry's major hope for commercially viable CO_2 emission controls still rests precariously with the experimental CCS technology.

Surface Mining

Coal mining, like coal combustion, entails multiple environmental hazards. Almost two thirds of all U.S. mined coal is now surface mined. Virtually all coal mined west of the Mississippi River and half the coal produced in Appalachia is surface mined. Surface mining rapidly has replaced underground mining because it is cheaper, more efficient, more profitable, and less labor intensive.[32] Unless rigorously regulated, however, surface mining is environmentally catastrophic. More than 1.5 million acres of U.S. land have been disturbed by coal surface mining; more than a million of these acres remain wrecked and ravaged wastelands, long abandoned by their destroyers. More than one thousand additional acres are disturbed each week by surface mining, and more than thirty states have been scarred by unreclaimed surface mines.

In Appalachia, surface miners roamed the hills virtually uncontrolled for decades. The evidence is written in the thousands of sterile acres, acidified streams and rivers, decapitated hills, and slopes scarred by abandoned mine highwalls. In the western prairies and grasslands, unregulated surface mining left thousands of barren, furrowed acres buried under spoil banks so hostile to revegetation that they seem like moonscapes to observers. After decades of resistance, the mining industry came reluctantly to recognize the necessity of federal regulation of surface mining, but vigorous controversy continues over the manner of this regulation and its effectiveness.

The Surface Mining Control and Reclamation Act. President Carter signed the Surface Mining Control and Reclamation Act (SMCRA) of 1977 and thereby created the first federal surface mining regulatory program. The act, strongly promoted by environmentalists against fierce resistance from the mining industry, is intended to control the environmental ravages of surface mining by restoring surface-mined land to productivity whenever possible.

The act's major features included the following:

- Environmental performance standards to which all surface miners were to comply in order to operate. Standards were to be established for the removal, storage, and redistribution of topsoil; siting and erosion control; drainage and protection of water quality; and many other matters affecting environmental quality.

- Requirements that mined land be returned, insofar as possible, to its original contours and to a use equal or superior to that before mining commenced.

- Protection of land unsuitable for mining from any mine activity.

SMCRA remains a troubled and underfunded program. The Office of Surface Mining Reclamation and Enforcement (OSMRE) and the states confront a hugely expensive and complex problem in protecting public health and safety on U.S. abandoned mine sites and active mining lands. Estimates suggest the total cost of restoring these ravaged and deserted acres is $8.6 billion.[33] Among other tasks, restoration requires the remediation of nine thousand acres of unstable waste piles and embankments, four million linear feet of dangerous highwalls, 8,200 acres of subsiding soil, and twenty-three thousand acres of clogged stream lands.[34] Until the Obama administration, a succession of directors passed through the OSMRE's revolving door, and improvement in program administration continues to be modest.

Surface Mining Has Been Intensely Controversial Wherever Practiced. The OSMRE has been persistently criticized—by environmentalists and their allies for lax enforcement of mining regulations and by mine owners for excessively costly and unnecessary regulation. One flashpoint of controversy revived by the Trump administration has been surface mining on federal lands, especially in the Powder

River Basin, the greatest regional producer of surface-mined coal. The Obama administration temporarily suspended new mining leases on federal lands in order to study its environmental impact. President Trump, condemning the Obama mining moratoria as more "war on coal," removed the mining ban on federal lands and instructed the DOI to reduce federally protected historic and wilderness areas, thus opening more land to mine leasing.[35]

Surface mining along mountaintops has steadily enlarged into a pervasive, intensely divisive issue as the practice spreads primarily through Appalachia and the Midwest. Science writer David Biello describes the impact of mountaintop removal:

> The litany of problems—both to the environment and human health—
> caused by a practice that involves blasting the top off a mountain to
> get at the coal beneath it more easily [includes] heavy metals, sulfuric
> acid and other mine contaminants in waterways and drinking-water
> wells; deformed fish carrying toxic levels of selenium found in 73 of
> 78 streams affected by mountaintop mining; entire streams filled in by
> blasted mountain rock; and forests cleared to get at the mountaintop
> beneath them. Add to that the fact that this form of mining has increased
> exponentially in the past 30 years, supplying roughly 10 percent of U.S.
> coal, and you have a recipe for much of the environmental devastation
> visible across northern Appalachia.[36]

Mining companies argue that it is the only way to get at many coal deposits. "Coal in these areas is found in very narrow seams, and the surrounding rock geology is less stable than in areas of layer seams," explained Carol Raulston, senior vice president of the National Mining Association. "It creates flat terrain on what was the top of the mountain but the mountain is still there."[37] Critics, however, say that the land is devastated, while people, property, and the environment endure severe collateral damage.

In mid-2015, the DOI proposed a new rule, scheduled for final adoption in late 2016, to protect streams from significant pollution created by mountaintop removal. The proposal would require coal companies to monitor and test stream quality near removal sites and to restore polluted waters to "the uses they were capable of supporting before mining activities."[38] The proposed rule provoked congressional Republican accusations that Obama was waging "a war on coal" and prompted the National Coal Association—the industry's trade group—to warn of severe unemployment and economic depression in coal-producing states if the rule becomes law. The mountaintop issue seems destined to stalk the White House, EPA, and OSMRE for many years and to assure abrasive confrontations between federal regulators and the coal industry indefinitely.

The Restoration Gamble. One ultimately important test of surface mine regulations is whether they result in an environmentally safer mining industry and a significant restoration of the many thousand acres of mining sites across the United States. The answer is elusive, partly because the restoration of surface mine sites is difficult under the best of circumstances, and public resources to underwrite much of the restoration cost remain unpredictable.

Restoration remains a gamble with nature. Technical studies suggest that the capacity of mining companies to restore mined land to conditions "equal or superior to their original condition"—as regulations require—is likely to be site specific, dependent on the particular biological and geological character of each mining site. Western mining sites are often ecologically fragile; relatively limited varieties of sustainable vegetation and scarce rainfall can make the ecological regeneration of the land difficult.

The prospects for restoration are less forbidding in Appalachia, where an abundance of precipitation, richer soil, and a greater diversity of native flora and fauna are available. Nonetheless, many experts believe that the disruption of subsurface hydrology and the drainage of acids and salts from the mines' spoil heaps may not be controlled easily even when surface revegetation is achieved. With more than four decades' experience with mine site restoration, the results remain ambiguous. Some sites have become restoration showpieces. In many instances, insufficient time has passed to demonstrate the vitality of restoration plans. In Appalachia, mountaintop mining creates especially challenging restoration problems, particularly when soil and mine wastes frequently threaten to contaminate surface and underground water flows.

An Emerging Issue: Coal Ash. The regulation of coal-burning emissions, mostly from electric power generation, annually creates 125 million to 130 million tons of toxic ash and sludge, enough to fill a million railcars; more than half this volume resides in ponds and pits, primarily on electricity utility property. This waste was virtually invisible politically until December 22, 2008, when an earthen dam containing a billion gallons of ash waste from the TVA Kingston Fossil power plant, near Kingston, Tennessee, failed. The released slurry erupted through the containment "like a volcano," reported one resident, flooding three hundred acres, including Kingston and the nearby Emery River, with sludge containing elevated levels of toxic metals (including arsenic, copper, barium, cadmium, chromium, lead, mercury, nickel, and thallium) and other pollutants.[39] Kingston residents claim the residue continues to create serious health problems. A rapid EPA national survey disclosed 431 similar facilities, of which forty-nine were considered "high hazard" because their failure could endanger human life. These containments are a portion of more than 1,300 sludge and ash pits estimated to exist nationally, most of them unregulated and unmonitored.[40]

Coal ash becomes a problem because it resides in a regulatory twilight zone. Depending on where it appears and what it contains, it can be considered a solid waste, water pollutant, toxic waste, groundwater contaminant, or even an air pollutant, and it is therefore subject to various federal and state regulations, or perhaps to no specific regulation or to conflicting laws. Consequently, although most states regulate some aspects of coal ash deposition, there is little consistency and considerable ambiguity about how environmental controls are applied and if the most effective management prevails.

In late 2014, the EPA issued, for the first time, a federal regulatory rule concerning coal ash, the result of six years' deliberation and public review. The new rule, like almost all the Obama administration's environmental regulatory proposals, ignited a politically polarized debate within Congress and divided environmentalist opinion. The EPA's final rule created federal requirements for the construction and maintenance of ash disposal ponds, required periodic containment monitoring, limited volume of some toxic waste in coal ash, and prohibited some chemical content, among other important regulations. The proposal, however, divided the environmental community, with many complaining that the rule was too weak.[41] "Your banana peel that you throw away has stronger protections when it winds up in a dump than coal ash does," complained a Sierra Club spokesman.[42]

The critics asserted that the EPA rule was flawed because it defined coal ash as a "solid waste" subject to the regulatory standards required by the Resource Conservation and Recovery Act (see Chapter 7), when it should have been defined as a "hazardous waste" and controlled with the much tougher regulatory rules of the Toxic Substances Control Act (see Chapter 7), an example of the important economic and environmental difference created when administrators exercise their discretionary authority to decide how and when to implement environmental regulations. In mid-2018, the Trump administration, at the request of the coal industry and over strenuous opposition from environmentalists, halted implementation of the Obama regulations from 2019 until 2022. The delay, explained EPA, would "provide states and utilities much-needed flexibility in the management of coal ash and save millions of dollars in regulatory costs."[43]

Can Deregulation Revive the Coal Industry?

The controversy over the Trump administration's plan to revive the coal industry by rolling back Obama-era regulation is, in many ways, a conflict between two competing visions of coal mining's future. Proponents of a regulatory rollback generally believe that deregulation can slow or halt coal's long economic decline, perhaps even reverse it. Additionally, advocates of ending a war on coal are typically unconvinced about the reality of global climate change and the magnitude—if any—of coal's contribution to climate warming. Proponents of coal deregulation often expect the electric power industry will eventually develop a clean coal technology; others believe that economic market forces will compel electric utilities, in any case, to adopt more efficient CO_2 controls than will government regulations.

Proponents of rigorous regulation, especially proponents of strong CO_2 emissions control, believe the coal industry is irreversibly lingering in an economic twilight as natural gas, renewable energy, and more energy-efficient technologies gradually displace coal combustion in the U.S. economy.[44] In 2018, most expert energy forecasts were predicting that coal's share of all national energy consumption will continue falling to about 22 percent, even without the proposed Obama-era[45] regulations. Coal use by the electric power industry, the major coal consumer, is anticipated to decrease more rapidly. The EIA, for example, predicts a decline from 39 percent in 2013 to 34 percent of all electric power fuel in 2040. Many electric utilities are also planning to reduce capacity.[46] And climate change continues to overshadow coal's economic future, posing the most potent long-term political and environmental threat ever to confront the industry.

FOSSIL FUEL ALTERNATIVES: NUCLEAR POWER AND RENEWABLE ENERGY

The environmental hazards and security problems inseparable from fossil fuel combustion have inspired both the federal government and the private sector to invest in the creation and commercialization of alternative energy technologies, which are asserted to be more environmentally benign and more robust because they depend less, if at all, on insecure or exhaustible fuels. Three of these technologies—nuclear power, wind power, and solar energy—dominate current national energy discourse and debate.

Nuclear Power's Fading Renaissance

The catastrophic tsunami that ravaged Japan's northeast coast on March 11, 2011, left in its wake a disastrous succession of unprecedented nuclear equipment failures, several reactor meltdowns, and dangerous radioactive emissions at the Fukushima Daiichi commercial nuclear power facility. It may also have shattered permanently the U.S. nuclear industry's cherished vision of a "nuclear renaissance." The Japanese disaster was another chapter in the crisis-driven history of the domestic nuclear power policy.

The Elusive Nuclear Revival

After decades of economic stagnation, the domestic nuclear power industry seemed, in 2010, about to revive. In 2000, statistics about commercial nuclear power read like the industry's obituary. Since 1980, the nuclear dream—the vision of almost unlimited, cheap electricity generated by hundreds of nuclear reactors—had been dying. The commercial nuclear power industry was failing under a burden of economic and technological misfortunes, an increasingly hostile political climate, inept public relations, persistent environmental risks, and mounting regulatory pressures.

By late 2010, however, industry leaders and supporters were speaking confidently about a "nuclear renaissance."[47] One potent source of this optimism might be called the "other greenhouse effect." Capitalizing on growing national and international attention to global climate change, in the 1990s the industry initiated an aggressive campaign to promote commercial nuclear power as the most desirable economic and environmental alternative to the greenhouse gas emissions associated with fossil fuel combustion to generate electric power. Another powerful stimulus was the federal government's vigorous political and economic initiatives since the George W. Bush administration.

The Renewal of Hope. In 2004, the George W. Bush administration proposed building fifty new power plants and prolonging the operating life of numerous existing facilities to the year 2020. Additionally, the Energy Policy Act (EPAct), sponsored by the Bush administration, promised a very substantial commitment to nuclear power development. In keeping with a half-century tradition of massive federal governmental subsidies, research grants, and other economic patronage, EPAct provided financial incentives for the construction of advanced nuclear plants amounting to $18.5 billion, which the industry requested be increased to $100 billion. Barack Obama added additional momentum to the nuclear resurgence when, much to the disappointment of environmentalists, his campaign platform endorsed the continued development of commercial nuclear power, a commitment reinforced when his 2010 State of the Union speech advocated "a new generation of safe, clean nuclear power plants" and proposed to triple public financing for nuclear power.[48]

Underlying these decisions had been rising public approval for commercial nuclear power to the point where, in mid-2009, a Gallup poll reported "new high levels of support," with 59 percent of Americans favoring domestic nuclear energy.[49] Added good news was an anticipated 30 percent escalation of the U.S. demand for electric power, a very substantial increase in nuclear output capacity, and the absence of a high-visibility facility accident or security lapse. The industry also anticipated that a planned new generation of reactor technologies (Generation III) would be considerably more efficient, safer, and economical than present operating models. As if to challenge history, moreover, the U.S. Nuclear Regulatory Commission (NRC), less than a year after the Fukushima disaster, approved construction of the first new commercial nuclear reactor since 1978 in Georgia.[50]

The Nuclear Dream Fades. Fukushima Daiichi, however, shattered visions of a bright commercial nuclear future. The Japanese tragedy—rated on the International Nuclear and Radiological Event Scale (INES) as comparable to the world's worst reactor accident at Chernobyl—seemed to dramatize globally the ominous predictions about commercial nuclear electric power so long voiced by its domestic critics. The domestic future of commercial nuclear power seemed blighted anew. Public support for commercial nuclear energy fell.[51] The disaster "shook confidence in nuclear power around the world," reported one contemporary survey.[52] The NRC rapidly initiated a safety survey of U.S. commercial nuclear reactors and concluded that, while domestic reactors were generally safe, they could be better prepared for a kind of damage inflicted by the Japanese tsunami.[53] "All of the nation's 104 [now ninety-eight] nuclear reactors will need to undergo analysis using cutting-edge technology and the most recent data to assess how well they can withstand earthquakes," the NRC also warned.[54] "We want to be able to manage the situation in which you lose all electric power and to maintain safety systems and instrumentation and control systems for a much longer period of time than what our plants are designed for right now," concluded NRC chairman Gregory Jaczko.[55] The sudden reversal of fortune after Fukushima Daiichi confronted the Obama administration with an issue relentlessly facing every presidency since Jimmy Carter arrived at the White House in 1978: what is to be done about commercial nuclear power. The issue is politically vexing because the federal government has been deeply implicated in commercial nuclear power development for more than a half century.

Commercial Nuclear's Federal Patron

Washington is largely responsible for the development of the nation's commercial nuclear power; federal policy has sustained the industry since its inception in the early 1950s, with aggressive promotion, benign regulation, and massive financial infusions of subsidies, development grants, and research promotion.

The industry prospered in its first several decades because of this benevolent regulation, generous federal funding, public and political favor, and unique governmental concessions never given its competitors such as ensuring that the industry would obtain the necessary insurance coverage. Until the 1970s, all but a handful of scientists, economists, and public officials associated with the new technology seemed, according to economists Irvin C. Bupp and Jean-Claude Derian, so "intoxicated" by the enterprise that they largely ignored grave technical and economic problems already apparent to a few critical observers.[56] When problems could not be ignored, they usually were hidden from public view; when critics arose, they were discredited by Washington's aggressive defense of the industry.

Despite the troubled history of the industry after the 1970s, by the beginning of the Obama presidency, the industry had received by conservative estimate more than $100 billion in federal subsidies—approximately 60 percent of the total federal energy research expenditures and far exceeding Washington's support for any other energy.[57] Critics have argued that, without these direct and indirect subsidies, the industry was unlikely to have been competitive in any market. "The nuclear power industry has benefited and continues to benefit from a vast array of preferential government subsidies," asserted the Union of Concerned Scientists (UCS). "Indeed . . . subsidies to the nuclear fuel cycle have often exceeded the value of the power produced."[58]

Federal financial backing is still the most potent driver of the nuclear industry's hope for a "renaissance," because this funding addresses the industry's chronically unsettled economic prospects. The largest current federal incentives for construction of new commercial nuclear facilities are provided by loan guarantees for new plant construction covering as much as 80 percent of construction cost and additional production tax credits.[59] Given the considerable economic risk involved in new plant construction, federal support is a crucial incentive for the construction of several first-starter facilities to prove the commercial viability of the new reactor generation; otherwise, the industry has scant motivation to plan future facilities.[60]

The Nuclear Industry Today

In 2018, there were ninety-eight operating nuclear reactors licensed to U.S. electrical utilities, down from a peak of 112 in 1990. Most reactors are located along the East Coast, in the Southeast, and in the Midwest (see Map 8.2). These reactors currently represent about 21 percent of U.S. net electricity-generating capacity. Under their original schedule, the licenses for these reactors were issued for forty years, and half of the reactors would have ended their legal operating lives between 2005 and 2015; the remainder would have shut down before 2075. In short, commercial nuclear power would disappear within a generation unless the present facility licenses were extended and new reactors were constructed, because U.S. utilities had ordered no new reactors since 1979 and simultaneously had cut back sharply on planned construction. In 2000, however, the NRC began to renew utility licenses through a prolonged process involving extensive NRC safety reviews, public meetings, and state consultation. By 2016, "the NRC had extended the licenses of 81 reactors (77 still operating), over three-quarters of the US total. The NRC is considering license renewal applications for 13 further units. Hence, almost all of the U.S. power reactors are likely to have 60-year lifetimes, with owners undertaking major capital works to upgrade them at around 30–40 years."[61]

Despite notable improvements in the industry's safety procedures, technology, and operating efficiency since Three Mile Island, its troubles remain substantial, including economic and technical difficulties, unsolved waste management problems, and a regulatory regime uneasy about the possibility of terrorist attacks on nuclear facilities.

The Problematic Economics of Nuclear Power. The gloss applied to the industry's public image by partisans of a nuclear renaissance cannot quite conceal its problematic economics. The cost of constructing and maintaining commercial nuclear power plants climbed so steeply after 1980 that private capital became increasingly scarce and costly. Even when an industry recovery seemed plausible after 2000, the managing director of a major national investment firm was warning that the "challenge of new construction is very difficult . . . project cost estimates have risen dramatically in the past year and are expected to continue rising. In the eyes of lenders and investors, these projects will face the potential risk of

MAP 8.2 ■ U.S. Operating Commercial Nuclear Power Reactors, 2014

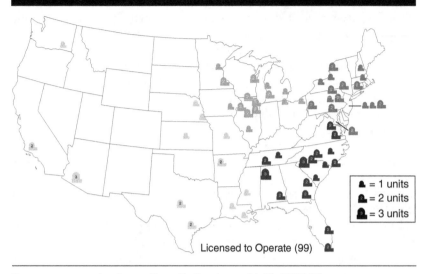

= 1 units
= 2 units
= 3 units

Licensed to Operate (99)

Source: www.nrc.gov/reading-rm/doc-collections/nuregs/staff/sr1542/v15/.

Note: There are no commercial reactors in Alaska or Hawaii.

serious delay and cost overruns."[62] Since 2008, Florida Power and Light's first estimate for a large new plant off the Florida Keys, for instance, reached $12 billion
to $18 billion and the facility was suspended indefinitely. [63] A still more ominous
portent for the industry, however, appeared in 2018 when Westinghouse, the lone
American manufacturer of commercial reactors, decided to take a $6 billion loss
and abandoned the domestic market.[64]

Another critical economic problem for the nuclear industry is the comparative costs of alternative fuels, such as natural gas and coal, which may often be
cheaper to utilities than nuclear energy. And new, competitive utilities may enter
an existing nuclear facility's market. Nuclear power has been competitive with
other fuels for electric generation primarily in the northeastern and southern
United States, where the domestic cost of competing fuels is highest. Expansion
into new geographic markets, however is unlikely, particularly while fracking
technology sustains a growing supply of competitive natural gas nationally.

Continuing Safety Issues. The NRC's public admission in the aftermath of
the 2011 Fukushima Daiichi disaster that the NRC lacked adequate information
about the vulnerability of U.S. commercial reactors to severe seismic shocks was
a reminder that the national debate about reactor safety remains alive and vigorous. A major reason—often *the* reason—for the cost escalation of new plant construction is concern about public safety and environmental protection. Despite

more recent efforts to streamline the review process, surmounting the regulatory hurdles still requires four to eight years and may involve almost one hundred different federal, state, and local governmental permits. Industry officials also complain about the costs imposed during plant construction through regulatory ratcheting by the NRC (its habit of requiring facilities to make new safety modifications or other expensive design changes many years after plant construction). Additional costs have also been imposed on many utilities by protracted litigation involving environmental groups and others challenging various aspects of plant design and safety.[65] And serious, expensive technical problems continue to beset the industry.

Proponents of nuclear power argue correctly that its safety record, notwithstanding the accident at Three Mile Island, is excellent and that critics have exaggerated its technical problems. However, continuing revelations of technical difficulties suggest serious deficiencies in the basic design and operation of the plants and frequent carelessness or incompetence in plant management.[66] Whatever their real significance, these problems have worked against the industry politically. Continuing admissions of safety risks and technical difficulties at a time of growing public apprehension about nuclear terrorism continue to inspire the opposition.

Materials and design standards for many plants currently have failed essential safety requirements. Reactor parts, for instance, have aged much faster than anticipated. Steam generators meant to last a plant's lifetime—approximately fifty years—are wearing out much sooner than expected; this is a particularly serious problem in New York, Florida, Virginia, Wisconsin, and South Carolina.[67] Mistakes have been made in plant specifications or construction. Pipes have cracked and "wasted" (become thinner) from extended exposure to radiation. Finally, continuing revelations of plant mismanagement, administrative bungling, and secrecy raise serious questions about the competence of plant managers and technicians.

Industry officials insist that critics have misrepresented the safety record of commercial nuclear utilities by seizing on highly publicized safety problems as if they characterized the entire industry. Indeed, many utilities have a virtually uninterrupted record of safe operations and skilled management. Still, after more than thirty years of operation, the industry continues to experience serious design, management, and engineering failures. The UCS's verdict seems fair:

> Is nuclear power in the United States safe enough today just because
> a reactor has not experienced a meltdown since 1979? The answer is a
> resounding no. . . . since the TMI [Three Mile Island] meltdown, 38 U.S.
> nuclear power reactors had to be shut down for at least one year while
> safety margins were restored to minimally acceptable levels. Seven of
> these reactors experienced two-year-plus outages. Though these reactors
> were shut down before they experienced a major accident, we cannot
> assume we will continue to be so lucky. [68]

The Continuing Problem of Nuclear Waste. The safe disposal of radioactive reactor waste has become an intractable problem blighting the nuclear industry's visions of an imminent revival. The high-level nuclear waste presently resting in cooling ponds at the nation's active and retired commercial nuclear power sites includes radioactive materials hazardous for thousands of years—in the case of plutonium-239, hazardous for more than 24,000 years.[69] By one estimate, this steadily increasing inventory of spent nuclear fuel rods accumulating in cooling ponds would easily cover a football field to a depth of about 20 feet.[70]

This waste problem was never anticipated when the federal government first promoted commercial nuclear power in the 1950s. To encourage the nation's public and private utilities to build nuclear power plants, Washington had assured the industry that the federal government would provide a "reprocessing" technology for the radioactive wastes contained in the spent nuclear fuel rods used to generate reactor power. Thus, existing and planned commercial facilities were designed to store temporarily no more than three years of accumulated spent fuel rods in cooling ponds. Excess fuel assemblies were to be removed from temporary onsite storage, reusable radioactive materials extracted, and the waste safely isolated elsewhere. However, the anticipated reprocessing proved an economic and technical failure.[71] Since the early 1970s, virtually all commercial spent fuel has remained in the onsite cooling ponds.[72] Until 1982, no comprehensive federal plan existed for the "permanent" storage of these nuclear wastes. Instead, federal and state governments had wrangled acrimoniously for more than a decade over the design and location of a permanent waste depository that no state wanted.

The Battle of Yucca Mountain. In 1982, Congress finally passed the Nuclear Waste Policy Act (NWPA), intended to create a process for designating and constructing the first permanent nuclear waste repository. The legislation assigned the site-selection task to the DOE and created what appeared to be a meticulously detailed, impartial, and open process by which all possible sites would be studied and reduced to a few from which the president would eventually select two for "permanent" repositories. However, the political leadership in every eligible state fought vehemently in Congress and the courts to prevent its designation as a possible waste site. Congress found a simple solution. In December 1987, Congress suddenly renounced NWPA procedures, summarily designated Yucca Mountain, Nevada, to be the first permanent depository site, and assured the nuclear power industry that Nevada would be ready by 1998 to accept delivery of the spent fuel rods cooling at reactor sites.

Nevada residents and political leaders have been outraged. Nevada continues unremitting resistance to the uncompleted Yucca Mountain facility with every available political and legal resource. This trench warfare, accompanied by fierce scientific controversy concerning Yucca Mountain's geologic safety, has slowed the facility's construction to a crawl.[73] The DOE abandoned its initial repository plan in 1989 because it lacked confidence in the technical quality of the proposal and predicted that the repository would be delayed until at least 2010, even though commercial utilities had already paid $3 billion in taxes to use the repository.[74] By 2007, it was evident that the DOE was unprepared to receive wastes at even a temporary repository. The Bush administration promised to open the site by 2010, requested a large budget increase to underwrite accelerated site construction, and was promptly sued by the state of Nevada and numerous other plaintiffs, thereby relegating the Yucca Mountain facility to a judicial limbo and an uncertain future while controversy continued over the facility's safety. In an effort to settle the matter, in 2010, Secretary of Energy Steven Chu recommended to President Obama that the facility be terminated. But the repository's destiny was further muddled when Obama pledged to eliminate its federal funding while simultaneously continuing its operation until the complex legal path to its termination is completed.

An Alternative Waste Plan. The prospective closing of the Yucca Mountain facility would require that some alternative storage space be available to accommodate the continuing deposit of new waste at reactor sites. Any near-term solution must necessarily be temporary, pending the outcome of federal–state negotiations over the final deposition of commercial nuclear waste or a judicial order. The most plausible solution for the temporary containment of the high-level wastes may be "dry cask storage" when nuclear utilities are no longer able to accommodate their existing waste at on-site cooling ponds.

"Dry cask storage," explains the NRC, "allows spent fuel that has already been cooled in the spent fuel pool for at least one year to be surrounded by inert gas inside a container called a cask. The casks are typically steel cylinders that are either welded or bolted closed. The steel cylinder provides a leak-tight containment of the spent fuel. Each cylinder is surrounded by additional steel, concrete, or other material to provide radiation shielding to workers and members of the public. Some of the cask designs can be used for both storage and transportation." Dry cask storage is already utilized in several states for high-level and low-level commercial waste. Debate lingers about the reliability of dry cask waste sequestration and cask vulnerability to terrorism. However, dry casks have been approved for waste storage by the NRC, the DOE, and an expert panel of the National Academy of Science.[75]

A number of states with commercial nuclear reactors, already uneasy about the safety of existing fuel rods that may remain in cooling ponds for at least several more decades, were further disconcerted when, in December 2010, the NRC modified its rules for on-site radioactive waste storage to double the storage time to sixty years after a facility goes out of service. The attorneys general of New York, Vermont, and Connecticut, expected to be the forerunners of future similar lawsuits by other states, have demanded that the NRC require commercial power companies to file environmental impact statements for the cooling ponds.[76] Thus, the contentious federalism that has characterized commercial nuclear power regulation for many decades seems destined to continue until and if the federal government can create a "permanent" nuclear waste depository.

The Nuclear Regulatory Commission. The NRC, whose regulatory responsibilities for commercial nuclear power reactors was described in Chapter 3, found no relief during the Obama administration from contention over the management of an ever-growing volume of commercial nuclear waste accumulating at commercial reactor sites and the continual appearance of new facility safety issues.[77] Defenders of the NRC assert that many of these continuing regulatory lapses and unresolved issues result from the NRC's chronic understaffing and underfunding and from the regulatory changes required by the NRC, which often take years for utilities to accomplish. Some observers argue that the NRC must be doing its job reasonably well, because it is such a frequent target of criticism from the nuclear power industry itself.[78] The most publicly and politically contentious issues on the NRC's agenda during the second Obama administration were the challenge to find a scientifically and publicly acceptable method for removal and safe storage of the reactor wastes now cooling at commercial nuclear sites and the emerging problem posed by the Japanese nuclear disaster. The Fukushima meltdown not only loosened a political backlash against the commercial nuclear power industry but also forced upon the NRC a multitude of sudden, unanticipated new regulatory issues involved with assessing and assuring the seismic safety of all existing commercial facilities.[79] And lingering over all else was the transcendent political question of whether the NRC and the Obama administration were presiding over the gradual extinction of the nuclear dream.[80]

Renewable Energy

Barack Obama's first election campaign had been rich in environmentalist substance and symbolism.[81] Obama had promised that his administration would create a policy pathway toward "a new energy future . . . embracing alternative and renewable energy, ending our addiction to foreign oil, addressing the global climate crisis and creating millions of new jobs that can't be shipped overseas."[82] This vision of a "new energy future," like virtually all public policy proposals to release the United States from a fossil fuels dependency, has been inspired by a common reliance on wind and solar energy as a technological foundation. Despite the powerful appeal of wind and solar technologies for energy conservation, all recent presidents have discovered that the practical politics of transforming a new energy era from vision into policy and the stubborn realities embedded in the U.S. energy economy pose inevitable, sometimes daunting challenges inherent to U.S. public policymaking.

Washington Slowly Warms to Renewables. At Barack Obama's inauguration in 2008, all forms of renewable energy provided only 7 percent of the nation's total energy consumption. Although national renewable energy consumption had risen by modest increments since 1970, the White House, Congress, and the public had feebly and inconstantly embraced renewable energy and energy conservation compared to the national investment in fossil fuels.

By 2008, the adverse impacts associated with the continued national dependence on imported oil and fossil fuels hastened passage of the EPAct. George W. Bush's most substantial commitment to promoting renewable energy and conservation, the Energy Policy Act, created numerous federal subsidies, tax incentives, and research support for the development of new, energy-efficient technologies and improved energy conservation practices in the domestic economy. The important energy conservation and efficiency features included $4.19 billion in tax credits for the production of renewable and increased energy efficiency in existing homes, new energy standards for a large variety of appliances, tax credits for hybrid vehicle purchases, and increased federal spending and tax incentives for production and blending of biofuels in domestic motor vehicles.

Although the Bush-era programs seem unambitious compared to the later Obama agenda, they were the foundation on which the Obama administration mounted its vastly more expansive and expensive energy renewal and conservation efforts.

Renewables' Environmental Benefits. The environmental appeal of renewable energy—especially the vision of renewable energy scaled-up to an integrated national energy system—has been enormously attractive yet often offset by the economic and technological obstacles to its rapid national deployment. In an era of global climate warming, wind- and solar-generated electric power have become especially important as potential substitutes for fossil fuels whose combustion by the U.S. electric sector produces about 29 percent of national climate-warming emissions.[83] Additionally, solar and wind power create no particulate emissions associated with air pollution and are infinitely available.

Conflicting Energy Policies: Trump vs. Obama. The Obama administration enormously enlarged the federal government's commitment to renewable energy. The American Recovery and Reinvestment Act (2009), Obama's huge investment in national recovery from the catastrophic 2008 recession, authorized more than $80 billion for the development of clean energy technologies and jobs. This included $36.7 billion to the DOE to support loans and subsidies for the manufacture and commercial distribution of advanced solar and wind technologies. The White House created an enormous political investment in the success of these renewable technologies despite formidable political risks, including a gamble on expensive, often unproven new technologies, huge federal budget deficits, and congressional Republicans' traditional ambivalence about massive spending for new renewable technologies.

By the time Donald Trump entered the White House, renewable energy had apparently achieved a secure place in the federal energy budget, but not the high priority given to fossil fuels by the Trump administration. Trump was no enthusiast for federally promoted renewable energy, but a Republican-dominated Congress was of a different mind. Growing corporate support, especially by electric utilities, for solar and wind energy combined with expanding state and local government investments in renewables, encouraged Congress to resist Trump's first budget proposal for huge cutbacks in federal funding for wind and solar technologies, biofuels, and energy-efficiency research, among other major renewable programs. The federal government's apparently continuing commitment to renewables seemed to assure a gradual but steady expansion of renewables in the nation's energy economy underway since 2000.

America's Increasing Renewable Energy. In mid-2018, the American Wind Energy Association reported what few energy experts would have expected only a few years earlier. Wind power was now producing almost a third of the electricity in Iowa, Kansas, Oklahoma, and South Dakota, while New Mexico was rapidly increasing its wind-power capacity faster than any other state in the previous year.[84] Significantly, this surge in wind-power consumption was led by state-based electric utilities and local communities, an indication that renewable energy was slowly rooting in state economies.

Since 2000, all forms of renewable energy, led by wind and solar power, have been slowly but steadily increasing in importance for both U.S energy production and consumption. At the turn of the century, renewables accounted for about 8.5 percent of total national energy production; by 2018, renewable energy was expected to reach about 13 percent of the domestic total. Equally important, solar and wind accounted for most of this growth in renewable energy creation, especially in the electric utility sector where renewables were slowly replacing fossil fuel to generate electricity.[85] This expansion of renewables is widely predicted to increase for several more decades: the respected Energy Information Administration, for example, has conservatively estimated that by 2050, renewables will combine with natural gas to become the primary source of growth in electric power generation—the major consumer of renewable energy and fossil fuels.

The Good Economic News About Renewables. The energy-saving potential of wind and solar technologies is substantial and widely advertised. Predictions about the beneficial impact of solar and wind technologies on the national energy economy have been significant:

- A quarter of the U.S. land area has winds strong enough to generate electricity at the same price as natural gas and coal.

- By 2018, solar power created more than 10 percent of electricity generation in California, Nevada, Hawaii, and Vermont.[86]

- The solar industry employs twice as many workers as the coal industry, almost five times as many as nuclear power, and nearly as many workers as the natural gas industry.[87]

- The total amount of electricity that could potentially be generated from wind in the United States has been estimated to be more than twice the electricity generated in the United States today.

Given favorable sites and economic incentives, large national corporations have been alert to the advantages of renewable energy:

- FedEx Corp has installed solar panels covering about three acres and capable of generating 2.42 megawatts of electricity atop its distribution hub in Woodbridge, New Jersey; it is expected to be the largest rooftop solar facility in the United States, producing about 30 percent of the facility's electricity needs.

- Walmart has announced an ultimate goal to produce 100 percent of its power with renewable energy and plans to bring its total solar installations to approximately 500 stores in twenty-two states and Puerto Rico by 2020.[88]

- The top ten corporate consumers of solar power in the United States, in addition to Walmart, include Apple, Amazon, Kohl's, and Target.

When Washington's commitment to renewable energy funding wavered between 2000 and 2010, the states seized the initiative and created, and continue to create, some of the most convincing demonstrations of public-sector confidence in renewables' potential.

By 2018, twenty-nine states and the District of Columbia had adopted Renewable Portfolio Standards requiring utilities to obtain a percentage of their electric power, varying among the states from 4 to 30 percent, from renewable energy, especially wind and solar technologies. California, often a leader in environmental innovation, has required that renewable energy produce at least 50 percent of its electric power by 2030 and appears likely to meet, or exceed, this goal.[89]

Renewables' Risks: Economic, Ecological, Technological. Renewable energy technologies such as wind and solar power also pose risks, and sometimes difficult trade-offs, to policymakers. One major economic concern is that renewable energy and its technologies are highly vulnerable to the uncertainties of the marketplace. The growth of U.S. renewable energy generation between 2012 and 2015, for example, was stimulated by high crude oil prices that made renewable energy competitive with fossil fuels for electric power generation—a favorable economic setting that could disappear if the decline of crude oil prices since 2015 were to continue for a long period. Changes in the price of competing fuels, unanticipated international trade events, the cost of technology development, and much else can produce chronic or sudden economic difficulties. Private investors still consider renewable technologies a risky enterprise. "For investors, deciding whether to invest money into renewable-energy projects can be difficult," notes one energy market analyst. "The issue is volatility: Wind-powered energy production, for instance, changes annually—and even weekly or daily—which creates uncertainty and investment risks. With limited options to accurately quantify that volatility, today's investors tend to act conservatively."[90]

Renewable technologies, especially wind and solar, also depend upon economic assistance from the federal government, such as subsidies, tax breaks, and research funding, to create a financially attractive image for investors. And what Washington gives, Washington can take away. Or Washington can create enough unpredictability to its renewables support to worry private investors and discourage long-term investments. In 2018, for example, the Trump administration raised the tariff on solar panels imported from China and lowered tax and investment credits for solar technologies, creating a significant slowdown in domestic solar installations and a decrease in the industry's employment.

Another persistent trade-off entailed by renewable energy technology development—and to environmentalists the most vexing—is the potential adverse environmental risks to be balanced against the attractions of renewables. The implications can pit environmental advocates against each other and arouse accusations of NIMBYism from one side or another. Here are some examples:

- "By 2030, environmental and lobby groups are pushing for the U.S. to be producing at least 20 percent of its electricity from wind. Meeting that goal, according to the Department of Energy, will require the U.S. to have about 300,000 megawatts of wind capacity, a 12-fold increase over 2008 levels. If that target is achieved, we can expect some 300,000 birds, at the least, to be killed by wind turbines each year."[91]

- The planned development of solar-panel farms covering thousands of desert acres in California, Arizona, Utah, and other western states has frequently been vigorously opposed by coalitions of environmentalists and local residents intent on preventing the intrusion into their lifestyles, the risk to endangered species, and the possible disruption of the native ecosystems.

- The manufacture and distribution of solar and wind technologies generates significant quantities of climate-warming CO_2 and related air emissions.

Finally, formidable technological obstacles stand between the present capacity of wind and solar technologies to generate electric power for communities and private use and the long-term goal of renewable advocates—the "holy grail of renewable energy"—the integration of renewable energy into the national electric power grid.[92] The most fundamental problem is developing a technology that efficiently stores intermittently created renewable energy. "With no current batteries constructed yet on a commercial scale, all electricity produced must meet the exact demand of the population—or the lights go out," explains a utility expert. "With [present] massive generators, even if a problem arises and a generator shuts down, the inertia of the hundreds of tons of spinning metal allows a window of time for the problem to be fixed or other generators to pick up the slack."[93]

CONCLUSION

The implications of current energy policy for the future are environmentally profound, creating compelling and difficult policy imperatives for U.S. policymakers. First, the United States today still depends primarily upon nonrenewable fossil fuels for most of its energy, with the environmental hazards entailed; policymakers are challenged to find a sure and plausible path to a rapid increase in renewable energy as a substitute for fossil fuels. While the federal government has greatly accelerated and enlarged its commitment to financing the development of new, efficient, renewable energy sources, such as wind and solar power, fossil fuels are certain to remain the nation's primary energy resource well beyond 2050.

Second, the rapid improvement and proliferation of fracking technology has initiated what is predicted to be a new natural gas "boom," which is gradually reducing the market price of natural gas and stimulating its increasing use, especially in the electric power industry. Although this apparent boom is anticipated to make the United States the world's leading exporter of petroleum by midcentury and to enhance U.S. energy security from foreign petroleum blockades, it will also encourage continued dependency upon fossil fuels as the foundation of the domestic energy economy.

Third, the well-known, severe adverse environmental impact of coal mining and combustion, now compounded by the recognition that coal combustion is the principle source of domestic climate change gases, creates a major challenge for U.S. policymakers because there is no readily available, inexpensive substitute for coal as a primary energy source for the next several decades. Moreover, the prospects for a rapidly available "clean coal" technology to diminish coal's environmental hazards seem bleak. Proponents of commercial nuclear power have promoted the technology as an environmentally attractive alternative to coal for power generation because nuclear energy creates no climate-change emissions, but the nuclear disaster at Fukushima Daiichi, the continuing problem of nuclear waste storage, and commercial nuclear power's bleak economics appear to have shattered any vision of a nuclear revival.

Finally, given the reality that no quick fix is politically or economically feasible to diminish rapidly U.S. dependence on fossil fuels, continuing aggressive, and perhaps more stringent, federal and state regulation of fossil fuel production and combustion is essential. The implementation of rigorous, and perhaps new, environmental controls of fossil fuel utilization will be a formidable political challenge to policymakers who will encounter persistent pressure from petroleum, coal, and natural gas producers to increase production as a strategy to combat the continuing adverse impact of the severe economic recession beginning in 2008. Despite the Trump administration's commitment to revive the coal industry, no energy sector now appears more vulnerable to an economic recession than does coal, and no industry poses a greater political challenge to federal and state policymakers to find a way to effectively balance new, imperative environmental regulations with the protection of coal mining's economic stability.

Suggested Readings

Aklin, Michael. *Renewables: The Politics of a Global Energy Transition*. Cambridge, MA: MIT Press, 2018.

Bakke, Gretchen. *The Grid: The Fraying Wires Between Americans and Our Energy Future*. New York: Bloomsbury, 2016.

Clemmer, Steve, Jeremy Richardson, Sandra Sattler, and Dave Lochbaum. *The Nuclear Power Dilemma*. Cambridge, MA: Union of Concerned Scientists, 2018.

Duffy, Robert J. *Nuclear Politics in America*. Lawrence: University Press of Kansas, 1997.

Flynn, James, James Chalmers, Doug Easterling, Roger Kasperson, Howard Kunreuther, C. K. Mertz, Alvin Mushkatel, K. David Pijawka, Paul Slovic, and Lydia Dotto. *One Hundred Centuries of Solitude: Redirecting America's High-Level Nuclear Waste Policy*. Boulder, CO: Westview Press, 1995.

Nye, David E. *Consuming Power: A Social History of American Energies*. Cambridge, MA: MIT Press, 1997.

Union of Concerned Scientists. *A Dwindling Role for Coal*. Cambridge, MA: Author, 2017, available at https://www.ucsusa.org/clean-energy/coal-and-other-fossil-fuels/coal-transition.

Notes

1. Frank Holmes, "U.S. Energy Is Breaking All Kinds of Records—Are You Participating?" *Forbes*, April 3, 2018, available at https://www.forbes.com/sites/greatspeculations/2018/04/03/u-s-energy-is-breaking-all-kinds-of-records-are-you-participating/#231bff8d4813.
2. U.S. Energy Information Administration, "Today in Energy," July 3, 2018, available at https://www.eia.gov/todayinenergy/detail.php?id=3661.
3. U.S. EPA, "Air Trends Report 2016: National Air Quality: Emissions by Source Category," available at https://gispub.epa.gov/air/trendsreport/2016/.
4. Ibid.
5. Energy Information Administration, "Energy and Environment Explained: Where Greenhouse Gases Come From," available at https://www.eia.gov/energyexplained/index.php?page=environment_where_ghg_come_from.
6. Energy Information Administration, Frequently Asked Questions: "How Much Oil Consumed by the United States Comes From Foreign Countries?" available at https://www.eia.gov/tools/faqs/faq.php?id=32&t=6.
7. IEA, *World Energy Outlook, 2002* (Paris, France: Author, 2002), 90, Table 3.1.

8. Marc Humphries, Document RL 33493, "Summary," in *Outer Continental Shelf: Debate Over Oil and Gas Leasing and Revenue Sharing* (Washington, DC: Congressional Reference Service, 2008). Another 86 billion barrels of oil and 420 tcf of natural gas are classified as undiscovered resources.

9. Ibid.

10. Joby Warrick, "Obama Administration Opens Up Southern Atlantic Coast to Offshore Drilling—But Restricts It in Alaska," *Washington Post*, January 27, 2015, available at https://www.washingtonpost.com/news/energy-environ ment/wp/2015/01/27/obama-administration-opens-up-southern-atlantic -coast-to-offshore-drilling-but-restricts-it-in-alaska/n.

11. Brittany Patterson and Zack Colman, "Trump Opens Vast Waters to Offshore Drilling," *Scientific American*, January 5, 2018, available at https://www.scien tificamerican.com/article/trump-opens-vast-waters-to-offshore-drilling/.

12. Proven reserves of natural gas are estimated quantities that analyses of geological and engineering data have demonstrated to be economically recoverable in future years from known reservoirs.

13. EIA, *Annual Energy Outlook, 2011 with Projections to 2035,* available at http:// www.eia.gov/forecasts/aeo/source_natural_gas.cfm.

14. Rebecca Smith, "Progress to Shutter 11 Plants Using Coal," *Wall Street Journal,* December 2, 2009, B4.

15. Natural gas is made up mostly of methane, which is a very potent green-house gas. Some methane leaks into the atmosphere from coal mines, oil and gas wells, natural gas storage tanks, pipelines, and processing plants. These leaks are the source of about 25 percent of total U.S. methane emis-sions but only about 3 percent of total U.S. greenhouse gas emissions.

16. A comprehensive discussion of the environmental issues associated with fracking can be found in U.S. Government, EPA, U.S. Geological Survey, *Risks and Rewards: The Controversy About Shale Gas Production and Hydraulic Fracturing, Ground Water Pollution, Toxic and Carcinogenic Chemical Dangers, Marcellus Shale, Hydrofrac and Fracking* (Progressive Management Publications, 2011), Amazon Digital Service.

17. Clifford Krauss, "Drilling Boom Revives Hopes for Natural Gas," *New York Times* (Late ed., East Coast), August 25, 2008, A.1.

18. Clifford Krauss, "Oil Boom Gives the U.S. New Edge in Energy and Diplomacy," *New York Times*, January 29, 2018, A1.

19. U.S. EPA, *Assessment of the Potential Impacts of Hydrologic Fracturing of Oil and Gas on Drinking Water Resources: Executive Summary* (Washington, DC: Environmental Protection Agency, 2015), ES-6.

20. Kirsten Korosec, "Mwaa Ha Ha! Fracking Fluid Is so Safe, Halliburton CEO Made a Peon Drink It," *Moneywatch*, August 23, 2011, available at https:// www.cbsnews.com/news/mwaa-ha-ha-fracking-fluid-is-so-safe-hallibur ton-ceo-made-a-peon-drink-it.

21. U.S. EPA, *Assessment of the Potential Impacts of Hydraulic Fracturing for Oil and Gas on Drinking Water Resources: Executive Summary.*

22. Lorraine Chow, "Trump Administration to Kill Fracking Rule on Public Lands," *EcoWatch*, March 16, 2017, available at https://www.ecowatch.com/trump-fracking-public-lands-2316672382.htm.

23. Energy Information Administration, "Annual Coal Report, November 2017," available at https://www.eia.gov/coal/annual/; and Devashree Saha, "Five Charts That Show Why Trump Can't Deliver on His Coal Promises," *Bookings: The Avenue*, December 6, 2016, available at https://www.brookings.edu/blog/the-avenue/2016/12/06/trump-cant-deliver-on-his-coal-promises.

24. Meghan Keneally, Jessica Hopper, and Evan Simon, "High Hopes in Coal Country With Trump's Climate Change Policy," *ABC News*, May 18, 2017, available at https://abcnews.go.com/Politics/wyoming-coal-miners-high-hopes-trump-amid-national/story?id=47465051.

25. Umair Irfan, "Trump's Perennial 'War on Coal' Claim, Fact-Checked," *Vox*, January 31, 2018, available at https://www.vox.com/2018/1/30/16953292/trump-war-on-coal-claim-fact-checked.

26. Jonathan L. Ramseur and James E. McCarthy, "Summary," EPA's Clean Power Plan: Highlights of the Final Rule, Congressional Reference Service Report R44145 (Washington, DC: Congressional Research Service, 2016).

27. Nicolas Loris, "The Many Problems of the EPA's Clean Power Plan and Climate Regulations: A Primer," *The Heritage Foundation Environment Report*, available at https://www.heritage.org/environment/report/the-many-problems-the-epas-clean-power-plan-and-climate-regulations-primer.

28. Center for American Progress, *Coal Capture and Sequestration*, 101, available at www.americanprogress.org/issues/2009/03/ccs_101.html.

29. David Biello, "Advanced CO_2 Capture Project Abandoned Due to 'Uncertain' U.S. Climate Policy," *Scientific American*, July 14, 2011, available at http://blogs.scientificamerican.com/observations/2011/07/14/advanced-c02-capture-project-abandoned-due-to-uncertain-u-s-climate-policy/.

30. Jamie Condliffe, "Clean Coal's Flagship Project Has Failed," *MIT Technology Review*, June 29, 2017, available at https://www.technologyreview.com/s/608191/clean-coals-flagship-project-has-failed/.

31. In 2009, for example, Summit Power Company's contemplated Odessa power plant with CCS would have cost an estimated $1.6 billion or about ten times as much as a modern gas-fired power plant. (Rebecca Smith, "U.S. News: States Vie for Share of Clean-Coal Cash," *Wall Street Journal* [Eastern ed.], Mar 23, 2009, A3.)

32. National Mining Association, "Statistics: Most Requested Statistics, U.S. Coal Industry," available at https://nma.org/2018/11/20/statistics-most-requested-statistics-u-s-coal-industry-2/.

33. U.S. DOI, OSMRE, "Abandoned Mine Land Reclamation: Update on the Reclamation of Abandoned Mine Land Affected by Mining That Took Place Before the Surface Mining Law Was Passed in 1977," Washington, DC, 2003, 20, available at http://www.osmre.gov/aml/remain/zintroun.htm.

34. Ibid.

35. Eric Lipton and Barry Meier, "Under Trump, Coal Mining Gets New Life on U.S. Lands," *New York Times*, August 7, 2017, A1.

36. David Biello, "Mountaintop Removal Mining: EPA Says Yes, Scientists Say No," *Scientific American Observations,* January 8, 2010, available at http://www.scientificamerican.com/blog/post.cfm?id=mountaintop-removal-mining-epa-says-2010-01-08. See also Margaret A. Palmer, E. S. Bernhardt, W. H. Schlesinger, K. N. Eshleman, E. Foufoula-Georgiou, M. S. Hendryx, A. D. Lemly, G. E. Likens, O. L. Loucks, M. E. Power, P. S. White, and P. R. Wilcock, "Mountaintop Mining Consequences," *Science* 327 (January 8, 2010): 148–149.

37. Jennifer Weeks, "Coal's Comeback," *CQ Researcher,* October 5, 2007, 825.

38. Nicholas Fandos, "U.S. Proposes New Rules to Protect Streams From Coal Pollution," *New York Times,* July 17, 2015, A14.

39. David A. Fahrenthold, "Still Unresolved, Tennessee Coal-Ash Spill Only One EPA Hurdle," *Washington Post,* December 22, 2009, A1.

40. Shaila Dewan, "Huge Coal Ash Spills Contaminating U.S. Water," *New York Times*, January 7, 2009, available at www.nytimes.com/2009/01/07/world/americas/07iht-sludge.4.19164565.html.

41. Samantha Page, "House Passes Bill That Would Allow Toxic Coal Ash Into Groundwater," *Climate Progress,* July 23, 2015, available at http://thinkprogress.org/climate/2015/07/23/3683507/house-passes-coal-ash-bill/.

42. Ben Adler, "Obama Blows a Chance to Crack Down on Coal," *Grist,* December 22, 2014, available at http://grist.org/climate-energy/obama-blows-a-chance-to-crack-down-on-coal/.

43. Dennis Romero and Associated Press, "Trump's EPA Rolls Back Obama-Era Coal Ash Regulations," *NBC News,* July 18, 2018, available at https://www.nbcnews.com/news/us-news/trump-s-epa-rolls-back-obama-era-coal-ash-regulations-n892586.

44. Devashree Saha, "Five Charts That Show Why Trump Can't Deliver on His Coal Promises," *Bookings: The Avenue*, December 6, 2016, available at https://www.brookings.edu/blog/the-avenue/2016/12/06/trump-cant-deliver-on-his-coal-promises.

45. U.S. Energy Information Administration, "Natural Gas, Renewables Projected to Provide Larger Shares of Electric Generation," *Today in Energy*, available at https://www.eia.gov/todayinenergy/detail.php?id=21072.

46. Brad Plumer and Nadja Popovich, "Trump Wants to Bail Out Coal and Nuclear Power—Here's Why That Will Be Hard," *New York Times*, June 13, 2018, available at https://www.nytimes.com/interactive/2018/06/13/climate/coal-nuclear-bailout.html.

47. See, for example: Matthew W. Wald, "After 35-Year Lull, Nuclear Power May Be in Early Stages of a Revival," *New York Times* (Late ed., East Coast), October 24, 2008, B3; Mark Williams, "The Renaissance of Nuclear Power Appears Inevitable: Nuclear Power Renaissance Faces Serious Obstacles," *Huffpost Green*, February 2, 2010, www.huffingtonpost.com/2010/02/26/nuclear-power-renaissance_n_477934.html; Sally Adee and Erico Guizzo, "Nuclear Reactor Renaissance," August 2010, http://spectrum.ieee.org/energy/nuclear/nuclear-reactor-renaissance.

48. World Nuclear Power Association, "Nuclear Power in the USA," available at http://world-nuclear.org/info/Country-Profiles/Countries-T-Z/USA--Nuclear-Power/.

49. Jeffrey M. Jones, "Support for Nuclear Energy Inches Up to New High, Majority Believes Nuclear Power Plants Are Safe," Gallup, March 20, 2009, available at www.gallup.com/poll/117025/support-nuclear-energy-inches-new-high.aspx.

50. Stephen Mufson, "NRC Approves Construction of First New Reactors Since 1978," *Washington Post*, February 9, 2012, available at www.washingtonpost.com/business/economy/nrc-approves-construction-of-new-nuclear-power-reactors-in-georgia/2012/02/09/glQA36wv1Q_story.html.

51. Marcia Clemmitt, "Nuclear Power: Can Nuclear Energy Answer Global Power Needs?" *CQ Researcher* 21, no. 2 (2011): 507, available at www.cqresearcher.com.

52. Christopher Joyce, "Commission: U.S. Must Make Nuclear Plants Safer," *NPR*, August 19, 2011, available at www.npr.org/2011/07/19/138513212/commission-u-s-must-redefine-nuclear-plant-safety.

53. Dr. Charles Miller, Amy Cubbage, Daniel Dorman, Jack Grobe, and Gary Holahan, *Near-Term Task Force Review of Insights From the Fukushima Dai-Ichi Accident: Recommendations for Enhancing Reactor Safety in the 21st Century* (Washington, DC: Nuclear Regulatory Commission, 2011).

54. U.S. NRC, *Briefing on NRC Response to Recent Nuclear Events in Japan*, March 21, 2011, available at www.nrc.gov/reading-rm/doc-collections/. . . /tr/ . . . /20110321.pdf.

55. Christopher Joyce, "U.S. Must Make Nuclear Plants Safer."

56. Irvin C. Bupp and Jean-Claude Derian, *The Failed Promise of Nuclear Power* (New York: Basic Books, 1978), chap. 5.

57. Estimates of federal nuclear power subsidies vary greatly because of different methods of calculation. Marshall Goldberg, "Federal Energy Subsidies: Not All Technologies Are Created Equal," Renewable Energy Policy Project Research Report No. 11 (Washington DC: Renewable Energy Policy Project, 2000). See also Doug Koplow, *Nuclear Power: Still Not Viable Without Subsidies* (Washington, DC: UCS, 2011).

58. Doug Koplow, *Nuclear Power*, 1.

59. Congressional Budget Office, *Nuclear Power's Role in Generating Electricity* (Washington, DC: Congressional Budget Office, May 2008), Publication No. 2986.

60. Notes the NRC of the National Academy of Sciences: "The handful of plants that could be built in the United States before 2020, given the long time needed for licensing and construction, would need to overcome several hurdles, including high construction costs, which have been rising rapidly across the energy sector in the last few years, and public concern about the long-term issues of storage and disposal of highly radioactive waste. If these hurdles are overcome, if the first new plants are constructed on budget and on schedule, and if the generated electricity is competitive in the market-place, the committee judges that it is likely that many more plants could follow these first plants. Otherwise, few new plants are likely to follow" (p. 447); see also UCS, *Nuclear Power: A Resurgence We Can't Afford.*

61. World Nuclear Power Association, "Nuclear Power in the USA."

62. John Gilbertson, Managing Director, Goldman Sacs. "Statement of John Gilbertson." Hearing of the Clean Air and Nuclear Safety Subcommittee of the Senate Environment and Public Works Committee. Subject: Nuclear Regulatory Commission's Licensing and Relicensing Processes for Nuclear Plants, available from www.neinuclearnotes.blogspot.com/2008_07_01_archive.html.

63. Rebecca Smith, "New Wave of Nuclear Plants Faces High Costs," *Wall Street Journal,* May 12, 2008, 1; Michael Grunwald, "Nuclear's Comeback: Still No Energy Panacea," *Time,* December 31, 2008, available at http://www.time.com/time/magazine/article/0,9171,1869203–1,00.html.

64. Diane Cardwell, "The Murky Future of Nuclear Power in the United States," *New York Times,* February 19, 2017, BU1.

65. EIA, *Annual Energy Review 2002* (Washington, DC: U.S. Government Printing Office, 2002), 254. See also Max Schulz, "Nuclear Power Is the Future," *Wilson Quarterly* (Autumn 2006): 98–107.

66. A concise, comprehensive discussion of reactor safety and related issues is found in Marcia Clemmitt, "Nuclear Power: Can Nuclear Energy Answer Global Power Needs?" *CQ Researcher* 21, no. 2 (2011), available at www.cqresearcher.com. See also David Lochbaum, *The NRC and Nuclear Power Plant Safety in 2010: A Brighter Spotlight Needed,* UCS, March 2011, available at www.ucsusa.org/assets/documents;nuclear_power/nrc-2010-full-report.pdf.

67. Matthew L. Wald, "As Nuclear Reactors Show Age, Owners Seek to Add to Usable Life," *New York Times,* June 22, 1989, A1.

68. David Lochbaum, *Nuclear Tightrope: Unlearned Lessons of Year-plus Reactor Outages* (Washington, DC: UCS, 2006), 1.

69. U.S. Nuclear Regulatory Commission, "Backgrounder on Radioactive Waste," available at https://www.nrc.gov/reading-rm/doc-collections/fact-sheets/radwaste.html.

70. Michael Wallace, George David Banks, and Alayna Rodriguez, "Finding a Solution to America's Nuclear Waste Problem," Center for Strategic and

International Studies: Commentary, August 2, 2013, available at https://www
.csis.org/analysis/finding-solution-america%E2%80%99s-nuclear-waste
-problem.

71. The federal government, in fact, gave surprisingly little attention to the
whole problem of reactor waste disposal. See Robert J. Duffy, *Nuclear
Politics in America* (Lawrence: University of Kansas Press, 1997), 184–189.

72. www.reuters.com/article/2011/06/13/idUS178883596820110613.

73. Among the major Yucca Mountain problems: the uranium in the fuel waste "in
SNF is not stable under the oxidizing conditions in Yucca Mountain and would
convert rather rapidly to more soluble higher oxides. Substantial amounts of
water exist in the pores and fractures of the volcanic tuff. The geologic complexity of the Yucca Mountain site, including seismicity and relatively recent
volcanism, and the proposed reliance on engineered barriers, notably titanium
drip shields to protect the casks from water, make the safety analysis complicated and less than convincing." (Rodney C. Ewing and Frank N. Von Hippel,
"Nuclear Waste Management in the United States—Starting Over," *Science*,
July 10, 2009, 151, available at www.sciencemag.org/content/325/5937/151.

74. NRC, *Fact Sheet on Decommissioning Nuclear Power Plant,* available at www
.nrc.gov/reading-rm/doc-collections/fact-sheets/decommissioning.html.

75. U.S. NRC, *Fact Sheet on Dry Cask Storage of Spent Nuclear Fuel,* 2009, available at http://www.nrc.gov/reading-rm/doc-collections/fact-sheets/dry
-cask-storage.html. See also National Academy of Sciences, Committee on
the Safety and Security of Commercial Spent Nuclear Fuel Storage, National
Research Council, *Safety and Security of Commercial Spent Nuclear Fuel
Storage: Public Report (2006),* available at www.nap.edu/catalog/11263.html.

76. Abby Luby, "As U.S. Moves Ahead with Nuclear Power, No Solution for
Radioactive Waste," *Inside Climate News,* March 3, 2011, available at
http://insideclimatenews.org/news/20110302/us-nuclear-power-energy
-radioactive-waste-storage-yucca-mountain.

77. U.S. NRC, "The Commission," available at http://www.nrc.gov/about-nrc/
organization/commfuncdesc.html.

78. Robert J. Duffy, *Nuclear Politics in America,* 171.

79. GAO, *NRC Has Made Progress in Implementing Its Reactor Oversight and
Licensing Processes but Continues to Face Challenges* (Washington, DC: GAO,
2007), Report No. GAO-08–114T, "Summary."

80. Stephen Tetreault, "NRC Staff Blasts Bid to Shutter Yucca Project," *Las
Vegas Review Journal,* June 24, 2011, available at http://www.lvrj.com/news/
nrc-staff-criticizes-jaczko-over-yucca-124522529.html.

81. On continuing concerns about oversight of existing commercial reactors,
see: "Near-Term Task Force Review of Insights From the Fukushima Dai-
Ichi Accident," in *Recommendations for Enhancing Reactor Safety in the 21st
Century* (Washington, DC: NRC, 2011) vi, vii.

82. Ibid.

83. Union of Concerned Scientists, "Benefits of Renewable Energy Use," December 20, 2017, available at https://www.ucsusa.org/clean-energy/renewable-energy/public-benefits-of-renewable-power.

84. American Wind Energy Association, "Wind Powers Forward to Reach 30 Percent in Four States," April 17, 2018, available at https://www.awea.org/AMR2017Press.

85. Energy Information Administration, *Annual Energy Outlook, 2017*, 79, 84.

86. V. John Weaver, "Solar Rises to Nearly 2% of U.S. Generation in 2017," *PV Magazine*, February 28, 2018, available at https://pv-magazine-usa.com/2018/02/28/solar-rises-to-nearly-2-of-u-s-generation-in-2017/.

87. The Solar Foundation, *National Solar Jobs Census, 2017*, available at https://www.thesolarfoundation.org/national/.

88. Marianne Wilson, "Walmart Ramps Up Renewable Energy Use," *Chain Store Age*, April 19, 2018, available at https://www.chainstoreage.com/store-spaces/walmart-ramps-renewable-energy-use/.

89. "California May Reach Its Renewable Energy Goal 10 Years Early," *Futurism*, November 17, 2017, available at https://futurism.com/california-reach-renewable-energy-goal-10-years-early/.

90. Rob Matheson, "Calculating the Financial Risks of Renewable Energy," *MIT News*, September 15, 2016, available at http://news.mit.edu/2016/startup-evervest-calculating-financial-risks-renewable-energy-0915.

91. Robert Bryce, "Windmills Are Killing Our Birds," *Wall Street Journal*, September 8, 2009, A19.

92. Samantha Gross, "The Fantasy of Quick and Easy Renewable Energy," *Brookings*, June 19, 2017, available at https://www.brookings.edu/blog/planetpolicy/2017/06/19/the-fantasy-of-quick-and-easy-renewable-energy/.

93. "The Problem With Renewable Energy (and Ways It's Being Fixed], *Interesting Engineering*, August 24, 2016, available at https://interestingengineering.com/the-problem-with-renewable-energy-fixed.

635 MILLION ACRES
OF POLITICS

The Contested Resources
of Public Lands

Early in the morning in mid-October 2017, an otherwise routine day at the Department of the Interior (DOI), a security officer on the roof at DOI raised the flag of Ryan Zinke, the Trump administration's new secretary of the Interior, up the flagstaff to signify that Zinke was at his office. When Zinke departed, the flag came down. It was not a routine day, however, because no previous cabinet member had ever displayed a personal flag at DOI or any place else in Washington. For DOI Secretary Ryan Zinke, however, the flag was extremely significant as a highly visible symbol and prophecy: a symbol that a very determined, new leadership had arrived at the DOI and a prophecy that America's vast public lands controlled by the DOI were destined for rapid and radical reorganization.[1]

Ryan Zinke, a former Montana congressman, an ardent Trump administrator, and man of strong will and convictions, had declared upon his appointment that he intended to enforce the Trump administration's aggressive reforms at DOI by "restoring honor and tradition to the department, whether it's flying the flag when [I am] in garrison or restoring traditional access to public lands."[2] That deliberately provocative promise to restore "traditional access to public lands" was certain to further inflame an unceasing conflict over the use of the public lands enduring almost as long as the DOI has existed.

Soon after his appointment, Zinke had declared that one of his first decisions would be to reverse the Obama administration's recent restrictions of energy exploration on the public lands including the nation's Outer Continental Shelf (OCS) and, especially, the huge Arctic National Wildlife Refuge (ANWR).

ANWR has been a political cauldron for decades, fueled by a history of intense economic, political, and regional conflicts inseparable from the management of the nation's public lands. Zinke's proposal to expand gas and oil exploration in ANWR was certain to infuriate environmentalists and conservationists and to sustain the Arctic wilderness as a flashpoint of the enduring struggle over control of the public domain that deeply engages environmentalists.

The ANWR conflict swirls about 19.6 million acres of pristine polar wilderness in the remote northeastern corner of Alaska, among the wildest and most inaccessible of U.S. public lands (see Map 9.1). ANWR is huge and resplendently wild, a sprawling panorama of tundra marshes and lagoons, interlaced with glacier-fed rivers and lodged between the foothills of the soaring Brooks Range and the expansive, frigid Beaufort Sea. All parties to the conflict agree—it is stunningly beautiful. They agree on little else. Beginning with a brief description of the actors and issues involved in the Alaskan dispute, this chapter explains why the nation's public lands have always been a battleground between advocates of contending and often sharply conflicting uses for the natural resources involved. The explanation involves the ambiguous and often confusing congressional legislation intended to determine which interests shall have access to these resources; the impact of the environmental movement on public land politics; and the constantly embattled federal agencies, especially the DOI and the U.S. Forest Service (part of the U.S. Department of Agriculture), which are responsible for the politically arduous job of simultaneously preserving these lands, promoting use of their resources, and protecting their most valuable ecological functions.

THE ARCTIC NATIONAL WILDLIFE REFUGE: PUBLIC LAND POLITICS AT A BOIL

U.S. energy industries generally regard proposals to promote energy exploration on the public lands, such as ANWR, to be long-term protection against potential energy shortages and a boost to the domestic economy. Environmentalists and conservationists frequently characterize ANWR as "the crown jewel of America's refuge system" and assume that further energy exploration there will result in catastrophic air pollution, habitat destruction, wildlife decimation, and ecological degradation. Arrayed among the other colliding forces contending over ANWR's fate are a multitude of interests that, in differing combination, are commonly drawn into disputes over the use of the public lands.[3]

ANWR's Multiple Purpose

As with most public lands owned by the federal government, ANWR's size and purpose are defined by Congress and the president, and the responsibility

MAP 9.1 ■ Arctic National Wildlife Refuge

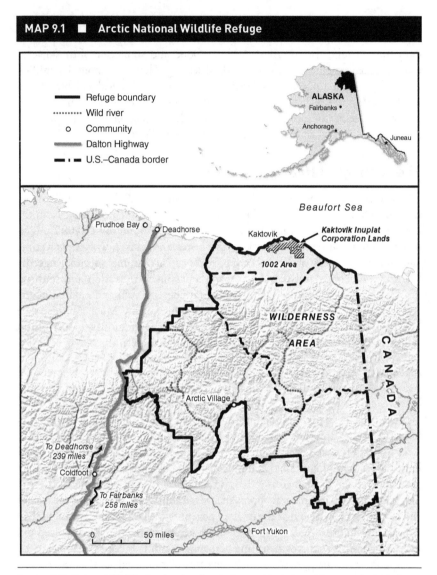

Source: U.S. Fish and Wildlife Service, http//arctic.fws.gov/shade.htm. Map reproduced by International Mapping Associates.

for its oversight is vested in the DOI. ANWR was created in 1980 from federal lands within Alaska for the purposes of wildlife conservation, habitat preservation, wilderness protection, promotion of recreation, and energy exploration—an example of a multiple-use designation that almost ensures a constant battle among the contenders for different uses. Much of ANWR's 19.6 million acres has been opened to oil and natural gas exploration. The Trans-Alaska pipeline, created in 1971, has been producing almost one million barrels of petroleum daily from Prudhoe Bay on Alaska's North Slope, and 90 percent of the adjacent coastal lands remain open for gas and oil leasing. However, about 1.5 million acres of the coastal plain, considered to be the most biologically rich and vulnerable within ANWR, has been restricted from energy exploration unless such activity is specifically authorized by Congress. This region, often called the 1002 Area, is the epicenter of the political conflict over ANWR.

The "Biological Heart" of ANWR

The ecological riches of the 1002 Area are undisputed. This natural endowment includes 160 bird species; the most important onshore denning area in the United States for polar bears; the principal calving ground for 130,000 migratory porcupine caribou; habitat for grizzly bears, arctic foxes, wolves, wolverine, and numerous whales; and many endangered plant and animal species. Ruggedly beautiful wilderness and vast Arctic panoramas invite recreation and tourism. This language of ecological values, biological conservation, and environmental aesthetics resonates powerfully among environmentalists. Much of this, they believe, would be sacrificed to produce exaggerated quantities of petroleum unlikely to alleviate significantly the nation's energy problems.[4]

A Disputed Energy Resource. Proponents of energy exploration in the 1002 Area speak primarily about national security, energy supply, the economy, and coexistence between energy production and environmental protection. They assert, for instance, that drilling in the area could yield as much as sixteen billion barrels of oil, an amount equal to thirty years of oil imports from Saudi Arabia. They also assert that newer, more efficient energy production technologies will limit the amount of land that would be disturbed by energy production to a few thousand acres and, in any case, that the ecological disruption involved is vastly exaggerated by environmental opponents. Most important, proponents of further energy production argue that the reserves now untapped under the 1002 Area will significantly improve U.S. security by decreasing dependence on imported oil, increasing domestic employment, and perhaps expanding U.S. petroleum exports.

Opponents to energy exploration believe that oil produced on ANWR's coastal plain will be unprofitable at current petroleum prices and emphasize that petroleum refiners already have many more Alaskan exploration leases than they have developed. It is the environmental risks, however, which incite the greatest opposition. "Drilling activities in the coastal plain would affect more than 300,000 acres of caribou calving areas," asserts a major environmental critic of ANWR development, and will "decrease the quality of 162,000 to 236,000 acres of snow goose staging habitat . . . [and] cause the loss of subsistence hunting opportunities on roughly half the coastal plain."[5] Additionally, many environmental critics are quick to recall the long history of environmentally hazardous Alaskan oil spills as an additional warning against ANWR energy leasing.

Congress, the White House, and ANWR

All public lands within the states, such as ANWR, were ceded to the federal government as a condition of state admission into the Union, and the federal courts have historically been unsympathetic to any state efforts to reclaim these lands. Any exploration for oil and gas on these lands, like the 1002 Area, requires both Congressional and presidential consent, and proposals to permit energy exploration within ANWR have been repeatedly introduced and rejected in Congress since 1992.[6] Barack Obama had voted in the Senate against ANWR exploration and drilling and reaffirmed that opposition during his presidency. Obama's Secretary of the Interior Salazar emphasized that the Obama administration would stand firm that the Alaska refuge "is a very special place" that must be protected and that he is not yet convinced that new drilling technology would meet that test, thus leaving the fate of the 1002 Area insecure and destined for continual contention among a multitude of political and economic interests.

Stakeholders in ANWR

The stakeholders in ANWR's resources include local, state, and federal governments; the federal bureaucracies administering the public lands; the economic interests seeking to exploit resources and the interests determined to protect them; and foreign governments, including Japan and China, that might become large consumers of the petroleum produced from the 1002 Area. Some of the stakeholders in the ANWR conflict have been highly visible; Congress, the White House, the DOI, environmental advocates, and energy industries rarely escape national attention. Congressional Republicans and Democrats have been divided over ANWR for two decades.

A very important stakeholder is the state of Alaska. Many states benefit from economic royalties received from resource exploitation on public lands in their jurisdiction, but Alaska's situation is unique. Alaska's economy is grounded on energy production: more than half Alaska's state income flows from oil and gas royalties. Every Alaskan resident—man, woman, and child—is reminded about this economic dependence by an annual check (currently about $1,100) representing his or her share of more than $660 million in annual dividends from state oil royalties.[7] Alaskans largely support energy exploration in the 1002 Area, believing energy production and environmental protection are compatible. Alaska's political leaders habitually equate oil and gas drilling with Alaskan prosperity. "It's about jobs and job creation. It's about wealth and wealth creation," exclaimed Alaskan Senator Lisa Murkowski (R), urging her colleagues to open the 1002 Area to energy exploration.[8] Many Alaskans also resent what they consider interference by Washington, D.C., and other interests, including environmentalists, in what they believe should be Alaska's own affair. Many of Alaska's Native Americans, however, were unlikely to agree. The Inupiat Eskimos and the Gwich'in Indians, an indigenous subsistence culture, are among the native tribes heavily dependent on the 1002 Area's continued ecological vitality for food and fuel. The state's commercial fishing interests were also disturbed by the possible degradation of their offshore stocks.

The Trump Administration and ANWR

Donald Trump had promised during his presidential campaign to achieve international "energy dominance" for America, and ANWR figured importantly in that plan. In 2017, the Republican-led Congress authorized the DOI to raise revenue by energy production in ANWR, and in mid-2018, DOI Secretary Ryan Zinke proposed to lease 1.6 million acres in ANWR's coastal plain for energy exploration. "The Trump administration's reckless dash to expedite drilling and destroy the Arctic National Wildlife Refuge will only hasten a trip to the court-house," predicted a major environmental advocacy leader.[9] And hasten it did. Like so many of the Trump administration's environmental initiatives, the ANWR leasing proposal was quickly opposed in the federal court by environmentalists and is apparently destined for a long sojourn in the federal judiciary where it faces a contested and uncertain future.

THE DEPARTMENT IN THE MIDDLE

As the battle over ANWR's energy resources illustrates, the DOI is frequently the epicenter of controversies over public land use because the DOI's land management agencies control most of the vast resources on the public domain. DOI's management and politics have a distinctly western character because most of these public lands lie west of the Mississippi River: almost 80 percent of Nevada and 60 percent of Alaska, for example, are federally owned. Secretaries of the Interior, invariably westerners, are highly attentive to the political and economic interests of the western states while, at the same time, they are expected to manage the public domain in trust for all people of the United States.

Moreover, from its inception, the laws DOI was expected to administer involved two different, and often competing, visions of land management: "reserving some federal lands (such as national forests and national parks) and selling or disposing of other lands to raise money or to encourage transportation, development, and settlement. From the earliest days, these policy views took on east/west overtones, with easterners more likely to view the lands as national public property and westerners more likely to view the lands as necessary for local use and development."[10] DOI's land management agencies usually work with quiet competence and dedication to their public mission, but these inconsistent and sometimes competing legislative mandates can create a volatile political setting ripe with potential for high-visibility political and economic conflicts.

THE PUBLIC LANDS

The controversy over ANWR renews a larger environmental struggle begun long before the concept of environmentalism was imagined. Fierce political contention over the use of the public domain runs like a dark and tangled thread throughout the fabric of U.S. history, reaching to the republic's inception. During the first century of U.S. independence, the conflict was largely between the states and private economic interests to obtain as much public land as possible for their own advantage. Only in 1976 did the government of the United States officially end its policy of conveying huge expanses of public lands to private control. By then, more than 1.1 billion acres of land, an expanse larger than Western Europe, had been surrendered to the states, farmers and trappers, railroads, veterans, loggers and miners, and canal builders—in other words, to any interest with the political strength to make a persuasive claim to Congress. With the mobilization of the conservation movement in the early twentieth century, the federal government began to restrict private control of the public domain in the interest of the U.S. people. Although vastly reduced, the public domain still remains an enormous physical expanse, embracing within its continental sprawl, often accidentally, some of the nation's most economically and ecologically significant resources, a biological and physical reserve still largely unexploited. The struggle to determine how this last great legacy shall be used constitutes, in large part, the substance of the political struggle over public lands.

All the public land is held in trust for the people of the nation and by Congress, in whom the Constitution vests the power to "dispose and make all needful Rules and Regulations respecting the Territory or other Property belonging to the United States."[11] Until the beginning of the twentieth century, Congress had been concerned primarily with rapidly divesting itself of the lands, turning them over to the states or to private interests in huge grants at bargain-basement prices. Only belatedly did Congress, powerfully pressured by the new U.S. conservation movement, awaken to the necessity of preserving the remaining natural resources in the public domain before they were wholly lost. By this time, most of the remaining public lands lay west of the Mississippi River; much was wilderness too remote and inaccessible to be exploited easily or was grasslands and rangelands seemingly devoid of economic attraction.

An Immense Public Domain

Today, the federal government owns approximately 635 million acres of land, about 28 percent of the total U.S. land area (Map 9.2). Many western states are largely public domain; more than half of Alaska, Idaho, Nevada, Oregon, Utah,

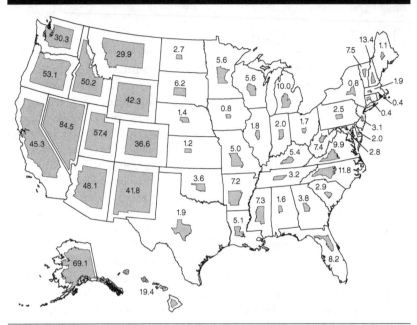

MAP 9.2 ■ Federal Lands as a Percentage of Total State Land Area (excluding trust properties)

Source: U.S. General Services Administration, Federal Real Property Profile, 2004, available at http://www.gsa.gov/Portal/gsa/ep/contentView.do?noc=T&contentType=GSA_DOCUMENT& contentId=13586 (accessed March 17, 2006).

and Wyoming are federally owned, and public lands constitute more than one third of Arizona, California, Colorado, and New Mexico. Much of this land, originally ceded back by the federal government to the western states after they joined the Union, was rejected by the states as useless for timbering, grazing, or farming; some was held in trust for Native American tribes by the federal government. Only later, well into the twentieth century, did exploration reveal that vast energy and mineral resources might reside under the tribal reservations, wilderness, timberland, and grasslands remaining in the public domain.

The economic value of public lands increased greatly in 1953, when the United States joined other nations in redefining the limits of national authority over offshore waters. Before 1953, the traditional standard had limited national sovereignty to three miles offshore. In 1953, Congress passed the Outer Continental Shelf Lands Act, despite the vigorous opposition of coastal states such as Florida and California. The act declared federal government ownership of OCS lands extending as far as two hundred miles offshore. The legislation, ratifying an international treaty negotiated by the State Department, ended a long-standing dispute between the federal and state governments over control of offshore energy resources by immediately vesting in the federal government control over almost all of the 1.1 billion acres of submerged continental shelf land. By accident and design, the spacious continental and offshore public lands, now controlled by the federal government, have become a public trust of potentially huge economic value. And the land is a money maker. In 2016, federal collections from user fees, mineral and fossil fuel extraction, land sales, timber production, and other economic activities added almost $7 billion to federal government income.[12]

An Unanticipated Bounty

The magnitude of mineral, timber, and energy reserves in the public domain remains uncertain. Many areas, including much of the gigantic Alaskan wilderness, have yet to be inventoried fully. Estimates of the resources on more accessible lands also can be controversial. However, commonly cited figures concerning estimated resources on public land suggest the reasons why public lands have assumed such importance to major economic interests in the United States:[13]

- 35 percent of U.S. petroleum

- 39 percent of U.S. natural gas

- 42 percent of U.S. coal

- 17 percent of hydropower

- 50 percent of geothermal energy

- 30 percent of untimbered forests

Beyond those resources on which a price can be placed, the public domain contains both incalculable natural treasures whose worth has become evident to generations—Yosemite, Yellowstone, the Grand Canyon, and the other national parks—and nameless wild and free places, the wilderness that the naturalist Aldo Leopold has called "the raw material out of which man has hammered the artifact called civilization" and to which, he reminds us, we need often return, in fact and imagination, as to a sanctuary.[14] Much of what remains undisturbed on U.S. soil still available to this generation in something like its original condition can be found only in federal wilderness areas. Whether wilderness is or should be a thing beyond price and beyond exploitation remains among the most bitterly controversial of all environmental issues.

Diversity Within the Public Domain

Public lands have been divided by Congress into different domains committed to different uses and administered by different executive agencies. The most important of these uses are the following:[15]

- *National Wilderness Preservation System.* The system currently comprises 110 million acres of land, including more than fifty million acres of Alaskan wilderness added in 1979. By legislative mandate, wilderness lands are to be set aside forever as undeveloped areas.

- *National Park System.* Created in 1872 with the designation of Yellowstone National Park, the system managed by DOI currently constitutes sixty-six national parks and 388 national monuments, historic sites, recreational areas, near-wilderness areas, seashores, and lakeshores, altogether embracing more than eighty-three million acres. Closed to mining, timbering, grazing, and most other economic uses, the system is to be available to the public for recreational purposes.

- *National Wildlife Refuge System.* The system, administered by DOI, currently includes more than ninety-six million acres, two thirds in Alaska but also distributed among all fifty states. The more than five hundred refuges are to provide habitat for migratory waterfowl and mammals, fish and waterfowl hatcheries, research stations, and related facilities.

- *National Forests.* Since 1897, Congress has reserved large forested areas of the public domain and has authorized the purchase of additional timberlands to create a forest reserve, to furnish continuous timber supplies for the nation, and to protect mountain watersheds. Forest lands are to be managed by the Department of Agriculture's Forest Service according to a multiple-use formula that requires a balance of recreation, timber, grazing, and conservation activities. Currently exceeding 190 million acres, national forests are found principally in the far western states, the Southeast, and Alaska.

- *National Rangelands.* The largest portion of the public domain, located primarily in the West and Alaska, is made up of grassland and prairie land, desert, scrub forest, and other open spaces collectively known as rangelands and managed by the Bureau of Land Management (BLM). Although often barren, a substantial portion of the 404.7 million acres of rangeland is suitable for grazing. The BLM issues permits to ranchers for this purpose.

Such a classification implies an orderly definition of the uses for the public domain and a supporting political consensus that do not exist. Behind the facade of congressionally assigned uses stretches a political terrain strewn with conflicts of historical proportions over which lands should be placed in different categories, which uses should prevail among competing demands on the land, how much economic exploitation should be permitted in the public domain, and how large the public domain should be.

The Land-Use Agencies

Four land management agencies control about 90 percent of all the land currently in the public domain. The Forest Service and the BLM control by far the largest portion of this collective jurisdiction. The Forest Service and the BLM are required by Congress to administer their huge public trusts under the doctrine of "multiple use." The two agencies come to this task with strikingly different political histories and territorial responsibilities.

The Forest Service. Created as part of the Department of Agriculture in 1905, the Forest Service is one of the proudest and most enduring monuments to the United States' first important conservation movement. Founded by Gifford Pinchot, one of the nation's greatest conservationists, the service has a long and distinguished history of forest management. Widely recognized and publicly respected, the service has been adept at cultivating vigorous congressional support and a favorable public image—who is not familiar with Smokey Bear and other service symbols of forest preservation? The service's jurisdiction covers 191 million acres of the land, including some grasslands, within the U.S. forest system. With more than 32,000 employees and a budget exceeding $4.5 billion, the Forest Service historically has possessed a strong sense of mission and high professional standards. "While the Forest Service has frequently been at the center of political maelstroms," political scientist Paul J. Culhane writes, "it has also been regarded as one of the most professional, best managed agencies in the federal government."[16] Operating through a highly decentralized system of forest administration, local forest rangers are vested with great discretion in interpreting how multiple-use principles will apply to specific forests within their jurisdictions.

The Bureau of Land Management. The BLM manages more than 264 million surface acres and about 700 million acres of subsurface public domain and leases another two hundred million acres in national forests and private lands, yet the bureau remains obscure outside the West.[17] The BLM's massive presence throughout the West is suggested by Map 9.3, which identifies the proportion of state lands currently managed by the agency and suggests, as well, why western political interests have been so deeply implicated in the BLM's political history. The BLM has struggled to establish standards of professionalism and conservation that would free it from its own long history of indifference to conservation values and from unflattering comparisons with the Forest Service.

The BLM was created in 1946 and, starting with responsibility for managing federal grasslands and grazing lands, gradually added to its jurisdiction other lands with mineral resources and, more recently, 78 million acres of Alaskan lands, including many large wilderness areas. This great diversity of lands has

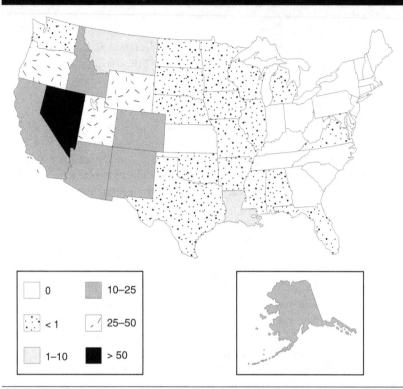

MAP 9.3 ■ Percentage of State Acreage Managed by the U.S. Bureau of Land Management, 2003

Legend:
- 0
- < 1
- 1–10
- 10–25
- 25–50
- > 50

Source: U.S. DOI, BLM, *Fiscal Year 2003 Annual Report: Shared Community Stewardship for America's Public Lands* (Washington, DC: U.S. Government Printing Office, 2003), 73.

different dominant uses: the Alaskan wilderness, more than 2.5 million acres of prime Douglas fir timber in western Oregon, and 146.9 million acres of grazing lands. The BLM also is responsible for arranging the leases for mineral exploration on all public domain lands and on the OCS.

Since 1970, two national public land policies have provoked the most significant public land conflicts: (1) the congressionally mandated practices of multiple use or "balanced use" for much of the public domain; and (2) the creation of vast tracts of highly restricted wilderness areas and roadless areas, precluding all or almost all human development. These conflicts characteristically pit federal resource management agencies, state and local governments, commodity producers and users, and environmentalists against one another over issues that long predate the first Earth Day.

CONFLICTS OVER MULTIPLE USE

Disputes over use of the public domain customarily evolve in roughly similar political settings and focus on land administered by one of the federal land management agencies. Struggling to interpret an ambiguous congressional mandate for land management, the resource agency will commonly find several parties in conflict over the interpretation of multiple use. These parties include the states within whose jurisdictions the land resides, the various private economic interests with a stake in the decision, congressional committees with jurisdiction over the agency's programs, and perhaps the White House. Especially since 1980, environmental interests have been important and predictable participants. Sometimes, the issues are resolved—if they are resolved—only by congressional reformulation of land-use policy.

The Multiple Use Mandate

In carrying out their assigned tasks, managers in the BLM and Forest Service often must walk an administrative tightrope fashioned from the inconsistencies and vagaries of their legislatively defined missions. Three different federal statutes charge the BLM and the Forest Service with administering the lands in their trust according to multiple-use principles. The most elaborate definition of the doctrine, ripe with the ambiguities that create so many problems in its implementation, is found in section 530 of the Multiple Use–Sustained Yield Act (1960):

> "Multiple use" means: the management of all the various renewable surface resources of the national forest so that they are utilized in the combination that will best meet the needs of the American people; making the most judicious use of the land for some or all of these resources or related services over areas large enough to provide sufficient latitude for periodic adjustments in use to conform to changing needs and conditions; that some land will be used for less than all of the resources; and harmonious and coordinated management of the various resources, each with the other, without impairment of the productivity of the land, with consideration being given to the relative values of the various resources, and not necessarily the combination of uses that will give the greatest dollar return or the greatest unit output.[18]

The intent of this complicated mandate is to make sure that in land management, "any use should be carried out to minimize interference with other uses of the same area and, if possible, to complement those other uses."[19] But it provides to agency managers scant information concerning how these differing values are to be defined and balanced when differing claims on land use must be resolved.

The BLM, for instance, has wrestled for years with managing desert areas east and north of Los Angeles to the satisfaction of both conservationists and vehicle-racing enthusiasts. Each year, the BLM processes more than one hundred applications for motorcycle races, some annual events with as many as three thousand competitors. Conservationists have argued that the races permanently scar the land, alternative ecological balances, and create noise and other disruptions for other recreationists.[20] The BLM must then determine the proper balance between recreation and conservation values in terms of these specific desert lands. The Forest Service is expected to protect the national forests from excessive timbering but at the same time assist state and private forest owners in obtaining access to federal forests. Wildlife refuges are supposed to protect and preserve the ecologically viable habitat for endangered species but also provide grazing, hunting, and perhaps mining opportunities to private interests.

But the multiple-use doctrine also leaves resource managers with the opportunity to balance and negotiate among interests claiming the use of public resources. It also promises constant pressure on the agencies to create or alter interpretations of multiple use by whatever interests feel that existing interpretations discriminate against their claims on the land.

Multiple Stakeholders in Multiple Use

The balance of forces in multiple-use conflict changes over time, but the conflict plays out across lines of political cleavage created by federalism, the separation of powers, and interest-group politics.

The Western States. The states have a large economic stake in multiple-use management. Approximately 20 percent of Forest Service receipts for timber sales are returned to local governments in lieu of property taxes on federal lands. More than one third of the BLM's annual receipts for mining royalties and other uses of its land is returned to the states.

The western states want a louder voice in determining grazing rights, in setting conditions for mineral exploration, in establishing timbering quotas, and in deciding how revenues from resource use in the public domain will be allocated. The conflict between the West and Washington over the public lands prevails no matter which party controls the White House or Congress or what the issue might be. "I'd love to say that this is a partisan issue and that if this [Obama] administration changes, it's going to be all sweetness and light," observed the head of the New Mexico Cattle Growers Association concerning its ongoing battle with Washington over grazing rights to the public lands. "But I have 22 years of experience telling me otherwise. It's not a partisan issue . . . People in Washington just don't understand the West. They don't understand the wide open spaces and how we live and how we manage the land."[21]

Despite angry protests over Washington's public land policies, the states are often guilty of doublethink about resources in the public domain. Eager to reap the economic advantages of greater resource use on lands within their domain—more royalties, more severance taxes, and greater industrial development—the states are equally determined not to pay calamitous ecological and economic costs for rapid resource exploitation. Thus, these states often seek an ideal, and often elusive, balance between resource development and environmental protection and waiver between supporting and opposing new federal land designations.

Every recent president has found the western public lands a tripwire, reviving the always-simmering public land controversies. President Clinton angered western states when he decided, without congressional cooperation, to designate forty-three million acres of western national forest lands as roadless areas, thereby virtually precluding any form of economic development. Western political interests again found a presidential champion in newly elected George W. Bush, himself a westerner, an oil man deeply committed to domestic energy development and a political conservative unsympathetic to the Clinton administration's restrictive public lands policies. Bush left no doubts about his political inclination by appointing Gale Norton as secretary of the Interior. Norton was a westerner, like all secretaries of DOI, and an outspoken critic of Washington's western land policies. Congressional conservatives, especially Republicans, were strongly encouraged by these congenial presidential signals to mount an aggressive legislative assault on the roadless-area designations that restricted access to federal wilderness and on other related Clinton land-use regulations.

This combative environment, prevailing throughout the Bush administration, was expected to turn considerably more benign with the advent of the Obama presidency. Optimistic expectations, however, often prove fragile in the volatile policy conflicts that sooner or later erupt between public land policymakers and environmentalists—often divided among themselves—during any presidency. It wasn't long before Obama was criticized for doing too little to protect the public lands when he approved limited oil and gas exploration in the Gulf of Mexico and opened new western public lands to more petroleum production in the West during his first administration.

Energy Users. Even the suggestion by any presidential administration that it might consider more energy exploration on public lands detonates an intense reaction among environmentalists and conservationists, who quickly suspect a needless raid on public resources. However, conflict between energy producers and environmentalists over access to energy resources is inevitable in light of the energy reserves that exist within the public domain. These lands are already big energy producers. The public domain currently yields about 41 percent of domestic coal, 18 percent of crude oil, and 17 percent of natural gas consumption. Much more lies beneath the surface but is currently inaccessible. For example, 62 percent of estimated national oil reserves reside below land presently restricted from energy exploration and development.

Barack Obama had aroused vigorous support from conservationists and environmentalists during his 2008 presidential campaign by a commitment to an expansive program of renewable energy development on the public lands and to ending the Bush administration's aggressive effort to open vast tracts of public land for oil and gas exploration. But Obama had inherited a severe economic recession, an imperative to stimulate employment, and a Congress deeply divided over energy policy—all of which compelled him to strike a difficult balance between energy conservation and energy production sure to disappoint proponents of a radical shift away from new energy production on the public lands during this first term. However, in the latter years of his first term, Obama, using his executive authority, instructed the DOI to protect several million acres of pristine western public domain from fossil fuel exploration by classifying the land as wilderness. The decision, which set up a howl of protest from the Republican congressional delegation and many western politicians, also initiated an unprecedented cascade of new public land designations reaching to the end of his second term.[22] During Obama's second term—especially in his last few months in office—the howls of protest from congressional Republicans and other legislative opponents grew even louder when Obama added millions of new acres of national parks, wilderness, and other areas restricted from energy exploration to the public domain. Relying on his executive authority to bypass Congress, by the end of his last term, Obama had unilaterally added more than 265 million acres of land and water to the public domain, thereby protecting more land by executive action than any other president. However, the future of these ambitious new public lands acquisitions immediately became problematic following the 2016 presidential election.

Donald Trump, an outspoken proponent of extensive new energy exploration on the public lands, had promised during his presidential campaign to roll back federal restrictions on oil and gas drilling in the public domain. Much to the satisfaction of congressional Republicans, major energy producers, and many western state leaders, Trump ordered his new secretary of the Interior, Ryan Zinke, to initiate measures to repeal many of Obama's land policies restricting energy exploration on western lands. In late 2017, Trump demonstrated his determination to reopen public lands to resource development by an unprecedented executive order scaling back by several million acres the size of the Obama administration's newly designated national monuments in Utah. "The public lands will once again be for public use," Trump observed, to emphasize the future direction of his public land policies.[23] The decision was strongly opposed by environmentalists, conservationists, and many Native American tribal leaders who hoped to overturn the president's order in the federal courts, where many battles over public land access are ultimately resolved.

Other Resource Users. Besides energy interests, each of the major federal land-use agencies has other "clientele" with a major economic or ideological stake in the agency's programs. In general, these resource users, such as lumber industries and stock grazers, want to expand their access to resources in the public domain, to use the resources as cheaply as possible, to protect the continuing availability of renewable resources, and to maintain or enhance their influence within the agencies making decisions about resources strategic to them. For example, sheep and cattle ranchers customarily participate actively in the political struggles over BLM rangeland regulations; individual timber companies, such as Weyerhaeuser and Crown Zellerbach, and timber trade associations, such as the National Forest Products Association, are involved in Forest Service determinations about allowable timber harvests.

Critics often assert that the land agencies are easily "captured" by their clientele, who then promote, for instance, greater timber production or more generous grazing rights at the sacrifice of balanced use and, particularly, with little regard for environmental values. The Forest Service's exemplary reputation has been no shield from accusations that it sanctions clear-cutting and other timber practices abhorrent to environmentalists, because the service allegedly has come to define its mission largely as timber production in response to commercial timber company demands. Agency administrators, however, often have a legislative mandate to promote resource use within their jurisdictions, and as a consequence, some community of interest with resource users is inevitable. Often, environmental and conservation groups constitute practically the only politically active and effective force for balanced use within the private pressure group system.

Environmentalists and Environmental Impact Statements

In the 1970s, environmentalists achieved a number of legislative and judicial victories that vastly expanded their influence in federal land management activities and compelled even the ecologically primitive BLM to develop, at least fitfully, an environmental conscience. Among the most important of these achievements was passage of the National Environmental Policy Act (NEPA) in 1970. NEPA required that environmental impact statements (EISs) be prepared by federal land management agencies for major land-use decisions affecting the environment—in effect, for most major land management planning. Draft statements had to be circulated for public review and comment prior to completion, and agency officials were obligated to give the statements careful consideration in all relevant decisions.

In practical terms, the EISs became an early warning system for environmental groups, alerting them to the implications of numerous agency policies whose importance might otherwise have gone unnoticed. Environmentalists had the opportunity to organize a political strategy for influencing land management decisions. In effect, the EIS enabled environmental interests to compel federal agencies to give them a voice in agency proceedings. Further, the statements often forced agencies, such as the BLM, to give greater attention to the ecological impacts of their management practices. Not least important, the EIS was a legally enforceable procedure; environmental groups skillfully exploited many opportunities to use the federal courts to delay or frustrate agency decisions they opposed by challenging the adequacy of impact statements.

Critics charged, sometimes justifiably, that environmentalists were seizing on these new strategies primarily to disrupt administrative procedures and thereby to harass their opponents even when their case lacked merit. But the environmental activities inspired by the enhanced standing as well as the impact statement procedures quite often resulted in valuable ecological improvements in federal land management and greater federal attention to the balanced use of land, to which many agency managers previously had given little more than lip service.

In many respects, the 110 million acres of pristine federal land now congressionally protected from development under the Wilderness Act are a monument to environmentalist activism and to the laws and administrative regulations that enormously enlarged the environmentalists' administrative and congressional influence.

In a political system in which localism usually dominates congressional life, this ascent of environmentalist power from the grassroots was an instance of capturing the political base from the opposition.

THE FATE OF THE FORESTS

More than one in every ten acres in the public domain could be used for commercial timber production. This land, about eighty-nine million acres, lies mostly within the jurisdiction of the Department of Agriculture's Forest Service. Since the end of World War II, pressure has been unremitting on the Forest Service to increase the size of the annual timber harvest from the national forests to satisfy the nation's growing demand for wood products. Recently, there has been increased pressure to open many undisturbed old-growth timber stands and wilderness areas to commercial logging. Against this economic pressure, the Forest Service is required not only to enforce the doctrine of multiple use, which forbids the service from allowing timber cutting that will preclude other forest uses, but also to manage timber cutting to ensure a "sustained yield" from any forest reserve used for commercial timbering. Congress has left to the Forest Service the difficult and politically contentious responsibility of defining how much timber cutting is compatible with multiple use and sustained yield.

The struggle over competing timber uses is fought in the arcane language of forest economics—"nondeclining, even-flow" formulas, "allowable cuts," and "allowable-cut effects"—but the larger interests and issues at stake are apparent. The struggle represents a collision between preservationist and developmental priorities for timber, between competing definitions of the nation's economic needs, and between differing definitions of the Forest Service's mission. It is a struggle likely to intensify well into the future.

A Disputed Treasure in Timber

About half of the nation's softwood sawtimber reserves and a substantial portion of its remaining hardwoods grow today in the national forests. The

Pacific Coast region, particularly the timbered hills and lowlands of the Pacific Northwest, contains the largest of these timber stands within the public domain; the area contains almost half the pine, spruce, fir, and other softwoods in the national forests. These timber reserves, more than three times the size of all the private commercial forests in the United States and currently worth more than $20 billion, will increase in value.

Although timber cutting was permitted in the national forests from their inception, the demand for commercial timber in the forests assumed major proportions only after World War II. In the early 1940s, the Forest Service sold about 1.5 billion board feet of timber per year; by 1973, the cut exceeded 12.3 billion board feet. Driven by the nation's ravenous postwar desire for new housing, the demand for wood products rose steadily in the three decades following 1945. Private timber companies, approaching the limits of their own production, began to look increasingly to the national forests as an untapped timber reserve. This demand, if wholly satisfied, would probably result in a doubling of the annual timber harvest from the national forests, in keeping with the industry's estimates that the U.S. demand for wood products would double by the early twenty-first century.

Pressure to expand the allowable timber cut has been particularly intense in the Pacific Northwest. Many of the Douglas fir forests in Oregon and Washington are old-growth stands, virgin forests never touched by a logger's saw, growing in a continuity of development many centuries old. These forests are among the most ecologically diverse and historically unique of all timber stands in North America, reminders of a continent once largely timbered with a profusion of species greater than all of Europe's. Many virgin forests, together with other less spectacular timberlands, are on Forest Service lands that are still classified or eligible for classification as wilderness. To many environmentalists and to organized preservation groups, such as the Sierra Club and the Wilderness Society, these lands are the living expression of the preservationist ethic, the values of the movement made visible. They are, in political terms, *gut issues.*

The Greening of Forest Policy

The environmental movement has profoundly changed forest management policies since 1970 by altering its political underpinnings. Before the 1970s, as political scientist George Hoberg observed, "the forest policy regime was characterized by a dominant administrative agency, a strong orientation toward the development of timber resources, and little input from the public."[24] By the early 1970s, the organized environmental movement had acquired political muscle and, together with its political allies, had promoted new environmental laws and new federal agencies to implement them. Environmentalists aggressively used their newly expanded judicial access to fashion litigation into a potent political weapon. New statutory and administrative provisions for public involvement in the implementation of forest policy and greater congressional oversight of Forest Service policies expanded environmentalist influence in day-to-day forest management. These changes meant a new pluralism in forest management politics, in which resource developers no longer dominated and in which environmentalists had become major players whose interests had to be acknowledged, along with their allies, in policymaking at all governmental levels.

Once again, as in other aspects of environmental policy, environmental organizations found the courts during the 1970s and early 1980s to be an effective ally. Especially important was the growing trend among federal courts to scrutinize carefully the Forest Service's management decisions to ensure they were compatible with newly enacted environmental laws rather than to defer, as the courts had done traditionally, to the Forest Service's professional expertise in cases in which the service's decisions were challenged. It was its success in overturning the historic Forest Service practice of clear-cutting in the early 1970s that demonstrated what this shift in judicial attitudes meant for environmentalists: Congress was forced by the federal courts to rewrite forest management laws to limit severely the once-common clear-cutting practices.

The Forest Service did not respond warmly to most of these early provocations. Professional foresters and the Forest Service's rank and file often resented the challenge to their professional judgment and the environmentalist insinuations that they were ecologically unenlightened. The rise of politically organized and powerful environmentalism, however, was evident when Congress passed the National Forest Management Act (NFMA) in 1976, compelling the Forest Service to open its forest management planning process from the lowest levels to environmentalist involvement and to set new standards for multiple-use decisions in which ecological values had to be given major consideration. Gradually, the Forest Service adapted to the new environmental realities, with the considerable assistance of progressive leaders within professional forestry itself. The academic training and recruitment of Forest Service professionals was transformed to include a much greater emphasis on environmental values and ecologically supportive practices in job preparation. The Forest Service adjusted its organizational structure and decision-making procedures to the new requirements of NEPA, NFMA, and other judicial and congressional mandates to better incorporate environmental values in its policymaking.

Still, the Forest Service, like other federal land management agencies, must live with the multiple-use laws as the fundamental calculus for its land-use decision-making, environmentalism notwithstanding. Thus, forest managers are never free of conflicting forces and values pressing constantly on them whenever major forest management policy must be formulated or implemented. Indeed, multiple-use legislation creates the fundamental political order out of which all forest management decisions must ultimately arise.

Multiple-Use Conflicts and the Forests

Because Congress has chosen not to specify how it expects foresters to define multiple use or sustained yield in specific jurisdictions, the Forest Service has been left with enormous discretion in translating these formulas into practice. As with the multiple-use doctrine, the congressional definition of sustained yield is open to diverse interpretations; as section 531 of the Multiple Use–Sustained Yield Act suggests, "Sustained yield . . . means the achievement and maintenance in perpetuity of a high-level annual or regular periodic output of the various renewable resources of the national forests without impairment of the productivity of the land."[25]

Both the sustained-yield and multiple-use doctrines are important to the commercial timber industry because they provide the basis for the Forest Service's determination of the allowable cut in a given timber reserve—the amount of timber that can be removed from a particular resource area in a given period. The Forest Service has interpreted sustained yield to require a nondeclining, even-flow policy, which limits the timber cut in a given area to a constant or increasing rate—but never a declining one. In effect, this has limited severely the cutting of old-growth forests, particularly in the Pacific Northwest, to the ire of the timber industry, local communities, and those economists who believe a larger cut of old-growth timber is more economically efficient and compatible with the multiple-use doctrine. Environmentalists generally support the protection of old-growth forests and advocate further reductions on the allowable cut elsewhere.[26]

In response to pressure from the timber industry by trade groups like the National Forest Products Association, the Forest Service began to increase the timber harvest substantially in the mid-1980s and to plan for increasing harvests thereafter. Between 1982 and 1989, the total timber cut in the national forests grew substantially from 6.7 million to 12.7 million board feet.[27] Forest Service professionals contended that this expansion was consistent with the statutory mandate to maintain a sustained yield. But the timber industry also wanted more production. With its own reserves being depleted rapidly, the industry contended that only a timber harvest from the national forests significantly above the currently projected levels would provide enough wood for the U.S. economy in the next several decades. Nonetheless, persistent pressure from environmental and conservation groups, especially through litigation in the federal courts, has diminished very substantially the size of the annual commercial timber yield from the National Forests. In their efforts to reduce the annual timber harvest, opponents have been especially successful in using the Endangered Species Act (ESA) to limit or halt many proposed timber sales because they placed protected species at risk of extinction. The decision by the Fish and Wildlife Service to list the northern spotted owl as endangered in 1988, soon to be described, is a classic example of how the ESA has become an environmentally protective restraint on commercial timbering on federal lands.

The Northern Spotted Owl Versus the Timber Industry

Environmentalists have long opposed the logging of old-growth forests. The battles tend to be fought on a forest-by-forest basis, as the Forest Service proposes the required long-range plans for each forest and then files the necessary EISs. George Bush's administration inherited one of these struggles, an especially emotional and public dispute provoked by Forest Service plans to permit greatly expanded timber cutting in old-growth northwestern forests. The plan might have succeeded, except for ecological serendipity in the form of the northern spotted owl.

The spotted owl is now an icon of U.S. resource politics, a symbol of the clash between competing approaches to valuing natural resources. In the mid-1980s, the Forest Service had planned to permit commercial timber companies to make substantial cuts in the old-growth Oregon forests, whose 2.3 million acres represent the last 1 percent of the nation's original forest cover. In 1985, biologists in the DOI's Fish and Wildlife Service reported to the departmental leadership that the northern spotted owl, whose habitat was almost exclusively northwestern old-growth forests, was fast disappearing and should be designated an endangered species. Estimates indicated that about 1,500 nesting pairs of owls remained, all in the first-growth stands. One consequence of this designation would be to protect this habitat, if geographically unique, from almost all forms of development. The DOI's leadership initially overruled this recommendation under considerable pressure from the timber industry and a variety of local Oregon and Washington interests, including timber mills, community leaders, unions, local congressional representatives, and timber industry workers.

Spokespeople for these interests argued that designating the northern spotted owl an endangered species would virtually end logging on 1.5 million acres of old-growth timber in Oregon and Washington. The federal government estimated that between 4,500 and 9,500 jobs would be lost, but the timber industry asserted that the actual figure was ten times that amount. "You're talking about complete devastation of communities," protested then-Senator Slade Gorton, R-WA. The president of the Northwest Forestry Association, a trade group, repeated a familiar refrain among local economic interests in Washington and Oregon: "To devastate a regional economy over the spotted owl seems absurd. You're talking about affecting half our industry."[28] The timber industry's outrage was exacerbated further because much of the old-growth softwood timber was exported, primarily to Japan, where it could command several times the domestic price.

Environmentalists had opposed commercial logging in old-growth forests long before the specific tracts in Oregon and Washington had entered the dispute. Environmentalists have argued that intensive logging in old-growth forests, with the building of logging roads and disruptive soil practices sure to attend it, will greatly reduce the forest's ability to conserve water and to prevent soil erosion, thus violating the principle of balanced use. Spokespeople for environmental organizations also contend that much of the old-growth timber is found in poor soil—at high elevations and on steep slopes—and exposure to weathering will cause rapid erosion after logging begins. Moreover, they assert, these forests support a unique ecosystem with a great variety of important and irreplaceable flora and fauna. Finally, environmentalists challenge the presumption that a major increase in the timber harvest would significantly decrease housing costs. In any case, many acceptable substitutes for wood exist in the U.S. economy that can be had without sacrificing virgin forests, they note.

Except for the northern spotted owl, these arguments might have succumbed to the political weight of the local, regional, and national interests defending commercial access to first-growth timber. In fall 1988, environmental organizations obtained a federal court order that instructed the secretary of the Interior to list the northern spotted owl as endangered, and in mid-1989, the DOI complied with the court's demand. The designation appeared almost to end commercial logging in northwestern first-growth forests, but it did nothing to diminish the rancor or the economic stakes involved in the continuing controversy over the appropriate use of the national forests.

HOW MUCH WILDERNESS IS ENOUGH?

More than 110 million acres of public land constitute the National Wilderness Preservation System. These wilderness areas are scattered among lands administered by Forest Service, National Park Service, Bureau of Land Management, and the Fish and Wildlife Service. A substantial portion of the sixty-five million undeveloped acres under the jurisdiction of the Forest Service—the "roadless regions"—is eligible for assignment to timber production. These roadless areas could also become part of the National Wilderness Preservation System and thereby be forever excluded from timbering and any other kind of development. Timber producers, environmentalists, the Forest Service, and Congress have disagreed since the 1980s over how much of this roadless area should be designated for multiple use—in other words, how much of the area should be open to timbering, mineral exploration, and other nonrecreational and nonconservation uses. Perhaps as much as a third of the whole national forest system, including many old-growth stands, is in these roadless areas.

Environmentalists would prefer that most of the roadless areas under the Forest Service's jurisdiction also be included in the National Wilderness Preservation System. Environmentalists have been apprehensive that any multiple-use designation for large, undeveloped roadless tracts will be an invitation not only to aggressive timbering but also to oil, natural gas, and coal exploration. They predict that energy industries, on locating energy reserves, will seek exceptions to environmental regulations. Air pollution from electric power plants and energy refining operations adjacent to public lands with energy reserves will result, and the quality of the lands will be degraded irreversibly. With some justification, environmentalists also allege that the Forest Service's strong commitment to its traditional multiple-use doctrine makes it reluctant to turn large tracts of roadless areas over to a single dominant use such as wilderness preservation. Nonetheless, the Multiple Use–Sustained Yield

Act requires the Forest Service to include wilderness protection among other multiple uses of land within its jurisdiction. The NFMA also requires the Forest Service to draw up a master plan for the use of land under its jurisdiction that includes the consideration of wilderness designation. Thus, the Forest Service was given both ample authority and explicit responsibility to recommend to Congress additional roadless areas for inclusion in the National Wilderness Preservation System. Although Congress alone possesses the authority to assign land to the system formally, the Forest Service's recommendations frequently influence the decisions. The White House, however, often has proposed its own plans for the roadless areas, sometimes at variance with Forest Service initiatives.

No presidential administration can avoid these wilderness controversies. George W. Bush, already deeply suspect among conservationists before he took office, earned their further animosity but also the enthusiastic approval of traditional exponents of public land development from his administration's "no more wilderness" policy. The policy resulted in 2003 from a federal court case involving the DOI. That litigation resulted in the DOI agreeing that the BLM would make no further inventory of possible wilderness areas within all the 256 million acres of federal public lands until Congress decided whether to create additional wilderness areas—an unlikely event in the politically polarized Congress. The Obama administration, however, determined to reverse this policy and, aided by Democratic majorities in both congressional chambers, signed in 2009 a legislative bill designating two million additional acres of public land as wilderness areas—just in time, from the viewpoint of conservationists, since Republicans regained control of the House of Representatives in 2010, making any further congressional approval of new wilderness designations unlikely for some time.

CONCLUSION

The struggles over energy exploration, mining, and timbering on public lands reveal a durable structure underlying the political conflicts over the use of public resources in the United States. The pattern tends to be repeated, because it grows from political realities inherent in the U.S. governmental system.

At the center of the conflict is a federal executive agency guarding the resource as a public trust and wrestling with an ambiguous mandate for its management. Most often, this agency will be part of the DOI or the Forest Service. The mandates will be vague because Congress must rely on a professional administrator to make expert resource decisions—hence the generality of the mandates—and ambiguous because Congress often shrinks from choosing between conflicting claims on resources. Thus, multiple-use prescriptions for forest or range management appear to offer something to recreationists, conservationists, and resource developers without really settling the competing claims. The administrative managers for the public resource inevitably will find their professional decisions politicized, as conflicting interests seek to influence technical decisions to their advantage. Technical decisions themselves can often be made and justified in different, scientifically defensible ways. All this means that resource administrators sometimes can exercise their professional judgment in the service of their own group and political loyalties. In all these ways, the resource management agency finds itself at the center of a political conflict over the public domain.

Further, both the White House and Congress will become partisan advocates of resource management policy, attempting to influence administrative decisions relevant to resource management and responding to pressure from organized interests with a stake in resource management. As we have observed in timber, wilderness, and energy development policies, Congress has the predictable tendency to intervene in administrative management to protect interests important to the legislators. So too, presidents Carter, Reagan, Bush, Clinton, George W. Bush, and indeed every president before them for a half century have directed the DOI and the Forest Service to pursue specific objectives in resource management compatible with their ideological biases and political commitments. Indeed, Congress and the White House often compete in attempting to influence administrative determinations affecting the public domain. The president, despite the illusory title of chief executive, has no guarantee of success in the struggle.

The plurality of organized interests involved in resource decisions means that Congress, the White House, and the administrative agencies are enmeshed in a process of coalition building with organized groups during resource policymaking. These organized interests, moreover, involve not only private interests but also the states within which the public domain resides and for which the use of the domain's resources have significant political and economic consequences.

Finally, policy struggles quite often are waged in the technical language of resource economics and scientific management. Perhaps more than most environmental issues, public resource management is an arcane business to most Americans, particularly those living where few public lands exist. In such circumstances, specialized private groups, such as environmentalists and resource users, tend to operate almost invisibly to the public. The outcome of the policy struggles depends particularly on the groups' organizational resources, technical expertise, and political adeptness in the administrative infighting and legal wrangling that often characterize resource policymaking. It is a political arena, more particularly, in which organized environmental groups often constitute practically the only expression of viewpoints not associated with resource users or administrators.

Suggested Readings

Clark, Jeanne N., and Daniel McCool. *Staking Out the Terrain: Power Differentials among Natural Resource Management Agencies*. 2nd ed. Albany, NY: SUNY Press, 2000.

Lowry, William R. *Dam Politics: Restoring America's Rivers*. Washington, DC: Georgetown University Press, 2003.

Nie, Martin A. *The Governance of Western Public Lands: Mapping Its Present and Future.* Lawrence: University of Kansas Press, 2009.

Reisner, Marc. *Cadillac Desert.* Rev. ed. New York: Penguin, 2001.

Vaughn, Jacqueline, and Hanna Cortner. *George W. Bush's Healthy Forests: Reframing the Environmental Debate.* Boulder: University Press of Colorado, 2005.

Notes

1. "Where's Zinke? The Interior Secretary's Special Flag Offers Clues," *Washington Post*, October 12, 2017, available at https://www.washington post.com/politics/wheres-zinke-the-interior-secretarys-special-flag -offers-clues/2017/10/12/68672476-aeb2-11e7-9e58-e6288544af98_story .html?utm_term=.ca723225a3bf.

2. Naomi Lim, "Special Flag Flown Over Interior Department When Ryan Zinke Is in the Building," *Washington Examiner*, October 12, 2017, https://www .washingtonexaminer.com/special-flag-flown-over-interior-department -when-ryan-zinke-is-in-the-building.

3. For a legislative history of the ANWR, see M. Lynne Corn, Michael Ratner, and Kristina Alexander, *Arctic National Wildlife Refuge (ANWR): A Primer for the 112th Congress,* February 14, 2012 (Washington DC: Congressional Research Service, 2012), Document RL33872, available at www.fas.org/sgp/ crs/misc/RL33872.pdf.

4. Defenders of Wildlife, "Arctic National Wildlife Refuge," available at http:// www.savearcticrefuge.org.

5. Matt Lee-Ashley, "The Energy Case Against Drilling in the Arctic National Wildlife Refuge," Energy and the Environment, Center for American Progress, November 13, 2017, available at www.americanprogress.org/ issues/green/news/2017/11/13/442603/energy-case-drilling-arctic-national -wildlife-refuge/.

6. For a legislative history of ANWR, see M. Lynne Corn and Bernard A. Gelb, "Arctic National Wildlife Refuge (ANWR): Controversies for the 108th Congress," Report no. 1B10111 (Washington, DC: Congressional Research Service, 2003).

7. Rachel D'Oro, "Alaska Environment, Development Co-Exist," November 17, 2003, available at www.lists.envirolink.org/pipermail/ar-news/Week-of -Mon-20031117/010930.html.

8. Juliet Eilperin, "Senate Votes to Raise Revenue by Drilling in the Arctic National Wildlife Refuge," *Washington Post*, October 19, 2017,

available at https://www.washingtonpost.com/news/energy-environment/wp/2017/10/19/senate-votes-to-raise-revenue-by-drilling-in-the-arctic-national-wildlife-refuge/?noredirect=on&utm_term=.5c1e61b20589.

9. Pamela King, "Trump Administration Takes First Steps Toward Drilling in Alaska's Arctic Refuge" *E&E News*, April 19, 2018, available at http://www.sciencemag.org/news/2018/04/trump-administration-takes-first-steps-toward-drilling-alaska-s-arctic-refuge.

10. Carol Hardy Vincent, Laura A. Hanson, and Carla N. Argueta, *Federal Land Ownership: Overview and Data*, CRS Report R42346 (Washington, DC: Congressional Reference Service, March 3, 2017), p.2.

11. Article IV, section 3, clause 2.

12. U.S. Department of the Interior, "Natural Resources Revenue Data 2016," available at https://revenuedata.doi.gov/explore/

13. Tom Arrandale, *The Battle for Natural Resources* (Washington, DC: Congressional Quarterly, 1983), chap. 1; U.S. DOI, "About the Department of the Interior: Quick Facts," available at http://www.doi.gov/facts.html.

14. Aldo Leopold, *A Sand County Almanac* (New York: Oxford University Press, 1949), 222.

15. A useful survey of public lands can be found in U.S. DOI, Bureau of Land Management, *Managing the Nation's Public Lands* (Washington, DC: U.S. Government Printing Office, 1983).

16. Paul J. Culhane, *Public Lands Politics* (Baltimore: Johns Hopkins University Press, 1981), 60.

17. U.S. Department of the Interior, Bureau of Land Management, *Public Land Statistics, 2014* (Washington, DC: Bureau of Land Management, 2015), Publication BLM/OC/ST-15/005+1165, P-108-4.

18. 16 U.S.C. § 530, 74 Stat. 215 (1960). On the impact of sustained use on the Forest Service, see Culhane, *Public Lands Politics*, chap. 2.

19. 16 U.S.C. § 530, 74 Stat. 215 (1960).

20. CEQ, *Environmental Quality, 1979* (Washington, DC: U.S. Government Printing Office, 1980), 309.

21. Ann O'Neill, "Spotted Owl Could Be a Game-Changer in Tombstone Water War," *CNN News*, June 9, 2012, available at www.cnn.com/2012/06/09/us/tombstone-shovel-brigade/index.html.

22. Scott Straeter, "'Wild Lands' Policy Stokes Flames of Dissent in Utah County," *New York Times*, January 6, 2011, available at www.nytimes.com/gwire/2011/01/06/06greenwire-wild-lands-policy-stokes-flames-of-dissent-in-92049.html?pagewanted=all.

23. Associated Press, "'Public Lands For Public Use': Pres. Trump Takes Unprecedented Step to Reduce National Monuments," December 4, 2017, available at https://fox6now.com/2017/12/04/public-lands-for-public-use-pres-trump-takes-unprecedented-step-to-reduce-national-monuments/.

24. George Hoberg, "From Localism to Legalism," in *Western Public Lands and Environmental Politics*, ed. Charles Davis (Boulder, CO: Westview Press, 1997), 48.

25. 16 U.S.C. § 530, 74 Stat. 215 (1960).

26. Culhane, *Public Lands Politics*, chap. 2.

27. U.S. Department of Commerce, Bureau of the Census, *Statistical Abstract of the United States, 1989* (Washington, DC: U.S. Government Printing Office, 1990), 656.

28. Timothy Egan, "U.S. Stand on Owl Seen Saving Trees in West," *New York Times*, April 27, 1989, A18.

THE POLITICS AND POLICY OF GLOBAL CLIMATE CHANGE

Very early in 2017, Washington, D.C., began to experience a unique type of climate change. At EPA websites, the words "greenhouse gases" and "climate change" were frequently replaced by terms such as "sustainability" and "emissions." At a website previously titled "Climate and Energy Resources for State and Local and Tribal Governments," the word "climate" disappeared from the title and fifteen other places where it had previously appeared.[1] Data related to climate change and carbon air emissions were sometimes removed from websites and archived at other locations. Language concerning U.S. commitments to mitigating international climate change vanished from several EPA websites.[2]

It was soon apparent that EPA wasn't exceptional, that the federal government seemed to be experiencing a gradual institutional amnesia about climate change. References to climate change, to numerous related words or phrases, to climate change policies, together with some significant climate-related data sets disappeared or became elusive at numerous other federal agency websites. The departments of State and Energy excised from their websites language concerning U.S. international obligations to abate climate warming. On the Department of Energy's *Website for Kids,* the sentence "Burning coal produces emissions that adversely affect the environment and human health" was deleted together with two pie charts relating to national coal combustion and national carbon dioxide emissions.[3] As 2017 progressed, the Trump administration steadfastly continued to reword or to eliminate the vocabulary of climate change science, policy, and research at federal websites.

Spokesmen for the Trump administration explained these changes by emphasizing that a new administration always had the freedom to highlight its new agenda, that the Trump agenda was advertising its commitment to repealing earlier federal climate change policies and promoting more exploration for gas and oil at the appropriate websites. At EPA, where the website edits seemed most prolific, a public affairs official noted: ". . . we are currently updating our website to reflect EPA's priorities under the leadership of President Trump and Administrator Pruitt . . . [and] we want to eliminate confusion by removing outdated language first and making room to discuss how we're protecting the environment. . . ."[4]

Environmental organizations quickly rallied into an intense opposition to these widespread changes, carefully tracked the web page alterations, and condemned the revisions as an unethical and indefensible censoring of scientific information inspired by partisan politics. "While there are many issues on which the administration has the right to declare its own policies," declared a prominent university scientist in *Scientific American* magazine, "a lot of what is going on here is that they're trying to erase awareness of the existence of the [climate change] issue itself, not promoting a different policy to address it, just erasing it."[5] The website edits generally angered scientists, especially climate experts, who consider climate change a scientific reality, not the problematic theory suggested by many early website revisions. The website controversy was a prelude to a profound and pervasive transformation in national climate change politics and policy initiated by the Trump administration.

SCIENCE AND CLIMATE WARMING

The intense controversy at the outset of the Trump administration over its treatment of climate science and policy has permeated virtually all contemporary aspects of the federal government's climate-related activities. Climate change has become the most publicly debated, politicized, and politically polarizing environmental issue since the first Earth Day. Even if climate change were not so highly charged with political and scientific controversy, it would be an especially formidable policy problem because its resolution involves not only domestic policy and politics but also international diplomacy and global science.

The Science of Atmospheric Warming

The catalyst to the ongoing controversy over the scientific validity of global climate change predictions has been the Intergovernmental Panel on Climate Change (IPCC), established in 1988 under the auspices of the United Nations Environment Programme and the World Meteorological Organization for the purpose of assessing "the scientific, technical and socioeconomic information relevant for the understanding of the risk of human-induced climate change."[6] The IPCC's periodic reports have each engaged more than 2,400 scientists across the globe in a continuing process of collecting, integrating, and evaluating the vast diversity of scientific research on virtually every aspect of climate change. The IPCC "does not carry out new research nor does it monitor climate-related data. It bases its assessment mainly on published and peer reviewed scientific technical literature."[7] The goal of these assessments is to inform international policy and negotiations on climate-related issues. The IPCC has become the most globally visible and consistently controversial of the scientific institutions associated with climate change research. Although the IPCC reports are as close to Holy Writ as exists within the scientific community associated with climate change advocacy, the IPCC has been consistently diligent to acknowledge explicitly the limitations that may be inherent to their assessment's data or conclusions, lest the reports lose their credibility.

The Five Intergovernmental Panels on Climate Change Assessments. The *First Assessment Report* of the IPCC (1990) as well as a supplemental report prepared in 1992 supported the establishment of the United Nations Framework Convention on Climate Change (UNFCCC) at the United Nations Conference on Environment and Development (UNCED, commonly known as "The Earth Summit") held in Rio de Janeiro, Brazil, in 1992. The UNFCCC treaty, which the United States has signed, serves as the foundation of international political efforts to combat global climate change.

The UNFCCC treaty also mandated periodic Conference of Parties (COP) held at regular intervals beginning in 1995, at different national locations—the last (COP 21) at Paris in April 2016. The COP conferences have been the venues where participating nations have negotiated the important international agreements on climate change mitigation and have defined their respective responsibilities for treaty implementation.

Each of the IPCC periodic reports have enriched the data base and expanded the temporal scope of its scientific conclusions. The *Fourth Assessment Report* (2007) and *Fifth Assessment Report* (2014) have become the most internationally influential scientific documents currently involved with climate change research, representing what most atmospheric scientists and related professionals consider to be a thorough, carefully explained view of the state of climate change science since 2001. Among all the IPCC reports, the *Fifth Assessment Report* included the most forceful affirmation of global climate change and its anthropomorphic (human) origin:

> Warming of the climate system is unequivocal, and since the 1950s, many of the observed changes are unprecedented over decades to millennia. The atmosphere and ocean have warmed, the amounts of snow and ice have diminished, sea level has risen, and the concentrations of greenhouse gases have increased. It is extremely likely that human influence has been the dominant cause of the observed warming since the mid-20th century."[8]

Changes of the magnitude predicted by the *Fifth Assessment Report* would profoundly and possibly catastrophically affect much of the world. Low-lying areas, including many economically underdeveloped countries in Africa and Asia, as well as island nations, would be inundated by seawater, their economic and ecological sustainability severely jeopardized. Economically and technologically advanced nations with exposed seacoasts or levee-protected lowlands would also confront formidable economic, engineering, and logistical problems in adjusting to rising sea levels. Generally, the world's temperate zones would probably shift further north, accelerating the desertification and deforestation of many continental areas in Asia, Africa, Europe, and North America, while transforming agricultural production in many others. Along with these transformations would come shifts in regional ecology and a multitude of other natural changes that are difficult to predict precisely. Not all the predicted changes would necessarily be adverse. Some experts have also predicted longer and more productive growing seasons for many crops as a result of increased ambient carbon dioxide, the transformation of some northern latitudes into new agricultural breadbaskets, and other benign consequences. In any event, the profound global alterations attending significant climate warming, however characterized, would apparently create a relatively swift, pervasive transformation of human societies and world ecosystems unprecedented in modern human history.

Since the first IPCC assessment report, numerous public and private institutions have also conducted extensive research that generally confirms the IPCC's major conclusions. Especially important domestically was the Third U.S. National Climate Assessment, a 2014 collaboration among thirteen major federal scientific agencies, which supported the IPCC reports and reaffirmed, especially, the existence and growing magnitude of global climate change and its anthropomorphic origins. The consequences of this global change are expected to profoundly alter almost every aspect of U.S. domestic life, a transformation on an ecological, economic, and social scale without historical precedent, as the conclusions in Box 10.1 suggest.

BOX 10.1 GLOBAL CLIMATE CHANGE IMPACTS IN THE UNITED STATES
KEY FINDINGS

1. Global warming is unequivocal and primarily human induced.

   Global temperature has increased over the past fifty years. This observed increase is due primarily to human-induced emissions of heat-trapping gases.

2. Climate changes are underway in the United States and are projected to grow.

   Climate-related changes are already observed in the United States and its coastal waters. These include increases in heavy downpours, rising temperature and sea level, rapidly retreating glaciers, thawing permafrost, lengthening growing seasons, lengthening ice-free seasons in the ocean and on lakes and rivers, earlier snowmelt, and alterations in river flows. These changes are projected to grow.

3. Widespread climate-related impacts are occurring now and are expected to increase.

   Climate changes are already affecting water, energy, transportation, agriculture, ecosystems, and health. These impacts are different from region to region and will grow under projected climate change.

4. Climate change will stress water resources.

   Water is an issue in every region, but the nature of the potential impacts varies. Drought, related to reduced precipitation, increased evaporation, and increased water loss from plants, is an important issue in many regions, especially in the West. Floods and water quality problems are likely to be amplified by climate changes in most regions. Declines in mountain snowpack are important in the West and Alaska, where snowpack provides vital natural water storage.

5. Crop and livestock production will be increasingly challenged.

   Agriculture is considered one of the sectors most adaptable to changes in climate. However, increased heat, pests, water stress, diseases, and weather extremes will pose adaptation challenges for crop and livestock production.

6. Coastal areas are at increasing risk from sea-level rise and storm surge.

   Sea-level rise and storm surge place many U.S. coastal areas at increasing risk of erosion and flooding, especially along the Atlantic and Gulf Coasts, Pacific Islands, and parts of Alaska. Energy and transportation infrastructure and other property in coastal areas are very likely to be adversely affected.

7. Threats to human health will increase.

   Health impacts of climate change are related to heat stress, waterborne diseases, poor air quality, extreme weather events, and diseases transmitted by insects and rodents. Robust public health infrastructure can reduce the potential for negative impacts.

8. Climate change will interact with many social and environmental stresses.

   Climate change will combine with pollution; population growth; overuse of resources; urbanization; and other social, economic, and environmental stresses to create larger impacts than from any of these factors alone.

9. Thresholds will be crossed, leading to changes in climate and ecosystems.

   There are a variety of thresholds in the climate system and ecosystems. These thresholds determine, for example, the presence of sea ice and permafrost and the survival of species, from fish to insect pests, with implications for society. With further climate change, the cross of additional thresholds is expected.

10. Future climate change and its impacts depend on choices made today.

    The amount and rate of future climate change depend primarily on current and future human-caused emissions of heat-trapping gases and airborne particles. Responses involve reducing emissions to limit future warming and adapting to the changes that are unavoidable.

Source: U.S. Global Climate Change Research Project, "Executive Summary," *Global Climate Change Impacts of the United States* (New York: Cambridge University Press, 2009), 12.

The Emissions Problem: Greenhouse Gases

The foundations of domestic climate change politics are human-created air emissions—the greenhouse gases (GHG)—and their sources. Emissions define what must be regulated; the sources identify which activities or interests must be regulated—in effect, the stakeholders in the politics of emissions regulation. The gases, by their proportion of domestic emissions, include

- *carbon dioxide* (CO_2) created by burning fossil fuels, solid waste, trees, and wood products, and also produced by some chemical reactions such as cement manufacturing (61 percent);

- *methane* (CH_4) produced during the production and transportation of coal, natural gas, and oil; from livestock and other agricultural practices, and from decay of organic waste in municipal solid waste landfills (10 percent);

- *nitrous oxide* (N_2O) created during agricultural and industrial activities and during fossil fuels and solid waste combustion (6 percent); and

- *fluorinated gases*, typically emitted in smaller quantities, but because they are potent greenhouse gases, they are sometimes referred to as High Global Warming Potential gases ("High GWP gases").[9]

Figure 10.1 illustrates that most major U.S. economic sectors are stakeholders in the politics of GHG regulation. Coal-burning industries, and especially electric utilities, have been extremely active politically because their emissions

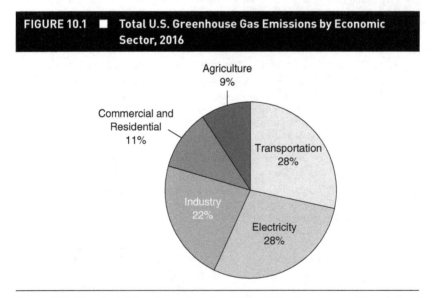

FIGURE 10.1 ■ Total U.S. Greenhouse Gas Emissions by Economic Sector, 2016

Agriculture 9%

Commercial and Residential 11%

Transportation 28%

Industry 22%

Electricity 28%

Source: EPA, "Overview of Greenhouse Gases" available at https://www.epa.gov/ghgemissions/overview-greenhouse-gases

are usually the most technologically difficult and expensive to control. The transportation sector, now the major source of GHG emissions, has been progressively expanding its investment in electric and hybrid engine technologies in anticipation of more tailpipe controls on gasoline and diesel fuels.

Climate Change Dissenters

The foundation for IPCC predictions about the magnitude of global climate change and its implications have been contested from the inception of international discussion about global climate change. The scientific debate has become increasingly strident, occasionally escalating into venomous exchanges within the scientific community. More often, these exchanges have taken place within the political arena, where the issue has transmuted into a polarizing partisan confrontation between contending factions promoting competing claims concerning the scientific validity and political acceptability of the proposed solutions. IPCC dissenters not only have contested the IPCC's major scientific conclusions and supporting research but, in some instances, also accused various scientific proponents and organizations of willfully conspiring to suppress and falsify scientific data inconsistent with the major premises of climate change.

Climate change dissenters (sometimes anointed "contrarians") range across a broad, extremely diverse social and scientific spectrum: some scientists engaged in climate research and related fields, other scientific professionals, political partisans ideologically hostile to the proposed social or economic solutions for climate change, and corporations vulnerable to the regulatory controls required to control climate-warming emissions. Proponents of the IPCC's conclusions and related initiatives have been especially vehement in asserting that many of the individuals and institutions opposing the IPCC's conclusions are proxies for the global petroleum corporation Exxon-Mobil, which has spent millions of dollars on its own corporate media campaign attacking the credibility of the IPCC and its allies. Moreover, Exxon-Mobil has a considerable number of corporate allies in the business of underwriting opposition to the IPCC, including numerous other corporations and advocacy groups associated with fossil fuel mining and combustion and with petroleum distillation and distribution.

The ongoing scientific debate swirls around a multitude of complex technical issues certain to confuse the public. The critics' favorite target has been the computer model used to generate climate change predictions, which have been assailed continually for faulty assumptions and inadequate data about current climate trends. Some experts have asserted that many computer models are based on inaccurate measurements of historical temperature change, that climate change models fail to describe the long-range physics of climate change, that other historical climate data are misconstrued or misapplied in climate modeling, and much more. Some experts cite other causes, such as solar activity and terrestrial volcanoes, to explain climate warming. Others rely on different models suggesting that the greenhouse effect is not inevitable. Still others do not believe sufficient evidence exists to make any responsible judgment about future climate change.

The Trump Administration Joins the Dissent

Donald Trump had long been an outspoken skeptic about climate change and critic of the Obama administration's climate change policies. "I believe in clean air. But I don't believe in climate change," he told a reporter in 2015 and proved it by rapidly and comprehensively populating his executive departments, especially the environmentally related agencies such as EPA, with like-minded leadership following his election. Within the first two years of the Trump presidency, the domestic and international foundations for a national climate change mitigation strategy created by the Obama administration were largely eradicated by cancellation of EPA's Clean Power Plan and the revocation of the U.S. commitment in 2016 to the Paris Accord for the reduction of global greenhouse gas emissions.

While past presidencies have sometimes created controversy about their management of environmentally important scientific information, the Trump administration's attitude toward environmental science unsupportive of their policy agenda and the scale of their website revisions have provoked unusually vehement and widespread opposition among numerous scientific organizations. "The Trump administration is attempting to delegitimize science," asserted the Union of Concerned Scientists, a major science advocacy group. "It is giving industries more ability to influence how and what science is used in policymaking, and it is creating a hostile environment for federal agency scientists. This is a new era in which political interference is more likely and more frequent . . ."[10] Proponents of the Trump administration's many changes in the use of scientific data and scientific experts throughout environmental agencies, and the EPA especially, have asserted that these reforms will create less anti-industry bias among scientific advisers, greater transparency in the management of scientific information, and reduce the pro-regulatory preferences common to federal environmental scientists.

The White House Confronts the National Climate Assessment

In late 2018, the persisting controversy provoked by Donald Trump's outspoken disbelief in the scientific basis of climate warming took an odd turn when the White House appeared to be arguing with itself before a national audience. The White House was forced by law to release the *Fourth Annual Climate Assessment,* a 1,600-page scientific document, the collaborative work of thirteen federal agencies including NASA and the Department of Defense, which predicted "the impacts of climate change will be more extensive than previously thought, leaving no region of the country insulated from the consequences of warming."[11] The report, including very recent scientific research, framed the climate issue primarily in terms of its American impact.

The report had important political implications. The *Assessment's* unsparing depiction of a grim American future in the absence of climate-warming mitigation became a national media event, vividly depicting the implications of climate change while keeping the climate issue in national attention. The report's prediction of climate warming's impact on the nation's infrastructure was typically graphic:

> Climate change and extreme weather events are expected to increasingly disrupt our Nation's energy and transportation systems, threatening more frequent and longer-lasting power outages, fuel shortages, and service disruptions, with cascading impacts on other critical sectors. . . . The continued increase in the frequency and extent of high-tide flooding due to sea level rise threatens America's trillion-dollar coastal property market and public infrastructure, with cascading impacts to the larger economy.[12]

The *Assessment's* publication also occurred almost simultaneously with the 2018 congressional elections, which returned a new Democratic majority to the House of Representatives. With the *Assessment's* conclusions broadcast nationally, congressional Democratic proponents of tough national GHG emissions regulation hoped to exploit the news as political capital for House Democrats intent on ending the Trump EPA's regulatory reversals.

Trump administrative spokesmen in the White House, EPA, and other important federal environmental agencies assailed the *Assessment's* scientific credibility. The president, however, was compelled to discuss the issue in the national media. "One of the problems that a lot of people like myself, we have a very high level of intelligence but we're not necessarily believers," the President told the *Washington Post*. "As to whether or not it's man-made and whether or not the effects that you're talking about are there, I don't see it," he explained.[13] The *Assessment's* release, however, created new scientific and political resources to sustain political proponents of stronger national GHG regulation.

THE DOMESTIC POLITICS OF CLIMATE CHANGE

Since 2000, global climate change science and policy have increasingly become defining issues that distinguish Republicans from Democrats in Congress, the White House, and the voting booth.[14] The polarizing impact of these partisan differences in Congress and the White House was dramatized by the abrupt reversal in national and international climate change policy between the Obama and Trump presidencies. Differences about climate science and policy are more moderate among less partisan voters and the general public but still influence political behavior and political perceptions.

The Public, Voters, and Climate Change

The great majority of Americans believe that global climate warming is real and that it is human created. On the eve of the 2016 presidential election, for example, a typical national survey cited by the Brookings Institution reported that 70 percent of Americans affirmed that solid evidence of global warming existed, 17 percent "did not see much evidence," and 13 percent were "not sure."[15] Gallup, like most public opinion analysts, found in another survey that most Americans also attributed climate change to human activities.[16] However, most public opinion polls also indicate that climate warming has seldom been a significant public preoccupation nor a high priority among the issues on the mind of most voters at the polls during presidential elections.[17]

Among party identifiers, and particularly among strong party partisans, attitudes about climate science and politics are divisive. Voters who participate most frequently in party primaries—the Americans most active in selecting presidential nominees, congressional candidates, and party candidates for state and local political office—are the most divided in climate attitudes. These partisan differences over most aspects of climate change were apparent in the 2016 presidential election. For example, a respected national survey comparing voters for Donald Trump and Hillary Clinton found that "just 25 percent of people who voted for Donald Trump believe climate change is occurring now and is caused by human activity . . . in comparison to the 90 percent of Hillary Clinton voters the survey says believe human-induced climate change is happening."[18] One important consequence of the wide partisan differences about climate issues among the most electorally active party voters is that elective officials—and especially members of Congress—often take their cues on policy issues from these highly polarized segments of the major parties. Thus, congressional voting on climate issues tends quite often to reproduce and to amplify the divisiveness of climate opinion among highly active Republican and Democratic voters.

The White House, Congress, and Climate Policy

The partisan divisions over climate policy in Congress and the White House have progressively widened and hardened since 1990. Democratic presidents and legislators have initiated policies to reduce domestic climate-warming emissions and to collaborate internationally on global climate-warming abatement. Republican presidents and most congressional Republicans have resisted efforts to commit the United States to binding international climate agreements and have firmly rejected any nationally legislated controls on domestic climate-warming emissions. The result has been a continuing congressional impasse in climate policymaking.

Studies of congressional voting since 2000 reveal a growing partisanship about most environmental issues, and especially pervasive over climate policy. In recent years, partisan battles have flared even over minor issues. Following the 2016 presidential election, for instance, party rivalry provoked a congressional face-off about renewing federal grants to help television meteorologists discuss climate warming in their weather reports. "Four Republican senators have called for an investigation, calling it indoctrination," reported the *New York Times*, while Democrats defended the funding awarded the National Science Foundation for the prior decade.[19] Thwarted by chronic congressional conflict, Democratic presidents have resorted since the early 1990s to their diplomatic powers and domestic regulatory authority in an unsuccessful effort to overcome Senate deadlock about climate change.

THE DIFFICULT QUEST FOR AN INTERNATIONAL CLIMATE AGREEMENT

The history of U.S. attempts to create and sign a binding international agreement limiting global climate-warming emissions is a narrative of prolonged and difficult global negotiations, obstructive party conflict, and repeated failure.

Early U.S. Climate Diplomacy

As early as 1972, the United States had agreed at the first Earth Summit in Stockholm to join with 113 other nations in identifying and controlling significant international environmental problems, including climate change. The U.S. commitments were largely symbolic but important in setting climate change as a priority for U.S. diplomacy. Scientific and diplomatic pressure, together with gradually emerging public concern about climate change, gradually compelled the White House to join other nations in prolonged, difficult negotiations of several international climate agreements intended to set specific national goals for reduction of climate-warming emissions.

In 1992, U.S. delegates attended the Rio Conference on Environment and Development with 179 other nations and actively participated in almost all its proceedings, but the delegation, representing the viewpoint of President George Bush and his Republican administration, was reluctant to lead in conference policymaking and agreed to only voluntary timetables and reduction goals for national GHG emissions. When it was evident that neither the United States nor several other industrialized nations would meet their voluntary emission abatement targets, President Clinton attempted to negotiate a binding climate treaty at the 1997 international climate conference in Kyoto, Japan. The United States seemed for the first time committed to join 192 other nations in a compulsory target-and-timetable GHG emissions agreement. But no consensus on the need for such a treaty existed within either congressional party or among the public, and the Senate overwhelmingly rejected the agreement. The subsequent presidential election of George W. Bush in 2000 virtually ended active U.S. domestic or international initiatives for comprehensive regulation of climate-warming emissions until Barack Obama's presidency.

The Obama Paris Accord

Obama entered the White House in 2008 and pledged to negotiate a strong, binding international treaty committing the United States to collaborate with other nations in reducing global GHG emissions. However, the severe economic recession beginning in 2008 compelled the White House to focus upon domestic economic recovery; climate diplomacy did not become a major presidential priority until after the 2012 presidential election. Then, relying upon his executive authority, Obama bypassed Republican opposition in the Senate and initiated new international climate negotiations that eventually resulted in the Paris Climate Accord, signed by the United States and 196 other nations in December 2015 at the United Nations.

Conference on Climate Change

The Paris Accord, widely acclaimed internationally, was surprisingly substantial after earlier decades of incremental and weakly enforceable global climate agreements. It seemed to set the United States on an accelerated trajectory toward a much greater commitment to global collaboration on climate change mitigation. Moreover, the Paris Accord was based upon an earlier treaty signed by the United States and ratified by the Senate and required no additional Senate approval. The agreement became legally binding when signed by nations representing at least 55 percent of global greenhouse gas emissions.

Essentially, by signing the Paris Climate Accord, the United States appeared committed to an ambitious, sustained program of progressive reductions in national climate-warming emissions; to specific emission reduction targets and deadlines; to involving the private sector in national emissions reductions; and to United Nations monitoring of U.S. compliance with its treaty obligations. The agreement was also controversial. To many critics, it was a fabric of voluntary national commitments stitched together by unenforceable, if well-intentioned, regulatory goals and financial investments. Many advocates of a global regulatory regime still criticized the agreement because its ambitious global climate goal was not compulsory and because rich nations were not contributing enough to mitigate climate-warming's impact upon poor and undeveloped countries. Some climate experts argued that an effective global climate regulatory regime required the stronger economic "bite" of a carbon tax and tougher, credible, compulsory global emission reduction monitoring and enforcement sanctions.[20] Senate Republicans, angered by Obama's refusal to consult the Senate and to require its approval to the agreement, were determined to overturn the Accord, looked to the 2016 election of a Republican president for a remedy, and were not disappointed.

The Paris Agreement Rejected

Donald Trump had promised during his presidential campaign to withdraw the United States from the Paris Accord, and he redeemed that pledge in June

2017. "The Paris Climate Accord is simply the latest example of Washington entering into an agreement that disadvantages the United States to the exclusive benefit of other countries," he explained in announcing his rejection of the treaty, "leaving American workers—who I love—and taxpayers to absorb the cost. . . ." Trump asserted the Paris Accord posed numerous threats to the United States, including lost jobs, reduced domestic manufacturing, and reduced energy development, while permitting other major industrial nations, particularly China, to increase their climate-warming emissions. Repeating a theme that had resonated strongly with his electorate, Trump linked rejection of the Paris Accord with revival of American economic growth: "The reality is that withdrawing is in America's economic interest and won't matter much to the climate," he asserted. "The United States, under the Trump administration, will continue to be the cleanest and most environmentally friendly country on Earth. We'll be the cleanest. We're going to have the cleanest air. We're going to have the cleanest water. We will be environmentally friendly, but we're not going to put our businesses out of work and we're not going to lose our jobs. We're going to grow; we're going to grow rapidly."[21]

Since 125 other nations had signed the Paris Agreement, the U.S. withdrawal did not prevent its global implementation, but it created considerable doubt concerning what role, if any, the United States would assume in future climate diplomacy and perpetuated the congressional deadlock over a new climate treaty.

DEADLOCK OVER DOMESTIC CLIMATE EMISSION CONTROLS

In the 1990s, President Clinton and congressional Democrats initiated unsuccessful proposals to regulate the domestic emission of climate-warming emissions, but Democrats lacked the congressional majorities sufficient to approve new regulatory proposals. The presidential election of George W. Bush in 2000 precluded further White House climate initiatives or any successful congressional climate regulatory legislation during Bush's two terms.

The inertia about climate emission controls ended when the Supreme Court compelled the federal government to act on the climate issue. In 2006, EPA's administrator ruled that CO_2 was not a pollutant that EPA was compelled to regulate under the Clean Air Act (CAA). A coalition of states, asserting that the CAA did compel EPA to regulate CO_2, immediately challenged the EPA's contrary interpretation in the federal courts. In a landmark decision, the Supreme Court ruled in *Massachusetts v. Environmental Protection Agency* (2007) that CO_2 could potentially endanger human health or the environment as defined by the CAA (the "endangerment finding"). The Court then instructed the EPA to determine whether CO_2 was, in fact, a threat to humans or the environment and, if so, to write appropriate regulations to control domestic CO_2 emissions. Meanwhile, Congress never came close to enacting any climate legislation before the end of Bush's second term.

The Obama Climate Regulations Bypass Congress

Barack Obama entered the White House in 2008 and pledged to revive federal climate change policy. With the advent of Democratic majorities in both congressional chambers and the Obama presidency, environmentalists expected a new congressional effort to enact the comprehensive climate bill. Throughout 2008 and early 2009, Congress ponderously struggled but failed to produce a climate bill. The 2010 congressional elections delivered a Republican majority in both congressional chambers and imposed a partisan deadlock precluding any congressional climate-warming legislation for the remainder of the Obama presidency. By 2012, however, EPA had ruled that domestic CO_2 emissions were a threat to human health and the environment. Armed with this EPA decision, and confronting the congressional impasse over climate legislation, Obama decided to bypass Congress and use his executive authority, acting through EPA, to propose the 2015 Clean Power Plan, discussed in Chapter 6, as an alternative approach to CO_2 regulation. These regulations created three important regulatory principles:

1. Setting new CO_2 emission standards for cars and light trucks (the Tailpipe Rule);

2. Determining that CO_2 emissions regulations applied to major stationary sources, such as power plants and cement factories; and

3. Permitting EPA to tailor its regulations to different types of emission sources, beginning with the largest power plant emissions sources, rather than pass a blanket rule applied to all sources.

The auto industry generally supported EPA's decision to create nationally uniform tailpipe emissions standards, which avoided the prospect of many different and economically burdensome state auto standards. But many other large industry groups, including electric utilities, coal mining, and petroleum refiners, joined with major commercial trade associations, such as the National Chambers of Commerce, in continued opposition to the EPA's aggressive approach to new climate emissions regulations. Joined by several states, including Texas and Arizona, this broad, politically potent coalition of industry, commerce, and states created an outpouring of legal challenges to the EPA's climate-warming regulations and perpetuated the battle within and outside Congress to thwart the second Obama administration's regulatory attack on domestic climate-warming emissions.

Trump's EPA Replaces Obama's Clean Power Plan

The 2016 presidential election was a contest between candidates with radically different, irreconcilable attitudes about domestic climate emissions controls. Donald Trump promised to suspend and replace the Obama Clean Power Plan; Hillary Clinton pledged to implement it. Following his election, Trump issued an executive order in March 2017 requiring the EPA's administrator to review the Obama Clean Power Plan and "determine whether to revise or withdraw the proposed rule"—in effect, to suspend its immediate implementation. A president, however, can revise but not revoke a regulation. Moreover, the Supreme Court's "impairment ruling," discussed previously, compelled the EPA to regulate carbon dioxide as a pollutant.

In April 2018, Trump's EPA proposed very different regulations to replace the suspended Obama rules. The new EPA regulations would reduce future U.S. carbon dioxide emissions and compel additional controls on many existing electric power plans, but their impact was expected to vary considerably from the Obama regulations. Among the major differences, the new regulations would:

- reduce future U.S. carbon dioxide emissions by an estimated 1 or 2 percent by 2035 rather than the estimated 32 percent in the Obama plan;

- permit aging, coal-fired power plants with less-efficient carbon dioxide emission controls to operate longer;

- create fewer incentives for electric utilities to use more renewable energy sources in planned future facilities; and

- allow the states more time, and greater freedom, to decide how electric utilities must achieve carbon dioxide emission controls.[22]

The new Trump regulations were enthusiastically welcomed by many electric utilities, the coal industry, and coal miners to whom Trump had made a campaign promise to end the war on coal symbolized by the Obama carbon emissions regulations. The new proposal, however, was coldly received by many state governors and energy regulators who had begun to implement the new Obama regulations and who asserted the new rules created inadequate incentives for state carbon emissions reductions. Joining with environmental organizations, some states turned to the federal courts to strike down the new Trump proposals through litigation—an assurance of a long judicial journey and an uncertain future for the Trump carbon emissions regulations.

The States and Climate Policy

By 2000, many state and local governments, impatient with Washington's political struggles over climate policy and aware of their own risks from climate warming, had assumed leadership in climate policy innovation while Washington faltered. When the Obama administration was inaugurated, sixteen states had already adopted GHG emissions reduction targets, thirty-nine states had joined the multistate Climate Registry to monitor and report their GHG emissions, and state partnerships had formed three regional cap-and-trade programs to facilitate emission control.[23] In addition, California had enacted a regulatory program that exceeded federal standards for GHG emissions from the transportation sector, and twelve other states proposed the adoption of the standards as well.

At the end of the Obama presidency, state policy innovations also included creation of state climate-warming commissions, state-based climate action plans, GHG inventories and emissions reporting, GHG emission standards for electric utilities, GHG performance standards for vehicles, and much else.[24] Most states welcomed, or at least accepted, the Obama regulations for national GHG emissions and were preparing to implement them when the Trump administration suspended the regulations. Numerous state and local governments were outspokenly critical of the Trump administration's new climate policies. The mayors of New York, Los Angeles, Houston, and seventy-two other cities, addressing an open letter to the president, declared, "[climate] change is both the greatest single threat we face, and our greatest economic opportunity" and affirmed "our cities' commitments to taking every action possible to achieve the principles and goals of the Paris Climate Agreement, and to engage states, businesses and other sectors to join us." The Democratic governors of California, Connecticut, Minnesota, New York, Oregon, and Washington warned that they would continue to work at cutting state carbon emissions despite Washington.[25] Thus, the regulatory stalemate in Washington appeared to create continuing incentives for policy innovation at the state and local level.

THE CLOUDED FUTURE OF U.S. CLIMATE POLICY

On the eve of the 2016 presidential election, the nation appeared at the threshold of a new era of domestic and international climate policymaking, politically controversial and technologically challenging but setting a clear direction and a plausible goal for national policymakers. After 2016, that threshold seemed to become a dead end as the Trump administration abruptly withdrew from the Paris Accord and suspended the Obama domestic climate emissions regulations, leaving no firm foundation of future climate policy

The Trump administration's policy agenda intended to define a new domestic and international climate regime for the United States. Much of this agenda, however, remained partially implemented, suspended in federal court litigation and still unenacted by 2019, leaving considerable uncertainty about the nation's national and international climate policy well into the latter years of the Trump presidency. Should the Trump administration's climate agenda emerge relatively intact after federal court litigation, bureaucratic rulemaking, and after the 2018 congressional elections—a risky assumption—the new climate policy regime will have some predictable impacts.

Reduced Pace and Size of Domestic Emissions Reductions

Even without federal or state regulation, national emissions of GHG are predicted to decline but at a much slower rate than would have been anticipated with the Obama Clean Power Plan. Many electric utilities and other industrial GHG emitters have already reduced their emissions, or plan to reduce emissions in new facilities, as natural gas and renewables replace coal energy for economic reasons. If the Trump substitute for the suspended Obama emissions regulations is fully implemented, further emission reductions will occur but at an estimated rate greatly reduced compared to the Obama power plan and insufficient to achieve national emission reductions needed to prevent an irreversible global climate warming predicted at mid-century by climate scientists.

The pace of future GHG emission reductions is likely to be reduced further if the EPA successfully retains the present auto emission standards and rejects the newer, stricter tailpipe standards proposed by the Obama EPA. Since the transportation sector is now the greatest source of domestic GHG emissions, the proposed new tailpipe standards were considered an essential component in achieving the ambitious emissions goal of the Obama administration.

Decline of U.S. Climate Diplomacy

American withdrawal from the 2017 Paris Accord did not preclude the treaty's implementation, since it was ratified by 181 other nations. Nor did the Trump administration's treaty rejection prevent continued American participation in other international climate deliberations such as the ongoing Conference of Parties to the original 1992 UNFCCC, a treaty signed by the United States. However, American rejection of the Paris Agreement greatly reduces the incentives for national collaboration in reducing domestic GHG emissions to a level considered essential to preventing a mid-century catastrophic rise in average climate temperature. Many critics have also asserted that the U.S. rejection of the Paris Accord diminishes its moral authority and political influence in future international environmental negotiations important to the United States.

Perhaps most important, disengagement from the Paris Accord suggests that the United States has abandoned leadership in international environmental diplomacy for the indefinite future.

The Risk of Federal Regulatory Inertia

The speed and scope of the Trump administration's climate policy reforms have caught virtually every related federal environmental department and agency in a flurry of reorganization, suspended and rewritten regulations, and new procedures. This rush of reform in federal climate policies has created in its slipstream an outpouring of litigation as well as delays when mandated bureaucratic reviews must occur. Especially important, many proposed revisions and revocations of EPA climate emission regulations, including enactment of new regulations, cannot be implemented by the president or EPA administrator without legally mandated judicial and administrative review. This evolving litigation and required administrative procedure confronts regulated interests with uncertainty about what future cost, technological requirements, and emission limits to anticipate. The implicit cost of this regulatory indecision is prolonged delay in achieving planned emission goals at a time when emission controls become increasingly important domestically and globally.

Growing State Climate Leadership

The Trump administration's revocation of the Obama administration's proposed climate regulations and retreat from the Paris Accord have encouraged growing initiative and innovation in climate policy among the states. Environmentalists are investing greater resources in state-based climate emission regulations and related policies, such as revised building codes, coastal protection, and flood management, in anticipation of long-term climate warming. Many state governments have created, or intend to create, regional climate pacts entailing negotiated climate emission limits, various strategies such as emissions trading to create economic incentives for emission reductions, and long-term water management plans based on climate change. This state assertion of climate policy leadership is epitomized by the U.S. Climate Alliance, a bipartisan coalition of major state governors that has created alternative venues for innovation and initiative in climate policy in the absence of federal leadership. Ultimately, however, the state contribution to climate-warming mitigation in all aspects— scientific, political, economic, and diplomatic—requires a deeply engaged and resourceful federal government in partnership with the states to realize the full potential of state-based climate policymaking.

CONCLUSION

Something profound yet vaguely conceived happened to political cognition in the latter third of the twentieth century. To this phenomenon, we have ascribed the inadequate word *environmentalism*. The artifacts of this movement are the most visible and, ultimately, the least important aspects of it. Beginning with Earth Day 1970 in the United States and comparable political stirrings elsewhere in the industrialized world, a structure of domestic laws, institutions, and cultural practices has evolved in the United States to translate environmentalism into a social force and presence. This already large and elaborate national structure (the focus of most of this book) has become a national pediment, among many throughout the world, on which a new regional and international regime of environmental management (the focus of this chapter) is emerging. This incipient globalization of environmental management is extremely tenuous and as yet largely unproven, still more symbol than monument. Yet it does exist, and it has never existed before in the history of human civilization. It is worth reflecting on the profound historical implications of an international protocol to manage climate change in the twilight of the twentieth century.

At the beginning of the new century, however, a better perspective on the future path of environmentalism might be gained by looking beyond its current political and governmental architecture, important as that may be, to its implications for our evolving national conceptions of political time, space, and causality. From this perspective, one of environmentalism's most profound impacts has been to accelerate the way in which science is transforming public policymaking. Environmental science, embodied in the technical underpinnings of current understandings of climate warming, ozone depletion, and intergenerational equity, is compelling policymakers to think in terms of policy problems and impacts, of the consequences of present decisions and future undertakings, and on a time scale almost unthinkable a few decades ago and unavoidable in the future. The genie of anticipatory environmental science is out of the bottle and, like the secrets of nuclear power, cannot now be ignored, however disconcerting it may be. Although our national political language has always been afflicted with vaporous rhetoric about "the future" and "concern for future generations," science today is providing policymakers with the intellectual tools and a scientific metric for characterizing the future impact of present public decision-making that impose a responsibility quite new to public life.

Added to this increasingly sophisticated ability to describe and anticipate the environmental consequences of present policies, environmentalism has also made us aware, sometimes acutely, of the need to think deliberately about the long-term risks of technological innovation. As the U.S. experience with nuclear power amply demonstrates, it is not only the scientific risks of technology development that need to be appraised but also the institutional risks—the questions about whether we have or can develop in appropriate ways the institutional means of managing satisfactorily the technologies we create domestically and internationally.

Most important, the evolving impact of environmentalism on our politics and culture has made an especially persuasive case, for those who will listen, that we are beginning a new century not only with the technological ability to destroy the cultural and biological conditions for the survival of human life on Earth but also with the capability to alter the genetic foundations of human life and thus consciously shape human evolution in materially and spiritually beneficial ways. Environmentalism at its best is a challenge to develop the moral and ethical sensibilities to leaven this power with an enlightened stewardship of Earth.

Suggested Readings

Chasek, Pamela S., ed. *Global Environmental Politics.* 4th ed. Boulder, CO: Westview Press, 2006.

Conca, Ken, and Geoffrey D. Dabelko, eds. *Green Planet Blues.* 4th ed. Boulder, CO: Westview Press, 2010.

Edwards, Paul N. *A Vast Machine: Computer Models, Climate Data, and the Politics of Global Warming.* Cambridge, MA: MIT Press, 2010.

Hulme, Mike. *Why We Disagree About Climate Change.* New York: Cambridge University Press, 2009.

Klein, Naomi. *This Changes Everything.* New York: Simon & Schuster, 2015.

Matez, Edmond A., and Jason E. Smerdon. *Climate Change: The Science of Global Warming and Our Energy.* New York: Columbia University Press, 2018.

Pachauri, Rajendra K., and Leo Meyer, eds. *Climate Change 2014 Synthesis Report.* Contribution of Working Groups I, II and III to the Fifth Assessment Report of the Intergovernmental Panel on Climate Change. Geneva, Switzerland: Simon & Schuster, 2014.

Voskoboynik, Daniel Macmillan. *The Memory We Could Be: Overcoming Fear to Create Our Ecological Future.* New York: New Society Publishers, 2018.

Notes

1. Tony Rinberg and Andrew Bergman, "Censoring Climate Change," *New York Times*, November 27, 2017, available at https://www.nytimes .com/2017/11/22/opinion/censoring-climate-change.html?action=click&pg type=Homepage&clickSource=story-heading&module=opinion-c-col-right -region&region=opinion-c-col-right-region&WT.nav=opinion-c-col -right-region.
2. Lisa Friedman, "E.P.A. Scrubs a Climate Website of 'Climate Change,'" *New York Times*, October 20, 2017, A10
3. Patrick Lee, "Child's Play: Team Trump Rewrites a Department of Energy Website for Kids," *Common Dreams*, February 19, 2017, available at https://www.commondreams.org/news/2017/02/19/childs-play-team -trump-rewrites-department-energy-website-kids.
4. Juliet Eilperin and Chris Mooney, "EPA Website Removes Climate Science Site From Public View After Two Decades," *Washington Post*, April 29, 2017, available at https://www.washingtonpost.com/news/energy-environment/

wp/2017/04/28/epa-website-removes-climate-science-site-from-public
-view-after-two-decades/?utm_term=.2ae8718782b9.

5. Scott Waldman, "Climate Web Pages Erased and Obscured Under Trump," *Scientific American*, January 10, 2018, available at https://www.scientificamer
ican.com/article/climate-web-pages-erased-and-obscured-under-trump/.

6. IPCC, "Climate Change 2007: Working Group I: The Physical Science Basis, IPCC Assessments of Climate Change and Uncertainties," 2007, available at www.ipcc.ch/publications_and_data/ar4/wg1/en/ch1s1–6.html.

7. Ibid.

8. Summarized in Pew Center for Climate and Energy Solutions, *IPCC: Growing Certainty on the Human Role in Climate Change*, available at http://www
.c2es.org/science-impacts/ipcc-summaries/growing-certainty; see also Intergovernmental Panel on Climate Change, Climate Change 2014, *Impacts, Adaptation, and Vulnerability: Summary for Policymakers*, available at http://www.ipcc.ch/.

9. Adapted from EPA, "Overview of Greenhouse Gases," available at https://www.epa.gov/ghgemissions/overview-greenhouse-gases.

10. Jacob Carter, Gretchen Goldman, Genna Reed, Peter Hansel, Michael Halpern, and Andrew Rosenberg, *Sidelining Science Since Day One* (Washington, DC: Union of Concerned Scientists, 2017), 1.

11. Umair Irfan, "Trump White House Issues Climate Change Report Undermining Its Own Policy," *Vox*, November 26, 2016, available at https://www.vox
.com/2018/11/26/18112505/national-climate-assessment-2018-trump.

12. U.S. Global Change Research Program, *Fourth National Climate Assessment, Volume II, Impacts, Risks, and Adaptation in the United States: Report-in-Brief*, (Washington, DC: Government Printing Office, 2018), 17.

13. Josh Dawsey, Brady Dennis, Philip Rucker, and Chris Mooney, "Trump Says He Is Among Those Who 'Have Very High Levels of Intelligence' But Are Not 'Believers' in Climate Change," *Chicago Tribune*, November 27, 2018, available at https://www.chicagotribune.com/news/nationworld/politics/ct
-trump-climate-change-20181127-story.html.

14. Matto Mildenberger, Jennifer Marlon, Peter Howe, Xinran Wang, and Anthony Leiserowitz, "Partisan Climate Opinion Maps 2016," Yale Program on Climate Change Communication, available at http://climatecommunica
tion.yale.edu/visualizations-data/partisan-maps-2016/?est=happening&gr
oup=dem&type=value&geo=c.

15. Christopher Borick, Sarah Mills, and Barry G. Rabe, "American Views on Climate Change at the Dawn of the Trump Presidency," *Brookings Education*, December 15, 2016, available at https://www.brookings.edu/blog/fixgov/2016/12/
15/views-on-climate-change-dawn-of-trump-presidency/.

16. Megan Brenan and Lydia Saad, "Global Warming Concern Steady Despite Some Partisan Shifts," *Gallup*, March 28, 2018, available at https://news.gallup
.com/poll/231530/global-warming-concern-steady-despite-partisan-shifts
.aspx?g_source=link_newsv9&g_campaign=item_231386&g_medium=copy.

17. On public issue priorities, see Pew Research Center, "Public's Policy Priorities for 2015," *U.S. Politics and Policy*, available at http://www.people-press.org/2015/01/15/publics-policy-priorities-reflect-changing-conditions-at-home-and-abroad/1-15-2015-priorities_01/; on long-term partisan differences about climate change, see Elaine Kamarck, "The Real Enemy to Progress on Climate Change Is Public Indifference," *Brookings FixGov*, December 3, 2015, available at http://www.brookings.edu/blogs/fixgov/posts/2015/12/03-public-indifference-politics-climate-change-paris-kamarck; and Pew Research Center, "Some of the Largest Gaps When It Comes to the Public's Priorities Are Over the Environment: Partisan Gaps on Environment and Global Warming," January 15, 2015, available at http://www.pewresearch.org/key-data-points/environment-energy-2/.

18. Chelsea Harvey, "Survey: Only a Quarter of Trump Voters Believe in Human-Caused Climate Change," *Washington Post*, February 2, 2017, available at https://www.washingtonpost.com/news/energy-environment/wp/2017/02/02/survey-only-a-quarter-of-trump-voters-believe-in-human-caused-climate-change/?utm_term=.676d593bf3c9.

19. Henry Fountain, Lisa Friedman, and Brad Plumer, "When Did Talking About Weather Become Political?" *New York Times*, July 18, 2018, available at https://www.nytimes.com/2018/07/18/climate/when-did-talking-about-the-weather-become-political.html.

20. Oliver Milman, "James Hansen, Father of Climate Change Awareness, Calls Paris Talks 'A Fraud,'" *The Guardian*, December 12, 2015, available at http://www.theguardian.com/environment/2015/dec/12/james-hansen-climate-change-paris-talks-fraud; other critiques include Naomi Klein, "We Are Out of Time: We Need to Take a Leap," *Moyers and Company*, December 11, 2015, available at http://billmoyers.com/story/we-are-out-of-time-we-need-to-take-a-leap; Ben Adler, "The Big Climate Agreement Won't Keep Fossil Fuels in the Ground," *Mother Jones*, December 9, 2015, available at http://www.motherjones.com/environment/2015/12/paris-climate-agreement-wont-keep-fossil-fuels-ground; and Durwood Zaelke, "Climate Agreement in Paris: Champagne Tonight, Hard Work, Fast Mitigation Tomorrow," available at http://www.igsd.org/climate-agreement-in-paris-champagne-tonight-hard-work-fast-mitigation-tomorrow/.

21. The White House, Briefings: "Statement by President Trump on the Paris Climate Accord," available at https://www.whitehouse.gov/briefings-statements/statement-president-trump-paris-climate-accord/.

22. Brian H. Potts, "What's Actually in President Trump's (Diet) Clean Power Plan?" *Forbes*, August 22, 2018, available at https://www.forbes.com/sites/brianpotts/2018/08/22/whats-actually-in-president-trumps-diet-clean-power-plan/#3682c1b23539.

23. Committee on Energy and Commerce, "Climate Change Legislation Design White Paper: Appropriate Roles for Different Levels of Government,"

Washington, DC, February 2008, available at http://energycommerce.house
.gov/Climate_Change/white%20paper%20st-lcl%20roles%20final%202–22
.pdf.

24. Adapted from "State Legislation From Around the Country," Pew Center on
Global Climate Change, available at www.pewclimate.org/what_s_being_
done/in_the_states/state_legislation.cfm.

25. Marianne Lavelle, "Climate Action Will Thrive on State and Local Level,
Leaders Vow After Trump Order," *Inside Climate News*, March 29,
2017, available at https://insideclimatenews.org/news/29032017/climate
-change-mayors-states-donald-trump-executive-order.

LIST OF ABBREVIATIONS

AFO	animal feeding operation
ALF	Animal Liberation Front
ANWR	Arctic National Wildlife Refuge
BCA	benefit–cost analysis
BINGOs	big, influential nongovernment organizations
BLM	Bureau of Land Management
CAA	Clean Air Act of 1970
CAFOs	concentrated animal feeding operations
CAGW	Citizens Against Government Waste
CCD	Colony Collapse Disorder
CCS	clean coal technology
CEQ	Council on Environmental Quality
CERCLA	Comprehensive Environmental Response, Compensation, and Liability Act of 1980 (Superfund)
COE	Army Corps of Engineers
COP	Conference of Parties
CPP	Clean Power Plan
CPSC	U.S. Consumer Product Safety Commission
CPSRA	Consumer Product Safety Reform Act
CWA	Clean Water Act of 1972
DDT	dichlorodiphenyltrichloroethane
DINP	diisononyl phthalate
DOE	Department of Energy
DOI	Department of the Interior
EIA	U.S. Energy Information Administration

EIS	environmental impact statement
ELF	Earth Liberation Front
EOP	Executive Office of the President
EPA	U.S. Environmental Protection Agency
EPAct	Energy Policy Act of 2005
EPCRA	Emergency Planning and Community Right-to-Know Act
FDA	Food and Drug Administration
FWPCAA	Federal Water Pollution Control Act Amendments of 1972
FWS	Fish and Wildlife Service
GAO	Government Accountability Office (until July 2004, Government Accounting Office)
GHG	greenhouse gases
IEA	International Energy Agency
INES	International Nuclear and Radiological Event Scale
IPCC	Intergovernmental Panel on Climate Change
IRIS	Integrated Risk Information System
MCLs	maximum contaminant limits
MMS	Minerals Management Service
NEPA	National Environmental Policy Act of 1969
NFMA	National Forest Management Act
NIMBY	Not In My Backyard
NPL	National Priority List
NRC	Nuclear Regulatory Commission
NWPA	Nuclear Waste Policy Act of 1982
OCS	outer continental shelf
OMB	Office of Management and Budget
OPEC	Organization of Petroleum Exporting Countries
OSHA	Occupational Safety and Health Administration
OSMRE	Office of Surface Mining Reclamation and Enforcement

OSTP	Office of Science and Technology Policy
PCBs	polychlorinated biphenyls
PSD	prevention of significant deterioration
RCRA	Resource Conservation and Recovery Act of 1976
RGGI	Regional Greenhouse Gas Initiative
RIA	regulatory impact analysis
RPS	Renewable Portfolio Standards
SDWA	Safe Drinking Water Act
SMCRA	Surface Mining Control and Reclamation Act
TCDD	2,3,7,8-tetrachloridibenzodioxin
TMDL	total maximum daily load
TRI	Toxics Release Inventory
TSCA	Toxic Substances Control Act of 1976
UCS	Union of Concerned Scientists
UNCED	United Nations Conference on Environment and Development (the Earth Summit)
UNFCCC	United Nations Framework Convention on Climate Change
USTs	underground storage tanks
VOCs	volatile organic compounds
WOTUS	waters of the United States

INDEX

CPSIA information can be obtained
at www.ICGtesting.com
Printed in the USA
BVHW042038100122
625922BV00005B/13